Coroners' Recommendations and the Promise of Saved Lives

This book is dedicated to:

- Rebecca Joyce Moore. Becky was born on 7 March 2013, during the data collection phase of this project.
- Joyce McDonald.
- Dr David Robinson.
- All the families who have appeared in the Coroner's Court.

Coroners' Recommendations and the Promise of Saved Lives

Dr Jennifer Moore, LLB, MA, PhD

Academic, Department of Preventive and Social Medicine and the Faculty of Law, The University of Otago, New Zealand, and a 2015–16 Harkness Fellow in Healthcare Policy and Practice, Stanford University, USA

Edward Elgar PUBLISHING

Cheltenham, UK • Northampton, MA, USA

Published by
Edward Elgar Publishing Limited
The Lypiatts
15 Lansdown Road
Cheltenham
Glos GL50 2JA
UK

Edward Elgar Publishing, Inc.
William Pratt House
9 Dewey Court
Northampton
Massachusetts 01060
USA

A catalogue record for this book
is available from the British Library

Library of Congress Control Number: 2016931774

This book is available electronically in the **Elgar**online
Law subject collection
DOI 10.4337/9781784711566

MIX
Paper from
responsible sources
FSC® C013056

ISBN 978 1 78471 155 9 (cased)
ISBN 978 1 78471 156 6 (ebook)

Typeset by Servis Filmsetting Ltd, Stockport, Cheshire
Printed and bound in Great Britain by TJ International Ltd, Padstow

New Zealand Law Foundation
Te Manatū a Ture o Aotearoa

The Law Foundation
NEW ZEALAND
SUPPORTING INDEPENDENT LEGAL THINKING.

The New Zealand Law Foundation – Te Manatū a Ture o Aotearoa – develops legal expertise on major and emerging public policy issues through its grants programme.

The Foundation is an independent charitable trust that fulfils a unique and important role in New Zealand's political and social development. The Foundation is proud of the success of the research projects it has funded, many of which have delivered ground-breaking legal research and supported the development of good public policy.

This is one of those projects; the research project that this book is based on was made possible by a grant from the Foundation. This research was the first to evaluate the rigour of coronial recommendations and their implementation since the Coroners Act was introduced in 2006. Already the Ministry of Justice in New Zealand has adopted several research findings which have also been incorporated into the Coroners Amendment Bill.

Contents

Figures

Tables

Acknowledgements and permissions

ACKNOWLEDGEMENTS

I would like to recognise and thank this study's participants, without whom this study could not have proceeded. Thank you sincerely for sharing with me your thoughts about this important topic. In particular, I owe special thanks to the Coronial Services of New Zealand, the former Chief Coroner, Judge Neil MacLean, and the Coroners for being incredibly helpful, encouraging and supportive throughout the research process.

It is also essential to mention the tremendous support that I received from the New Zealand Law Foundation. Without their generous funding of this research, the project would not have proceeded. I would like to express my gratitude to the Director, Lynda Hagen, for her support, enthusiasm and advice. I also wish to thank Dianne Gallagher for her friendly, helpful support and assistance.

I am particularly grateful to Ben Booth and the wonderful team at Edward Elgar. Thank you for supporting this project.

I am infinitely grateful to the Dean of Law, University of Otago, Professor Mark Henaghan. I have been fortunate to have three superb heads of department at the University of Otago: Professor Peter Crampton, Professor Mark Henaghan and Professor Robin Gauld. Peter, Mark and Robin have all nurtured, encouraged, supported and inspired me. Professor Rex Ahdar deserves special mention because he spent hours reading a draft of this book and made invaluable suggestions. I am also grateful to many other academic colleagues, such as Professor Kate Diesfeld, Associate Professor Colin Gavaghan, Professor Ron Paterson, Professor Peter Skegg, Louise Delany, Dr Marie Bismark, Professor David Studdert, Professor Michelle Mello, and Professor Hank Weiss. Dr John Rutherford (Wellington pathologist) has been a wonderful mentor. Special thanks must also go to Professor Ian Freckelton QC (a coronial law expert) for being generous with his time and for providing excellent advice. I was lucky to have two wonderful research assistants: Steve Thomson and Catey Boyce. I am particularly grateful to Steve and Catey for their assistance with Chapter 6.

My literature searching was aided by fabulous support from the

University of Otago law librarians and the CSNZ staff, particularly Dean Skachill, Lily Nunweek and Jackie Andrews. I am particularly thankful to Dean, Lily and their colleagues, who spent many hours putting full coronial findings onto a USB drive for me.

A constant source of inspiration came from the University of Melbourne's public health law team, who has also been researching the Coroners Act 2008 (Vic) and the implementation of coroners' recommendations. I have benefitted from numerous conversations with them. Another source of inspiration and encouragement is: Dr Bugeja (Coronial Prevention Unit, Coroner's Court of Victoria, Australia). I am grateful for your guidance and conversations about the research.

Portions of Chapters 5 and 6 were published in Jennifer Moore, "An Empirical Approach to the New Zealand Government's Review of the Coronial Jurisdiction" (2014) 21 JLM 602–26. Portions of Chapter 3 were published in Jennifer Moore, "Coroners' Recommendations about Healthcare-related Deaths as a Potential Tool for Improving Patient Safety and Quality of Care" (2014) 127(1398) NZ Medical Journal 35. I gratefully acknowledge permission from the *New Zealand Medical Journal* and the *Journal of Law and Medicine* to reproduce portions of these articles in revised form. Portions of Chapters 2–7 were submitted to the NZ Law Foundation as a final report about the research findings. I gratefully acknowledge permission from the NZ Law Foundation and Lynda Hagen to reproduce portions of the report.

Finally, I wish to thank those people who have helped me to survive the research process. Thank you to the dream team – Dr David Kent and Joanne Kent! I am immensely grateful to Joanne Kent, who skilfully cared for Rebecca while I wrote this book. David cured Rebecca's illnesses on numerous occasions, particularly during the winter in 2014. I would like to acknowledge my family, who are my unfailing support network. Thank you particularly to Rob, who spent many hours caring for our daughter, Rebecca, when she was born during the data collection phase of this project. Completion of this book, without Rob's continual (and free) IT support, would have been much more arduous. Grandpa (Malcolm McDonald) and Grandma (Dr Jill Wolfgang) played a vital babysitting role, allowing me to spend hours writing. Sue and Dr David Robinson were fantastic proof readers of earlier drafts. I am grateful to Captain Ted Moore and Maryanne Moore for providing support during the final stages of writing. Thank you to Maryanne for babysitting in October 2015 while I was a Harkness Fellow in Healthcare Policy at Stanford Law School.

PERMISSIONS

Grateful acknowledgment is made for permissions to reprint the following material:

Excerpts from: Jennifer Moore "An Empirical Approach to the New Zealand Government's Review of the Coronial Jurisdiction" (2014) 21 JLM 602. Reprinted by permission of Thomson Reuters.

Excerpts from: Jennifer Moore "Coroners' Recommendations about Healthcare-related Deaths as a Potential Tool for Improving Patient Safety and Quality of Care" (2014) 127(1398) *NZ Medical Journal* 35. Reprinted by permission of the *New Zealand Medical Journal.*

Excerpts from: Jennifer Moore and Mark Henaghan *New Zealand Coroners' Recommendations, 2007–2012* (Final report, Dunedin, 2014). Reprinted by permission of the New Zealand Law Foundation and Lynda Hagen, the director of the New Zealand Law Foundation.

Every effort has been made to trace copyright holders and to obtain their permission for the use of copyright material. The publisher apologises for any errors or omissions in the above list and would be grateful for notification of any corrections that should be incorporated in future reprints or editions of this book.

Abbreviations

ACT	Australian Capital Territory
BAC	blood alcohol concentration
CDC	Centers for Disease Control and Prevention
CAA	Civil Aviation Authority
CPU	Coroners Prevention Unit
CLS	Clinical Liaison Service
CMS	case management system
COPD	chronic obstructive pulmonary disease
CSNZ	Coronial Services of New Zealand
CTO	compulsory treatment order
CYMRC	Child and Youth Mortality Review Committee
DHB	District Health Board
ED	emergency department
HDC	Health and Disability Commissioner
HQSC	Health Quality and Safety Commission
ICD 10	International Statistical Classification of Diseases and Related Health Problems, 10th Revision
IRHACE	Institute of Refrigeration, Heating and Air Conditioning Engineers of NZ
MRC	Mortality Review Committee
NCIS	National Coronial Information System
NZNO	New Zealand Nurses' Organisation
NSW	New South Wales, Australia
NT	Northern Territory, Australia
NVDRS	National Violent Death Reporting System
NZ	New Zealand
NZLII	New Zealand Legal Information Institute
NZTA	New Zealand Transport Agency
PVLRC	Parliament of Victoria Law Reform Committee
QLD	Queensland, Australia
SUDI	sudden unexplained death of an infant
TISG	Transport Industry Safety Group
UK	United Kingdom
US	United States

VIC	Victoria, Australia
WA	Western Australia
WHO	World Health Organization

Table of cases

Table of statutes and regulations

1. Learning from death

We were at the Coroner's Court so New Zealand could learn from Adam's death. We did not want Adam's life to be a waste.[1]

The inquest at least gave us some answers to our questions about how the pregnancy was managed and the death of our baby daughter Ava Mae. . . Hopefully the verdict of HM Coroner will be taken to heart and acted upon by the hospital so that other parents will be spared the pain and emotional turmoil that we have had to endure simply to discover the truth about why our little baby girl's life was so short.[2]

1.1 INTRODUCTION

In February 2011, in a New Zealand (NZ) coronial inquiry that attracted widespread media attention, Robert Barlow, father of the deceased baby, Adam, explained:[3]

> We don't want our son to be remembered as the baby who died at the hands of a flawed maternity system. We want him to be remembered as the baby who brought about positive change in the maternity sector for the good of future mothers and babies.

Coroner Matenga found that baby Adam died after a "series of failures" by the midwife contributed to a hypoxic intrauterine environment during a prolonged second stage of labour due to foetal malposition.[4] During the

---

1 Interview with Robert Barlow (Jennifer Moore, 11 October 2012). Participants could elect to be named or anonymous. Pseudonyms are used throughout this book for all coroners, apart from the then Chief Coroner, who chose to be named. Those organisations and interested parties who elected to remain anonymous have been given pseudonyms.

2 "Baby Born Alive 'Wrongly' Recorded as Stillborn" *The Telegraph* (31 October 2012). <http://www.telegraph.co.uk/health/healthnews/9646068/Baby-born-alive-wrongly-recorded-as-stillborn.html>.

3 *Barlow* [2012] NZCorC 87.

4 *Barlow*, above n 3; Maryanne Twentyman "Midwife rejects baby death ruling" *Stuff* (New Zealand, 9 May 2012).

pregnancy, Linda Barlow (Adam's mother) had conveyed her concern about her baby's posterior position to her midwife. Adam's parents felt that the care they received from the midwife who looked after Linda at the time of Adam's birth had contributed to the death of their son.

The Barlows' experience began in 2008 when they relocated to NZ from the United Kingdom (UK). In an interview with me, Robert described their decision-making:[5]

> We felt that it would be a better place for our children to grow up, which is a bit ironic. There are good things about maternity here and over there [the UK]. The system we have here [in NZ] was put into place 20 years ago and there has been no review to see whether it is working. In Hamilton there are no obstetricians anymore. I think there should be a choice for people.

In NZ, Linda became pregnant with baby Adam. On 24 October 2009, Linda's waters broke and her contractions began. The Barlows met their midwife at River Ridge East Birth Centre, in Hamilton, NZ. The midwife assessed Linda as being in early labour and she was sent home, despite her wanting to remain at River Ridge. Linda became fully dilated at home and an ambulance returned her to River Ridge. Because of a lack of progress in labour, Linda was transferred to Waikato Hospital.

The midwife did not communicate any urgency to the hospital midwives regarding the labour and little clinical information was provided. There was confusion about whether the responsibility for primary care remained with the midwife or the hospital midwives. After complaining of not being able to breathe, Linda was rushed to theatre for an emergency caesarean section. Adam was born by emergency caesarean section at 3.00pm and died shortly after birth.

In his findings, Coroner Matenga considered the procedural issue of jurisdiction.[6] NZ, English and Australian coroners do not have jurisdiction to investigate stillbirths.[7] Despite the paediatrician's conclusion that Adam was stillborn, the coroner received evidence that Adam had been assessed by nurses as having a faint heart beat when born. This is a sign of life and, therefore, Adam could not be classed as a stillborn child. The coroner concluded he had jurisdiction to open an inquiry.[8]

During the inquest, an obstetrician who gave expert evidence described

---

5 *Barlow*, above n 1.

6 *Barlow* [2012] NZCorC 87.

7 Ian Freckelton "Stillbirth and the Law: Options for Law Reform and Issues for the Coronial Jurisdiction" (2013) 21 JLM 7; Coroners Act 2006 (NZ) s 9.

8 *Barlow* [2012] NZCorC 87.

Adam's death as "needless" and stated that Mrs Barlow had experienced "gross neglect in labour".[9] The then NZ Minister of Health, Tony Ryall, described the case as "deeply distressing".[10] In 2012, Coroner Matenga directed three recommendations to the NZ Ministry of Health, one recommendation to the Waikato District Health Board and five recommendations to the Midwifery Council of NZ.[11]

After the tragic death of their baby, the Barlows hoped that the lessons from their experience would prevent similar deaths. In my interview with Robert, he explained that he and Linda viewed the coronial process, especially the coroner's recommendations, as a way to achieve this goal and to ensure that Adam's life was not a "waste".[12]

Coroners in NZ can make recommendations that may reduce the chances of occurrence of similar deaths in the future.[13] Likewise, coroners in many other jurisdictions (such as England, Australia and Canada) may make public health and safety recommendations.[14] Like the Barlows, a common refrain of those who have lost family members to preventable death is that they want the coronial system to ensure that "this doesn't happen to anyone else".[15] Many NZ families believe and hope that coroners' findings and recommendations can "make a massive difference to saving people's lives".[16]

Similarly, families in many other parts of the world hope that coroners' findings will save other people's lives in the future, so that other families "will be spared the pain and emotional turmoil that [they] have had to endure".[17] Mr and Mrs Charlton made this comment after the tragic death of their baby daughter, Ava Mae. Ava Mae Charlton was born in England in September 2009, but died shortly after she was born, following a delayed emergency caesarean. Ava Mae's death was recorded as a

---

9 *Barlow*, above n 3.

10 Twentyman, above n 4.

11 *Barlow*, above n 3.

12 *Barlow*, above n 1.

13 Coroners Act 2006 (NZ) s 3(1)(b).

14 For example, see the Coroners Act 1985 (Vic, Australia) s 19(2); Coroners Act 1997 (ACT, Australia) s 52(4); Coroners Act RSO 1990 (Ontario, Canada) c C-37, s 313(3); Coroners (Amendment) Rules 2008 (England and Wales) Rule 43.

15 Cliff Taylor "Toxic gas death inquiry" *The New Zealand Herald* (Auckland, 15 June 2008).

16 Kim Thomas "Call for wider licence review powers" *Stuff* (New Zealand, 25 February 2009).

17 "Baby born alive wrongly recorded as stillborn" *The Telegraph* (London, 31 October 2012).

stillbirth. The distraught parents fought for two years to get their baby's death investigated. The mother, Mrs Charlton, explained that the inquest "at least gave us some answers to our questions about how the pregnancy was managed and the death of our baby daughter Ava Mae".[18] Like NZ families, this English family also wants coronial inquiries to be the catalyst for change. Their wish – that we can learn from death – is at the heart of this book.

For many organisations that receive coroners' recommendations, it is important that their health and safety messages are aligned with the coronial preventive purpose. They, too, are motivated by a desire to prevent fatalities. According to the NZ Electricity Engineers' Association:[19]

> Everybody is really interested in this research and the Government's review . . . because what coroners say, and dealing with their recommendations, is actually really important in terms of how we run our business and how we run our industry.

Coronial information is of particular importance to policymakers, organisations, practitioners and researchers who have an interest in mortality and morbidity prevention. Many organisations analyse coroners' recommendations for patterns, so that these trends can inform, and improve, their work. However, adverse comments in coronial recommendations can cause reputational harm to organisations. It is unsurprising, then, that coroners' recommendations have an important impact on the way that businesses and industries are managed.

The public interest in coroners' recommendations can be demonstrated by the frequency of media items about coronial inquiries. This research generated widespread media attention. On 18 July 2014, there were 23 media items about this project.[20] The coroners interviewed for this study commented that the media play an important role in publicising the health and safety messages in coronial recommendations.

---

[18] "Baby born alive wrongly recorded as stillborn" *The Telegraph* (London, 31 October 2012).

[19] Interview with Electricity Engineers' Association (Jennifer Moore, 7 February 2013).

[20] For example, see Vaimoana Tapaleao "Findings by Coroners Fall on Deaf Ears" *The New Zealand Herald* (Auckland, 18 July 2014); David Loughrey "Chief Coroner Welcomes Study" *Otago Daily Times* (Dunedin, 18 July 2014); Collette Devlin and Tessa Johnstone "Report Highlights Failings of Coronial System" *Dominion Post* (Wellington, 18 July 2014).

However, not all media coverage of the Coronial Services of NZ (CSNZ) is favourable. For example, Sir Bob Jones (a NZ property developer) expressed his frustration about the quality of coronial recommendations by issuing his own recommendations for coroners. Specifically, he asserted that:[21]

> At the next coroners' annual conference, instead of speeches they should have half a dozen ex-All Black forwards present to line them up, bend them over and render hourly bum-kicking sessions which hopefully will bring them to their senses.

This comment was primarily prompted by a coronial finding about the death of a woman from cardiac arrhythmia, which was attributed, in part, to her excessive consumption of Coca-Cola.[22] The coroner found that the woman's consumption of six to ten litres of Coca-Cola per day was a substantial contributor to the development of the imbalances that caused her arrhythmia. The coroner made recommendations to the NZ Ministry of Health and Coca-Cola:

> To: The Ministry of Health
>
> I. That it be considered, in consultation with ESR and other appropriate experts, whether, in light of the evidence given to the Inquest Hearing, that the warning labels on carbonated beverages give sufficient protection to consumers. The hazards to the health of the consumers of excessive quantities of sugar and caffeine contained in carbonated beverages could be more clearly emphasised.
>
> II. It is noted that the caffeine content for "formulated caffeine beverages" defined as those containing 145 milligrams/L or more (Standard 2.6.4), is regulated. Consideration could be given to either the lowering of the caffeine percentage limit or creating a more specific warning such as those printed on cans containing "formulated caffeine beverages," produced and marketed by Coca-Cola. It may also be considered appropriate to review standard 2.6.4 to reduce the caffeine content threshold to enable more specific advice to consumers to be given.
>
> To: The Coco-Cola Company – Coca-Cola Amital (NZ) Limited, Coca-Cola Oceania Limited

21 Bob Jones "Bob Jones: Coroners should shut up and do their jobs" *The New Zealand Herald* (Auckland, 19 February 2013).

22 *Harris* [2013] NZCorC 46.

I. That consideration is given to the inclusion of advice as to the quantity of caffeine on the labels to its products and of the adding to the labels appropriate warnings related to the dangers of consuming excessive quantities of the products.

These coronial recommendations not only generated media comment from Sir Bob Jones, but also from Michael Laws (a NZ writer, broadcaster and politician). Laws asserted that the deceased's "stupid" lifestyle choices caused her cardiac arrhythmia.[23] He also argued that:[24]

> The problem with this new breed of coroners created by the 2006 Coroners Act [is that] they are becoming increasingly draconian in their recommendations – linking one odd death or one accidental fatality to some kind of systemic failing in our society.

In keeping with Laws' complaints, a commonly cited weakness of coroners' recommendations is that they focus on an isolated case. There has been a tendency for some coroners to extrapolate a generic recommendation based on an individual case (or in some instances, grouped clusters of cases). In their critiques of the coroner's recommendations about Coca-Cola, many other commentators similarly focused on the limitations of using a single case to inform recommendations. One commentator contended that coroners "ignore the extreme oddity of the circumstances and ascribe them to the community at large" and "too often fail to recognise freak accidents as simply that, namely freak".[25]

In contrast to these views, Professor Sellman of the National Addiction Centre at the University of Otago in NZ supported the coroner's recommendations and advocated for an overhaul of food labelling in NZ.[26] Recent public health research demonstrates that the proposed overhaul of food labelling in NZ has support from industry, policymakers and non-government organisations.[27]

---

[23] Michael Laws "Individual Stupidity No Reason to Curb Our Freedoms" *Sunday Star Times* (17 February 2013) A11.

[24] Laws, above n 23.

[25] Cameron Slater "Bob Jones on Idiot Coroners, They Deserve a Good Bum Kicking" (21 February 2013) Whale Oil Beef Hooked <http://www.whaleoil.co.nz/tag/natasha-harris/>.

[26] TVNZ "Professor backs coded food labels after Coca-Cola death – National News | TVNZ" (14 February 2013) TVNZ <http://tvnz.co.nz/national-news/professor-backs-coded-food-labels-after-coca-cola-death-5341540>.

[27] Louise Signal and others "Front-of-pack Nutrition Labelling of Food in New Zealand: An Exploration of Stakeholder Views about Research and Implementation" (2012) 23 Health Promotion Journal of Australia 48.

In this context of apparent controversy about coronial inquiries, I embarked upon exploration of the veracity of commentators' assertions about coroners' recommendations. In particular, my research is concerned with providing evidence-based answers to four overarching questions: (1) What is the nature of coronial recommendations? (2) Who are the recipients of coroners' recommendations? (3) Is NZ's coronial law achieving its full preventive potential? and (4) Should a regime requiring responses to coroners' recommendations be part of NZ law?

Described as "the ombudsman for the dead",[28] the coroner's role is to identify the causes and circumstances of sudden or unexplained deaths, or deaths in special circumstances, such as deaths of people under compulsory detention. Coronial death investigations cover deaths in widely varying circumstances, from deaths as a result of criminal activity, missing persons who are suspected to have died, and deaths that occur in the course of clinical care. The coroner may hold an inquiry into a death to determine the deceased's identity, and when, where, how and why s/he died.[29] The coroner makes decisions about whether to order a post-mortem and whether to retain or release body parts and tissue samples.

Not all deaths reported to the coroner result in an investigation or inquiry. In 2010, the NZ Coroner's Office had 5645 deaths reported where there was uncertainty as to whether a medical certificate of the cause of death could be issued.[30] The coroner accepted jurisdiction in respect of 3343 of those cases. In the remaining 2302 cases, the coroner and doctor discussed the case and a medical certificate of cause of death was issued rather than commencing a coronial investigation. In practical terms the coroner will usually discuss the death with the consultant and make a judgement call whether the case warrants investigation.

If a coroner undertakes an inquiry (either by inquest or in chambers), s/he is not required to make recommendations or comments to prevent the occurrence of future similar deaths. If a coroner does make recommendations, a copy of the findings (including the recommendations) is sent to the organisation/s stated in the coroner's decisions to those entities by the coroner's administrative staff. When a NZ coroner directs a recommendation to an organisation, there is no statutory requirement for that organisation to respond to the coroner (or any entity) about

---

[28] R.C. Bennett "The Changing Role of the Coroner" (1978) 118 CMA 1133 at 1133.

[29] Coroners Act 2006, s 4(2).

[30] Email from CSNZ to Jennifer Moore regarding number of deaths in the coronial jurisdiction (2 February 2011).

what, if anything, they propose to do. However, some organisations do voluntarily write letters in response to coroners' recommendations. Those responses are often described in the CSNZ *Recommendations Recap*.[31]

NZ's recent disasters, such as Pike River and the Christchurch earthquakes, have brought mortality into focus.[32] There are approximately 29 000 deaths in NZ per year.[33] About 20% of those deaths must be reported to the coroner.[34] According to John Fogarty QC, "there can be no doubt that the Coroners Act saves lives, and establishes a process whereby the community can have confidence of an independent inquiry into unusual death where no one . . . can hide from scrutiny."[35]

There is no NZ empirical research, and limited international research, about the extent of organisations' implementation of coroners' recommendations. A recent Australian study explored the implementation of coroners' recommendations in Victoria.[36] This book is the first NZ project to investigate the rigour of coronial recommendations, and the extent of their impact and implementation. The findings have informed the debate about whether law reform is required to enable coroners to fulfil their statutory prophylactic function. An evaluation of whether coroners' findings have the potential to save lives is lacking and is well overdue.

This book uses NZ data, but it has international dimensions because it also includes analysis of literature, Coroner's Court findings and appellate litigation from jurisdictions such as England, Canada, Australia and Scotland. In the next section, I explore the literature from around the world that has examined the coronial jurisdiction.

---

31 Coronial Services of New Zealand "Recommendations Recap — Coroners Court" Coronial Services of New Zealand <http://www.justice.govt.nz/courts/coroners-court/publications/recommendations-recap>.

32 "Christchurch earthquake" *Stuff* (New Zealand, 22 February 2012); "Pike River: Our darkest hour" *Stuff* (New Zealand, 24 November 2012).

33 Statistics New Zealand *Births and Deaths* (2012).

34 Sue Johnson "Births, Deaths and Coroners' Inquiries" in *Health Care and the Law* (4th ed., Brookers, Wellington, 2010).

35 John Fogarty "A Chief Coroner" [2000] NZLJ 316 at 316.

36 Georgina Sutherland and others "What Happens to Coroners' Recommendations for Improving Public Health and Safety? Organisational Responses Under a Mandatory Response Regime in Victoria, Australia" (2014) 14 BMC Public Health 732.

1.2 RESEARCH ON CORONERS AND CORONERS' RECOMMENDATIONS

Given the high public profile of coroners, it is surprising that little is known about coroners' decision-making or their recommendations. Numerous scholars have observed that the work of coroners remains largely under-researched.[37] For instance, Bugeja and Ranson observe that despite the "significance of coroners' recommendations for public health and safety, they are a relatively unexplored area of socio-legal and medico-legal research".[38] In 2006, in their authoritative text on coronial law, Freckelton and Ranson noted that it is "remarkable that no empirical base" has yet been generated.[39] There is limited empirical research about the formulation, nature, purpose and implementation of coroners' recommendations.

Empirical research about coroners, their procedures and recommendations is recent. Research in Australia and the UK has quantified the frequency of coroners' recommendations,[40] investigated coronial inquiries about healthcare-related deaths,[41] conducted case studies on specific categories of death,[42] and provided legal and forensic descriptions of death investigations.[43] A 2011 NZ LLB(Hons)

---

[37] For example, see Susanne Langer, Jonathan Scourfield and Ben Fincham "Documenting the Quick and the Dead: A Study of Suicide Case Files in a Coroner's Office" (2008) 56 The Sociological Review 293 at 294; Ian Freckelton and David Ranson *Death Investigation and the Coroner's Inquest* (Oxford University Press, Melbourne, 2006); Ray Watterson, Penny Brown and John McKenzie "Coronial Recommendations and the Prevention of Indigenous Death" (2008) 12 Special Edition 2 Australian Indigenous Law Review 4; David Studdert and Stephen Cordner "Impact of Coronial Investigations on Manner and Cause of Death Determinations in Australia, 2000–2007" (2010) 192 MJA 444.

[38] Lyndal Bugeja and David Ranson "Coroners' Recommendations: Do They Lead to Positive Public Health Outcomes?" (2003) 10 JLM 399 at 399.

[39] Freckelton and Ranson, above n 37, at 742.

[40] Lyndal Bugeja "Determinants of Coroners' Recommendations on External Cause Deaths in Victoria, Australia" (PhD, Monash University, 2011); Bugeja and others "Application of a Public Health Framework to Examine the Characteristics of Coroners' Recommendations for Injury Prevention" [2012] 18 Injury Prevention 326.

[41] Carol Grech "Coronial Inquiries into Fatal Adverse Events in South Australian Hospitals: From Inquest to Practice" (PhD, The University of Adelaide, 2004).

[42] Boronia Halstead *Coroners' Recommendations and the Prevention of Deaths in Custody: A Victorian Case Study* (1995).

[43] Freckelton and Ranson, above n 37.

thesis explored coronial recommendations, but it was not empirical research.[44]

The University of Melbourne's Public Health Law group recently published their first article about research on the introduction of Victoria's mandatory response regime for coronial recommendations.[45] Despite speculative commentary about organisations' responses to coroners' recommendations, there is limited empirical research about the extent of implementation of coronial recommendations. Prior to the Melbourne study, in 2008, Watterson et al. sent letters to several hundred organisations, located in every Australian jurisdiction except Queensland, following their receipt of coroners' recommendations, to inquire how they had responded.[46]

Queensland, the state omitted from the Watterson et al. study, undertook its own review of organisations' responses to coroners' recommendations in 2006.[47] This review focused on recommendations made to public sector agencies. The review found a relatively high rate of implementation (68% fully or partially implemented), but there was no distinction made between action taken before or after recommendations were handed down. The review outlined the main reasons for rejection: concerns that recommendations were too costly, inappropriate or unrealistic, or not within the organisation's power to implement. This Queensland study, the Melbourne research and my NZ project endeavour to tackle "the greatest challenge that remains, [which] is to understand the reasons for the apparent low implementation rate of coroners' recommendations, despite repeated instances of similar fatalities".[48]

Social scientists have undertaken empirical analyses of coronial work. Atkinson's classic 1970s research explored the social organisation of sudden death.[49] More recently, Timmermans has examined the professional authority of medical examiners' determinations on suicide and undertaken ethnography research in a medical examiner's

---

[44] Kate Tidbury "Coronial Recommendations: Ensuring the Dead Really do Speak to Protect the Living" (LLB(Hons), Auckland University, 2011).

[45] Sutherland and others, above n 36.

[46] Watterson, Brown and McKenzie, above n 37.

[47] Queensland Ombudsman *The Coronial Recommendations Project: An Investigation into the Administrative Practice of Queensland Public Sector Agencies in Assisting Coronial Inquiries and Responding to Coronial Recommendations* (2006).

[48] Bugeja, above n 40.

[49] Maxwell Atkinson *Discovering Suicide: Studies in the Social Organization of Sudden Death* (MacMillan, London, 1978).

office.[50] Social scientists have also analysed families' experiences of inquests[51] and how coroners' decisions classify natural versus unnatural death.[52]

There is much non-empirical commentary about coroners, their work and recommendations.[53] An Australian, Professor Ian Freckelton QC, is one of the most prolific scholars of coronial law.[54] Coroner or medical examiner information has also been used as the primary data source for descriptive and analytic research to examine and report the nature, extent, determinants and interventions for the prevention of external-cause deaths.[55] Coronial records have also been used for historical research about suicides in NZ.[56]

---

[50] Stefan Timmermans *Post Mortem: How Medical Examiners Explain Suspicious Deaths* (University of Chicago Press, Chicago, 2007); Stefan Timmermans "Suicide Determination and the Professional Authority of Medical Examiners" (2005) 70 American Sociological Review 311.

[51] Lucy Biddle "Public Hazards or Private Tragedies? An Exploratory Study of the Effect of Coroners' Procedures on Those Bereaved by Suicide" (2003) 56 Social Science and Medicine 1033.

[52] Lindsay Prior "The Good, the Bad and the Unnatural: A Study of Coroners' Decisions in Northern Ireland" (1985) 33 Sociological Review 64.

[53] Justin Malbon "Institutional Responses to Coronial Recommendations" (1998) 6 JLM 35; Hugh Selby *The Inquest Handbook* (The Federation Press, Sydney, 1998).

[54] For example, see Ian Freckelton "Anglo-Australian Coronial Law Reform: The Widening Gap" (2010) 17 JLM 471; Ian Freckelton "Coronership Under Challenge: The Evolving Institution of the Modern Coroner" (The Greek Legal and Medical Conference, Corfu, Greece, 2009); Ian Freckelton "Reforming Coronership: International Perspectives and Contemporary Developments" (2008) 16 JLM 379; Ian Freckelton "The Myers Oration 2005: Untimely Death, Law and Suicidality" (2005) 12 Psychiatry, Psychology and Law 265; Ian Freckelton "International Trends in Death Investigation" (World Association of Medical Law Conference, Brazil, 8 August 2012); Freckelton and Ranson, above n 37; Ian Freckelton "Death Investigation and the Evolving Role of the Coroner" (2008) 11 Otago LR 565; Ian Freckelton "Death Investigation, the Coroner and Therapeutic Jurisprudence" (2007) 15 JLM 242.

[55] For example, see Randy Hanzlick "The Role of Medical Examiners and Coroners in Public Health Surveillance and Epidemiologic Research" (1996) 17 *Annual Review of Public Health* 383.

[56] John Weaver *Sorrows of a Century: Interpreting Suicide in New Zealand, 1900–2000* (Bridget Williams Books and McGill-Queen's University Press, Wellington and Montreal, 2014).

1.3 RESEARCH AIMS, OBJECTIVES AND SIGNIFICANCE

This research, the first of its kind in NZ, aimed to describe, quantify and investigate the nature, recipients and preventive potential of NZ coroners' recommendations from 1 July 2007 to 30 June 2012. 1 July 2007 was chosen as the commencement date because that is when the Coroners Act 2006 (NZ) came into force.

Quantifying the number of recommendations for my five-year study period was a useful aim in itself. On the basis of estimates provided by the CSNZ, my 2012 research proposal estimated that my study period would include approximately 1060 recommendations. My research findings aimed to provide an exact quantification of the number of recommendations for my study period.

Identifying and interviewing the recipients of coroners' recommendations during my study period was a useful objective. I needed to identify the recipients of recommendations in order to examine their rate of implementation. The most prevalent concern is that coroners' recommendations are ineffective because the organisations to which they are directed ignore them.[57] My research assessed the veracity of this concern.

My project also aimed to investigate the preventive potential of coronial recommendations. Coroners spend time making recommendations, and considerable financial resources are spent on public inquests and the administration of the NZ Act. The NZ Ministry of Justice spent $16.57 million to administer the Act in 2010/11.[58] The outlay of funds is justified, partly, on the basis that coroners' recommendations contribute to preventive public health goals. Yet, no research had assessed the public health impact of coroners' recommendations. Is the preventive purpose of the Act being achieved? How can coroners' statutory roles as "public health officials" be effectively fulfilled?[59] A key purpose of my research was to provide evidence-based answers to these questions.

Additional research aims were to:

- analyse the rigour of coronial recommendations
- explore the relationship between coroners' recommendations and morbidity and mortality prevention

---

57 Sutherland and others, above n 36.

58 Email from CSNZ to Jennifer Moore regarding cost to administer the Coroners Act 2006 (2 August 2011).

59 Freckelton, above n 54, at 244.

- analyse what improvements, if any, are required to maximise the preventive potential of coroners' recommendations
- examine the factors that affect the implementation of coronial recommendations
- provide an exploratory project to a field which is important, yet under-researched
- contribute to coronial practice and provide feedback to the CSNZ
- inform law reform, particularly about whether a mandatory response regime should be introduced in NZ.

The research objectives were to:

1. Analyse NZ coroners' recommendations from 2007 to 2012.
2. Conduct semi-structured interviews with coroners, recipients of recommendations and interested parties.
3. Survey recipients of recommendations who received coroners' recommendations during the study period and who were not interviewed.
4. Analyse appellate litigation about coroners' recommendations and their preventive function.

As Pickering has commented, studying practices (as this project does) can contribute to the "development of critical and policy-oriented perspectives".[60] My purpose was to bridge the research–practice and research–policy divides. Such research–practice translation includes feedback to research participants. Twelve of the fifteen coroners I interviewed reported that they are largely unaware of their colleagues' practices. One coroner explained that he "doesn't talk as freely . . . to my fellow coroners as I am to you [the interviewer]" and that he "would love to see, to know, more about how other coroners do their work".[61] This research seeks to provide some insight into coronial practice, particularly their decision-making about recommendations.

---

[60] Andrew Pickering "From Science as Knowledge to Science as Practice" in *Science as Practice and Culture* (University of Chicago Press, Chicago and London, 1992) 1 at 6.

[61] Interview with Coroner Dymond (Jennifer Moore, 16 October 2012).

1.4 STUDY METHODS AND UNDER-REPORTING IN THE NZ CORONIAL JURISDICTION

While the topic of this book is legal, I use methods from public health and health sociology.[62] The research questions cannot be answered using legal methods alone. As Freckelton and Ranson have pointed out, it is "unlikely that the available data sets will be mined in a way that their potential would allow . . . unless specialists in epidemiological analysis [public health researchers] are employed by Coroner's offices on a regular basis".[63]

This book is based on the following data:

1. coroners' recommendations
2. interview transcripts
3. questionnaire responses
4. appellate decisions.

1.4.1 Coroners' Recommendations

The aims of the textual analysis of coroners' recommendations were to describe the:

- nature of NZ coroners' recommendations
- nature of the recipients of coroners' recommendations.

The study population comprised deaths reported to, and investigated by, the CSNZ for the five-year study period 1 July 2007 – 30 June 2012, where one or more recommendations were made by coroners in their findings. A coroner's finding is a report written by the coroner about the facts of a death. The finding will include who the deceased was, where, when, and how s/he died. The finding is a public document. Members of the public can request copies, although there may be prohibition orders.

Comments or recommendations arising from coronial investigations are usually located at the end of the finding. The recipients to be sent one or more recommendations are usually specified in the recommendation or comment itself. However, coroners differ in the way that they write their findings, the frequency that they make recommendations and the scope of

---

[62] The author of this book is a lawyer, health scientist and social scientist with a PhD in Public Health from the University of Melbourne's Faculty of Medicine.

[63] Freckelton and Ranson, above n 37, at 741.

those recommendations.[64] There is a template for NZ coronial findings, but it is not used by all coroners. The following template was proposed by Harding J:[65]

IN THE CORONERS COURT

AT [*Location*] **CSU-201**

UNDER	THE CORONERS ACT 2006
AND	
IN THE MATTER	of an Inquiry into the death of [*Name of deceased*]

Date(s) of Hearing: [*Date*]

Appearances:

Date of Findings:

FINDINGS OF CORONER [initials and surname]

INTRODUCTION

[1] xxx

FACTS

[2] xxx

ISSUES

[3] xxx

DISCUSSION

[4] xxx

CONCLUSIONS

[5] xxx

FORMAL FINDINGS

[6] xxx

COMMENTS/RECOMMENDATIONS

[7] xxx

RESTRICTION OF PUBLICATION

[8] xxx **Coroner [initials and surname]**

---

64 This variation in coronial findings and recommendations is also evident in Australian states and territories. For example, see Federation of Community Legal Centres, Victoria *Saving Lives by Joining up Justice: Why Australia Needs Coronial Reform and How to Achieve it* (2013) at 27.

65 I am grateful to Coroner McElrea for drawing my attention to this template.

Many researchers, particularly in public health and social science, regard coronial information as a rich source of data.[66] However, it is not necessarily easy to access coronial data. Coronial websites in NZ and Australia do not provide automatic access to all coroners' findings. An Australian report concluded that "there are significant limitations to most of the publicly available information".[67] The report highlights the access difficulties faced by "advocates and researchers trying to prevent future deaths . . . via accessing findings and recommendations for all similar deaths" because the "information sought is often not publicly accessible via the internet".[68]

Given the limitations of the coronial data sources, what coronial information was used for this study and how was it accessed? If a researcher cannot source the data from the internet, could s/he access the information from the NZ Coroner's Court Law Reports? There are no formal law reports for the NZ Coroner's Court, even though the NZ Coroner's Court is a Court of Record.[69] Commentators have identified under-reporting, and the undesirable consequences such as inconsistent decision-making, as problematic for the coronial jurisdiction.[70]

Without the extremely helpful and competent assistance of the then NZ Chief Coroner and the CSNZ staff, this research would not have been possible.[71] With their assistance, the information for this study was available from four sources:

1. the CSNZ and their case management system (CMS)
2. the CSNZ website
3. New Zealand Legal Information Institute (NZLII)
4. *Recommendations Recap*.

---

[66] Timothy Robert Driscoll "The Epidemiology of Work-related Fatalities in Australia" (Doctor of Philosophy, University of Sydney, 2002); Bugeja, above n 40, at 107–8.

[67] Federation of Community Legal Centres, Victoria, above n 64, at 24.

[68] At 24–5.

[69] For example, see *Newton v Coroner's Court* HC Christchurch CIV–2004–409–2173, 7 October 2004, where it was held that the Coroner's Court is a court of record and, as such, is subject to the general rule that proceedings ought to be heard in public unless there is a strong countervailing public interest overriding the need to disseminate information.

[70] For example, see Jennifer Moore "An Empirical Approach to the New Zealand Government's Review of the Coronial Jurisdiction" (2014) 21 JLM; Freckelton and Ranson, above n 37, at ch 7.

[71] I am particularly grateful to Judge Neil MacLean, the Research Counsel, Jackie Andrews, Wendy Proffitt and Dean Skachill.

I have discussed these data sources and their limitations in detail elsewhere.[72] Here, I raise the issue to illustrate that the "data sources" and "data collection" phases of this study were not straightforward tasks.

Researchers can contact the CSNZ and request a search of the CMS. The CMS is a national database for NZ coronial cases.[73] Information about every death reported to a coroner since 1 July 2007 is stored on the system. If the researcher requires coronial cases pre-2007, the CSNZ will need to undertake a much more complicated and time-consuming task.

Researchers can also search the National Coronial Information System (NCIS). The NCIS is a data storage and retrieval system for coronial information for Australian cases and which, from July 2013, now also includes some NZ coronial data.[74] However, the full text of coroners' findings and recommendations is not publicly available from the NCIS. If a researcher wishes to access information from the NCIS, s/he must make an application to the NCIS, which is then subject to approval by the NCIS Research Committee and the Victorian Department of Justice Research Ethics Committee.[75] A fee of \$1000–\$2750 is payable.[76] The standard online fee for universities is \$2750.[77] The application process can take at least two months.

Another option is for the researcher to search the CSNZ website for information. There are a small number of full coroners' findings on the CSNZ website. Thirty-eight full findings of "public interest" are available on the website.[78] If the desired finding is not in this list of 38 coroners'

---

72 Jennifer Moore and Mark Henaghan *New Zealand Coroners' Recommendations, 2007–2012 (final report)* (2014) at chapter 2.

73 Coronial Services of New Zealand "Coronial data collection – Coroners Court" (14 February 2014) Coronial Services of New Zealand <http://www.justice.govt.nz/courts/coroners-court/publications/findings-recommendations-and-records/coronial-data-collection>.

74 National Coronial Information System "About the NCIS | National Coronial Information System" (14 February 2014) National Coronial Information System NCIS <http://www.ncis.org.au/data-collection/>.

75 National Coronial Information System "How to access data? | National Coronial Information System" National Coronial Information System NCIS <http://www.ncis.org.au/how-to-access-data-on-the-ncis/>.

76 Email from Joanna Cotsonis (Access Liaison Officer, NCIS) regarding fees for access to NCIS (26 July 2013).

77 Cotsonis, above n 76.

78 Coronial Services of New Zealand "Findings of public Interest – Coroners Court" Coronial Services of New Zealand <http://www.justice.govt.nz/courts/coroners-court/media-centre/findings-of-public-interest/findings-of-public-interest>.

findings, the researcher must email the Operations Manager at the CSNZ to request the required information.[79]

If a researcher does not require full coronial findings, there is more information accessible. Since late 2013, it has been possible to access most coroners' recommendations (not the full findings) from 1 July 2007 on either the CSNZ website or the NZLII.[80] While this is an improvement, for legal researchers and practitioners, it is not a substitute for formal law reports. For this research, I was unable to rely on NZLII or the CSNZ website because I required the full findings.

The information provided in an individual summary of a recommendation on NZLII includes:

- the name of the case
- the date of the last update of the information
- date of the finding
- "summary of recommendation"
- recommendations or comments made by the coroner.

The "summary of recommendation" is typically only a few sentences which describes information about the case such as the cause of death. The information provided on NZLII is minimal. An example of the information provided on NZLII is as follows:[81]

> **Bellingham [2009] NZCorC 6 (17 February 2009)**
> Last Updated: 21 May 2012
> Date of Finding: 17th February 2009
>
> SUMMARY OF RECOMMENDATIONS
>
> Todd Stancy Bellingham, 18 years of age at the time of this tragedy on Sunday the 26th of August 2007, died as a result of multiple injuries sustained in a car crash while participating in a rally sprint event organised by the Waiuku Dirt Track Club in the Waiuku Forest on this day.

---

[79] Coronial Services of New Zealand "Findings and Recommendations — Coroners Court" Coronial Services of New Zealand <http://www.justice.govt.nz/courts/coroners-court/publications/findings-recommendations-and-records/>.

[80] NZLII "New Zealand Coroners Court Decisions" NZLII <http://www.nzlii.org/nz/cases/NZCorC/>.

[81] *Bellingham* [2009] NZCorC 6.

RECOMMENDATIONS MADE BY CORONER BRANDT SHORTLAND

I. The only recommendation we can suggest is irrespective of budget constraints or policy decisions, there should always be sufficient medical expertise on course to deal with the worst case scenario in any form of motor racing. Cases such as this run the risk of an overhaul of racing rules and safety procedures.
II. We take the view that an overhaul is not warranted. There needs to be better contingent medical attention for the serious crash.

It is helpful to have this information online. I could not, though, rely on such limited information. NZLII does not even state whether the inquiry was by inquest or a chambers finding. Therefore, the full coronial findings provided by the CSNZ CMS were invaluable.

I cross-checked the recommendations on NZLII against the same findings that were on the USB drive provided by the CSNZ. This cross-checking was important because sometimes NZLII referred to a coronial statement as a recommendation, whereas the original coroner's finding referred to the same statement as a comment. For example, in the *Bellingham* case above, is Coroner Shortland's second recommendation actually a comment? In the first recommendation Coroner Shortland states that "the only recommendation [he] can suggest is. . . ." This statement suggests that he will only make one recommendation, yet NZLII lists both statements as recommendations under a heading "recommendations made by Coroner Brandt Shortland". Given that there is a difference between a recommendation and a comment, and this study's inclusion criterion is recommendations, it was vital that I did not inappropriately code a comment as a recommendation.

Researchers and members of the public can also access a document called *Recommendations Recap* on the CSNZ website.[82] Since late 2011, the CSNZ has been publishing this document. The *Recommendations Recaps*, which appear every three months, are summaries of coroners' recommendations.[83] The *Recommendations Recap* is a useful initiative, but it is not a substitute for official law reports. They are summaries of the recommendations, not the complete findings. They do not include findings in which recommendations were not made.

The data gathered comprised the variables which I have analysed in detail elsewhere, and also the free text of the coroners' recommendations

[82] *Recommendations Recap* documents are available from the Coronial Service of New Zealand website: <http://www.justice.govt.nz/courts/coroners-court/publications/recommendations-recap>.

[83] See the Coronial Service of New Zealand website.

and comments for each coronial inquiry.[84] The variables were used to classify the data in Microsoft Excel. The data analysis procedure included, broadly, assessment of the:

- number of coroners' recommendations and comments
- recipients to which recommendations were directed
- organisations' responses to recommendations
- number of coroners' references to previous, similar cases.

As Bugeja has explained, the "analysis was complex as some incidents resulted in various combinations of multiple deaths, recommendations made and organisations sent recommendations".[85] For instance, a coroner may direct a single recommendation to one recipient, or multiple recipients. Alternatively, a coroner may direct many recommendations to one recipient, or multiple recommendations to many different organisations.

My final estimate of the number of coroners' recommendations is different from the number generated by the CSNZ because of our different counting rules. For example, as outlined above, I classified certain coronial statements as comments, whereas the same statements were classified by the CSNZ on NZLII as recommendations. After reading the full finding for *Collings*, for instance, I counted one coronial statement as a recommendation and the other as a comment, whereas NZLII has coded the two statements as recommendations.[86] I encountered another scenario where NZLII recorded coronial statements as comments, but they were actually recommendations. For example, NZLII used a heading "comments made by coroner" but when I read the comments I discovered that one or more was actually a recommendation. In *Keenan*, for example, NZLII states "comments made by Coroner RG McElrea" and goes on to note these comments as:[87]

> It is likely that, although the neoprene chest waders Mr Keenan was wearing are designed to give buoyancy, his chances of survival would have been enhanced if he had been wearing an inflatable life vest, preferably in conjunction with a belt. Water Safety New Zealand (WSNZ) recommends the use of neoprene chest waders. These should be worn with a belt and personal floatation device. *We recommend that WSNZ gives publicity* to the desirability of using neoprene chest waders in conjunction with a belt and personal floatation device, by suitable publicity to members of the public and specialist suppliers and users of such products.

---

84 Moore and Henaghan, above n 72 at chapter 2.

85 Bugeja, above n 40, at 201.

86 *Collings* [2009] NZCorC 163.

87 *Keenan* [2010] NZCorC 6 (author's emphasis).

When one reads these supposed coronial comments, it is not difficult to notice that the coroner makes a recommendation when he states: "we recommend that WSNZ. . . ." In these scenarios, I coded the appropriate comments as recommendations, ignoring the headings on the NZLII. Presumably, however, the CSNZ and the NZLII have counted these coronial statements as comments, thereby generating further differences between my quantification of coroners' recommendations and theirs.

Also, sometimes coroners' findings do not specify whether their statements are comments or recommendations. In this scenario, I coded these according to the statutory definition and the definitions of comment and recommendation described during interviews with the coroners.

The total number, range and average number of recommendations and comments per inquiry during the study period were calculated. The number and proportion of recipients to which recommendations were directed during the study period was calculated. The types of recipients sent coroners' recommendations were also described by calculating the proportion of government, not-for-profit, for-profit, individual and untargeted recipients. The number of organisations' responses to recommendations was also calculated. The data analysis also included description of the following:

- the method of case completion, by calculating the proportion of inquest or chambers inquiries
- the classification of types of deaths, by calculating the proportion of ICD-10 external cause and natural cause deaths
- the number of comments per incident
- the number of recommendations and comments per coroner
- the number of recommendations per year for the five-year study period.

After much of the data analysis of the coroners' recommendations component of the research was completed, I began the interviews.

1.4.2 Interviews

I interviewed 15 coroners, 79 organisations and 8 interested parties. Overall, 17 coroners were approached and 15 agreed to participate. The response rate for all coroners is 88%.[88]

---

88 A study in Victoria, Australia which included interviews of coroners had a response rate of 29.3%. See Bugeja, above n 40, at 294.

Table 1.1 Recipients of coroners' recommendations, by category, NZ, 1 July 2007 – 30 June 2012

Recipients	n	%
Government	121	39%
Not-for-profit and/or non-government	67	22%
For-profit	44	14%
Individuals	5	2%
Untargeted	72	23%

The organisations were identified from the sample of coroners' recommendations. All coroners' findings from the study sample (1 July 2007 to 30 June 2012) were read. The name/s of the recipient/s to which each coroner's recommendation was directed was entered into Microsoft Excel into a column called 'recipient'. The recipient could be single or multiple and of various types. Coroners direct their recommendations to identifiable organisations (government, not-for-profit or for-profit) or individuals. Coroners also direct their recommendations to a single recipient or multiple recipients. For instance, one recommendation can be directed to the Ministry of Health; whereas another recommendation can be directed to the Ministry of Health, the Health and Disability Commissioner, and Plunket.

Sometimes coroners direct their recommendations to groups. I coded these as 'untargeted'. This group includes recipients of recommendations where there is no identifiable organisation or individual. For instance, coroners directed recommendations to "hunters",[89] "recreational divers"[90] and "candidates for licences".[91]

A dataset of 309 recipients was identified. Table 1.1 and Figure 1.1 describe the recipients of coroners' recommendations in the study sample. The highest number of recommendations were directed to government organisations (n=121, 39%). The smallest number of recommendations were directed to individuals (n=5, 2%). Although coroners "are trying to ensure that a recommendation is targeted and that it says *who* it is to go to", a significant proportion (n=72, 23%) were untargeted.[92]

89 *Timms* [2008] NZCorC 62.
90 *Ngapera* [2010] NZCorC 126.
91 *Lewis* [2011] NZCorC 186.
92 Interview with the Chief Coroner (Jennifer Moore, 12 September 2012).

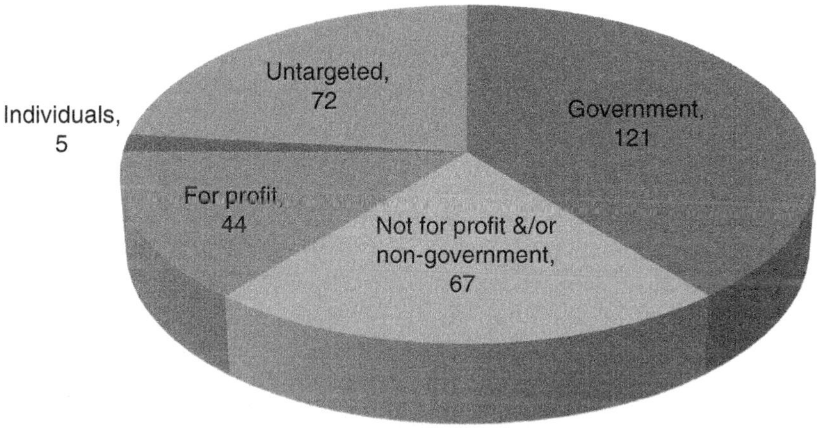

Figure 1.1 Recipients of NZ coroners' recommendations

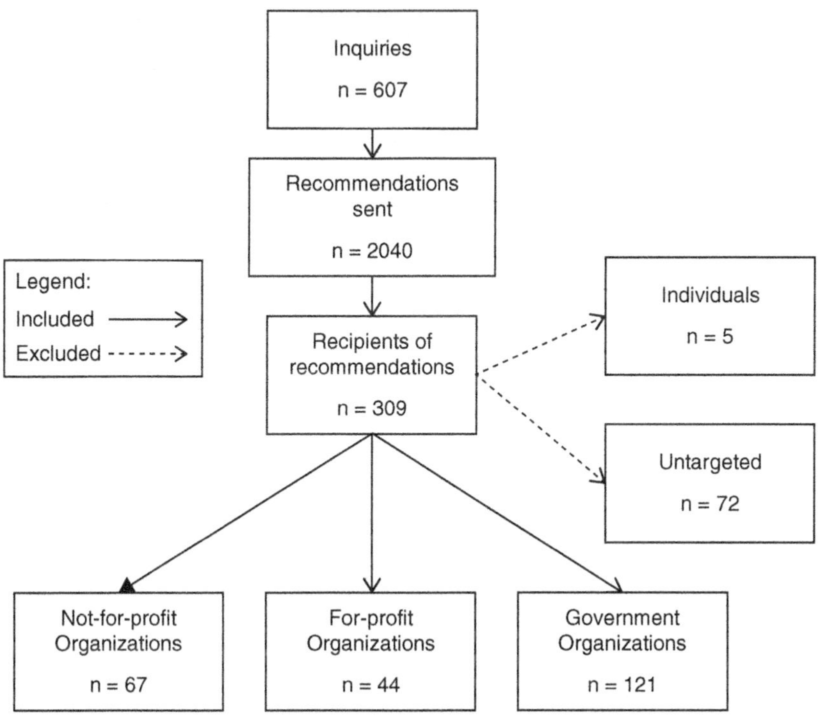

Figure 1.2 Summary of recipients of recommendations included in and excluded from the qualitative study

Table 1.2 Number and percentage of organisations sent NZ coroners' recommendations, by type, 1 July 2007 – 30 June 2012

Organisations	n	%
Government	121	52%
Not for profit and/or non-government	67	29%
For profit	44	19%
	232	

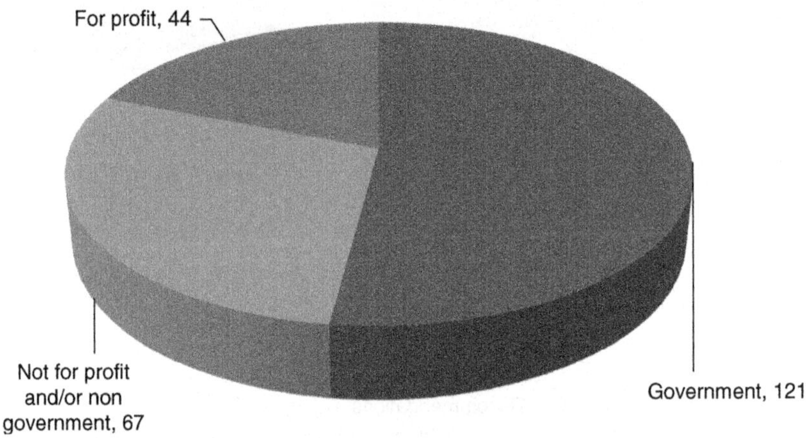

Figure 1.3 Number of organisations sent NZ coroners' recommendations, by type

Only identifiable organisations were included in the qualitative study.[93] Individuals and untargeted recipients were excluded because it is not possible to contact and interview the recipients of untargeted recommendations (Figure 1.2).

The remaining dataset included 232 organisations. Table 1.2 and Figure 1.3 describe the type of organisations that were sent coroners' recommendations in the study sample. Just over half of coroners' recommendations were directed to government organisations (n=121, 52%).

The inclusion criterion was organisations that were sent coroners' recommendations during the study period. Some organisations (16)

[93] Although untargeted recommendations were excluded from the qualitative study, they were included in our study of coroners' recommendations and analysed in chapter 3.

contacted me, offering to participate. The remaining 216 organisations were contacted.

Seventy-nine of the 232 organisations were able to participate. I conducted 100 interviews with senior individuals from organisations because sometimes I interviewed more than one person from a single organisation. This is because several people are typically involved in considering coroners' recommendations. For example, at some district health boards (DHBs) it is usual for the Chief Legal Advisor, the Coronial Liaison Officer, the Chief Medical Officer, and the CEO to be involved in reviewing coroners' recommendations.

The eight interested parties include two medical professionals, three lawyers, three families and one organisation with an interest in coroners' recommendations. The sample of interested parties is not representative, nor can it be generalised to all NZ lawyers, medical professionals or families that are involved in the coronial jurisdiction. The interested parties were included because of the depth of their experience with the Coroner's Court. They also provide a different perspective on coroners' recommendations than the views garnered from organisations and coroners.

1.4.3 Questionnaire

As I explained in section 1.4.2 above, 79 of the 232 organisations were able to participate in the interviews. During the interviews, participants were asked for their views about the introduction of a mandatory statutory regime whereby organisations would be required to respond to coroners' recommendations. All coroners interviewed were in favour of the introduction of a mandatory response regime. Only two organisations did not support such law reform. The NZ Courts Minister's review also considered whether to include this law reform option in its review.[94] The media focused on the perceived problems caused by absence of a mandatory response regime under the current Coroners Act.[95]

Given the public interest in this law reform option, and the strong support garnered during interviews, I decided to investigate the views of those organisations that had declined to be interviewed. I wondered

---

[94] Cabinet Paper *Coroners Act Review: Proposals for Reform – Paper 1* (2013) at [21].

[95] For example, see Scott Inglis "Safety Must be Prime Concern" *Bay of Plenty Times* (31 January 2014) <http://www.nzherald.co.nz/bay-of-plenty-times/news/article.cfm?c_id=1503343&objectid=11194832> where the author argues that "coroners should be given greater powers to compel people and organisations to make changes when it comes to safety".

whether the organisations that declined to participate in the study did not wish to be interviewed because they do not consider or respond to coroners' recommendations. I also wanted to know how many organisations that were not interviewed would agree with the introduction of a mandatory response regime for coroners' recommendations. Without the questionnaire data, a limitation of the research may have been that only those organisations that respond to coroners' recommendations participated in the study, providing unbalanced results. Combining the questionnaire data with the interview data provided a clearer picture of organisations' views about law reform options.

I devised a two-page questionnaire that asked participants (senior individuals from organisations) for their views on coroners' recommendations. The questionnaire comprised three sections. In the first section, participants were asked to respond to ten statements about coroners' recommendations using a five-point Likert scale, with 1 being 'strongly agree' and 5 being 'strongly disagree'.[96] In the second section, participants were asked to state whether they believe any changes need to be made to the coronial system (yes or no option) and asked them to explain why or why not. Finally, I asked participants to explain why they did or did not support the introduction of a system which required organisations to respond to coroners' recommendations.

Forty-two of the 153 organisations returned completed questionnaires. That is a response rate of 27.4%.

1.4.4 Appellate Cases

I reviewed appellate litigation about coroners' recommendations and the coronial preventive function. I analysed cases from NZ, Australia, Canada, England, Ireland and Scotland. The dataset included judgments over the last ten years (January 2005 – June 2015) and several significant precedents from the 1980s and 1990s. Discussion of the cases is organised thematically and, thus, appears in several sections throughout this book.

---

[96] Research shows that a five-point scale is optimal for closed questions: Martin Tolich and Carl Davidson "Collecting Data" in *Social Science Research in New Zealand* (Pearson, North Shore, 2007) at 146. For further information about Likert scales, see DA de Vaus *Surveys in Social Research* (5th ed., Allen and Unwin, New South Wales, 2002) at 102 and 182–6.

1.5 STRUCTURAL OVERVIEW OF BOOK

In Chapter 2, I explore the coronial jurisdictions in Australia, England, Scotland, Ireland, Canada, the United States and NZ. This analysis provides the context for the next chapter's discussion of coronial recommendations.

In Chapter 3, I describe and quantify the NZ coroners' recommendations in my study period. Given the limitations of the coronial information that I outline in Chapter 1, an important contribution of this study is quantifying the number of recommendations from 2007–12. The results and discussion in this chapter address my research objective to describe the nature, frequency and recipients of NZ coroners' recommendations, 1 July 2007 – 30 June 2012.

In Chapter 4 I analyse the organisations' responses to my interview questions about what action (if any) they took upon receipt of coronial recommendations and what factors influenced their decision. I explain that little is known about whether and how organisations that receive recommendations act on them. But there is much speculation that most coronial recommendations are not implemented. The most prevalent concern (expressed by coroners, public inquiries, the media and the public) is that coroners' recommendations are ineffective and have little or no preventive impact because the organisations to which they are directed ignore them. This chapter provides landmark data on the actual rate of implementation of NZ coronial recommendations.

Chapter 5 traces the origins of coroners' statutory prophylactic function. It also analyses the key barriers to maximising this function and strategies for improvement. This chapter highlights that the majority of research participants are supportive of the statutory preventive function. While there have been improvements since the introduction of the Coroners Act 2006 (NZ), the findings suggest that the prophylactic potential of coroners' recommendations has not yet been fully realised in NZ. The empirical evidence in this chapter suggests that recommendations could be improved by encouraging more coroners to consider similar cases, undertaking analysis of patterns and comparative risks.

The preventive potential of coroners' recommendations could also be improved by the introduction of a mandatory response regime, which is the topic of Chapter 6. I analyse the debate about whether mandatory response regimes should be included in NZ coronial legislation, drawing from overseas experiences. This chapter describes the participants' overwhelming support for the introduction of such a regime. I highlight that introduction of a mandatory response regime cannot be a replacement for early consultation with organisations and interested parties *during* the coronial process. I argue that the Coroners Act 2006 (NZ) should be amended to include a mandatory response regime and that the NZ Government's review (which excludes this proposal) is inconsistent with the empirical evidence.

Chapter 7 brings together the important threads from the preceding chapters. This chapter presents a summary of my findings, an analysis of the limitations of my research and a call for further research. It also discusses the implications of my findings and how they might inform coronial practice and law reform.

2. Coronial jurisdictions

2.1 THE INTERNATIONAL LEGAL CONTEXT

Freckelton and Ranson have warned that evaluation of death investigation systems in different jurisdictions in order to identify a model system, may be difficult because of variations in organisational structures and professional bases across jurisdictions.[1] This chapter does not attempt to repeat Freckelton and Ranson's detailed discussion of Coroner's Courts around the world.[2] Rather, this chapter summarises the coronial systems in Australia, England, Scotland, Ireland, Canada and the United States in order to provide an international legal context for this book's analysis of recommendations.

2.1.1 Australia

England's coronial system was received by Australia at the time of settlement in 1788.[3] The coroner's primary role then, as it is now, was the investigation of sudden death.

Unlike NZ, Australia has no national coronial regime.[4] Rather, each state or territory has its own regime controlling coronial processes, including the making of recommendations to prevent deaths.

Victorian coronial law is contained in the Coroners Act 2008 (Vic). Like New Zealand's legislation, a central purpose of the Act is to contribute to a reduction in the number of preventable deaths.[5] The review

---

[1] Ian Freckelton and David Ranson *Death Investigation and the Coroner's Inquest* (Oxford University Press, Melbourne, 2006) at 94.

[2] Freckelton and Ranson, above n 1.

[3] Freckelton and Ranson, above n 1.

[4] Although some systems related to coroners do function at the national level. For example, the National Coronial Information Service (NCIS), an Internet-based data storage and retrieval system for Australian coronial cases. See the National Coronial Information Service website, available at <http://www.ncis.org.au>.

[5] Coroners Act 2008 (VIC), s(1)(c).

of the Coroners Act 1958 (Vic) resulted in major reforms to the Victorian coronial system and the introduction of the Coroners Act 1985 (Vic).[6]

The 1985 Act established an Office of the State Coroner and a centralised coronial service which houses the State Coroner's Office and the Victorian Institute of Forensic Medicine. The rationale for this arrangement was to enhance death investigations and contribute to prevention.[7] Most importantly for prevention, Section 21(2) of the 1985 Act provided that coroners can make recommendations to the Attorney General on any matter connected to the death, including public health and safety and the administration of justice relating to death.

Victoria is the most advanced Australian jurisdiction in terms of its coronial services and is recognised as a leader of coronial reform.[8] Freckelton predicted that the report of the Parliament of Victoria Law Reform Committee (PVLRC) would provide a "blueprint for a new generation of coronial law reform"[9] and, given the recent or ongoing reforms in NSW, Western Australia, the Northern Territory and the Australian Capital Territory, this appears to be the case. Indeed, the Victorian Coroners Act 1985 formed the basis for the enactment of similar legislation in a number of other Australian states.[10]

Both New South Wales and Queensland adopted new coronial legislation in the last decade. The Coroners Act 2003 (QLD) has death prevention through the making of coroners' recommendations as a primary object. The Coroners Act 2009 (NSW) enshrines the importance of death prevention by providing for coroners' recommendations on matters including public health.[11] Both Acts allow coroners to make recommendations directed at relevant entities for preventive purposes.[12]

Northern Territory coroners are also vested with a statutory prophylactic function. The Coroners Act 1993 (NT) allows coroners to make recommendations to the Attorney General on any matter connected with

---

6 Parliament of Victoria Law Reform Committee *Coroners Act 1985 Review Final Report* (2006).

7 Graeme Johnstone "An Avenue for Death and Injury Prevention" in Hugh Selby (ed.) *The Aftermath of Death* (Leichhardt Federation Press, New South Wales, 1992) 140.

8 Rebecca Scott Bray "New Victorian Coroners Act" (2009) 34 Alt LJ 207, at 207.

9 Ian Freckelton "Coronial Law Reform: The New Wave" (2006) 14 JLM 151, at 152.

10 Lyndal Bugeja "Determinants of Coroners' Recommendations on External Cause Deaths in Victoria, Australia" (PhD, Monash University, 2011).

11 Coroners Act 2009 (NSW), s 3(e); Coroners Act 2003 (QLD), s 3(d).

12 Coroners Act 2009 (NSW), s 82; Coroners Act 2003 (QLD), s 46.

an investigated death or disaster, including public health or safety or the administration of justice.[13] Likewise, legislation in South Australia, Western Australia and the Australian Capital Territory also allows for coronial recommendations. The Western Australian coronial system was recently reviewed by the Law Reform Commission of Western Australia.[14]

Coroners in Tasmania have a duty to make recommendations in order to prevent further deaths: "A coroner *must*, whenever appropriate, make recommendations with respect to ways of preventing further deaths and on any other matter that the coroner considers appropriate."[15] Tasmanian coroners are thus compelled to make preventive recommendations, where appropriate, unlike in most other jurisdictions where the legislation is framed in terms of a discretionary power to make recommendations or comment in respect of preventable deaths.

2.1.2 England

England's is the oldest coronial regime in the world. Coronership is an ancient judicial office. It has been described as "shape-shifting" because of its dramatic evolution over the centuries.[16] There is some evidence that a coroner existed as early as the ninth century.[17] However, it is generally accepted that the office of the coroner was established in 1194 with the Articles of Eyre.[18] An element of the coroner's role entailed providing information to Richard I's judges as they toured the country. The coroner's main duty was as a tax gatherer.[19] The medieval coroner held inquests, heard appeals and confessions of felons. These were the "crown pleas" which the coroner had to "keep" and he did so by safeguarding lands and goods, arresting witnesses and suspects and recording all the details.[20]

Coroners were elected in the county court by the knights and freeholders of the shire from the county gentry and middle classes.[21] The basis of

---

13 Coroners Act 1993 (NT), s 35(2).

14 Law Reform Commission of Western Australia and Tatum L. Hands *Review of Coronial Practice in Western Australia: Final Report Project 100* (2012).

15 Coroners Act 1995 (Tas), s 28(2).

16 Freckelton and Ranson, above n 1, at v.

17 At 4.

18 Paul Matthews *Jervis on Coroners* (Sweet and Maxwell, London, 2002) at 1.

19 R.F. Hunnisett *The Medieval Coroner* (Cambridge University Press, Cambridge, 1961) at 1.

20 Hunnisett, above n 19.

21 Jill McKeough "Origins of the Coronial Jurisdiction" (1983) 6 UNSWLJ 191.

the election of coroners was land ownership, reputation as wise, lawful men and residence in the district.[22] Coroners were not required to have legal or medical knowledge and they enjoyed tenure for life.[23]

The De Officio Coronatoris 1276 was the first description of the English coroner's death investigation duties.[24] This included a primitive version of the post-mortem examination, where the coroner would inspect and feel the naked body for wounds, bruises or signs of injury.[25]

The coroner's legal inquiry was the *inquisitor* (inquest). The inquest was held with a jury to ascertain the cause of death.[26] The coroner recorded the proceedings on the roll for presentment.

The coroner's status declined in the fourteenth century.[27] The centralisation of justice in the fifteenth and sixteenth centuries in the King's Courts, the creation of the Escheators and Justices of the Peace, caused further decline in coronial work.[28] The consequence was that the coronial inquest was largely confined to cases of death.

Despite this narrowing of the coroner's role, it was not until the Births and Deaths Registration Act 1836 that there was a formal obligation for coroners to notify local registrars of deaths.[29] The County Coroners Act 1860 provided for coroners to be paid a salary.[30]

In modern England, the Coroners Act 1980 (UK) disposed of English coroners' historic ability to add "riders" or comments to coronial findings, removing the preventive aspect of the coroner's role. This occurred because of a perception that coroners and juries were abusing the power to add riders to findings, often expressing opinions on matters irrelevant to, or insufficiently supported by, the evidence.[31]

Rule 43 of the Coroners Rules 1984 (UK) altered this situation by creating the power for a coroner to report a matter to a relevant authority where a coroner believed that action should be taken to prevent the recurrence of fatalities similar to the one under inquest.[32] While, strictly

---

22 Carol Grech "Coronial Inquiries into Fatal Adverse Events in South Australian Hospitals: From Inquest to Practice" (PhD, The University of Adelaide, 2004).
23 McKeough, above n 21.
24 Grech, above n 22.
25 Grech, above n 22.
26 McKeough, above n 21.
27 Freckelton and Ranson, above n 1, at 11.
28 Matthews, above n 18.
29 Births and Deaths Registration Act (UK) 1836 6 & 7 Will IV c 86, s 25.
30 County Coroners Act 1860 (UK) 23 & 24 Vict c 116, s 4.
31 Matthews, above n 18, at 13–54.
32 Coroners (Amendment) Rules 2008 (England and Wales) Rule 43.

speaking, this power to report is not a power to make particular recommendations, such recommendations may be informally made within official reports.[33] This delegated legislation was updated in 2008 in order to give greater prominence and importance to coroners' reports to improve public health and safety.[34] For example, coroners were given a wider remit to make reports to prevent future deaths; it did not have to be related to a similar death.[35]

The current legislation is the Coroners and Justice Act 2009 (UK). Under this new Act, the coroner must report matters to the newly established Chief Coroner and all "interested persons" where there is a risk that other, similar deaths may occur and the coroner believes action should be taken to prevent such an occurrence.[36] The Chief Coroner acts as a centralised figure for the coronial system, with functions that include ensuring that reports and responses made in relation to deaths in one coronial district are not overlooked in another, so that preventable deaths are less likely to occur.[37] This is to be achieved through the publication of six-monthly summaries of Rule 43 reports (which are renamed as "Reports on Action to Prevent Future Deaths")[38] and their corresponding responses on the Ministry of Justice website and also in the Chief Coroner's annual report. The summaries include trends, reports with wider implications, and annexes giving details of the number of reports issued by each coroner district, organisations which have not responded to the coroner, and all reports received.[39]

---

33 Christopher Dorries *Coroners' Court: A Guide to Law and Practice* (2nd ed., Oxford University Press, Oxford, 2004).

34 UK Ministry of Justice *Guidance for Coroners on Changes to Rule 43: Coroner Reports to Prevent Future Deaths* (2008).

35 Ministry of Justice *Guidance for Coroners on Changes to Rule 43: Coroner Reports to Prevent Future Deaths* (2008) at 3.

36 Coroners and Justice Act 2009 (UK), Sch 5, s 7. See also reg 28(4) of the Coroners (Investigations) Regulations 2013, which came into effect on 25 July 2013. The coroner may also send a copy of the report to any other person who the coroner believes may find it useful or of interest.

37 Ministry of Justice *Guidance for Coroners on Changes to Rule 43: Coroner Reports to Prevent Future Deaths* (2008).

38 Office of the Chief Coroner *Guidance No. 5: Reports to prevent future deaths*. For simplicity, this book will continue to use the term "Rule 43 reports" to refer to Reports on Action to Prevent Future Deaths.

39 These summaries can be accessed from the Ministry of Justice's website, at <http://www.justice.gov.uk/coroners-burial-cremation/coroners/rule-43>.

2.1.3 Scotland

Freckelton has observed that the Lockerbie disaster highlighted the significant differences between death investigation in Scotland and coronial jurisdictions elsewhere in the world.[40] In jurisdictions, such as Scotland, that follow the civil code system derived from Roman law, sudden deaths are not investigated by a coronial system. Instead, death investigation in Scotland is carried out by the Office of the Procurator Fiscal and the sheriff courts.

The office of the Procurator Fiscal was first established in the sixteenth century with the single responsibility of collecting sheriffs' fines.[41] However, its function has since shifted. Procurators Fiscal are now qualified lawyers, employed by the Crown Office and Procurator Fiscal Service.[42] The Procurator Fiscal is an independent public prosecutor. The police and other agencies report crimes to him/her which s/he must consider and decide whether to take criminal proceedings in the public interest. The modern Procurator Fiscal's role at common law and under statute covers three areas: most importantly, the prosecution of crime in Scotland, but also the investigation of deaths which are sudden, unexplained or suspicious and complaints against the police.[43]

Certain types of death require a fatal accident inquiry, requiring a sheriff in the Sheriff's Court to set out the circumstances of death.[44] The Fatal Accidents and Sudden Deaths Inquiry (Scotland) Act 1976 prescribes that fatal accident inquiries will be held before a sheriff without a jury.

Pursuant to section 6(1), the sheriff must determine the cause of death, any reasonable precautions that might have been taken so as to prevent the death and any defects in a system that contributed to the death or to an accident resulting in the death. The sheriff holds the inquiry, generally at the application of the procurator fiscal.[45] The sheriff presiding over a fatal accident inquiry determines matters relating to legal representation,

---

40 Freckelton and Ranson, above n 1.

41 "Historical development of the office of Procurator Fiscal", Crown Office and Procurator Fiscal Service. <http://www.copfs.gov.uk/News/Historical/HistDevPF>.

42 "The Role of the Procurator Fiscal in the Investigation of Deaths", Crown Office and Procurator Fiscal Service. <http://www.crownoffice.gov.uk/sites/default/files/Publications/Resource/Doc/13556/0000589.pdf>.

43 "About Crown Office and Procurator Fiscal Service", Crown Office and Procurator Fiscal Service. <http://www.copfs.gov.uk/about/about-crown-office-and-procurator-fiscal-service>.

44 Fatal Accidents and Sudden Deaths Inquiry (Scotland) Act 1976, s 6(1).

45 Freckelton and Ranson, above n 1.

access to and the provision of relevant and material evidence and the scope of cross-examination of witnesses.[46] Section 6(1)(c) provides the sheriff with the power to determine reasonable precautions, if any, whereby the death might have been avoided.

Sheriffs make recommendations in around one-third of cases.[47] Upon making a determination, a sheriff must send a copy of the determinations reached to the Lord Advocate,[48] and to the parties to the proceeding,[49] and the Government maintains a website where some recommendations are published in brief.[50] Freckelton asserts that while the procurator fiscal's role includes prevention, "evaluation of criminality remains a central part of the office".[51]

A Scottish Government-commissioned review of fatal accident inquiries was published in late 2009, promoting an explicit preventive purpose achieved through a recommendatory power.[52] At the time of writing, the Scottish Government was still considering the report.[53] The Scottish Parliament has not yet made a legislative response to this report.

2.1.4 Ireland

Although the first recorded mention of the Irish Coroner was in 1264, the office may have existed since 1212.[54] Historically, Irish coroners held inquests into sudden and violent deaths. They were also expert witnesses at assizes and could operate as sheriffs. The reforms between 1829 and 1908 brought the Irish Coroner "into the modern era".[55] The Coroners

---

[46] *Kennedy & Anor v Lord Advocate & The Scottish Ministers* [2009] CSOH 01 (Outer House) at para 24.

[47] Lord Cullen of Whitekirk KT – *Review of Fatal Accident Inquiry Legislation: The Report* <http://www.scotland.gov.uk/Resource/Doc/290392/0089246.pdf>.

[48] Fatal Accidents and Sudden Deaths Inquiry (Scotland) Act 1976, s 6(4)(a).

[49] Fatal Accidents and Sudden Deaths Inquiry Procedure (Scotland) Rules 1977, r 11(3).

[50] See the Scottish Government's website at <http://www.scotland.gov.uk/Topics/Justice/law/fatalaccidentinquiries/Recommend>.

[51] Freckelton and Ranson, above n 1, at 82.

[52] Lord Cullen of Whitekirk KT – *Review of Fatal Accident Inquiry Legislation: The Report* <http://www.scotland.gov.uk/Resource/Doc/290392/0089246.pdf> at 3.32 and 8.25.

[53] "Review of Fatal Accident Inquiry Legislation", The Scottish Government. <http://www.scotland.gov.uk/About/Review/fatal-accident-review>.

[54] Freckelton and Ranson, above n 1, at 82.

[55] Freckelton and Ranson, above n 1, at 83.

(Ireland) Act 1881 permitted medical practitioners, barristers, solicitors or justices of the peace to become coroners.

In Ireland today, pursuant to the Coroners Act 1962 (Ir), coroners are independent officials who investigate sudden and unexplained deaths. Coroners must be medical practitioners or practising barristers or solicitors with five years' experience.[56] There are 47 Coroner districts in Ireland.[57] The Civil Law (Miscellaneous Provisions) Act 2011 amended the legislation to allow for the Coroner districts of Dublin city and Dublin county to be amalgamated.

The Irish Coroner's Court is inquisitorial and is similar to its English counterpart. The inquiry is initially concerned with determining whether the death was due to natural causes. If the cause of death is unnatural, an inquest must be held.[58]

While the principal legislation is the Coroners Act 1962 (Ir), the Coroners Amendment Act 2005 provides for increased sanctions for those who refuse to cooperate with the conduct of an inquest. Recommendations "of a general character designed to prevent further fatalities may be appended to the verdict at any inquest".[59]

In 1998, the Irish Government established a working group to review the coronial service. In 2000, the group published its report, concluding that there are many shortcomings with the Irish coronial system. Academic commentators have similarly noted the weaknesses in the Irish coronial system, such as under-resourcing.[60] Many of these issues have been observed in other coronial jurisdictions such as NZ. For example, under-reporting minimises the preventive potential of coroners' recommendations in many jurisdictions, including Ireland. According to McGovern, it is "time to implement change" in the Irish coronial system, not least because:[61]

> The data which coroners collect on population morbidity is an invaluable resource, that still remains unused at a national level in this country. The scattered storage and different methods of preserving documents have made it

---

[56] Coroners Act 1962 (Ir), s 14(1).

[57] Coroners Act 1962 (Ir) (Ireland IE), s 6(1); Coroner Service, Department of Justice and Equality "Coroner Service: Who are Coroners?" Coroner Service, Department of Justice and Equality <http://www.coroners.ie/en/CS/Pages/Who%20Are%20Coroners>.

[58] Coroners Act 1962 (Ir), s 17.

[59] Coroners Act 1962 (Ir), s 31(2).

[60] Cliona McGovern "The Coroner Service in Ireland – Time to Implement Change" (2007) 13 Medico-Legal Journal of Ireland 2.

[61] McGovern, above n 60, 6.

> an almost impossible task to allow for a proper analysis of the files. It would be of great advantage were they all to be stored and archived in one location. Additionally, it would allow for proper statistical analysis and enable death investigators to identify other similar cases which have occurred in the country.

The Working Group's report included 110 recommendations.[62] Although it was expected that the new legislation, to implement many of these recommendations, would be introduced the following year, the Coroners Bill was introduced in 2007. At the time of writing, the Coroners Act 1962 (Ir) remained in force.

In *Lawlor & Anor v Geraghty*, the High Court of Ireland commented on the coroner's role.[63] Referring to the 2005 Supreme Court of Ireland decision, *Magee v Farrell*, the Court observed that the "role of the coroner is judicial in nature".[64] Further, the coroner enjoys "a relatively wide jurisdiction in terms of enquiring into the circumstances surrounding a person's death".[65]

In *Lawlor*, the applicants were the parents of the deceased who had died in 2007 while undergoing elective cosmetic surgery in Colombia. The applicants sought an order to quash the decision of the respondent coroner to refuse their application for adjournment of the inquest on the grounds that the coroner had not exhausted all efforts to obtain medical notes about their son's treatment. The Court held that the coroner ought to have adjourned the inquest to endeavour to obtain the hospital records. Kearns P stated:[66]

> It is difficult to imagine a more obvious case than this one where a family in the particular circumstances would require clarification about the circumstances surrounding the death of the deceased, not least because it would afford the family an opportunity for some emotional closure on family tragedy and provide also an opportunity for the making of suitable recommendations at the conclusion of the inquest. None of these things occurred or were allowed to occur.

This highlights the importance of coronial information-gathering which may assist investigation into the circumstances of death and the formulation of preventive recommendations.

---

62 Department of Justice, Equality and Law Reform, Ireland *Review of the Coroners Service: Report of the Working Group* (2000).

63 *Lawlor & Anor v Geraghty* High Court, 20 May 2010.

64 *Lawlor & Anor v Geraghty*, above n 63, at 4.

65 *Lawlor & Anor v Geraghty*, above n 63, at 6.

66 *Lawlor & Anor v Geraghty*, above n 63, at 12.

2.1.5 Canada

Inherited from England, the coronial system for death investigation still exists in the Canadian provinces.[67] However, unlike other jurisdictions such as Australia and NZ, whose coronial system origins are English, most Canadian coroners are medical practitioners, not lawyers appointed as judicial officers. For example, in Alberta, death investigations are undertaken by medical examiners (doctors) who are assisted by medical examiners' investigators. In Saskatchewan, by contrast, not all of the province's coroners are medical practitioners. They come from a "wide variety of backgrounds including medical, legal, business and investigations".[68]

In Ontario, all coroners have medical qualifications. According to Freckelton and Ranson:[69]

> Canadian systems for death investigation have received considerable approbation, in particular that of Ontario. The innovative approaches taken in this jurisdiction with respect to death prevention and coroners' recommendations have been particularly effective, and this has occurred in a setting where coroners are for the most part medical practitioners with a focus on public health, rather than legal practitioners.

The Ontario coronial regime's public health orientation was noted by an Ontario judge who stated that coroners with a medical orientation "bring to their task their medical experience and their situation-sense of patients, families, illnesses, medical record confidentiality, medical institutions and medical care".[70] This focus is strengthened by the joint leadership that the Ontario Chief Coroner and Chief Forensic Pathologist provide to the regime.[71] The Ontario Office of the Chief Coroner's focus on death prevention is clear from its motto: "We speak for the dead to protect the living."[72]

Inquests in Ontario inquire into the circumstances of the death and

---

67 Freckelton and Ranson, above n 1, at 75.

68 Government of Saskatchewan "Frequently Asked Questions – Ministry of Justice – Government of Saskatchewan" <http://www.justice.gov.sk.ca/coroner-faq>.

69 Freckelton and Ranson, above n 1, at 79.

70 *People First of Ontario v Porter, Regional Coroner Niagara* (1991) 5 OR (3d) 609; [1991] OJ No. 3389 (Div Ct).

71 See Ministry of Community Safety and Correctional Services' website: <http://www.mcscs.jus.gov.on.ca/english/DeathInvestigations/AboutDeathInvestigationsinOntario/DI_intro.html>.

72 See the Office of the Chief Coroner's website: <http://www.mcscs.jus.gov.on.ca/english/DeathInvestigations/office_coroner/coroner.html>.

determine who the deceased was, and how, when, where and by what means the deceased died.[73] The strict rules of evidence do not apply. Inquests are held with juries. Parties address the jury with suggestions about their findings and potential recommendations. The jury makes recommendations that may prevent similar deaths.[74] In Chapter 6, I explore the Canadian provinces' prevention-focused death investigation systems further, focusing in particular on their approach to recommendations and organisational responses to recommendations.

2.1.6 United States of America

The English coronial system was imported to the US with the first British immigrants.[75] The first recorded American inquest took place in 1635. Coroners were elected and inquests were held with juries. Over time, coroners in the US were discredited. Corruption was rife, the office politicised and coroners tended to be unqualified occupants of minor political office, farmers or undertakers.[76] The anti-corruption and medical lobbies pushed for reform. The result was that many states replaced coroners with the medical examiner system of death investigation.

Today, the medical examiner system has been established in many US states. However, as commentators have recorded, the variation and large number of independent jurisdictions handling death investigations in the US "makes a clear overall description of the medical examiner system impossible".[77] The fragmented, disparate death investigation system in the US has generated complaints and formal reviews.[78]

According to the US Department of Justice, as of 2004, 16 states had a centralised state-wide medical examiner system.[79] Fourteen states had a county coroner system, seven had a county medical examiner system, and 13 had a mixed county medical examiner and coroner system. Eight states with decentralised death investigation systems also had a state medical

---

73 Coroners Act RSO 1990, c C-37, s 31(1).

74 Ontario Ministry of Community Safety and Correctional Services "Ministry of Community Safety and Correctional Services: About Death Investigations in Ontario" <http://www.mcscs.jus.gov.on.ca/english/DeathInvestigations/About DeathInvestigationsinOntario/DI_intro.html>.

75 Freckelton and Ranson, above n 1, at 70.

76 At 71.

77 At 72; Randy Hanzlick and Debra Combs "Medical Examiner and Coroner Systems: History and Trends" (1998) 279 *JAMA* 870; Matthew J. Hickman and others *Medical Examiners' and Coroners' Offices, 2004* (NCJ 216756 2007).

78 Freckelton and Ranson, above n 1, at 73.

79 Hickman and others, above n 77, at 1.

examiner office performing medico-legal duties (Alabama, Arkansas, Georgia, Iowa, Kentucky, Montana, North Dakota and Tennessee).[80] The District of Columbia reported a city medical examiner office, which functioned similarly to a state-wide system.

Where a coronial role does exist, it is an elected position, and a wide range of individuals may hold the office of coroner, many of them funeral directors and most non-physicians. Some counties in South Carolina and Indiana have elected forensic nurses to the role, but they are not judicial officers.[81] Some coroners may also hold other official positions, particularly law enforcement positions, which can raise conflicts of interest with their role as coroner.[82] For all US coronial systems, the responsibility of coroners is primarily to determine the time, cause and manner of death. In carrying out this function, coroners retain quasi-judicial powers, including the power to subpoena and in some states to empanel juries, although they are not judicial officers, instead being regarded "executive branch officials".[83]

Medical examiners have no power to hold hearings or inquests.[84] Instead, the investigation records are treated as documents which may be discovered and used in evidence in civil or criminal proceedings. The 1971 British review of death certification found that the medical examiner system is not regarded as sufficiently thorough in removing public doubts and suspicions.[85]

Medical examiners bring the sort of medical expertise to death investigation for which Anglo-Australasian, legally trained coroners must rely upon independent experts. Legally trained coroners, however, are better placed to marshal evidence and oversee the often complicated inquests that death investigations involve, including dealing with witnesses and interested third parties.

It is beyond the scope of this book to engage fully with the debate as to whether a medical examiner model or coronial system is superior. New Zealand's Law Commission considered and rejected proposals to reform New Zealand's death investigation system to adopt medical examiners.[86] In addition, such a change was not included in the current

---

80 At 1.

81 Freckelton and Ranson, above n 1, at 73.

82 Freckelton and Ranson, above n 1.

83 At 73.

84 At 73.

85 Brodrick Committee *Report of the Committee on Death Certification and Coroners* (1971).

86 New Zealand Law Commission *Coroners* (NZLC R62 2000) para 148.

NZ Government's terms of reference for review of the coronial system. Moreover, "the pressures that have been generated in the United States for replacement of coroners by medical examiners have not been experienced to the same degree in other countries with coroners' jurisdictions."[87] The debate in the US as to which system is more appropriate for death investigation "does not translate well into other coronial systems around the world".[88] This perhaps is partly because the present focus of American death investigation systems is primarily criminal justice rather than public health and death prevention,[89] although there are indications that this is changing[90] and there is sharing of coronial information for prevention purposes.[91]

This study's participants identified either Victoria, Australia (88/123) or Ontario, Canada (35/123) as the prevention-focused "Rolls Royce", "gold standard" systems.[92] It is possible that the Victorian system was more frequently identified by participants as their preferred jurisdiction because it is physically close to NZ and, like NZ, has legally qualified coroners.

2.2 NEW ZEALAND CORONIAL JURISDICTION

2.2.1 Historical Origins

New Zealand inherited the English coronial system, and in 1846, adopted its own coronial legislation with the passing of the Coroners Ordinance 1846.[93] The Ordinance was repealed by the Coroners Act 1858 (NZ).[94]

---

87 Freckelton and Ranson, above n 1, at 74.

88 At 75.

89 In other words, American death investigations are performed mainly to detect criminal activity and to collect evidence relating to causes of deaths for use in predominantly criminal proceedings. See Randy Hanzlick "Medical Examiners, Coroners and Public Health: A Review and Update" (2006) 130 Arch Pathol Lab Med 1274.

90 For example, the findings of medical examiners and coroners are increasingly being used by public health and other organisations to improve product or environmental safety. See Hanzlick, above n 89.

91 Randy Hanzlick "The Centres for Disease Control and Prevention's Medical Examiner/Coroner Information Sharing Program (MecISP)" (1997) 42(3) Journal of Forensic Science 531.

92 For example, Interview with HealthCareOrganisation214 (Jennifer Moore, 13 March 2013); Interview with Coroner Price (Jennifer Moore, 12 October 2012).

93 Freckelton and Ranson, above n 1.

94 Coroners Act 1858 (NZ), s 13.

The Coroners Act 1867 (NZ) followed. This Act provided for inquests to be held with a jury with a minimum of 12 members. The 1867 Act was amended in 1908, removing the requirement that a coroner sit with a jury when holding an inquest. The Coroners Act 1951 (NZ) consolidated the New Zealand and English law of the time.[95] Coroners' juries were abolished and the Act gave coroners the same powers, privileges, immunities and authorities as Justices of the Peace.

The 1984 *Final Report of the Working Party on Delays in the Release of Bodies for Burial* was the catalyst for the next redraft of coronial legislation.[96] The Working Party's findings were reflected in the Coroners Act 1988 (NZ), which remained the key piece of coronial legislation until the overhaul of the coronial system in 2006.[97]

The introduction of the 2006 Act was prompted by a Law Commission report published in 2000, which made recommendations for reform.[98] This report concluded that the coronial system was under-resourced, insufficiently valued, lacking in leadership and culturally insensitive. The Act, which came into force on 1 July 2007, provides the legislative framework for the operation of the coronial jurisdiction in New Zealand. The purpose of the Act is to help prevent deaths and to promote justice through:[99]

(a) investigations, and the identification of the causes and circumstances of sudden and unexplained deaths, or deaths in special circumstances, and
(b) the making of specified recommendations or comments that, if drawn to public attention, may reduce the chance of occurrence of other deaths in circumstances similar to those in which those deaths occurred.

2.2.2 Modern Coronial Services of New Zealand

(a) What is the CSNZ?

Prior to the overhaul of the coronial jurisdiction in the mid-2000s, there were 74 coroners located throughout NZ.[100] The Law Commission's 2000 report on the coronial jurisdiction documented differing views about

---

95 "(29 November 1951)" 296 New Zealand Parliamentary Debates 1184.
96 "(14 July 1987)" 482 New Zealand Parliamentary Debates 10430.
97 (14 July 1987), above n 96.
98 New Zealand Law Commission, above n 86.
99 Coroners Act 2006 (NZ), s 3(1)(a), (b).
100 New Zealand Law Commission, above n 86, at 18.

whether to centralise the coronial districts.[101] The report revealed that coroners were balancing their coronial duties with other legal work.[102] The Department of Courts submission to the Law Commission reported that 20% of the coroners did 80% of the work.[103] The Law Commission envisaged the centralisation of coronial districts with full-time, and better resourced and remunerated coroners. The Coroners Act 2006 (NZ) ushered in this vision. Today, NZ has 16 full-time coroners and a Chief Coroner, who work in a centralised coronial system – the Coronial Services of NZ.

The Coronial Services of New Zealand (CSNZ) primarily comprises the Office of the Chief Coroner, the regional offices and coroners' chambers and the Coronial Services Unit (CSU). The CSNZ is part of the Ministry of Justice. The Coronial Services Unit provides "case management and administrative support to the coroners to help them fulfil their duties".[104] The CSU also liaises with families of the deceased as they navigate through the coronial process.[105]

The Coronial Services Operations Manager is located in Auckland and oversees coronial operations throughout NZ. The Chief Coroner's chambers are also in Auckland, but the Chief Coroner travels regularly throughout New Zealand. The national office is located in Wellington. There are nine regional offices: Whangarei, Auckland, Hamilton, Rotorua, Hastings, Palmerston North, Wellington, Christchurch, and Dunedin.[106]

(b) Who is the CSNZ?

(i) Chief Coroner The current Chief Coroner, Judge Deborah Marshall, was appointed in February 2015. She was a coroner in Auckland from January 2013 to February 2015. The former Chief Coroner, Judge Neil MacLean, served as a Christchurch Coroner from 1978 to 1993. He began his role as NZ's first Chief Coroner in February 2007. The 2007 Coroners' Orientation Programme highlighted that the previous coronial system "lacked leadership".[107] The creation of a Chief Coroner sought to remedy this problem by providing leadership and coordination.

---

101 At 18.

102 At 17–18.

103 At 17–18.

104 Coronial Services of New Zealand "Coronial Services Staff" <www.justice.govt.nz/courts/coroners-court>.

105 Ibid.

106 Coronial Services of New Zealand "Local Offices" <www.justice.govt.nz/courts/coroners-court/contact-us/local-offices>.

107 David Baragwanath "How We Got Here: Law Commission Report 62 and

The Chief Coroner is appointed by the Governor General.[108] The appointment is made on the advice of the Attorney General, after consultation with the Minister of Justice.[109] The Coroners Act 2006 (NZ) requires that "the person appointed as Chief Coroner must be a District Court Judge, or a coroner immediately before being appointed Chief Coroner, or appointed as a Coroner when appointed as the Chief Coroner".[110] The appointment as Chief Coroner must be for a period not exceeding eight years.[111] There is no opportunity for reappointment.[112] NZ's current Chief Coroner, Judge Deborah Marshall, took office in February 2015. The former Chief Coroner, Judge Neil MacLean, was in office from February 2007 to February 2015.

The Chief Coroner's main function is to ensure the integrity and effectiveness of the coronial system provided for in the Coroners Act 2006 (NZ).[113] The Act outlines 14 additional functions which enable the Chief Coroner to carry out their main functions.[114] For example, the Chief Coroner oversees coroners' inquiries to ensure they are orderly and expeditious[115] and promotes consistency in coronial decision-making.[116]

(ii) Coroners New Zealand coroners are lawyers appointed as judicial officers. Coroners must have at least five years' experience as a barrister or solicitor before appointment.[117] In jurisdictions with the "medical examiner" system, the death investigators are qualified doctors, not lawyers. In NZ, two coroners are dually qualified as nurses and lawyers. Several coroners hold postgraduate qualifications and many hold bachelor's degrees in disciplines such as engineering, social sciences and Maori studies.

During interviews for this study, some participants expressed surprise upon learning that coroners are lawyers, not doctors. The confusion may be related to the so-called "CSI effect", whereby television depicts medical

---

the Coroners Act 2006" (paper presented to Coroners Orientation Programme, Wellington, 18 June 2007) at 2.

108 Coroners Act 2006, s 105(1).
109 Coroners Act 2006, s 105(3).
110 Coroners Act 2006, s 105(2).
111 Coroners Act 2006, s 105(4).
112 Ibid.
113 Coroners Act 2006, s 7.
114 Coroners Act 2006, s 7(a) – (n).
115 Coroners Act 2006, s 7(a).
116 Coroners Act 2006, s 7(h).
117 Coroners Act 2006, s 103.

examiners and pathologists undertaking death investigation. These portrayals suggest to the public that coroners are doctors. Two coroners who were interviewed asserted that in the future, all NZ coroners will, or should, be trained in health/science and law,[118] or at least be medico-legal specialists.[119] Given the size of NZ, it may not be realistic to recommend that *all* coroners *must* be trained in health and law. However, the data highlight that coroners should have access to appropriately qualified public health researchers and clinicians.

Coroners are appointed by the Governor General, on the advice of the Attorney General, after consultation with the Minister of Justice. The Coronial Services of NZ website explains the appointment procedure as follows:[120]

> As vacancies occur the usual practice is for a request for expressions of interest to be advertised in the relevant metropolitan newspaper/s and other appropriate legal publications, to which the legal profession has access. The response form used in the past covers contact details, clarification of citizenship and residence status, gender and ethnic information (optional) age etc together with at least three nominated referees who can vouch for character and accuracy of the information supplied. A statutory declaration is also required confirming no criminal convictions or disciplinary actions or unresolved complaints. Also that the applicant is financially secure with no bankruptcy or related issues. [sic] Also that there is no other matter which might affect credibility in office. [sic]

Although there is no specific age requirement, many NZ coroners are in their 40s and 50s. Section 103 of the Coroners Act 2006 (NZ) provides for security of tenure, while section 110 states that coroners' salaries are to be determined by the Remuneration Authority. NZ coroners are full-time, unless they are authorised by the Attorney General to act as part-time coroners.[121]

There is a statutory cap for a maximum of 20 full-time coroners.[122] There are currently 16 coroners, plus the Chief Coroner. They are located in the nine centres with regional offices that were listed above in the section "What is the CSNZ?" There are four coroners in Auckland: Coroners Katharine Greig, Morag McDowell, Sarn Herdson and Debra

---

118 Price, above n 92.

119 Price, above n 92; Interview with Coroner Reid (Jennifer Moore, 30 October 2012).

120 Coronial Services of New Zealand "Frequently Asked Questions" <www.justice.govt.nz/courts/coroners-court/frequently-asked-questions>.

121 Coroners Act 2006, s 108.

122 Coroners Act 2006, s 109(1).

Bell. They cover Auckland, Henderson, Manukau, Papakura, Pukekohe and Takapuna.[123]

Four of the regional centres have two coroners in each location.[124] Coroner Matenga is based in Hamilton and covers Hamilton, Cambridge, Huntly, Matamata, Te Aroha, Paeroa, Te Awamutu, Te Kuiti, Thames and Waihi. The areas Hawera, Levin, Kaikoura, Marlborough, Marton, Motueka, Nelson, New Plymouth, Ohakune, Palmerston North, Taihape, Taumaranui, Wanganui, and Waverley are covered by Coroners Carla na Nagara and Tim Scott. The Wellington coroner Peter Ryan covers Kapiti, Lower Hutt, Masterton, Porirua, Upper Hutt, Wellington and the Chatham Islands. The coroners based in Christchurch are Sue Johnson and Richard McElrea. They cover Ashburton, Christchurch, Rangiora, Timaru, Waimate, Greymouth, Hokitika, Westport and Ross Dependency.

Dunedin, Hastings, Rotorua and Whangarei have one coroner each.[125] Dunedin's Coroner, David Crerar, covers Alexandra, Balclutha, Cromwell, Dunedin, Gore, Invercargill, Oamaru, Queenstown, Te Anau and Wanaka. Dannevirke, Eketahuna, Gisborne, Hastings, Napier, Ruatoria, Waipukurau and Wairoa are covered by Coroner Christopher Devonport, who is based in Hastings. Rotorua's Coroner, Wallace Bain, covers Putaruru, Rotorua, Taupo, Tauranga, Tokoroa and Whakatane. Dargaville, Kaikohe, Kaitaia, Kerikeri, Warkworth, Whangarei and Raoul Island (Kermedec Group) are covered by Coroner Brandt Shortland.

The Chief Coroner can designate other coroners to conduct inquiries where there is a good reason why the coroners to whom the deaths have been reported should not conduct them.[126]

Every coroner vacates that office, if s/he has not earlier done so in another way, upon attaining the age of 70 years.[127] However, a former coroner of, or over, the age of 70 years may from time to time be reappointed for a term not exceeding 12 months.[128] The Governor-General may, if s/he thinks fit, remove a coroner from office for inability or misbehaviour.[129]

---

123 Coronial Services of New Zealand "Local Offices" <www.justice.govt.nz/courts/coroners-court/contact-us/local-offices>.

124 Ibid.

125 Ibid.

126 Coroners Act 2006, s 7(e).

127 Coroners Act 2006, s 103(4).

128 Coroners Act 2006, s 103(5).

129 Coroners Act 2006, s 114(1).

(iii) Support staff The CSNZ has different staff positions throughout the country. Coronial Case Managers assist coroners and families. They help coroners by managing each case from the time the deceased is released from the mortuary until the coroner's finding is distributed to all parties.[130] Families involved in the coronial process will also often interact with Coronial Case Managers after their loved ones have been released from the mortuary.

The National Initial Investigation Office Senior Coordinator and Coordinators include staff who:[131]

> work at a centralised location to receive and manage any newly reported death. They deal with the coronial process from the report of a new death up to when the person is released from the mortuary. They assist the coroner by ensuring the initial coronial process is managed and that families are kept informed on what is happening in relation to a post mortem, the notification of body tissue retention and when the person is released from the mortuary.

Coronial Service Administrators fulfil a variety of support roles. They answer telephone calls from families who ring the regional offices.[132] Regional staff assist families through the coronial process and ensure "proper processes are followed".[133]

The media are able to report on most aspects of the Coroner's Court. A dedicated staff member deals with enquiries from the media.

In addition to administrative staff, the coroners are supported by a Judicial Support Manager and two Research Counsel. Information services are provided to coroners and members of the public who have requests for coronial findings.

2.2.3 The Coroner's Role and the Death Investigation Process

The NZ coroner's role is described in section 4 of the Coroners Act 2006 (NZ). The coroner's task commences once a report of a death is received from the NZ Police. Anyone who finds a body in NZ must report the death to the NZ Police.[134] The Police are responsible for determining whether the death should be reported to the coroner.

NZ coroners investigate sudden, unnatural and violent deaths. Deaths

---

130 Coronial Services of New Zealand "Coronial Services Staff" <www.justice.govt.nz/courts/coroners-court/contact-us/coronial-services-staff>.
131 Ibid.
132 Ibid.
133 Ibid.
134 Coroners Act 2006, s 14.

that "must" be reported under the Coroners Act 2006 (NZ) include deaths:[135]

- without known cause, suicide, or unnatural or violent
- for which no doctor's certificate is given
- during medical, surgical, dental or similar operation or procedure
- in official custody or care.

Sections 13(1)(c) and 13(1)(d) include numerous subsections. For example, reportable deaths under section 13(1)(c)(iv) that occur during "medical, surgical, dental or similar operation or procedure" include "every death . . . that occurred while that person was affected by an anaesthetic".

Section 63 of the Coroners Act 2006 (NZ) states that coroners can decide whether to open and conduct an inquiry and, in doing so, they must have regard to several matters such as whether the death "appears to have been unnatural or violent" and "the existence and extent of any allegations, rumours, suspicions, or public concern, about the death. . .".

Once the death has been reported to the coroner, s/he must determine whether to direct a post-mortem, and if one is directed, determine who, other than the pathologist, may attend. The coroner is also responsible for authorising the release of a body after the post-mortem. The coroner decides whether to open an inquiry, and if an inquiry is to be conducted, whether an inquest should be held. Pursuant to section 80 of the Coroners Act 2006 (NZ), a coroner who decides to open an inquiry may decide to hold an inquest or undertake a chambers ("on the papers") investigation. However, if the death appears to have occurred in official custody or care (as defined in section 9) the coroner "must" hold an inquest.

The coroner must open and conduct an inquest for the three purposes stated in section 4(2): to determine the details of the death; to make recommendations to reduce the chances of the occurrence of future deaths in similar circumstances; and to determine whether the coroner is in fact the correct authority to investigate the death.[136]

An inquest is not an opportunity to undertake a "roving Royal Commission".[137] The nature of a coronial inquest is described as follows:[138]

> A Coroner's Inquest is a judicial hearing presided over by a warranted judicial officer, who has most of the ancillary powers of a District Court Judge.

---

135 Coroners Act 2006, s 13(1)(a) and (b).
136 Coroners Act 2006, s 4(2).
137 *Re Doogan; Ex parte Lucas-Smith* (2005) 193 FLR 239 at 28.
138 LexisNexis *Coroners, The Laws of New Zealand* (LexisNexis) vol 8 at 25.

> An inquest is a fact-finding exercise rather than a method of apportioning guilt. The procedures and rules of evidence that are suitable for one exercise are unsuitable for the other. . . . It is an inquisitorial process, a process of investigation quite unlike a trial.

Contemporary coronial law reform in Australia has sought to define the boundaries of the coronial role more effectively. The Law Reform Commission of Western Australia's review of their coronial jurisdiction revealed concerns about "wide-ranging inquests" and "broad recommendations tenuously connected to deaths".[139]

Section 4 defines the coroner's role, but it is only a "general guide".[140] Their role is much broader than conducting inquests. Coroners liaise with other investigators such as the Health and Disability Commissioner. They are proactive about speaking to the public, appearing in the media and playing crucial roles in the aftermath of disasters such as the Christchurch earthquakes.

In jurisdictions such as NZ, Australia and Canada, coroners have statutory preventive roles. According to Freckelton, the course of the NZ coroner as "a quasi-public health official appears set".[141]

In its review of the Western Australian coronial jurisdiction, the Law Reform Commission of Western Australia concluded that:[142]

> The coroner continues to play a valuable role by ensuring that deaths that fall outside the remit of specialist bodies are not ignored, by enabling the independent exploration of unanswered questions about a death in a public forum and by raising public awareness about circumstances leading to particular deaths.

In NZ, a number of agencies have a specific interest in death reporting and analysing trends and causes of death. In addition to the CSNZ, the following organisations are involved in death prevention: the Office of the Health and Disability Commissioner, the Accident Compensation Corporation, District Health Boards (specifically their internal sentinel event reviews), and the Health Quality and Safety Commission, including the mortality review committees such as the Perinatal and Maternal Mortality Review

---

[139] Law Reform Commission of Western Australia and Hands, above n 14, at 45; Rebecca Scott Bray "Coronial Law Reform" (2010) 35 AltLJ 232.

[140] Coroners Act 2006, s 4(3).

[141] Ian Freckelton "Death Investigation and the Evolving Role of the Coroner" (2008) 11 Otago LR 565, at 583.

[142] Tatum L. Hands "Under the Microscope: Reforming Western Australia's Coronial System" (2012) 39 Brief: Journal of the Law Society of Western Australia 12, at 15.

Committee, Perioperative Mortality Review Committee, Child and Youth Mortality Review Committee, and the Family Violence Death Review Committee.

Although the mortality committees review individual deaths, they analyse and interpret information in the context of population-wide mortality trends and advice is formulated with these broader trends in mind. Mortality committee members provide clinical and epidemiological expertise and can design recommendations that are both evidence-based and feasible.

This contrasts with the narrower construction adapted to the facts of a specific case, which is the primary focus for the coronial process and is aligned to the public accountability/justice aspect of the coroner's role. The Health and Disability Commissioner (HDC) investigative process focuses on the individual acts of specific health practitioners and can result in disciplinary action, and has an outward public focus on practitioner accountability for actions (albeit that practitioners are not always named).

The coronial process serves the interests of justice and assures the public that there is independent scrutiny of unexpected or unexplained death. The coronial process can identify key facts, the proximate cause of death and general context in which the death occurred.

When investigating a case, the coroner is statutorily required to consider whether the death ought to be investigated by other authorities where such investigations form part of their functions, powers and duties. The coroner liaises with the other investigative bodies about the scope and timing of death investigations. Agencies with a formal statutory investigative (and often a disciplinary or prosecutory) function include:

- Police (criminal activity)
- Children's Commissioner (child death)
- Civil Aviation Authority (aviation-related deaths, could result in prosecutions being laid under the CAA Act)
- ACC (to ascertain whether the patient received treatment injury and/or determine any claim for eligibility (for survivor's compensation))
- Director (and Deputy Director) of Mental Health and District Inspectors under the Intellectual Disability (Compulsory Care and Rehabilitation) Act 2003 and Mental Health (Compulsory Assessment and Treatment) Act 1992 (for deaths of patients who are subject to a compulsory treatment order (CTO). Investigations focus on the care provided to the patient and systemic learnings)
- Health and Disability Commissioner (investigating complaints about the appropriateness and quality of healthcare provided to

patients. This may result in Human Rights Review Tribunal or Health Practitioner Disciplinary Tribunal charges being laid against health practitioners)

- Mortality Review Committees established under the New Zealand Public Health and Disability Act 2000
- Medical Officers of Health appointed under the Health Act 1956 (in respect of deaths resulting from communicable diseases)
- Director or officer appointed under the Food Act 1981 (deaths due to a food-borne disease outbreak)
- Inspectors appointed under the Health and Safety in Employment Act 1992 (deaths occurring in the workplace, with a focus on whether all practicable steps had been taken to avoid such injury or death)
- NZTA (road traffic accident deaths)
- Maritime NZ (maritime deaths)
- Independent Police Conduct Authority (deaths of persons detained by the Police or killed by the Police in the course of the Police executing their duties)
- Transport Accident Investigation Commission (land, maritime and aviation deaths)
- Royal Commissions of Inquiry.

Investigations undertaken by any of the above agencies often delay the commencement of the coronial inquiry.

2.2.4 Positive Feedback about the Coronial Jurisdiction

Although this book highlights aspects of the coronial jurisdiction that could be improved, research participants also pointed out elements of the current system which work well. Almost all participants (121/123) reported that the coronial jurisdiction improved after the introduction of the Coroners Act 2006 (NZ). There was a perception that there are "fewer random recommendations than we used to see".[143] Organisations stated that they "take coroners' recommendations seriously" and that the "coronial process is important".[144] Many participants described their "respect" and "admiration" for the coronial jurisdiction.[145]

---

143 Interview with NZ Transport Agency (Jennifer Moore, 12 February 2013).

144 Interview with GovtOrg02 (Jennifer Moore, 5 February 2013).

145 Interview with Clancys (Jennifer Moore, 11 October 2012); Interview with GovtOrg03 (Jennifer Moore, 1 March 2013).

The Clancy family (who tragically lost their baby, Hunter Warwick, following a prolonged second stage of labour) described the positive aspects of the coronial inquest into their baby's death as follows:[146]

> We admire the coroners. Matenga was great. There was so much information and yet he got it. He said that there should have been monitoring. He also raised the issue that I was 35 and that should have been seen as high risk and maybe a hospital birth was more appropriate.

Many participants appreciated the inquisitorial nature of the coronial jurisdiction:[147]

> Our view still is that it's a wonderful service . . . there are strengths because it's an inquiry and not adversarial. When they're done well, they are the most complete as far as an investigation into a road trauma . . . a well-constructed coroner's report is the best information.

Similarly, the College of Midwives commented:[148]

> I went to a coroner's investigation that was run by Judge MacLean. And it was a really great experience because he did the questioning, and I thought that was a much better system. . . . I felt that you got to the truth.

Robert Barlow (whose son, Adam, was pronounced stillborn and died due to intrapartum asphyxia) explained that:[149]

> It was good to be able to make closing statements. Not all coroners allow that. We felt that after ten days of evidence and medical jargon it was good to recap that we were there for our little boy.

Participants also appreciated the independence and objectivity of a coronial inquiry.[150] The following government organisation's view captures these sentiments:[151]

---

146 Clancys, above n 145; *Clancy* [2010] NZCorC 115.

147 NZ Transport Agency, above n 143.

148 Interview with NZ College of Midwives (Jennifer Moore, 22 January 2013).

149 Interview with Robert Barlow (Jennifer Moore, 11 October 2012); *Barlow* [2012] NZCorC 87.

150 For example, Interview with GovtOrg04 (Jennifer Moore); Interview with Lawyer04 (Jennifer Moore, 5 February 2013); Interview with Sean Goddard (Department of Conservation) (Jennifer Moore, 14 May 2013).

151 Interview with GovtOrg01 (Jennifer Moore, 28 February 2013).

> It is right that we have the coronial process. I like the idea that we have someone independent who can take that step back and look down on something with few constraints.

The ability of the coronial process to identify themes for preventive purposes was mentioned by many participants:[152]

> They are sometimes like canaries in a mine. A good example was the coroner who picked up early that snow tyres were an issue, earlier than anybody else. So we do want them to be asking the questions.

Likewise, the Wellington City Council asserted that:[153]

> "The coroner" is probably the one institution that has an insight into what themes are emerging that haven't been seen before. Personally I welcome the coroner's discussion about those things.

Participants typically described coroners' unique position to review things from a different angle.

Participants welcomed coroners' sensitivity towards the emotional nature of the jurisdiction.[154] Organisations often commented favourably about specific coroners:[155]

> Look at Sue's training and background. From the bottom–up, she knows how the health system works, knows about injustice, knows about misogyny, knows about all the gender issues. She knows about all that, and is compassionate, and she has an understanding about the family dynamic. . . . Katherine Greig's good too . . . so is Carla from Palmerston North.

Participants also appreciated inquiries into clusters of cycling or quad bike deaths, or coroners with experience in a specific category of death focusing on that category.

It was common for participants to prefer their local coroners. For example, participants made comments such as "we are blessed in Auckland. We have competent coroners here."[156] Participants frequently commented

---

152 NZ Transport Agency, above n 143.

153 Interview with Wellington City Council (Jennifer Moore, 31 January 2013).

154 For example, Interview with GovtOrg10 (Jennifer Moore, 1 May 2013); Interview with Professor Werry (Jennifer Moore, 12 November 2012).

155 NZ College of Midwives, above n 148.

156 Interview with HealthCareOrganisation01 (Jennifer Moore, 4 December 2012); Lawyer04, above n 150; Interview with Surf Life Saving NZ (Jennifer Moore, 11 February 2013).

on the variability across coroners, observing that "there are some who are very, very good and make great recommendations. However, there are others who do not fit into that same category. It would be good to have some performance assessment monitoring."[157]

Organisations valued their relationships with coroners and appreciated that coronial information could inform their work:[158]

> I have usually found, despite my caveats, coroners' findings useful and they assist me in my job. We look for patterns and commonalities in the findings either in one area or across the country. . . . The Mortality Review Committees find coroners' findings useful. The public of NZ should be reassured that there are processes that go looking for common issues.

Similarly, the following description reflects other organisations' experiences:[159]

> Well what coroners do is really important in terms of the family, in terms of the event, and from our perspective, in terms of actually reinforcing and supporting good change within processes and procedures for an industry or a company or whatever. So this is pretty important stuff!

Most organisations' overall perception of the CSNZ was that they were "impressed" with the work coroners achieve given the "resourcing issues".[160] In Chapter 5 I analyse under-resourcing in the coronial services in detail.

2.3 NZ GOVERNMENT'S 2012–14 REVIEW

2.3.1 Background and Catalyst

On 31 July 2012, the Courts Minister announced a targeted review of the CSNZ.[161] A principal catalyst for the government review was the Law

---

157 Interview with David Cliff (Police) (Jennifer Moore, 22 April 2013).

158 Interview with HealthCareOrganisation199 (Jennifer Moore, 15 February 2013).

159 Interview with Electricity Engineers' Association (Jennifer Moore, 7 February 2013).

160 Interview with GovtOrg07 (Jennifer Moore, 20 February 2013).

161 Chester Borrows "Changes to Coroner's Court Signalled" *Press Release* (26 June 2013); Jennifer Moore "An Empirical Approach to the New Zealand Government's Review of the Coronial Jurisdiction" (2014) 21 JLM 602.

Commission's finding, during its review of the Burial and Cremation Act 1964, that there is potential duplication between the CSNZ and other investigation bodies, and that clarification for reportable deaths is needed.[162] An examination of the overlap between investigation services is one of the aims of the review. The terms of reference are to:[163]

- better balance the needs of grieving families, including the cultural needs of Maori whanau, with the public interest in understanding the causes and circumstances of deaths
- improve the quality, consistency and timeliness of coronial investigations and decision-making
- clarify the role of coroners and reduce duplication between coroners and other authorities that investigate deaths and accidents
- clarify the role coroners have in making recommendations to prevent future deaths and the relationship to agencies that have policy and operational responsibility in those areas, and
- ensure resources are used effectively.

Prior to the July announcement, in May 2012, the Minister's advisor contacted me after reading about my research in the media.[164] The original terms of reference for the Government's review did not include coroners' recommendations, but after discussion with me and the Chief Coroner, coroners' recommendations were included.[165] The inclusion is significant because the government review revealed that coroners' recommendations are one of the most important aspects of the review.[166]

---

162 In 2011 and 2012, I worked at the Law Commission on the review of the Burial and Cremation Act 1964. That review is ongoing: <http://www.lawcom.govt.nz/project/review-burial-and-cremation-act-1964>. The Burial and Cremation Act 1964 intersects with the Coroners Act 2006.

163 Borrows, above n 161.

164 Email from Oliver Searle Private Secretary (Advisory) to Hon Borrows to Jennifer Moore regarding the Law Foundation-funded coroners' recommendations research and the New Zealand Government review (16 May 2012); Vaughan Elder "Coroner welcomes Otago study" (16 May 2012) <http://www.odt.co.nz/news/dunedin/209423/coroner-welcomes-otago-study>.

165 Email from Oliver Searle Private Secretary (Advisory) to Hon Borrows to Jennifer Moore regarding the scope of the Law Foundation-funded research compared with the scope of the New Zealand Government review (31 July 2012).

166 Cabinet Paper *Coroners Act Review: Proposals for Reform – Paper 1* (2013) at 5.

2.3.2 Cabinet Papers

The first Cabinet Paper reports that the Ministry of Justice wrote to 168 stakeholders seeking feedback about the coronial system. Forty-nine submissions were received.[167] In keeping with the review's terms of reference, the submissions were about the following topics:[168]

- consistency, timeliness and efficiency
- reporting deaths and post-mortem examinations
- relationship with other investigating bodies
- the nature of coroners' recommendations
- Maori and cultural needs, and
- other matters such as the reporting of suicide.

Although the review found that coroners' recommendations are one of the most significant areas requiring reform, an analysis of the textual recommendations was not undertaken. The review was concerned with the "needs of grieving families".[169] However, the targeted review excluded the public voice. Had families been included in the review, it is probable that submissions would have called for the introduction of a mandatory response regime for coroners' recommendations. The empirical evidence suggests that families would be supportive of this law reform. Numerous media articles also report that families would like coroners' recommendation powers to be strengthened. There will be an opportunity for public submissions during the parliamentary select committee phase.

On 26 June 2013, the Courts Minister announced proposals to reform the CSNZ.[170] These proposals were considered in two stages. The first stage covers the following:

1. improving processes within the coronial system to ensure they are timely and consistent
2. improving coroners' recommendations, and
3. clarifying which cases need to be reported to the coroner.

The 2000 Law Commission report raised concerns about the lack of consistency of practice between coroners. This concern was echoed in the

---

167 A summary of submissions can be found at: <http://www.justice.govt.nz/courts/coroners-court/media-centre/news/summary-of-submissions>.

168 Ibid.

169 Cabinet Paper, above n 166.

170 Borrows, above n 161.

current review's submissions. Strengthening the Chief Coroner's role to spread workloads and, therefore, reduce delays is proposed. Reduction of duplication with other investigating authorities is also proposed, with the use of memoranda of understanding.

The Minister proposes amendments to coroners' powers to make recommendations. In particular, submissions highlighted that organisations and interested parties desire enhanced engagement with the CSNZ during inquiries. A definition of "interested parties" will be inserted by amendment into the Coroners Act 2006 (NZ).

The reforms will also involve redrafting the statutory provisions relating to reportable deaths, particularly healthcare-related deaths. Concerns about the interpretation of medical deaths have led to confusion amongst medical practitioners about which deaths should be reported. This issue arose during the Law Commission's review of the Burial and Cremation Act.

The second stage, announced on 17 October 2013,[171] focuses on:[172]

1. improving accountability, transparency and leadership
2. clarifying the management of tissue samples taken as part of a post-mortem to make the process clearer and more responsive to families
3. clarifying that coroners only have jurisdiction to investigate deaths that occur outside of New Zealand in certain circumstances, and
4. improving and clarifying a number of provisions in the Act.

There are two paragraphs about coroners' recommendations in the second paper.[173] The Minister will "monitor" the situation before "considering whether further changes are necessary".[174] The paper refers to the "continued public discussion"[175] about whether legislation should require agencies to respond to coroners' recommendations. The Minister does not commit to the introduction of such changes. Instead, he states that he "expects that reasonable coronial recommendations will voluntarily get a response from government agencies".[176]

---

171 The Hon Chester Borrows "Further Changes to Coronial System Announced" *Press Release* (17 October 2013).

172 NZ Ministry of Justice *Coroners Act Review: Proposal for Reform – Cabinet Paper 2* (2013).

173 At 33, 34.

174 At 33.

175 At 34.

176 At 34.

2.3.3 Bill

In June 2013, the Government expected to introduce a Bill to implement all the changes in the second quarter of 2014.[177] On 31 July 2014, the Coroners Amendment Bill 2014 was introduced to Parliament.[178] The Bill had its first reading in February 2015. The NZ Justice and Electoral Committee report was published in August 2015. The Bill had its second reading on 20 October 2015.[179] I have analysed the Government's review of the coronial jurisdiction elsewhere.[180]

2.4 CORONERS' FUNCTIONS AND RECOMMENDATIONS

2.4.1 Coroners' Preventive and Investigative Functions

The literature generally identifies the following coronial functions:[181]

- investigative
- preventive
- administrative
- judicial
- therapeutic
- educational
- disaster management.

---

[177] Email from Oliver Searle (Private Secretary (Advisory) to Hon Borrows) to Jennifer Moore regarding date for introduction of the Bill (27 June 2013).

[178] "New Zealand Parliament – Coroners Amendment Bill 2014: Bills Digest No 2161" New Zealand Parliament <http://www.parliament.nz/en-nz/pb/legislation/bills/digests/50PLLaw21611/coroners-amendment-bill-2014-bills-digest-no-2161>.

[179] "New Zealand Parliament – Coroners Amendment Bill" <http://www.parliament.nz/en-nz/pb/legislation/bills/00DBHOH_BILL56949_1/coroners-amendment-bill>.

[180] Moore, above n 161.

[181] For example, see Freckelton and Ranson, above n 1, at 59; K.M. Waller *Coronial Law and Practice in New South Wales* (3rd ed., Law Book Company, Sydney, 1994) at 8; Gordon Tait and Belinda Carpenter "Suicide and the Therapeutic Coroner: Inquests, Governance and the Grieving Family" (2013) 2 International Journal for Crime, Justice and Social Democracy 92.

During interviews, when I asked coroners to describe their functions, they typically highlighted their judicial investigative function. For example, coroners used the following descriptions:[182]

- "judicial officer who has an investigative role"
- "independent, judicial investigator"
- "conductor of evidence . . . investigating the facts."

Similarly, the 2012 Canadian Supreme Court of Yukon case, *Silverfox v Chief Coroner*, states that the "coroner's task is dual: she is responsible for both marshalling the evidence and presiding over the inquest."[183]

NZ coroners also likened their functions to a "public watchdog", "fact finder", "story teller", "social geographer".[184] Two coroners emphasised the importance of their therapeutic function, explaining that they are the "advocates for the deceased and his/her family".[185] Coroners conceptualised themselves as the "experts in death".[186]

Coroners' recommendation-making power is linked to their preventive function. Much of the appellate case law concerns the investigative, administrative and preventive functions. In the 2014 Supreme Court of Queensland decision *Goldsborough v Bentley*, the scope of coronial functions was discussed.[187] The case concerned a challenge to the conduct of an inquest which investigated the death of a tourist in 2011. The tourist drowned in a waterhole which was owned by a company. The death was investigated by a branch of the Queensland government, Fair and Safe Work Queensland. The agency decided not to prosecute the company. The issue was whether the coroner could investigate the reasoning of the agency's decision not to prosecute. The applicant argued that such an investigative power was beyond the coronial jurisdiction. The coroner contended that such investigation was permissible because it was concerned with prevention of future deaths, and prevention is a coronial function.

---

[182] Interview with Coroner Clarke (Jennifer Moore, 29 October 2012); Interview with Coroner Atwood (Jennifer Moore, 11 December 2012); Interview with Coroner Aitken (Jennifer Moore, 22 January 2013).

[183] *Silverfox v Yukon (Chief Coroner)* Yukon Territory Court of Appeal Vancouver 2011 YKCA 9, 14 October 2011 at para 34.

[184] Clarke, above n 182; Interview with Coroner Fitzpatrick (Jennifer Moore, 25 September 2012); Interview with Coroner Owen (Jennifer Moore, 3 October 2012); Interview with Coroner Pennell (Jennifer Moore, 13 October 2012).

[185] Atwood, above n 182; Interview with Coroner Dymond (Jennifer Moore, 16 October 2012).

[186] Atwood, above n 182; Interview with Coroner Frank (Jennifer Moore, 10 October 2012).

[187] *Goldsborough v Bentley* [2014] QSC 141 (Supreme Court of Queensland).

The Court favourably cited *Doomadgee*, in which Muir J reasoned that the legislative boundaries and scope of the coroner's role are "indefinite".[188] Similarly, the Supreme Court observed that "'public health or safety' and 'the administration of justice' are also broad subject matters with indefinite boundaries".[189] Therefore, although coronial recommendations must be *connected with* the death under investigation, there are many ways to make such a connection because recommendations are concerned with the broad topics of public health or safety and the administration of justice.[190] Furthermore, "connected with" does not only mean *directly* connected with.[191] The Supreme Court of Queensland held that it was within the coronial jurisdiction to investigate the agency's decision because such investigation was connected with the public health/ preventive coronial function.

In Canada, the courts have also discussed the various coronial functions and their boundaries. For instance, the Ontario Court of Appeal stated that the coroner's inquest has two functions: "a narrow investigative function and a broader public interest function".[192] The public interest function encompasses the coronial recommendation-making power. The Ontario Court of Appeal commented that recent case law has emphasised the importance of the public interest and preventive functions, particularly in exposing systemic failings that cause death. The following oft-quoted statement from *People First of Ontario v Ontario (Niagara Regional Coroner)* was cited with approval:[193]

> A separate and wider function is becoming increasingly significant; the vindication of the public interest in the prevention of death by the public exposure of conditions that threaten life. The separate role of the jury in recommending systemic changes to prevent death has become more and more important.

---

188 *Goldsborough v Bentley*, above n 187, at para 19.

189 *Goldsborough v Bentley*, above n 187, at para 32.

190 For comparison, see *Ontario (Provincial Advocate for Children & Youth) v Evans*, No 2011 CarswellOnt 4374, 2011 ONSC 3354, 278 O.A.C. 262, 30 Admin. L.R. (5th) 297, 203 A.C.W.S. (3d) 64 (Ontario Superior Court 3 June 2011) at paras 30 and 36. The Court found that the recommendations proposed by a party granted standing at the inquest were not sufficiently connected to the death under investigation, or the scope of the inquest.

191 *Thales Australia Limited v The Coroners Court & Ors* Victoria Supreme Court Melbourne [2011] VSC 133, 11 April 2011 at para 75.

192 *Nishnawbe Aski Nation v Eden*, No 2009 CarswellOnt 3404, [2009] 3 C.N.L.R. 233, 97 O.R. (3d) 382, 254 O.A.C. 224, 178 A.C.W.S. (3d) 359 (Ontario Superior Court 29 May 2009) at para 21.

193 *People First of Ontario v Porter, Regional Coroner Niagara* [1991] 5 OR 609 at para 33.

> The social and preventive function of the inquest which focuses on the public interest has become, in some cases, just as important as the distinctly separate function of investigating the individual facts of individual deaths and the personal roles of individuals involved in the death.

In *People First of Ontario*, the court noted the potential tension between the coronial investigative and preventive functions. This tension exists despite the "clear distinction in statute" between the two functions.[194] The Court noted that the tension is especially "acute when there is a potentially adversarial conflict between a public interest advocacy group and those directly connected with the deceased".[195]

Likewise, academic commentators have observed the tension between the various coronial functions. Tait and Carpenter, in their observation of 20 English inquests, noted the "significant tension between the governmental and the pastoral functions of the Coroner, between what appears to be an investigative and preventative role . . . and the therapeutic role – in looking after the well-being of bereaved families".[196] They express concern that the coronial therapeutic function is hindering coroners' ability to fulfil their other functions. The authors conclude that the tension, and "confusion", between the coronial functions requires "formal clarification",[197] perhaps by legislative amendment, although the authors do not canvass that option. The tension between coronial functions is apparent in appellate litigation which debates which coronial function is primary (investigative or preventive?) and whether coroners *should* have made recommendations in particular cases. I discuss these topics in the next section.

2.4.2 International Approaches to Coronial Recommendations

Historically, decisions of the Coroner's Court were called "inquisitions". Today, in NZ and elsewhere, coroners' decisions are called "findings" or "verdicts".[198] The structure and formulation of coroners' findings varies. According to Coroner Stewart:[199]

---

194 *People First of Ontario v Porter, Regional Coroner Niagara*, above n 193, at para 40.

195 *People First of Ontario v Porter, Regional Coroner Niagara*, above n 193, at para 45.

196 Gordon Tait and Belinda Carpenter "Suicide and the Therapeutic Coroner: Inquests, Governance and the Grieving Family" (2013) 2 International Journal for Crime, Justice and Social Democracy 92 at 97.

197 Ibid., at 102.

198 Some commentators refer to coroners' findings as "reports".

199 Interview with Coroner Stewart (Jennifer Moore, 12 October 2012).

> Speaking for the dead is a big part [of our role] in the sense that we try to establish what happened. My findings are a bit lengthier than others because, for me, it's about recording the circumstances of the death for the future. That's not necessarily with prevention in mind. It's more as a record of what happened in that unexplained death.

Coroners' findings typically include information such as the findings of fact, the deceased's identity, the cause and circumstances of the death, and prophylactic recommendations.[200] Sometimes inquests do not include transcripts of evidence.

Traditionally, coroners or coroners' juries have added "riders" to their findings. These riders are aimed at reducing similar fatalities in the future. Case law in the 1980s and 1990s noted that the power to make recommendations was "ancillary to the inquest procedure"[201] and "subordinate to the mandatory power to make findings relating to how the deaths occurred".[202] Freckelton and Ranson argue that *Harmsworth v State Coroner* "narrows the extent to which an Australian inquest can be directed towards facilitating a coroner's wish to delve and to make recommendations or comments".[203] More recent Australian case law appears to have applied a broader interpretation:[204]

> The power of a coroner to make recommendations about matters of public health and safety seems apt to enable the coroner to consider matters outside the scope of what may be considered necessary to determine the manner and cause of death.

In addition, Freckelton and Ranson have observed that riders (or recommendations) are a "major focus" of coronial inquiries in Australia, NZ and Canada.[205] For example, in Ontario, Canada, the "ultimate objective of each investigation is to gain knowledge to prevent similar deaths".[206] The importance of coronial recommendations is captured in the Canadian literature about jury charges which states that "the jury should be encouraged

---

200 Examples of summaries of coroners' findings can be found on the CSNZ website: <http://www.justice.govt.nz/courts/coroners-court/publications>.

201 *Re Kelly (deceased)* (1996) 161 JP 417 at 423.

202 *Harmsworth v State Coroner* [1989] 989 VR at 996.

203 Freckelton and Ranson, above n 1, at 548.

204 *Josephine Conway v Mary Jerram, Magistrate and NSW State Coroner & Anor* NSW Supreme Court Sydney [2010] NSWSC 371, 3 May 2010 at para 63.

205 Freckelton and Ranson, above n 1, at 1133.

206 R.C. Bennett "The Changing Role of the Coroner" (1978) 118 CMA 1133.

to make recommendations".[207] In *Nishnawbe*, the Ontario Court of Appeal commented that recommendations must be made by a jury that is representative of the community, including First Nations people.[208]

Despite the courts' recognition of the importance of coronial recommendations, caution has been expressed. The following statement from an important Canadian decision is frequently cited with approval:[209]

> Notwithstanding the emerging public interest in the jury recommendations in the modern Ontario inquest, an inquest is not a Royal commission; an inquest is not a public platform; an inquest is not a campaign or a lobby; an inquest is not a crusade.

Inquests, and appellate litigation in Australia, NZ and Canada, often focus on whether recommendations should, or should not, be issued.[210] For example, in *R (Smith) v Oxfordshire Assistant Deputy Coroner*, the claimant claimed judicial review of the inquest into the death of her son who had died of hyperthermia while serving in the army in Iraq.[211] The claimant claimed various orders, one of which:[212]

> Required the coroner to make recommendations under Rule 43 of the Coroners Rules 1984, where such recommendations were in the coroner's view necessary to prevent the occurrence of the circumstances that led to the deceased's death.

The ground for this claim was that the coroner had erred in law by failing to make recommendations under Rule 43. In another English case that considered whether coronial recommendations should have been made,

---

[207] Justice T. David Marshall *Canadian Law of Inquests: A Handbook for Coroners, Medical Examiners, Counsel and the Police* (2nd ed., Scarborough: Thomson Professional Publishing, 1991); *Silverfox v Chief Coroner* [2012] YKSC 74 at para 103.

[208] *Nishnawbe Aski Nation v Eden*, No 2011 CarswellOnt 1474, 2011 ONCA 187, 104 O.R. (3d) 321, [2011] 2 C.N.L.R. 168, 21 Admin. L.R. (5th) 121, 281 O.A.C. 102 (Ontario Court of Appeal 10 March 2011) at 18 and 31.

[209] *People First of Ontario v Ontario (Niagara Regional Coroner)* (1991), 5 O.R. (3d) 609 (Ont. Div. Ct.) at 622.

[210] For example, see *R (on the application of Butler) v HM Coroner for the Black Country District* High Court (Administrative Court) London [2010] EWHC 43 (Admin), 21 January 2010.

[211] *R (on the application of Smith) v Oxfordshire Assistant Deputy Coroner*, [2009] EWCA Civ 441.

[212] *R (on the application of Smith) v Oxfordshire Assistant Deputy Coroner*, above n 211, at para 1.

three applications were linked.[213] All three cases involved prisoners who had hanged themselves in their cells. In the first case, the claimant challenged the coroner's ruling that the jury could not consider questions relating to the actions of the Prison Service after the deceased was found hanging in his cell as these did not directly relate to the cause of death or a contribution to it. As a result, the coroner was unable to make any recommendations regarding:

- the prison not providing suicide prevention training or any other relevant training to the patrolling officer who found the deceased
- the prison not equipping the officers with a safe instrument for cutting a ligature
- the prison appearing to have given conflicting guidance to the officers as to what to do when confronted with a detainee in a life-threatening situation.

The claimant challenged the coroner's decision not to make a Rule 43 recommendation regarding the above matters.

Likewise, in a 2011 English case about a fatal road traffic accident, the claimant (the sister of the deceased) sought to quash the verdict and have a fresh inquest for four reasons, including that the "coroner should have made recommendations so as to prevent a repeat of this tragic accident".[214] Silber J noted that before making a recommendation, the coroner must be satisfied that action should be taken to prevent the occurrence or continuation of such circumstances or to eliminate or reduce the risk of death created by such circumstances.[215] Moreover, the judge also noted that whether the coroner chooses to report the circumstances to a person who s/he believes has the power to take such action is at the coroner's discretion.[216]

The judge found that there were no facts that indicated that it was Wednesbury unreasonable[217] for the coroner not to have made a

---

[213] *R (on the application of Lewis) v HM Coroner for the North and Mid Division of the County of Shropshire* High Court (Administrative Court) London [2009] EWHC 661 (Admin), 3 April 2009.

[214] *R (on the application of Cairns) v HM Deputy Coroner for Inner West London* High Court (Administrative Court) London [2011] EWHC 2890 (Admin), 7 November 2011 at para 1.

[215] *R (on the application of Cairns) v HM Deputy Coroner for Inner West London*, above n 214, at para 74.

[216] *R (on the application of Cairns) v HM Deputy Coroner for Inner West London*, above n 214, at para 75.

[217] A reasoning or decision is "Wednesbury unreasonable" if it is so unreasonable that no reasonable person acting reasonably could have made it. See

recommendation under Rule 43.[218] He noted that the local authority had indicated that it did not wish for the inquest to be adjourned in order to ascertain if there had been other accidents at the time. In addition, the judge noted that the collision investigator was unaware of anything which could be done to prevent recurrent deaths of cyclists that come into close proximity to large vehicles. Therefore, the coroner had not erred in declining to make a Rule 43 report because there was no evidence that the tragedy could be prevented.

Similarly, in the Australian case, *Taing*, the two plaintiffs sought orders from the Supreme Court of the Northern Territory that inquests be held into their husbands' deaths, in part, to determine whether coronial recommendations should be made.[219] The deceased persons were self-employed fishermen who lived at the remote Dugong Creek camp.[220] Their remains were found at the camp. The first attendants on the scene observed the burnt wreckage of the camp. The deaths were initially treated as suspicious. However, the pathologist and coroner found that the cause of death was undetermined. Nevertheless, the wives insisted that their husbands' deaths were suspicious.

The plaintiffs argued that coronial recommendations should be made in relation to fuel containers and storage.[221] However, the Court held that it was reasonable that the coroner did not make recommendations. The Coroner was:[222]

> Unable to find the cause of the fire so to make a recommendation about the storage or management of fuel or related work practices would not be consistent with her conclusion. In any event, making a comment is a discretionary matter. It is not a reason in this case to order an inquest to be held.

Although litigants do ask the courts to quash coroners' recommendations, the power of a Supreme Court to do so is unclear.[223] For example, in a

---

Associated Provincial Picture Houses Ltd v Wednesbury Corporation (1948) 1 KB 223.

218 *R (on the application of Cairns) v HM Deputy Coroner for Inner West London*, above n 214, at para 76.

219 *Taing & Nuon v The Territory Coroner and Attorney-General for the Northern Territory* (2011) NTSC 58 SC.

220 *Taing & Nuon v The Territory Coroner and Attorney-General for the Northern Territory*, above n 219, at para 2.

221 *Taing & Nuon v The Territory Coroner and Attorney-General for the Northern Territory*, above n 219, at para 34.

222 *Taing & Nuon v The Territory Coroner and Attorney-General for the Northern Territory*, above n 219, at para 71.

223 *Canadian Chiropractic Assn v McLellan*, No 2011 CarswellOnt 12092, 2011 ONSC 6014, 209 A.C.W.S. (3d) 551, 285 O.A.C. 122 (Ontario Superior Court 9 November 2011).

2011 Canadian case, the deceased died after suffering a stroke which took place one week after she had received chiropractic neck manipulation. The jury made recommendations. The applicants, the Canadian Chiropractic Association, commenced judicial review to quash the verdict and its recommendations. The Court did not quash the recommendations, but its main reason for that decision was due to the inordinate delay in filing the case.[224]

Freckelton and Ranson have pointed out that there is limited capacity to apply for review of recommendations, as opposed to coroners' findings.[225] In 2011, in the Supreme Court of South Australia case, *Onuma v Coroner's Court of South Australia*, the respondent coroner similarly argued that the Supreme Court had no jurisdiction to hear an appeal against a Coroner's Court recommendation because the legislation clearly distinguished between a finding of the court (which provided a right of appeal) and a recommendation of the court (which did not expressly provide a right of appeal).[226] The Supreme Court disagreed with the earlier (2008) statement of principle in *Saraf* about the power of the court to set aside coronial recommendations.[227] In *Saraf*, the Supreme Court of South Australia noted that coroners' recommendations should be interpreted as a "subset of the findings" and that there is a right of appeal against recommendations:[228]

> There is, therefore, an obvious and close connection between the findings made by the Coroner's Court and any recommendation. In some cases, the recommendation will depend on the findings that have been made. The recommendations might fairly be considered to be a subset of the findings. In order to understand the recommendation it might be necessary to examine the finding. Thus, while s 25 draws a distinction between the finding and a recommendation, I do not think that Parliament intended that the right of appeal in s 27(1) should be limited to a finding so that there was no right of appeal against a recommendation.
>
> Policy reasons reinforce that conclusion. First, it would be curious indeed if there was a right of appeal against a finding but no right of appeal against a recommendation. If the Solicitor-General is correct and a coroner has made recommendations quite beyond his powers, there would be no appeal against that excess of power. That would be an entirely unsatisfactory result leaving

---

224 *Canadian Chiropractic Assn v McLellan*, above n 223, at para 63.

225 Freckelton and Ranson, above n 1, at 691.

226 *Onuma v Coroner's Court of South Australia* South Australia Supreme Court South Australia [2011] SASC 218, 9 December 2011.

227 *Onuma v Coroner's Court of South Australia*, above n 226, at para 8.

228 *Saraf and Another v Johns*, No 101 SASR 87 (Supreme Court of South Australia 23 June 2008) at paras 33 and 34.

> an aggrieved person without remedy by way of appeal. Secondly, while it would be possible for a person with a sufficient interest to institute an application for judicial review seeking orders quashing the recommendations on the ground the Coroner's Court had acted beyond its power, it is unsatisfactory to require that person to resort to two remedies, an appeal against a finding of the Coroner's Court and an application for judicial review to quash a recommendation. The firm policy of the law is to put an end to litigation as speedily as justice allows.

However, in *Onuma*, the Supreme Court of South Australia rejected the *Saraf* statement:[229]

> I cannot agree that the objects of the Act are advanced by disregarding the plain wording of the Act in that way. The Act itself has drawn a clear distinction between findings on the one hand and recommendations on the other.
>
> There is in my view a good reason for that. Any recommendation made by the Coroner must be for the purpose of, and only for the purpose of, the matters set out in s 25(2), namely, for the purpose of preventing or reducing the likelihood of a recurrence of an event similar to the event that was the subject of the inquest. That subsection very clearly defines the parameters in which a Coroner may make any recommendation. The recommendation itself does not establish, create or extinguish any legal right, liability or entitlement. It has no legal force or effect on any person. A Coroner making a recommendation cannot compel anyone to do anything and apart from the procedural requirements in s 25(4) and (5), no action is necessary as a consequence of any recommendation made by the Coroner.
>
> . . .Such a construction of the Act is, in my view, more likely to advance the public interest which is protected and enhanced by coronial investigations, than a construction which would permit appeals to be brought to the Supreme Court by any person aggrieved by a recommendation made by the Coroner. Further, such a construction would have the potential to create an open-ended class of litigants who might be aggrieved by a Coroner's recommendation.

The Supreme Court concluded that Parliament did not intend to extend a right of appeal against coroners' recommendations. However, parties with sufficient interest in a coroner's recommendation may have a remedy by way of judicial review. The Court also noted that "if there is no basis at all in the evidence before the Coroner which could justify or explain a recommendation, then that recommendation would have no weight."[230] Freckelton and Ranson have argued that if coronial recommendations

---

229 *Onuma v Coroner's Court of South Australia*, above n 226, at paras 76, 78, 79 and 82.

230 *Onuma v Coroner's Court of South Australia*, above n 226, at para 84.

are not reasonably open on the evidence, there may be a power to quash them.[231]

2.4.3 NZ Coroners' Recommendations

In NZ, coroners can make "specified recommendations or comments". "Recommendations" and "comments" are not defined separately in the NZ Act. Recommendations are typically "more formal and specific, for example about the details of a particular safety procedure".[232] This book analyses recommendations because I am concerned with evaluating the rigour and public health impact of the formal statements relating to the prevention of deaths.

"Recommendations or comments" are defined in section 9 of the Coroners Act 2006 (NZ) as "recommendations or comments about the avoidance of circumstances similar to those in which the death occurred or the way in which any people should act in circumstances of that kind". This definition allows coroners to consider a wide range of factors relating to a death.

However, the section 9 definition contains two limiting clauses: "in circumstances similar to those in which the death occurred", also found in sections 4 and 57, and "in circumstances of that kind". Recommendations should relate to the circumstances in which the particular death occurred, preventing a coroner from viewing the death too broadly. The NZ government review proposes amending the Act to "ensure coroners' recommendations or comments are specific to the case and evidence before the coroner".[233] The two limiting clauses in section 9 should encourage coroners to make recommendations that are specific to the case.

All coroners interviewed for this project explained that there is a difference between a recommendation and a comment. A "comment" is a general observation that does not usually call for a response. A "recommendation" should be targeted to a specific organisation and it will usually call for change and/or a response.

Despite the misconceptions of some participants, coroners are not *required* to make recommendations. One of the coroner's tasks is to decide whether recommendation/s and/or comment/s should be made. Coroners sometimes discuss their decision-making in their findings. For example, in *Hancock*, Coroner Ryan stated:[234]

---

231 Freckelton and Ranson, above n 1, at 662.

232 Email from CSNZ to Jennifer Moore "regarding the difference between recommendations and comments" (13 January 2012).

233 Cabinet Paper, above n 166, at 27.1.

234 *Hancock* [2008] NZCorC 14, at para 14.

> I have considered whether I can make any useful recommendation that may help to prevent further deaths occurring in similar circumstances, but am unable to do so. This is because there were no environmental factors nor defects in Mrs Inch's vehicle which may have contributed to the crash occurring.

The coroner's observations apply a public health injury prevention approach: assessment of whether environmental factors (physical or social) create the risk of fatal injury. If such an environmental factor is found, countermeasures (to counter the damage done by environmental hazards) should be applied. In this case no environmental hazards (or other issues, for example defects in the vehicle) were identified by the coroner. Therefore, he decided that a recommendation was not required.

Many NZ coroners (11/15) reported that they will often make comments if a recommendation is not required, but there are important observations that should be formally recorded. For instance, in an inquiry into a death caused by a fall from an electricity pylon, the coroner made the following comments:[235]

> I. I note that Counties Power Limited, which maintains the electricity network that this particular pylon forms a part of, has now installed barbed wire climbing deterrents on all three pylons in this vicinity. I commend the company for undertaking such preventive measures, particularly as these pylons are located in a relatively remote site in a low population area with gated access. In view of this remedial action, I do not consider there are any recommendations that I could usefully make which might prevent further deaths occurring in the future in similar circumstances.
>
> II. I accept the view of Counties Power Limited, that it is common knowledge that climbing electricity pylons with power lines attached is extremely hazardous. In addition, the pylon also had standard danger signage mounted on it, although the sign was weathered. I do not consider, therefore, that Kheirrson was ignorant of the dangers faced when he climbed the pylon.
>
> III. This death highlights the very real danger facing any person who attempts to climb an electricity pylon. The Police inform that this continues to be a problem, particularly with people attempting to steal the copper wire power lines. Kheirrson's death, although apparently unrelated to such criminal activity, should serve as a warning to any person who considers climbing pylons, that they face potentially fatal consequences.

In this case, the coroner endorsed the work undertaken by Counties Power Limited to prevent similar fatalities in the future. Many coroners that I interviewed (13/15) reported that it is common for them to choose to comment (rather than issue recommendations) when organisations have already remedied the issues. The coroner in *Pukeroa* highlights that the

---

235 *Pukeroa* [2012] NZCorC 4.

electricity pylon had danger signage warning the public about the potential risks. In interviews, coroners reported (9/15) that they are unlikely to make recommendations if members of the public choose to take risks when the risks are known and warnings are in place. For example, when an experienced kayaker died of cardiopulmonary congestion consistent with drowning while at sea in extreme weather conditions, Coroner Bain commented as follows:[236]

> It is hoped that these comments will ring true to other people when thinking about kayaking in extreme conditions particularly when they are predicted. I do not see that there is any useful recommendation that can be made because the stupidness of what they did is obvious. Apart from a blanket ban being imposed in certain weather conditions you cannot stop people from being fools unto themselves.
>
> This was an entirely avoidable tragedy and the life of a very experienced and renowned rafter, kayaker, outrigger canoeist and photographer has been lost. It is a salutary lesson to all and hopefully it is a salutary lesson to those involved. I am critical of all four men for venturing into the ocean on that fateful day. Hopefully they have learnt their lesson and others within their sport will heed the foolishness of their misplaced bravado.

Coroners frequently expressed frustration about sudden unexplained deaths in infancy (SUDI). This is a category of death where recommendations have been repeated and many of the risks (such as an intoxicated adult co-sleeping with a child) are well known. In an inquiry into a SUDI death, Coroner Ryan chose not to make an untargeted recommendation to "the world at large" for the following reasons:[237]

> I have considered whether or not there is any recommendation that I could usefully make to help prevent further deaths occurring in similar circumstances in the future. However, any recommendation would be simply to the world at large and would therefore not be useful. Instead I would like to endorse the efforts of all public interest groups who are promoting the education of parents as to the dangers of SIDS and measures that parents can take to reduce the risk to their children. In particular I support all efforts being made to educate parents as to the danger of drinking to excess while caring for infants because of the effect of alcohol impairing the parents' ability to ensure their children are safe and well.

In another SUDI case involving an unsafe sleeping environment, Coroner McDowell similarly chose not to make recommendations. Instead, she made comments and sent a copy of the findings to the Ministry of Health

---

236 *Moore* [2009] NZCorC 99.

237 *Marriott-Oneroa* [2009] NZCorC 60.

to consider alongside previous coronial recommendations about SUDI. Coroner McDowell's reasoning was as follows:[238]

> I. In my previous decision relating to the death of Baby Leonydas Tukariri, I referred to expert advice provided by Professor Ed Mitchell, Paediatrician and Professor of Child Health Research at Auckland University, about SIDS' risk factors. There are a number of risks and protective factors relating to SIDS and not all factors are equally weighted. The most significant factor is sleep position, maternal smoking during pregnancy, bed sharing, and the interaction between bed sharing and smoking. There is now overwhelming evidence that bed sharing is a major risk for SIDS in infants of mothers who smoked during pregnancy. The mechanism by which bed sharing is associated with SIDS is unknown, there being a number of postulated mechanisms, including: airway obstruction, entrapment (where the chest wall cannot move normally during respiration), thermal stress and re-breathing of expired gases. Additionally, Dr Mitchell has also previously provided evidence that it is inappropriate for adult sized pillows to be used in the first year of life as they represent a potentially unsafe sleeping environment.
>
> II. Having regard to the identified SIDS risk factors a number of factors were obviously present for Tamati including, his age, that his mother smoked in pregnancy, his post-natal cigarette exposure, and bed-sharing with others, including an adult. Although it cannot be established to any degree of certainty whether the pillow contributed to or caused his death, the use of an adult pillow for Tamati was also potentially unsafe.
>
> III. In order to prevent the tragedy of sudden unexpected deaths in infancy, it is vital that parents are provided with information about the principles of safe sleeping essential to protecting the life of their baby. This includes the need for the message to be made explicit that laying babies to sleep in the first year of life on an adult pillow is a hazard that increases the risk of infant death. I consider it important also to reiterate the message that bed sharing by adults with infants exposes the infant to the risk of death and should be avoided for *every* sleep.
>
> IV. Recent coronial decisions have made recommendations to the Ministry of Health aimed at ensuring that public health advice in relation to safe infant care practices and safe sleeping environments are strengthened, broadened and consistent among public health educators and health professionals so as to make it clear that bed sharing with infants should be avoided. Accordingly, a copy of these Findings will be sent to the Ministry of Health to consider in the context of these previous recommendations regarding bed sharing.

In this case, Coroner McDowell refers to previous recommendations about SUDI and bed sharing. Coroners (13/15), organisations (76/79) and interested parties (8/8) noted that, where possible, coroners' findings

---

238 *Rawhiti* [2011] NZCorC 179.

should refer to previous similar cases in order to increase the preventive potential of recommendations.

In an inquiry into the death of a 2-year-old from positional asphyxia in a bunk bed, the coroner's recommendations flow from her analysis of the previous similar cases, relevant standards, legislation and evidence. The coroner's evidence-based finding explains why recommendations are necessary:[239]

> [1] There have also been other recent deaths of children by asphyxiation involving bunk beds – albeit in different circumstances to Luca's. In May 2008, 6 year old Taytana Lasini fell from a top bunk and caught her neck in a dressing gown belt tied to the bunk. In April 2009 10 year old Sarah Smith slid under the guardrail of a top bunk and accidentally got caught in clothing hanging from the rail.
> [2] That deaths and injuries of children involving bunks are occurring, and that safety messages are inconsistent in my view warrants further scrutiny from accident prevention, and product safety authorities, particularly with a view to determining whether the standard pertaining to bunks should be made mandatory. Product safety standards are generally made mandatory by regulation under s 29 of the Fair Trading Act 1986.
> **Recommendations**
> [3] I therefore recommend to the Ministry of Economic Development and the Ministry of Consumer Affairs that consideration be given to making the standard "Bunk beds and other elevated beds AS/NZS 4220:2010" (and subsequent variations), mandatory.
> [4] I recommend to the Ministry of Economic Development, the Ministry of Consumer Affairs, and Safekids New Zealand that they review their safety literature regarding bunk beds to ensure that it is consistent with the standard "Bunk beds and other elevated beds AS/NZS 4220:2010".

By contrast, the recommendations in *Thacker* were frequently cited by participants as examples of non-evidence-based recommendations.[240] In this case, a woman died from a head injury sustained when she fell from the tray of a farm tractor. The coroner made the following comments:[241]

> Prior to investigating Lois' death I had not heard of a fatality or indeed accident occurring in similar circumstances. I had ridden on a tractor tray in similar ways many times and I had never thought of the particular dangers that might be associated with that. Lois' death has caused me to reflect and reconsider. As a consequence I consider that publication and recommendation would be worthwhile.

---

239 *Gibson* [2011] NZCorC 43.
240 *Thacker* [2010] NZCorC 146.
241 *Thacker*, above n 240.

> A copy of this finding will be forwarded – as is routine – to the local media. In addition however, a copy will be forwarded to the New Zealand Farmer magazine – or if no such publication presently exists – any similar magazine published to the farming community. That would enable the editor of such magazine to give this finding such publicity as he or she thinks fit.

The coroner states he "had not heard of a fatality . . . in similar circumstances". The finding does not refer to previous similar cases, but it is unclear whether any research was undertaken to identify such cases. Rather than citing the evidence, the coroner notes his personal experiences of tractor trays. His experience informs his decision that a recommendation "would be worthwhile". In addition, investigation of the appropriate magazine at which to direct the findings was not undertaken. Such limitations inhibit the preventive potential of the coroner's recommendation, which was:[242]

> I recommend that any person reading the details of this decision, who is in the practise [sic] of transporting or being transported in similar circumstances to review this practice. It is clearly potentially dangerous – potentially fatal.

It is unlikely that this recommendation has been, or will be, implemented. It does not target a specific, identifiable organisation. Instead, it is directed to "any person reading the details of this decision, who is in the practice of transporting or being transported in similar circumstances". Such a vague direction is unlikely to reach its intended audience. In Chapter 3, I discuss this issue in detail and identify all untargeted recommendations in my study period.

Most participants (111/123) viewed coroners' recommendations as the most important aspect of coronial inquiries. The following remark captures participants' sentiments:[243]

> I believe that the value of recommendations, or their lack of value, speaks volumes about the entire set-up.

As I pointed out in the previous section, if coronial recommendations are not reasonably open on the evidence, there may be a power to quash them. For example, in the 2012 NZ High Court decision, *Smith v Jamieson*, the plaintiffs sought orders to quash aspects of Coroner Jamieson's findings.[244]

---

242 *Thacker*, above n 240.

243 Cliff (Police), above n 157.

244 *Smith v Jamieson* High Court Wellington CIV 2011–485–1680, 21 May 2012.

The deceased, Edward Magalogo (an 18-year-old), died after being dragged out to sea while on a school trip to Muriwai beach, Auckland. The coroner made an interim ruling, acknowledging section 58 of the Coroners Act 2006 (NZ) applied to adverse comments.[245] He gave three teachers an opportunity to comment. The teachers submitted their comments after the deadline. The coroner's ruling was formalised without considering their submissions. The teachers argued that the circumstances of non-consideration amounted to a breach of natural justice, and that the coroner's adverse comment was at any rate wholly unsupported by the evidence.

Simon France J held that no evidence supported a causative link between the adequacy of the teacher's supervision and Magalogo's death.[246] Therefore, statements to that effect were quashed. Adverse comments about the circumstances of the event (but that did not suggest causation) stand as discrete, legitimate observations. Simon France J also held that even though Coroner Jamieson did not make inquiries when the teachers failed to meet the submission deadline (despite indicating they would make a submission), it was not obvious whether there was a breach of natural justice. However, even if there was a breach, his Honour declined relief because the submissions had been considered in this substantive hearing, and the coroner had since retired.[247]

245 *Smith v Jamieson*, above n 244, at para 4.
246 *Smith v Jamieson*, above n 244, at para 27 and 42.
247 *Smith v Jamieson*, above n 244, at paras 34–41.

3. Coroners' recommendations

3.1 INTRODUCTION

In Chapter 1, and elsewhere,[1] I have described the limitations of coronial data sources and the difficulties in accessing complete datasets of full coroners' findings. In several jurisdictions abroad, government organisations compile basic statistics about Coroner's Courts and coronial recommendations.[2] Despite the introduction of the *Recommendations Recap*, a common complaint during interviews was that the shortcomings in access to publicly available full findings in NZ have meant that it has been difficult to compile accurate statistics about coronial findings.

This chapter attempts to address some of these problems by providing descriptive quantifications of NZ coronial recommendations during the study period. The results and discussion in this chapter address my research objective to describe the nature, frequency and recipients of NZ coroners' recommendations, 1 July 2007 – 30 June 2012.

The chapter is divided into three main parts. First, I outline the historical origins of coronial recommendations and the legislative recommendation-making power. Secondly, I describe the number and nature of coroners' recommendations. Finally, I examine the recipients of coronial recommendations.

3.2 HISTORICAL ORIGIN

Coronial recommendations were originally called "riders". Riders were "expressions of opinion" added to the verdict to make "suggestions of

---

[1] Jennifer Moore and Mark Henaghan *New Zealand Coroners' Recommendations, 2007–2012 (final report)* (2014).

[2] Judge Ian Gray *2011–12 Annual Report of the Coroner's Court of Victoria* (2013) at 55; Ministry of Justice *Coroner Statistics 2010 England and Wales* (2011); Office of the Chief Coroner Ontario *Office of the Chief Coroner of Ontario 2010 Report on Inquests* (2012); Ministry of Justice *Summary of Reports and Responses under Rule 43 of the Coroners Rules: Ninth Report: For period 1 October 2012 – 31 March 2013* (2013).

measures which should be taken to reduce the incidence of needless deaths similar to that which was the subject of the inquest".[3]

As McKeough has observed, "adding a rider to a coroner's verdict is a time-honoured method of making comments on matters of public interest."[4] The addition of riders to coroners' verdicts is indeed "time-honoured", with one of the earliest records of a rider from 1821 in England following the death of a man who suffocated:[5]

> ... in a certain pond by certain gas water which is thrown into the said pond by persons employed by a certain gas company to the jurors unknown. That the throwing of the said gas water appears to the said jurors to be a serious evil; and the said jurors recommend to the parish aforesaid (St Matthew Bethnal Green) to take proper measures to remedy the said evil.

Riders were appended to the coronial inquisition and were not technically considered part of the verdict.[6]

It is by way of riders that coronial systems made recommendations to appropriate entities about how to avoid preventable deaths in the future. This preventive potential was recognised as early as 1842 in England by the Registrar General of Births, Deaths and Marriages.[7] In 1915, an English medical practitioner and barrister, Dr William Brend, highlighted that coronial data could be deployed for public health purposes and concluded that "[i]f prevention of deaths is not now regarded as the main purpose to be served by inquests, the inquiry becomes of relatively little value."[8]

In NZ, the first recorded rider was made in 1845 in Auckland at an inquest into the death of a child who fell down a tan pit and drowned.[9] The jury recommended that there be "some regulation obliging proprietors

---

[3] Ian Freckelton and David Ranson *Death Investigation and the Coroner's Inquest* (Oxford University Press, Melbourne, 2006) at 655.

[4] Jill McKeough "Origins of the Coronial Jurisdiction" (1983) 6 UNSWLJ 191 at 206.

[5] Thomas R. Forbes "Coroners' Inquests in the County of Middlesex, England, 1819–42" (1977) 32 Journal of the History of Medicine 375, at 378.

[6] John Jervis *Jervis on Coroners* (Sweet and Maxwell, London, 1946).

[7] Graeme Johnstone "An Avenue for Death and Injury Prevention" in Hugh Selby (ed.) *The Aftermath of Death* (Leichhardt Federation Press, New South Wales, 1992) 140.

[8] William Brend *An Inquiry into the Statistics of Deaths from Violence and Unnatural Causes in the United Kingdom* (Charles Griffin and Co, London, 1915); William Brend "Bills of Mortality" (1907) 5 Trans Med-Legal Society 140.

[9] Laurie Gluckman *Touching on Deaths: A Medical History of Early Auckland Based on the First 384 Inquests* (Doppelganger, Auckland, 2000) at 134.

to have wells or water holes upon their premises carefully enclosed".[10] Writing in 1868, after the first recorded rider, it is interesting that Coroner Alexander Johnston does not mention riders in his *Handy Book for the Coroners of New Zealand*.[11]

Foreshadowing modern recommendations, riders were made in the interests of public health. In one death attributed to cholera, the following rider was added to the verdict:[12]

> To call the attention of the authorities to the fact that the neighbourhood in which this man died is impregnated with foul air and that from the medical evidence it is likely to predispose to diseases of this nature.

This rider is reflective of contemporaneous medical knowledge. Cholera was considered a miasmatic until science established cholera as a water-borne disease. There was widespread fear of the disease not only because of the sudden onset of serious symptoms, but also because there had been three pandemics before 1850. The rider is vaguely directed to "the authorities". My analysis of modern untargeted recommendations in this chapter should highlight that failure to direct recommendations to specific entities was not restricted to riders from 1800s NZ.[13]

Riders in 1800s NZ also reflected concerns about workplace health and safety. After an apprentice died in 1860 during dangerous engineering works, the jury recommended that:[14]

> [T]he Coroner call the attention of the Authorities to a more strict supervision of works which, from the manner in which they are conduced, or otherwise, are likely to be attended with danger to the public.

Like modern recommendations, early riders were repeated about particular causes of death such as drowning.[15] In the next section, I describe the origins of the legislative power to make coronial recommendations.

---

10 At 134.

11 Alexander J. Johnston *A Handy Book for the Coroners of New Zealand Containing Provisions of the Coroners Act 1867* (Government Printer, Wellington, New Zealand, 1868).

12 Gluckman, above n 9, at 103.

13 See this chapter at section 3.6.3.

14 Gluckman, above n 9, at 266.

15 At 104.

3.3 LEGISLATIVE POWER TO MAKE RECOMMENDATIONS

Coronial preventive functions and recommendation-making powers were explored in the 1970s and 1980s in the United Kingdom, Canada and Australia. The 1971 United Kingdom Brodrick Report recommended that riders should not form part of the coroner's verdict because the facts of the case would speak for themselves.[16] In 1980, riders were abolished in England and Wales.[17] The introduction of Rule 43 changed the situation, creating the power for a coroner to report a matter to a relevant authority where a coroner believed that action should be taken to prevent the recurrence of fatalities similar to the one under inquest.[18]

The legislative power to make recommendations has had a different history in Ontario, Canada. The Ontario Law Reform Commission's 1971 report supported an extension of the coroner's work to include investigation of preventable deaths.[19] These different approaches to death prevention became a "central point of departure" between the jurisdictions as recommendations increasingly play a pivotal role in coronial inquiries in Canada, Australia and New Zealand.[20]

In Victoria, Australia, Norris's review of their 1958 Coroners Act recognised the preventive role of the coroner.[21] The Victorian Coroners Act 1985 implemented many of the Norris report recommendations. Section 21(2) of the Act provided Victorian coroners with the power to make recommendations. All other Australian states and territories have also enacted provisions which allow the coroner or jury to make comments or recommendations.[22] In South Australia, for instance, the Coroner's Court may add any recommendation that might prevent or reduce the likelihood of a recurrence of an event similar to the event that was the subject of the inquest.[23]

Despite the long history of riders in England, a legislative recommen-

---

16 Brodrick Committee *Report of the Committee on Death Certification and Coroners* (1971).

17 Freckelton and Ranson, above n 3, at 617.

18 Coroners (Amendment) Rules 2008 (England and Wales) Rule 43; Coroners and Justice Act 2009 (England and Wales).

19 Ontario Law Reform Commission *Report on the Coroner System in Ontario* (1971).

20 Freckelton and Ranson, above n 3, at 617 and 654.

21 John Norris *The Coroners Act 1958 – A General Review* (1981).

22 For example, see Coroners Act 1997 (ACT) 1997 s 52(4); Coroners Act 1993 (NT) 1993 s 26(2).

23 Coroners Act 2003 (SA) s 25(2).

dation-making power for coroners is a comparatively recent addition in NZ. The Coroners Act 1908 and the Coroners Act 1951 did not provide coroners with recommendation-making powers. With the abolition of juries under the Coroners Act 1951, we know little about the frequency of riders from that time, but there has been speculation that riders were made informally.[24]

A provision to allow coroners to make recommendations was included in section 15 of the Coroners Act 1988. This section provided that a purpose of the inquest was to make:

> any recommendations or comments on the avoidance of circumstances similar to those in which the death occurred, or on the manner in which any persons should act in such circumstances, that, in the opinion of the coroner, may, if drawn to public attention, reduce the chances of the occurrence of other deaths in such circumstances.

The current legislative power to make recommendations is similar to the provision in the 1988 Act. Section 57 of the Coroners Act 2006 (NZ) states that the purpose of an inquiry, and any related inquest, is to make:

> specified recommendations or comments (as defined in section 9) that, in the coroner's opinion, may, if drawn to public attention, reduce the chances of the occurrence of other deaths in circumstances similar to those in which the death occurred.

Echoing the Brodrick report's conclusion that coroners should not make riders, there are New Zealanders who argue that coroners should not have legislative power to make recommendations. For example, a lawyer interviewed for this study commented:[25]

> This raises the question of the function of the coroner and the jurisdiction. Is the function of the coroner to serve a broader public health and safety interest, or is it more about the community's responsibility towards a deceased individual? I think their primary role is the fact-finding role, establishing the cause and circumstances of the death. There is a huge amount of broader public interest and personal dignity in the community, through the coronial jurisdiction, honouring the dead person by determining exactly what happened and asking: how did this person die? Everything that follows from that – are there other people dying the same way, are there ways to prevent future deaths? All those second

---

[24] Kate Tidbury "Coronial Recommendations: Ensuring the Dead Really do Speak to Protect the Living" (LLB(Hons), Auckland University, 2011) at 9.

[25] Interview with Lawyer04 (Jennifer Moore, 5 February 2013).

> tier issues are better moved away from the coronial jurisdiction so that you could get some research base or epidemiology, or Mortality Review Committee that could analyse all the data and draw conclusions. In this way, you protect the coronial jurisdiction by limiting its scope to a fact-finding exercise. The Western common law system is very good at doing some things and very poor at doing others. So it is very good at ensuring due process and fact finding, but not very good when it comes to inquisitorial, analytical output.

There were another five participants who shared this lawyer's view that the coroner's function should be restricted to fact-finding. However, there was overwhelming support for coroners to maintain their preventive function and power to make recommendations. All these participants reported that coronial recommendations must be improved, but they wanted coroners to maintain their legislative power to make recommendations. The following account from a government organisation interviewed is reflective of these participants' views:[26]

> We coordinated a meeting with coroners, the judiciary, academics and agencies. It was not an easy meeting. There was a divergence of views about suicide. . . . Coroners had direct experience of young people killing themselves after receiving break up text messages. Coroners added value there. Don't strip coroners of their role to make recommendations because they can make useful observations based on their direct experiences. And often they are the first to see these trends. Sure, there are some stupid recommendations and they're not perfect, but don't strip them of the power to make recommendations.

The current New Zealand Government's review of the Coroners Act 2006 (NZ) does not propose to remove the legislative power to make recommendations. An amendment to the Act is proposed to "ensure coroners' recommendations or comments are specific to the case and evidence before the coroner".[27]

3.4 NUMBER OF RECOMMENDATIONS AND COMMENTS

Some jurisdictions document the frequency of coronial recommendations in reviews or annual reports.[28] Comparisons of the frequency of

---

[26] Interview with GovtOrg09 (Jennifer Moore, 12 February 2013).

[27] Cabinet Paper *Coroners Act Review: Proposals for Reform – Paper 1* (2013) at 5.

[28] Law Reform Commission of Western Australia and Tatum L. Hands *Review of Coronial Practice in Western Australia: Background Paper Project 100*

coronial recommendations between NZ and overseas jurisdictions must be made with caution because of the different population sizes and coronial systems. For instance, in Western Australia there are approximately 13 000 deaths per year, of which around 15% are reportable, whereas in NZ about 20% of the 29 000 deaths per year are reportable.[29]

As part of its review of the coronial system, the Western Australian Law Reform Commission undertook an investigation of inquests performed in 2007.[30] There were recommendations made in 22 of the 39 inquests. The total number of recommendations for 2007 was 88.[31] From 2000–09, 565 recommendations were made by Western Australian coroners.[32]

The Coroner's Court of Victoria's Annual Reports describe the number of findings and recommendations for each reporting period.[33] Of the 4620 coronial findings made from 1 July 2011 to 30 June 2012, there were a total of 217 recommendations.[34]

In Canada, the Office of the Chief Coroner of Ontario *2010 Report on Inquests* states that in 2010 there were 58 inquests which resulted in 282 recommendations.[35] The report also describes the average number of recommendations per inquest over a seven-year period from 2004–10.[36] The average number of recommendations per inquest in 2009 and 2010 was 4.9.[37]

Between October 2010 and March 2011 in England, there were 203 inquests which resulted in 189 Rule 43 reports.[38] The English statistical summaries include the breakdown of the Rule 43 reports issued under the "broad categories of subject", or underlying causes of death, upon which each report was based.[39]

(2010); Ministry of Justice, above n 2; Office of the Chief Coroner Ontario, above n 2; Coronial Council of Victoria *Coronial Council of Victoria Annual Report 2010–2011* (2011).

29 Tatum L. Hands "Under the Microscope: Reforming Western Australia's Coronial System" (2012) 39 Brief: Journal of the Law Society of Western Australia 12.

30 Law Reform Commission of Western Australia and Hands, above n 28, at 21.

31 At 21–2.

32 At 37.

33 Gray, above n 2, at 55.

34 At 55.

35 Office of the Chief Coroner Ontario, above n 2, at 3.

36 At 35.

37 At 35.

38 Ministry of Justice *Summary of Reports and Responses under Rule 43 of the Coroners Rules: Fifth Report* (2011) at 4.

39 At 4.

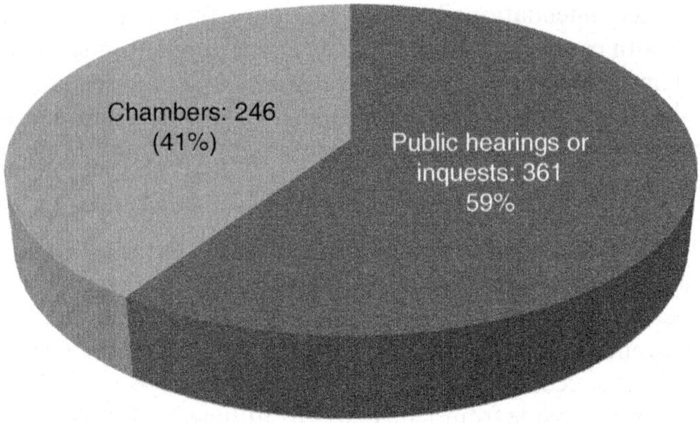

Figure 3.1 *Method of case completion for NZ coronial inquiries, 1 July 2007 – 30 June 2012*

The CSNZ does not produce annual reports with statistical summaries. The *Recommendations Recaps* summarise the recommendations that were made during the quarterly reporting period, but they do not include statistical summaries of the annual frequency of coronial recommendations.

My study examined coronial recommendations over a five-year period to gather information about the number of recommendations and comments that are not currently included in the CSNZ publications.

3.4.1 Number of Recommendations and Comments

In NZ, during the five-year study period, there were 607 coronial inquiries. Almost 60% of these inquiries were public hearings, or inquests, and 41% were completed on the papers in chambers (Figure 3.1).

This study's method of case completion finding is interesting because there was a perception among a number of participants (43/123) that there have been fewer inquests since the introduction of the 2006 Act. For example, one lawyer's view was that:[40]

> In the last year there haven't been many hearings. Anecdotal evidence from the Police seems to support this. Why? Could this be due to pressure on court time? Or maybe there are more chambers findings.

40 Interview with Mr Dawson (lawyer) (Jennifer Moore, 10 September 2012).

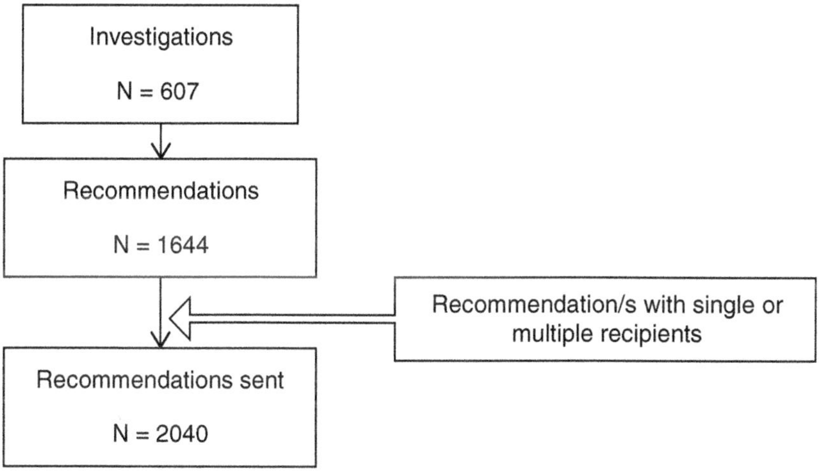

Source: Reproduced with permission from the *NZ Medical Journal*: Jennifer Moore "Coroners' Recommendations about Healthcare-related Deaths as a Potential Tool for Improving Patient Safety and Quality of Care" (2014) 127(1398) NZMJ 35, 38.

Figure 3.2 Summary of coronial investigations and recommendations during the study

Similarly, some organisations believed that the rate of inquests has decreased:[41]

> We just haven't been seeing the same number of inquests in recent years. I'm sure there used to be more when there were part-time coroners. I think the media contributes to the misconception that there are more inquests than there really are. I think more coroner's investigations are being held without an inquest these days.

While more cases were completed by inquest, there were a significant proportion of in-chambers findings, which may explain the participants' perceptions.

The 607 coronial inquiries resulted in 1644 recommendations (Figure 3.2).

The total number of recommendations sent to recipients was 2040 because coroners made single or multiple recommendations to one or more recipients (Figure 3.2). Figure 3.3 describes the scenarios for analysis of recommendations.

---

[41] Interview with GovtOrg02 (Jennifer Moore, 5 February 2013).

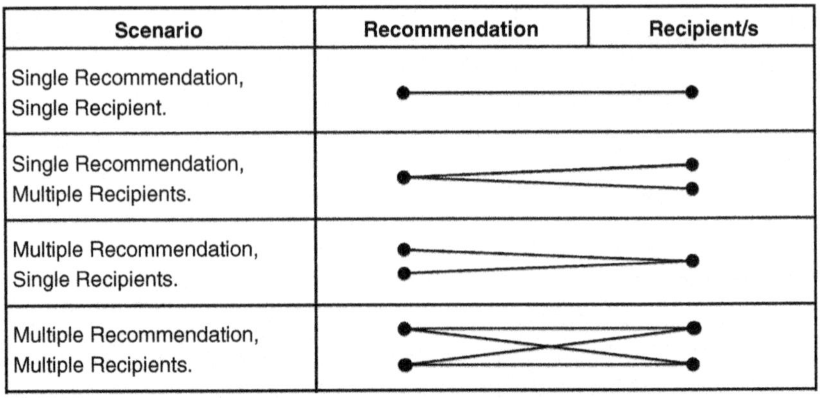

Source: Figure 3.3 is modelled on a similar one in Lyndal Bugeja "Determinants of Coroners' Recommendations on External Cause Deaths in Victoria, Australia" (PhD, Monash University, 2011) at 201.

Figure 3.3 Scenario for analysis of recommendations directed to recipients

Eighty-nine per cent of the 232 organisations received between one and ten recommendations. Occasionally organisations received ten or more recommendations, but this was comparatively rare. Thirty-seven per cent of organisations received one coronial recommendation during the study period. Seventeen per cent of organisations received two recommendations during my study period. Thirty-four per cent of organisations received between three and ten recommendations during the study period.

The number of recommendations per year for the study period is described in Table 3.1.

There were only five recommendations in 2007 because the Act came into force in July of that year and "it took some time for the coroners to start producing findings with recommendations".[42] From 2008, the number of recommendations increases each year, until the drop in 2011. 2010 produced an unusually high number of recommendations.

In my study period, the average number of recommendations per inquest was 2.7. This rate may be compared with Western Australian coroners, who typically issue four recommendations per inquest.[43] Commentators

42 Email from Lily Nunweek to Jennifer Moore regarding dataset of coronial recommendations (20 December 2013).

43 Law Reform Commission of Western Australia and Hands, above n 28, at 37.

Table 3.1 Number of recommendations per year, NZ, 1 July 2007 – 30 June 2012

Year	N
2007*	5
2008	161
2009	386
2010	558
2011	368
2012*	166

Note: *half year.

have noticed that sometimes high profile public cases result in more recommendations.[44] Similarly, it is possible that the media interest in certain coronial inquiries in NZ was a factor in those cases which produced particularly high numbers of recommendations. For instance, there was a lot of media attention following the "Tongariro River tragedy", where six teenage students and their teacher drowned while undertaking an adventure exercise with the Sir Edmund Hillary Outdoor Pursuit Centre.[45] The coronial inquiry into the incident produced 29 recommendations, which was the highest number of recommendations issued by a coronial inquiry in my study period.[46]

In the first 384 inquests held in Auckland between 1841 and 1864, recommendations were made in 21 (5.5%) inquests.[47] The frequency of recommendations is now much higher than in the nineteenth century. For example, in 2009, recommendations were made in 17% of the 1027 inquests held, while recommendations were made in 15.5% of the 1198 inquests in 2010.[48]

Although the focus of this study is recommendations, I also counted the number of coronial comments in order to provide an exploratory picture of the relative numbers. I only counted comments that were made alongside recommendations in coronial inquiries. Coronial inquiries that

44 For example, see: Freckelton and Ranson, above n 3.

45 For example, see: Mike Barrington "Tongariro drownings aftermath" *The Northern Advocate* (17 April 2008); Kim Knight "Fatality, near-misses preceded gorge deaths" *Sunday Star Times* (21 February 2010).

46 *McClean* [2010] NZCorC 48.

47 Gluckman, above n 9, at 115–323.

48 Tidbury, above n 24, at 11.

resulted in comments only (that is, no recommendations were made) were excluded because the focus of my study is recommendations.

The interpretation section of the Coroners Act 2006 (NZ) provides that:[49]

> specified recommendations or comments means, in relation to a death, recommendations or comments by the designated coroner on either or both of the following:
> (a) Avoidance of circumstances similar to those in which the death occurred;
> (b) The way in which any people should act in circumstances of that kind.

"Comments" is not defined separately. Does the "or" suggest that recommendations and comments are different? All coroners who were interviewed for this study reported that there is a difference between recommendations and comments. Participants' definitions of "comments" were similar. For example, the former NZ Chief Coroner, Judge MacLean, explained that:[50]

> Recommendations are generally specific as to what a coroner believes should have been done differently, or should be done differently, in the future. So they are generally targeted and they can be responded to by organisations or people who can say: "yes we agree, no we don't, or we partly agree, and this is what we are doing about it." Comments are more like passing observations that don't necessarily call for a response.

Coroners typically differentiated recommendations from comments on the basis that comments generally do not invite responses or action from organisations. A few (3/15) coroners highlighted the advantages of making comments instead of recommendations. For instance, one coroner explained that when:[51]

> The facts speak for themselves, you don't have to go overboard and recommend the obvious. For example, in the case involving the drowning, they had drunk a couple of bourbons before going in the water. I didn't want to recommend that people never drink before going in boats, but the facts speak for themselves.
>
> In a case involving an infant death . . . I had made comments there that three of the six people living at the address were cigarette smokers. The mother smoked during the pregnancy. So I highlighted the smoking aspect in my comments . . . I did not make a recommendation. One coroner makes recommendations: "I recommend that the findings be sent to such and such" but that is

---

49 Coroners Act 2006 (NZ), s 9.

50 Interview with the former Chief Coroner (Jennifer Moore, 12 September 2012).

51 Interview with Coroner Reid (Jennifer Moore, 30 October 2012).

> not a recommendation in terms of section 57. It devalues the recommendation process. You can accommodate that without it being a recommendation. And you can get the safety message through via comments.

It was common (10/15) for coroners to report that high rates of recommendation-making "devalue" the recommendation process and that, therefore, coroners should consider whether making a comment may be more appropriate.

In addition, some coroners (5/15) reported that they sometimes deliberately elect to make a comment, rather than a recommendation, in order to enable the organisation to make decisions about the best way to prevent similar deaths in the future. For example, in an inquiry about recreational diving, the coroner endorsed the recommendations made in the Police National Dive Squad Report and he made the following comment:[52]

> I believe a version of the report with some of the details of the equipment and problems with it could usefully be made available with the recommendations to the diving community. However, I will leave that up to the Police National Dive Squad as to what information they provide along with the recommendations and conclusions of their report.

During my study period, coroners made 670 comments (Figure 3.4). Although coroners made more recommendations, 670 is a significant number of comments. It is beyond the scope of this study to provide in-depth analysis of the nature of coronial comments. However, the number of coronial comments and the coroners' descriptions of their decision-making suggest that further investigation would be useful.

The number of comments and recommendations, by coroner, is described in Figure 3.5.

3.4.2 Unique and Repeated Recommendations

I adopted Bugeja's definition of "original or repeated recommendation", which was "whether the recommendation was original to the cohort (i.e. made only once) or was a repeat of a recommendation made in another case in the cohort".[53] Repeated recommendations were those that were identical in wording. There may have been repetitive themes amongst the recommendations. However, common themes were not excluded. As Bugeja points out, the impact of this approach is that there may be an

---

52 *Schumacher* [2010] NZCorC 213.

53 Lyndal Bugeja "Determinants of Coroners' Recommendations on External Cause Deaths in Victoria, Australia" (PhD, Monash University, 2011) at 185.

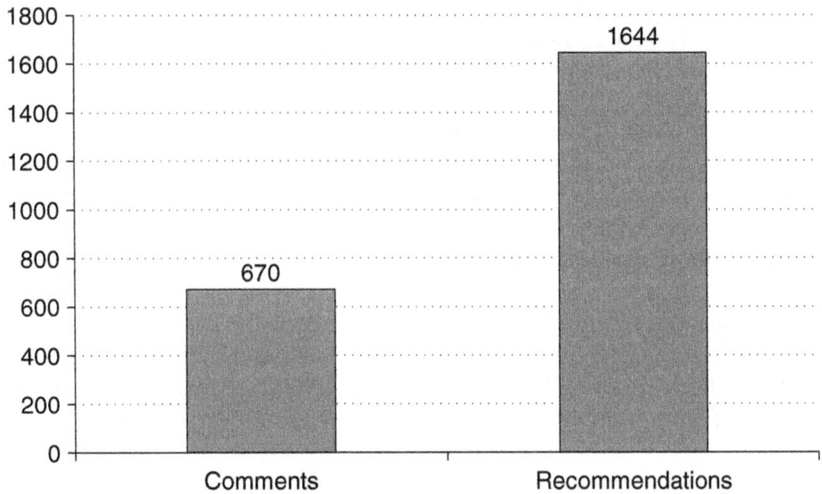

Figure 3.4 Total number of comments and recommendations in 607 inquiries

overestimate of the reported frequency of original recommendations.[54] It is necessary to identify repeated recommendations in order to accurately determine the number of recommendations in my study period. Failure to exclude repeated recommendations overestimates the number.

In my study period, 324 of the 1644 coronial recommendations were identical repeated recommendations (Figure 3.6). In other words, there were 1320 unique recommendations in my study period.

Participants reported that the cumulative effect of repeated recommendations aids the uptake of coronial recommendations. This finding is consistent with previous research.[55] As such, I wanted to investigate the number and nature of repeated recommendations.

It is also useful to isolate the repeated recommendations in order to identify the underlying causes of death that attract frequent coronial recommendations. The underlying cause of death categories that attracted the greatest number of repeated recommendations are described in Figure 3.7.

---

[54] At 191.

[55] Ray Watterson, Penny Brown and John McKenzie "Coronial Recommendations and the Prevention of Indigenous Death" (2008) 12 Special Edition 2 Australian Indigenous Law Review 4 at 167; Bugeja, above n 53, at 91.

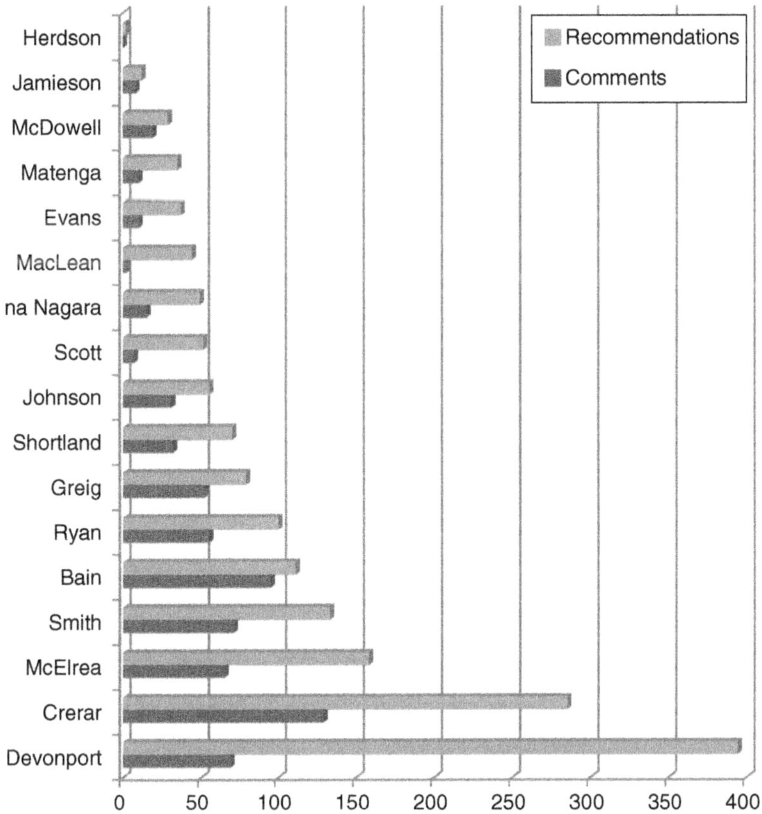

Figure 3.5 *Number of recommendations and comments per coroner*

3.4.3 Underlying Cause of Deaths

According to the World Health Organization, in high-income jurisdictions like NZ, heart disease is the top, and cancers high, among the top ten leading causes of death.[56] In NZ, like other industrialised countries, transport accidents are a major cause of mortality.[57] NZ also has a comparatively high rate of intentional self-harm, particularly among males.

---

[56] World Health Organization *The Global Burden of Disease: 2004 Update* (2008).

[57] New Zealand Ministry of Health *Mortality and Demographic Data 2010* (2013) at 11.

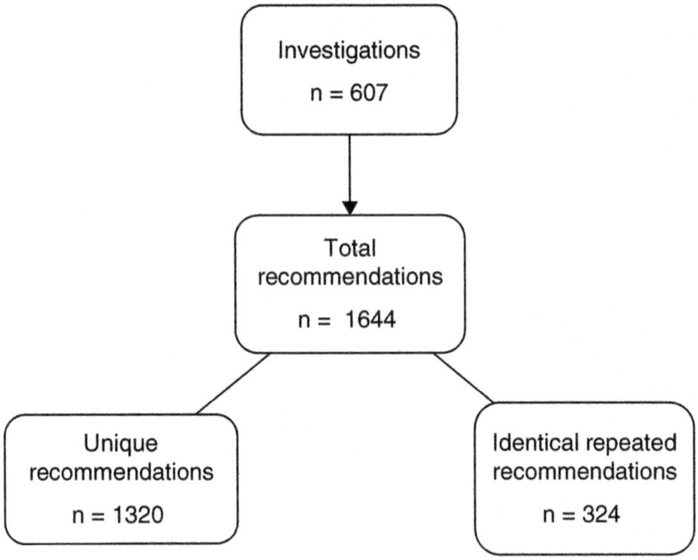

Source: Reproduced with permission from the *NZ Medical Journal*: Jennifer Moore "Coroners' Recommendations about Healthcare-related Deaths as a Potential Tool for Improving Patient Safety and Quality of Care" (2014) 127(1398) NZMJ 35, 40.

Figure 3.6 Summary of coronial investigations, unique and repeated recommendations, 1 July 2007 – 30 June 2012

The underlying cause of death categories that the coroners investigated during the study period are described in Figure 3.8.

Given NZ's mortality statistics, it is arguably not surprising that many coronial investigations concern transport accidents and intentional self-harm. Fifty-eight of the 607 coronial inquiries concerned deaths attributed to complications of medical and/or surgical care. The burden of injury is not evenly distributed amongst ethnicity or age groups. For example, young children have a higher proportion of death due to drowning compared with other age groups. "Exposure to and poisoning by noxious substances" is an ICD-10 classification which includes fatal exposure to narcotics and alcohol.

In their investigations about these underlying causes of death, what were the typical characteristics of coronial recommendations? The following section explores the nature of coroners' recommendations during my study period.

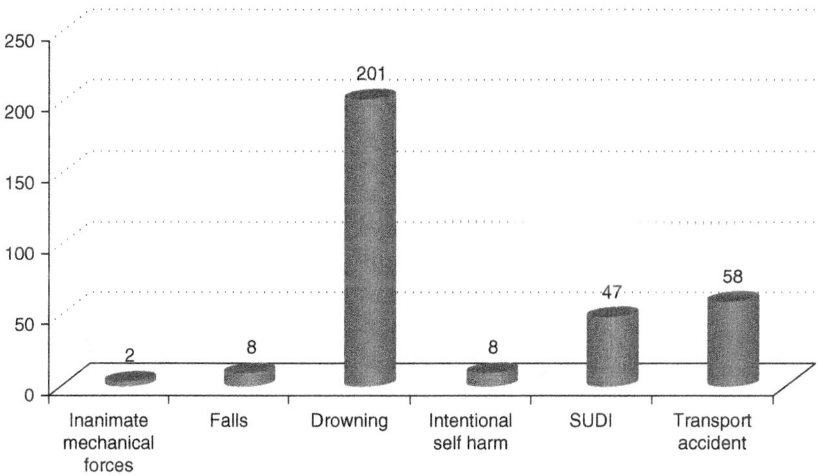

Source: Reproduced with permission from the *NZ Medical Journal*: Jennifer Moore "Coroners' Recommendations about Healthcare-related Deaths as a Potential Tool for Improving Patient Safety and Quality of Care" (2014) 127(1398) NZMJ 35, 40.

Figure 3.7 Summary and number of identical repeated recommendations, 1 July 2007 – 30 June 2012

3.5 NATURE OF RECOMMENDATIONS

This section provides a qualitative overview of the nature of coroners' recommendations in my study period. The structure of coronial recommendations is not standardised. However, coroners' recommendations are typically shaped according to overarching formats. It is usual for a coroner to make a recommendation in one of the following categories:

- Category 1: that the recipient review its practices, policies and/or procedures
- Category 2: that the recipient change its practices, policies and/or procedures
- Category 3: for immediate law reform, or a review of the current legal framework
- Category 4: for publicity about an issue.

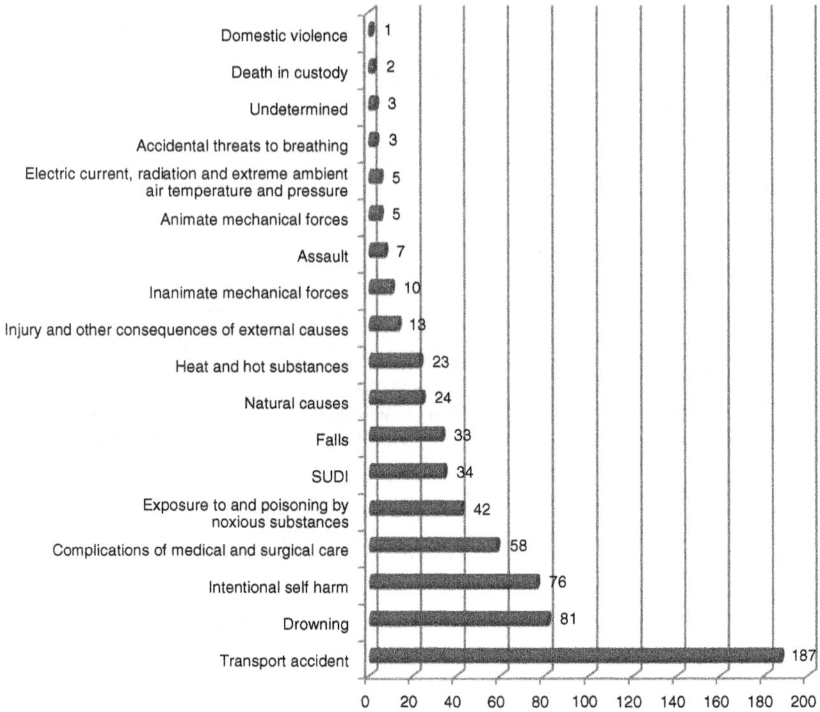

Source: Reproduced with permission from the *NZ Medical Journal*: Jennifer Moore "Coroners' Recommendations about Healthcare-related Deaths as a Potential Tool for Improving Patient Safety and Quality of Care" (2014) 127(1398) NZMJ 35, 39.

Figure 3.8 Underlying causes of death categories investigated by NZ coroners, 1 July 2007 – 30 June 2012

I classified 562/1644 coroners' recommendations as category 1. An example of category 1 is:[58]

> That the Department of Corrections review its institutional protocols so that in the event a prison proposes to transfer a prisoner, processes are in place to ensure that the transfer will not prejudice the prisoner's opportunity to attend an appointment for medical treatment or testing outside of the prison.

Some coroners (7/15) reported that they prefer to restrict their recommendations to reviews of organisational policies and procedures because

---

[58] *Kahu* [2008] NZCorC 5.

only the agencies have the necessary institutional knowledge to make appropriate organisational changes. Using healthcare-related deaths as an example, Coroner Stewart explained that:[59]

> Hospitals have their own investigation processes. Often by the time the case gets to us, they have had their internal review and they have put in place the necessary steps and corrections. To an extent, they are the experts on how to improve their own systems. So other than endorsing what they have already put in place, it is not usual to make a recommendation. Having said that, there have been cases where I have got independent expert advice (someone who is independent of the agency involved) and the expert has come up with an alternative proposal and that has been put forward as a recommendation. It depends on the case. An example is a hospital death involving pulmonary embolism. At that stage they hadn't finished their guidelines. I had a review from an independent expert who made some suggestions about the hospital's draft guidelines and how they could be improved. I suggested to the hospital that they may wish to consider the suggestions about their guidelines which were made by my expert.

Coroner Stewart (and the other coroners who prefer category 1 recommendations) often described organisations as the "experts" on their own systems. Therefore, recommendations that state that organisations should change their policies and procedures (category 2 above) are perceived as unwise because coroners lack the information that would be required to formulate the precise details of the suggested change. That is why some coroners prefer to make general recommendations which allow the organisation to make decisions about the details. For example, the following category 1 recommendation suggests that the organisation decide "upon the exact words" and how to implement the recommendation:[60]

> I make that recommendation. I leave it to the DHB to implement it and to hit upon the exact words. I say again that to be effective it needs to be concise and easy to understand. In my view more is seldom good and if a notice is a lengthy one and difficult to understand, people simply do not read it.

691/1644 coroners' recommendations were category 2. An example of a category 2 recommendation (that an organisation change its policies, procedures and practices) is:[61]

---

59 Interview with Coroner Stewart (Jennifer Moore, 12 October 2012).
60 *Halbert* [2009] NZCorC 123.
61 *Moore* [2009] NZCorC 17.

> That the . . . District Health Board formally adopts and implements a separate form for the initial assessment of risk a patient poses to him or herself or to others on admission to a mental health facility.
>
> That the . . . District Health Board amends its procedures relating to searches for missing patients from any mental health facility to ensure that a thorough search of the entire grounds of the facility is undertaken as soon as a patient is noted to be missing.

Category 1 and 2 recommendations were often directed to health sector organisations and addressed matters such as:[62]

- reviews of hospital or clinic policies and practices
- reviews of telephone triage systems
- changes to clinical policies, procedures and practices, including:
    - the introduction of, or changes to, guidelines, pathways, protocols, checklists and/or standard operating procedures
    - increased supervision of junior doctors in specific areas of practice
    - improving medical record-keeping and note-taking practices
    - training and education
    - the procedures during changeovers such as improving communication between health care workers from different specialities or professions.

In addition to healthcare-related deaths, category 2 recommendations are also particularly common in transport-related deaths. For example, coroners have recommended:[63]

> That Transit New Zealand erect warning signs around this particular stretch of road advising motorists that this is a particularly dangerous stretch and that it has a high crash rate.

Coroners have also made category 2 recommendations such as:[64]

> That Western Bay Transport upgrade their documentation of Hazard Identification and controls for any significant hazard identified.

---

[62] Jennifer Moore "Coroners' Recommendations about Healthcare-related Deaths as a Potential Tool for Improving Patient Safety and Quality of Care" (2014) 127(1398) NZ Medical Journal 35.

[63] *Paynter* [2009] NZCorC 20.

[64] *Hallmond* [2009] NZCorC 91.

> That they maintain documentation of all formal and informal (on the job) training provided and keep a register of qualifications for all employees.

Given that NZ coroners are qualified lawyers appointed as judicial officers, it is not surprising that I found that 141 recommendations were category 3 recommendations (that is, recommendations which suggest immediate law reform, or a review of the current legal framework). An example of a category 3 recommendation which suggests amendments to the law is:[65]

> That the government amend the law in relation to school buses to require all school buses to be fitted with a system of flashing warning lights to indicate to other road users that the school bus is stationary for the purposes of either receiving or discharging passengers, and that these flashing lights be automatically activated when a school bus on its run comes to a halt for either of those purposes.

Coroners sometimes endorse law reform recommendations that are suggested to them by organisations or experts during an inquiry. For example, this coroner made the following statement:[66]

> I endorse the recommendation for the introduction of legislation which creates an offence when a driver of a motor vehicle uses a hand held mobile phone while driving.

Coroners also made their own suggestions for law reform such as that:[67]

> The New Zealand Firearms Safety Code should be incorporated into legislation and its observance have statutory force.

Sometimes coroners recommend that an organisation investigate their proposal so that legislative change may occur in the future. For example, an all-terrain vehicle (ATV) accident prompted the following recommendation:[68]

> The Court endorses the new educational and enforcement programme being proposed by the Department of Labour, but considers that both Ministries undertake an immediate investigation to consider the mandatory installation of:
>
> a. The compulsory wearing of helmets when operating ATVs in any circumstances; and
> b. The installation of a roll bar on all ATVs/quad bikes; and
> c. The installation of lap belts on all ATVs/quad bikes.

---

65 *Aldworth* [2009] NZCorC 67.
66 *Keating* [2008] NZCorC 18.
67 *Timms* [2008] NZCorC 62.
68 *Santos* [2011] NZCorC 3.

An example of a coroner's recommendation to amend the current legal framework is:[69]

> I also recommend that included in the new legislation is a provision, similar to that in section 7A of the Mental Health (Compulsory Assessment and Treatment) Act 1992 for consultation with the family or whānau of the proposed patient.

An example of a coroner's recommendation which calls for a review of the regulatory framework is:[70]

> That the Ministry of Transport review the policies underpinning rule 7.12 of the Land Transport (Road User) Rules 2004 with a view to amending the rule so that riders of motorised skateboards are required to wear safety helmets when riding their boards.

Category 4 coronial recommendations call for publicity about an issue. There were 250 category 4 recommendations. Coroners may direct that a recommendation is for "the public at large"[71] or general "public attention":[72]

> I intend to circulate this Finding to the media to draw public attention to the tragic consequences of alcohol-and-cannabis-affected drivers in charge of vehicles travelling at high speeds.

Alternatively, coroners may make recommendations to a specific group, such as families with newborn babies:[73]

> That continued publicity be given to unsafe sleeping environments for babies (including co-sleeping with the mother).

Another category 4 example is a recommendation directed to a specific profession in order to publicise or "raise awareness" about rare presentations or unusual issues:[74]

> That the Royal NZ College of General Practitioners promulgates information to Fellows of the College to raise awareness of the issues raised in this case, particularly in relation to sudden cardiac deaths in young people.

---

69 *Kennett* [2011] NZCorC 66.
70 *White* [2008] NZCorC 65.
71 *Araos-Elevancini* [2008] NZCorC 54.
72 *McKenzie* [2012] NZCorC 56.
73 *Huata* [2009] NZCorC 63.
74 *Burgess* [2010] NZCorC 66.

Similarly, coroners often request a specific organisation to give publicity to an issue. For example, for deaths due to drowning, coroners sometimes recommend that Water Safety NZ (WSNZ) publicise an issue:[75]

> I recommend that WSNZ gives publicity to the desirability of using neoprene chest waders in conjunction with a belt and personal floatation device, by suitable publicity to members of the public and specialist suppliers and users of such products.

Coroners often adopt category 4 recommendations in order to educate the public. For example, coroners frequently call for education of parents concerning safe sleeping for babies:[76]

> My recommendation is for better education to young parents and families who for a variety of reasons decide to have all family members sleep in the one bed with the presence of an infant or baby.

3.6 RECIPIENTS OF RECOMMENDATIONS

This section provides an overview of all the recipients of coronial recommendations during my study period. I classified the recipients as "organisations", "individuals" and "untargeted".

There are a small number of overseas studies which have examined the recipients of coronial recommendations. A landmark study in Victoria, Australia, provided descriptive statistics for the organisations that were sent coroners' recommendations from 2000–05.[77] Three hundred and eighty organisations were sent recommendations during the study period.[78]

While some studies provide primarily speculative discussion about organisations' responses to recommendations, a small number note the recipients of recommendations and monitor their responses and implementation.[79] In the only Australian academic study to analyse the implementation of recommendations, the researchers analysed the responses of government organisations to 484 recommendations from 185 inquests in Australia, mostly in 2004.[80] In 2006, the Queensland Ombudsman reported on the

---

75 *Keenan* [2010] NZCorC 6.

76 *Howard* [2008] NZCorC 45.

77 Bugeja, above n 53, at 259.

78 At 259.

79 Justin Malbon "Institutional Responses to Coronial Recommendations" (1998) 6 JLM 35.

80 Watterson, Brown and McKenzie, above n 55.

public sector agencies that received and responded to coroners' recommendations.[81] The report discusses 72 inquest reports prepared by Queensland coroners in 2002 and 2003 involving 23 public sector agencies.

The jurisdictions (for example, Ontario, Canada and England) which compile responses to coronial recommendations in their annual reports have also tracked the recipients of recommendations.[82] The CPU in Victoria records and monitors coronial recommendations and recipients' responses. The Coroner's Court of Victoria Annual Reports provide statistics about recommendations, recipients and responses.[83]

The CSNZ does not produce a public document which outlines the recipients of coronial recommendations. My study provides the first description of the recipients of NZ coronial recommendations. In NZ for my study period, there were 309 recipients of coroners' recommendations (Figure 3.9).

Of the 2040 recommendations that were directed to recipients, the majority (1114) were sent to government organisations. Figure 3.10 describes the number of recommendations sent to organisations by recipient type.

3.6.1 Organisations

This section discusses the recipients of recommendations that were organisations: government, non-government not-for-profit and for-profit. As described in Figure 3.10, there were 232 organisations: 121 government, 67 non-government not-for-profit and 44 for-profit. My finding that government organisations received the highest number of recommendations is consistent with other research.[84]

As I outlined earlier in this chapter, transport accidents cause a significant proportion of mortality in NZ. Therefore, it is not a surprising finding that the NZ Transport Agency received the highest proportion of unique coroners' recommendations (Figure 3.11).

It is probable that the research revealed that coroners typically sent recommendations to government organisations, and that the MOH received the second-highest proportion of recommendations, because these entities are responsible for the development of legislation, policies and

---

[81] Queensland Ombudsman *The Coronial Recommendations Project: An Investigation into the Administrative Practice of Queensland Public Sector Agencies in Assisting Coronial Inquiries and Responding to Coronial Recommendations* (2006).

[82] Office of the Chief Coroner Ontario, above n 2; Ministry of Justice, above n 2.

[83] Gray, above n 2.

[84] For example, see: Bugeja, above n 53, at 265.

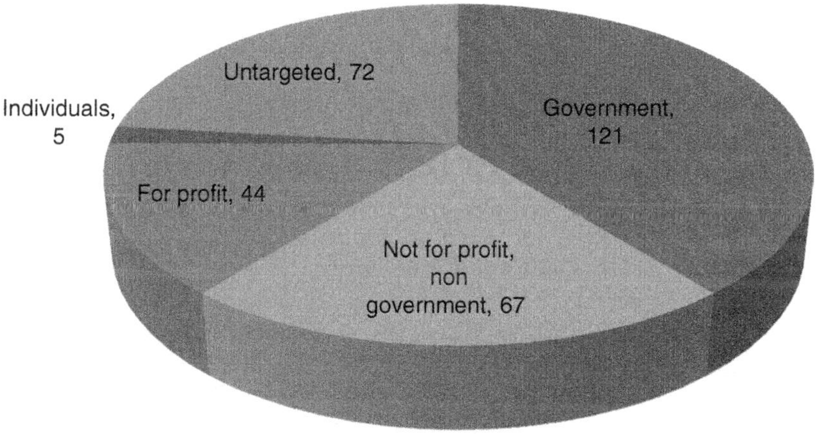

Source: Reproduced with permission from the *NZ Medical Journal*: Jennifer Moore "Coroners' Recommendations about Healthcare-related Deaths as a Potential Tool for Improving Patient Safety and Quality of Care" (2014) 127(1398) NZMJ 35, 41.

Figure 3.9 Summary and number of recipients of coroners' recommendations by type, 1 July 2007 – 30 June 2012

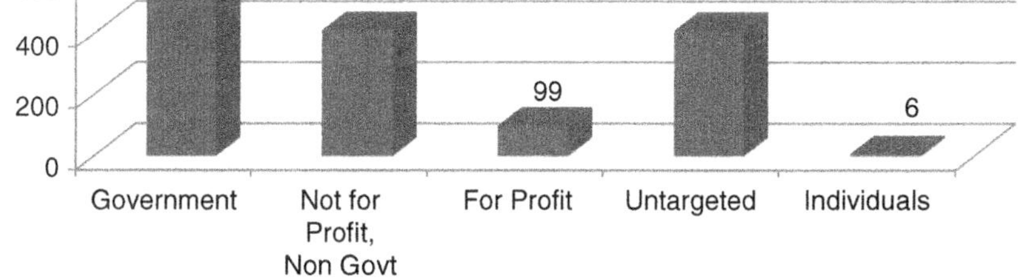

Figure 3.10 Number of recommendations directed to recipients by type, NZ 1 July 2007 – 30 June 2012

programmes designed to manage public health. Fifty-six of the 232 organisations were health agencies, such as Plunket, St John and the National Addiction Centre.[85]

The Sir Edmund Hillary Outdoor Pursuit Centre received the highest number of total recommendations (161), but relatively few unique recommendations (23) because of the number of people who died in a single incident (Figure 3.11). On 30 March 2010, a teacher and six students died while undertaking an adventure challenge exercise conducted by the Sir Edmund Hillary Outdoor Pursuit Centre.

Figure 3.12 depicts the unique and the total number of recommendations that were directed to organisations by type. The total number of recommendations depicted in the figure sums to less than 2040 (my total dataset for recommendations directed to recipients) because this figure excludes the untargeted and individual recipients. Government organisations received 303 repeated recommendations. Not-for-profit organisations received 182 repeated recommendations and for-profit received 11 repeated recommendations.

It is useful to identify repeated recommendations in order to enable further investigation into why repeated recommendations were necessary and what action, if any, was taken by organisations that received repeated recommendations. These figures do not reveal whether the repeated recommendations were feasible or evidence-based. However, they provide an exploratory indication of the incidence and recipients of repeated recommendations.

3.6.2 Individuals

In this section, I describe the individuals who were the recipients of coronial recommendations. As described in Figure 3.9, five of the 309 recipients were individuals. The five individuals were:

1. "Medical Officer of Health"[86]
2. "Attorney General"[87]
3. "Dr David Hoadley"[88]
4. "Dr Vause"[89]
5. "Midwife, Sue Bolton".[90]

---

85 Moore, above 62.
86 *Taana* [2011] NZCorC 168.
87 *Fenton* [2012] NZCorC 96.
88 *Farrell* [2010] NZCorC 75.
89 *Dunlop* [2012] NZCorC 20.
90 *Clancy* [2010] NZCorC 115.

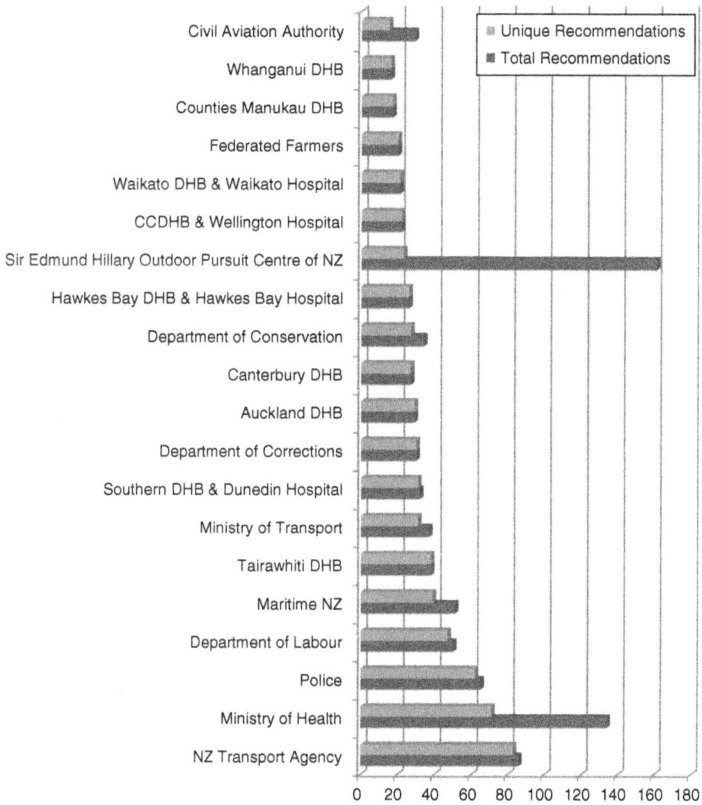

Source: Reproduced with permission from the *NZ Medical Journal*: Jennifer Moore "Coroners' Recommendations about Healthcare-related Deaths as a Potential Tool for Improving Patient Safety and Quality of Care" (2014) 127(1398) NZMJ 35, 42.

Figure 3.11 Number of recommendations (15 or more unique and total) sent to organisations, NZ 1 July 2007 – 30 June 2012

Apart from the Attorney General, all individuals are health practitioners. Even when the health practitioners were affiliated with health care organisations, the coroners preferred to direct these recommendations to the individual practitioners.

3.6.3 Untargeted

As I explained earlier in this chapter, the nature of coronial recommendations varies. Sometimes coroners fail to state to whom a recommendation

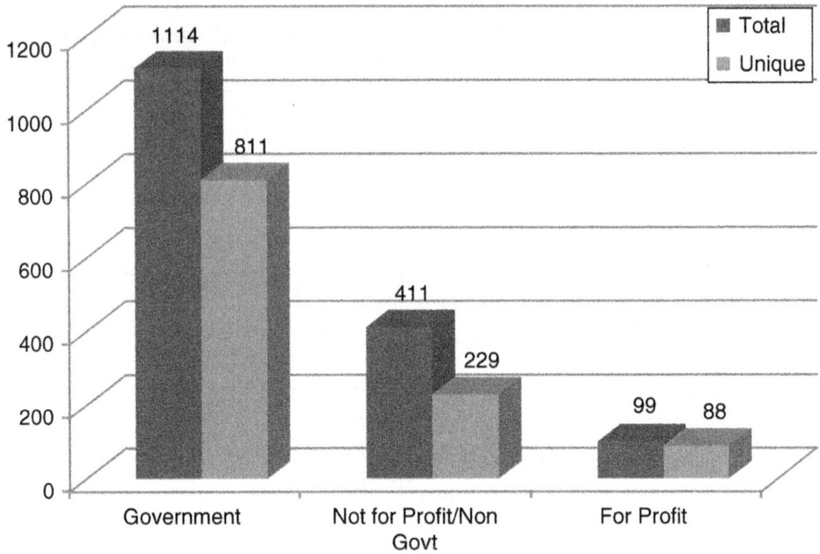

Figure 3.12 Total and unique number of recommendations received by organisations, by type

is directed. The NZ Chief Coroner, Judge MacLean, acknowledges that while there are some "sweeping" recommendations, "the aim is to produce well targeted recommendations".[91]

A targeted recommendation identifies a specific organisation/s. By contrast, an "untargeted" recommendation is a recommendation which is not directed to an identifiable organisation. For example, I have classified recommendations that were directed to "any person reading . . . this decision"[92] or "persons taking drugs"[93] as untargeted.

All untargeted recommendations are described in Table 3.2. Many identically worded untargeted recommendations appear in multiple coronial inquiries. For example, "the government", or variations such as "appropriate government agency" or "relevant government agency", were repeated 29 times. I have only counted each unique phrase once in order to avoid overestimating the total number of untargeted recommendations.

[91] "Ask Me Anything: Chief Coroner Judge Neil MacLean" *The National Business Review* (New Zealand, 14 December 2012) 31.
[92] *Thacker* [2010] NZCorC 146.
[93] *Osborne* [2011] NZCorC 138.

Table 3.2 NZ coronial untargeted recommendations, 1 July 2007 – 30 June 2012

No.	Untargeted recommendation	Total N	Date
1	"adventure race promotion and organisation industry"	1	22 June 2010.[94]
2	"all buses used for transporting school pupils"	1	20 July 2009.[95]
3	"all owners and/or operators of motorised vehicles"; "all drivers"; "all drivers of all cars"; "all motor vehicle drivers"; "motorcyclists"	5	1 (12 November 2008);[96] 1 (30 September 2009);[97] 1 (10 November 2009);[98] 1 (8 December 2009);[99] 1 (3 June 2010).[100]
4	"all merchants"	1	16 September 2009.[101]
5	"all parents of newborn children"	2	31 October 2008.[102]
6	"all persons close to a person who is showing signs of depression"	1	15 October 2008.[103]
7	"all persons travelling in small boats"	1	8 August 2008.[104]
8	"all persons using ladders"	1	24 November 2009.[105]
9	"retailers" [of Delonghi products]	3	6 June 2008.[106]
10	"all rural-based general practitioners"	1	1 September 2010.[107]

94 *Schriek* [2010] NZCorC 140.
95 *Aldworth*, above n 65.
96 *Wilson-Tui* [2008] NZCorC 64.
97 *Hale* [2009] NZCorC 119.
98 *Noble* [2009] NZCorC 145.
99 *Struthers* [2009] NZCorC 172.
100 *MacDonald* [2010] NZCorC 111.
101 *Melville* [2009] NZCorC 109.
102 *Leisi* [2008] NZCorC 58.
103 *Araos-Elevancini*, above n 71.
104 *Dewes* [2008] NZCorC 44.
105 *Burns* [2009] NZCorC 157.
106 *Pearson* [2008] NZCorC 20.
107 *Williams* [2010] NZCorC 148.

Table 3.2 (continued)

No.	Untargeted recommendation	Total N	Date
11	"all rural schools"	1	20 July 2009.[108]
12	"all whitebaiters"	1	28 July 2008.[109]
13	"ambulance and fire services"; "ambulance sector"	2	1 (3 November 2009);[110] 1 (1 November 2011).[111]
14	"any dive operator in Milford Sound"	1	19 August 2010.[112]
15	"any person reading the details of this decision"	1	3 September 2010.[113]
16	"anyone"; "no one"; "someone"	3	1 (21 December 2007);[114] 1 (11 August 2008);[115] 1 (27 August 2009).[116]
17	"appropriate farm workers' union"	1	29 May 2009.[117]
18	"relevant safety organisations"	1	11 February 2011.[118]
19	"appropriate government agency"; "relevant government agency"; "the appropriate Minister/s"; "appropriate government department"; "the	29	1 (8 August 2008);[119] 1 (21 August 2008);[120] 1 (15 October 2008);[121] 1 (29 May 2009);[122] 1 (2 July 2008);[123] 1 (2 July 2008);[124] 5 (9 April 2009);[125] 1 (20 July 2009);[126]

108 *Aldworth*, above n 65.
109 *Kelly* [2008] NZCorC 34.
110 *Laing* [2009] NZCorC 139.
111 *Gravatt* [2011] NZCorC 122.
112 *Houghton* [2010] NZCorC 145.
113 *Thacker*, above n 92.
114 *Chambers* [2007] NZCorC 14.
115 *McWhinnie* [2008] NZCorC 23.
116 *Kailahi* [2009] NZCorC 101.
117 *Frank* [2009] NZCorC 39.
118 *McGahan* [2011] NZCorC 27.
119 *Norris* [2008] NZCorC 41.
120 *Singh* [2008] NZCorC 39.
121 *Donald* [2008] NZCorC 48.
122 *Frank*, above n 117.
123 *Sicely* [2008] NZCorC 32.
124 *Muru* [2008] NZCorC 6.
125 *Scott-Collins* [2009] NZCorC 189.
126 *Aldworth*, above n 65.

Table 3.2 (continued)

No.	Untargeted recommendation	Total N	Date
19	government"; "local leaders and MPs"; "appropriate regulatory agency"	29	14 (30 March 2010) [7 deaths, same incident];[127] 1 (12 August 2010);[128] 1 (15 November 2010);[129] 1 (8 February 2011).[130]
20	"all candidates for licenses"	2	1 September 2011.[131]
21	"caregivers at the day base centre"	2	12 November 2008.[132]
22	"an Emergency Department of any hospital"	1	15 December 2008.[133]
23	"All employees in a rural workplace"; "immigrant workers" [on farms]	6	5 (30 November 2009);[134] 1 (8 March 2010).[135]
24	"all employers"	1	30 October 2009.[136]
25	"farming community"; "all self employed farmers and their employees"	3	1 (28 July 2008);[137] 1 (15 October 2008);[138] 1 (26 February 2010).[139]
26	"free divers"; "all dive industry and recreational divers"; "recreational divers"; "divers undertaking technical dives"	38	1 (9 July 2010);[140] 10 (19 July 2010);[141] 13 (16 September 2010);[142] 9 (15 November 2010);[143] 5 (3 November 2011).[144]

127 *McClean*, above n 46.
128 *Campbell* [2010] NZCorC 118.
129 *Fernandez* [2010] NZCorC 190.
130 *McGregor* [2011] NZCorC 24.
131 *Lewis* [2011] NZCorC 186.
132 *Roos* [2008] NZCorC 80.
133 *Puaca-Stevanovic* [2008] NZCorC 82.
134 *Sewell* [2009] NZCorC 112.
135 *Modi* [2010] NZCorC 28.
136 *Mbatha* [2009] NZCorC 136.
137 *Oosten* [2008] NZCorC 31.
138 *Donald*, above n 121.
139 *Butt* [2010] NZCorC 22.
140 *de Thierry* [2010] NZCorC 120.
141 *Ngapera* [2010] NZCorC 126.
142 *Schumacher*, above n 52.
143 *Tipene* [2010] NZCorC 188.
144 *Bailey* [2011] NZCorC 117.

Table 3.2 (continued)

No.	Untargeted recommendation	Total N	Date
27	"funeral directors"	1	22 June 2010.[145]
28	"Head Office of dairy companies in NZ"	1	28 July 2008.[146]
29	"health practitioners"	1	18 March 2009.[147]
30	"doctors"	1	18 June 2009.[148]
31	"regional hospitals in Auckland"	1	22 March 2010.[149]
32	"hunters"	4	11 November 2008.[150]
33	"landlords"	1	21 June 2010.[151]
34	"Lead Maternity Carers"	1	28 April 2009.[152]
35	"lines company"	1	5 August 2009.[153]
36	"manufacturers of gas heaters"	1	6 June 2008.[154]
37	"maternity care staff"	1	28 April 2009.[155]
38	"manufacturers and suppliers of the Vicon baler"	2	13 January 2012.[156]
39	"midwives"	3	1 July 2010.[157]
40	"mountaineering and abseiling community"	1	17 June 2008.[158]
41	"mountaineers"	6	3 (29 July 2009);[159] 3 (30 April 2012).[160]
42	"fishermen"	1	30 November 2010.[161]

145 *Koefoed* [2010] NZCorC 106.
146 *Skinner* [2008] NZCorC 30.
147 *Wallace* [2009] NZCorC 15.
148 *Mr H* [2009] NZCorC 52.
149 *Ervine* [2010] NZCorC 44.
150 *Timms*, above n 67.
151 *Colcord-Smit* [2010] NZCorC 113.
152 *Riki* [2009] NZCorC 28.
153 *McOnie* [2009] NZCorC 82.
154 *Pearson*, above n 106.
155 *Riki*, above n 152.
156 *Rolton* [2012] NZCorC 13.
157 *Morris* [2010] NZCorC 112.
158 *MacDonald* [2008] NZCorC 29.
159 *Pawson* [2009] NZCorC 78.
160 *Ong* [2012] NZCorC 52.
161 *Herbert* [2010] NZCorC 200.

Table 3.2 (continued)

No.	Untargeted recommendation	Total N	Date
43	"operators of commercial snorkelling activities (including swimming with dolphin activities)"	11	20 April 2012.[162]
44	"all operators of powered recreational vessels or maritime products"	1	1 September 2011.[163]
45	"others with an interest in outdoor safety"	1	27 July 2009.[164]
46	"all owners of properties with swimming pools"	1	3 August 2009.[165]
47	"pedestrian"	2	27 August 2009.[166]
48	"those persons taking drugs"	1	2 August 2011.[167]
49	"persons who prescribe anti-depressant medication"	1	23 October 2008.[168]
50	"persons working around vintage farm machinery"	5	14 August 2008.[169]
51	"skiers and snowboarders"; "commercial ski areas"	4	2 (8 September 2011);[170] 2 (22 September 2011).[171]
52	"public health service"	1	18 June 2009.[172]
53	"publicity"; "public attention"; "media publicity"; "to the media to	19	1 (7 July 2009);[173] 1 (15 October 2008);[174] 1 (12 December 2008);[175] 1 (22 January 2009);[176] 1 (18 June 2009);[177]

162 *Harper* [2012] NZCorC 48.
163 *Lewis*, above n 131.
164 *Okin* [2009] NZCorC 76.
165 *Calvey* [2009] NZCorC 80.
166 *Bach* [2009] NZCorC 100.
167 *Osborne*, above n 93.
168 *Harris* [2008] NZCorC 56.
169 *Eunson* [2008] NZCorC 36.
170 *Swett* [2011] NZCorC 153.
171 *Donaggio* [2011] NZCorC 152.
172 *Warren-King* [2009] NZCorC 53.
173 *Huata*, above n 73.
174 *Donald*, above n 121.
175 *McLean* [2008] NZCorC 72.
176 *Keen* [2009] NZCorC 3.
177 *Stephen* [2009] NZCorC 54.

Table 3.2 (continued)

No.	Untargeted recommendation	Total N	Date
53	draw public attention to"; "appropriate publicity"; "public at large"	19	1 (29 July 2009);[178] 1 (10 November 2009);[179] 1 (25 February 2010);[180] 2 (3 June 2010);[181] 1 (12 August 2010);[182] 1 (7 September 2010);[183] 1 (4 October 2010);[184] 1 (25 October 2011);[185] 1 (23 March 2012);[186] 1 (30 April 2012);[187] 1 (17 April 2008);[188] 1 (3 November 2009);[189] 1 (15 October 2008).[190]
54	"residential property managers"	1	18 May 2009.[191]
55	"agencies such as schools, welfare and parental advisory agencies"	1	21 June 2010.[192]
56	"snow boarder and skier user groups"	1	12 August 2010.[193]
57	"specialist consultants and staff"	1	22 October 2009.[194]
58	"supervising adults"	1	13 March 2012.[195]

178 *Ellis* [2009] NZCorC 94.
179 *Brown* [2009] NZCorC 144.
180 *Donoghue* [2010] NZCorC 21.
181 *MacDonald*, above n 100.
182 *Campbell*, above n 128.
183 *Ladbrook* [2010] NZCorC 149.
184 *Seol* [2010] NZCorC 177.
185 *Taylor* [2011] NZCorC 198.
186 *Morris* [2012] NZCorC 27.
187 *McKenzie*, above n 72.
188 *Giddens* [2008] NZCorC 10.
189 *Chambers* [2009] NZCorC 138.
190 *Araos-Elevancini*, above n 71.
191 *Bowling* [2009] NZCorC 40.
192 *Colcord* [2010] NZCorC 114.
193 *Campbell*, above n 128.
194 *McCrone* [2009] NZCorC 133.
195 *Siaea* [2012] NZCorC 39.

Table 3.2 (continued)

No.	Untargeted recommendation	Total N	Date
59	"the appropriate health authority"; "the appropriate health service"	2	1 (22 July 2009);[196] 1 (13 March 2012).[197]
60	"the organisers of events on the motorcycling calendar"	1	10 January 2011.[198]
61	"the outdoor recreation retail industry and clubs"	1	27 July 2009.[199]
62	"the relevant territorial authority"; "the local authority responsible"; "the local authority/ies"; "the territorial authority responsible"	6	1 (24 July 2008);[200] 1 (11 June 2010);[201] 1 (6 July 2010);[202] 1 (12 August 2010);[203] 1 (4 August 2011);[204] 1 (25 January 2011).[205]
63	"the roading authority/ies"; "road controlling authority"; "responsible roading authorities"	15	3 (1 July 2008);[206] 3 (4 July 2008);[207] 1 (17 June 2009);[208] 1 (10 August 2010);[209] 2 (18 October 2011);[210] 1 (19 April 2012);[211] 2 (5 August 2009);[212] 2 (30 September 2009).[213]
64	"those that drive long haul trucks"	1	22 June 2009.[214]

196 *Robertson* [2009] NZCorC 71.
197 *Evaroa-Snowden* [2012] NZCorC 8.
198 *Going* [2011] NZCorC 6.
199 *Okin*, above n 164.
200 *Tauatevalue* [2008] NZCorC 27.
201 *Chambers* [2010] NZCorC 97.
202 *Kerrison* [2010] NZCorC 117.
203 *Campbell*, above n 128.
204 *Mita* [2011] NZCorC 137.
205 *Graham* [2011] NZCorC 9.
206 *Flutey* [2008] NZCorC 25.
207 *Mwale* [2008] NZCorC 26.
208 *Nasau* [2009] NZCorC 62.
209 *Ahn* [2010] NZCorC 141.
210 *Fong* [2011] NZCorC 194.
211 *Wallbank* [2012] NZCorC 43.
212 *McOnie*, above n 153.
213 *Crooks* [2009] NZCorC 118.
214 *Thorburn* [2009] NZCorC 56.

Table 3.2 (continued)

No.	Untargeted recommendation	Total N	Date
65	"trampers"; "tramping and mountaineering community"	6	5 (30 April 2008);[215] 1 (15 March 2010).[216]
66	"the relevant utilities"	1	5 August 2009.[217]
67	"vehicle manufacturers"	1	23 July 2010.[218]
68	"all marae committees"	1	8 October 2012.[219]
69	"road controlling authorities with responsibility for roads that are prone to winter ice condition"	5	19 June 2012.[220]
70	"users of 4 x 4 farm vehicles"	1	20 December 2007.[221]
71	"the law makers of NZ"	1	9 April 2009.[222]
72	Nothing specified (that is, no identifiable organisation, individual, group or category specified)	27	2 (12 June 2008);[223] 1 (30 July 2008);[224] 3 (20 August 2008);[225] 2 (9 September 2008);[226] 2 (20 October 2008);[227] 3 (17 November 2008);[228] 1 (17 February 2009);[229] 1 (20 April 2009);[230] 1 (4 May 2009);[231] 1 (10 August 2009);[232] 1 (2 September 2009);[233]

215 *Lee* [2008] NZCorC 11.
216 *Yun* [2010] NZCorC 217.
217 *McOnie*, above n 153.
218 *Grant* [2010] NZCorC 128.
219 *Baby A* [2012] NZCorC 205.
220 *Pearson* [2012] NZCorC 84.
221 *Lewis* [2007] NZCorC 9.
222 *Scott-Collins*, above n 125.
223 *Keating*, above n 66.
224 *Barlow* [2008] NZCorC 35.
225 *Kim* [2008] NZCorC 38.
226 *Erepeta* [2008] NZCorC 43.
227 *Pene* [2008] NZCorC 53.
228 *Moat* [2008] NZCorC 67.
229 *Bellingham* [2009] NZCorC 6.
230 *Wu* [2009] NZCorC 191.
231 *Kupa* [2009] NZCorC 31.
232 *Brown* [2009] NZCorC 85.
233 *Connell* [2009] NZCorC 103.

Table 3.2 (continued)

No.	Untargeted recommendation	Total N	Date
			1 (15 September 2009);[234] 1 (12 October 2009);[235] 1 (1 September 2011);[236] 1 (15 September 2011);[237] 1 (23 March 2012);[238] 1 (3 April 2012);[239] 3 (16 May 2012).[240]

A review of the NZ coronial recommendations released in 2011 suggested that "almost all recommendations are directed to an organisation".[241] However, as depicted in Table 3.2, my research found that 72/309 recipients of coronial recommendations were untargeted.

I also found that there were a total of 258 untargeted recommendations (that is, the sum of column three in Table 3.2). The sum of this column is greater than 72 because many unique untargeted recommendations were directed to multiple organisations. For example, the unique untargeted recommendation "the government" (or variations such as "the appropriate government agency") was directed to organisations on 29 occasions. There were a significant proportion of untargeted recommendations that I classified as "nothing specified" (27), where I was unable to identify a specific organisation, individual, group or category to which the recommendations were directed. An example of a recommendation that I categorised as "nothing specified" is:[242]

> I. This is another example of a driver's attention being diverted while using a hand held mobile phone for texting.
> II. I endorse the recommendation for the introduction of legislation, which creates an offence when a driver of a motor vehicle uses a hand held mobile phone while driving.

---

234 *Page* [2009] NZCorC 107.
235 *Barr* [2009] NZCorC 130.
236 *Lewis*, above n 131.
237 *Bergh* [2011] NZCorC 149.
238 *Sinclair* [2012] NZCorC 62.
239 *Vaimalu* [2012] NZCorC 37.
240 *Stantiall* [2012] NZCorC 68.
241 Tidbury, above n 24, at 21.
242 *Keating*, above n 66.

Similarly, I also categorised recommendations as untargeted "nothing specified" when they were formulated as follows:[243]

> The only feasible recommendation I can make as a result of this inquest is that installation of smoke alarms throughout New Zealand properties should be hard wired to avoid any tampering or malfunction as a result of human intervention when it is really needed. The hard-wired alarm will probably save lives and avoid deaths like this.

My findings about untargeted recommendations suggest that there are opportunities for NZ coroners to improve their processes for identifying the appropriate organisation/s to which to direct recommendations. The former NZ Chief Coroner, Judge MacLean, has recognised that this is an area that needs improvement. He has stated that coroners:[244]

> have let ourselves down in the past by not targeting properly or not even sending them [recommendations]. That was a process issue at our end because our staff did not understand that it was their responsibility. Sometimes we uncovered that coroner X made a recommendation and that coroner got a response from the agency, but that coroner X never passed that information on to me. Again, we have been working on that.

Fourteen of the coroners interviewed thought that coroners should target their recommendations to a specific person or organisation. By contrast, one coroner, Coroner Reid, argued that untargeted recommendations may have a positive public health impact:

> The coroner has a mandate to make specified recommendations or comments that "if drawn to public attention" may reduce the chances of the occurrence of other deaths in circumstances similar to those in which the death occurred. There is a place for evidenced-based recommendations directed to a category of persons (say cyclists) at changing behaviour in a certain way, and reliant on media or specialist publications to promote them. The measurement of success of such recommendations is ultimately statistical. Just because they cannot be precisely measured (and I believe there are parallels with the work of, say, psychiatrists in reducing the incidence of suicide) does not make them less effective. I accept poorly thought-through, general, wide-ranging recommendations are likely to be ineffective.

It is important to recognise that untargeted recommendations also feature in coronial jurisdictions abroad. For example, a study in Victoria, Australia

---

[243] *Barlow*, above n 224.
[244] Coroner, above n 50.

which identified the organisations that were sent coronial recommendations from 1 July 2000 – 30 June 2005 found that 71 recommendations did not specify an organisation (that is, were untargeted).[245] Similarly, in the Australian observational documentary series *Outback Coroner*, it is not uncommon for coroners to make untargeted recommendations, for example to "professional fishermen".[246]

My study reinforces prior research findings that vaguely directed recommendations (for example, "to the government") receive poor or no responses and have little or no preventive impact.[247] If a recommendation is inappropriately directed, its preventive potential is undermined because it does not reach the organisation that can consider and/or implement it. A failure to address a recommendation to a specific organisation or person arguably invites organisations to ignore recommendations. Organisations can argue that the recommendation was not directed at them and therefore does not require any action, which, in turn, limits the effectiveness and preventive potential of recommendations.

The organisations that I interviewed often (52/79) reported that coronial recommendations suggest that coroners fail to understand organisations' roles and functions. An independent crown entity explained that some coronial recommendations appear to take a "shotgun approach", possibly because "they don't understand our role".[248] Similarly, Medsafe explained that some coronial recommendations are not appropriately targeted, partly because of a lack of understanding about health organisations' different functions:[249]

> . . .the Coronial Service don't necessarily understand the difference, or differentiate between, Medsafe and Pharmac, which is pretty fundamental. They just see the Ministry of Health (MOH) and think that someone there will be responsible for implementing the recommendation. That is a big blind spot. It makes a lot of assumptions about what the role of the MOH is. That is one of the weaknesses. The messages may not be targeted at the right people. An example would be a recommendation that will come to the MOH saying "clinicians should do something". The Ministry is not responsible for the behaviour of clinicians. That recommendation would have been better directed at Colleges. So the MOH ends up playing this middle man role because we have to pass that information on. That is okay. But the system is never corrected. We become a convenient post box for coroners. It's better to direct the recom-

---

245 Bugeja, above n 53, at 259.
246 "Gadd Knight" on *Outback Coroner* (2013).
247 Law Reform Commission of Western Australia and Hands, above n 28, at 71.
248 Interview with NZ Law Commission (Jennifer Moore, 13 February 2013).
249 Interview with Medsafe (Jennifer Moore, 8 February 2013).

> mendation to the right people in the first instance because it makes everyone lift their game. . . . The problem is that this actually undermines the credibility of the Coronial Services. . . . It undermines our willingness to implement or to participate. . . . Different coroners seem to have different levels of understanding.

Medsafe's comments highlight that some coronial recommendations fail to recognise that the Ministry of Health "is not responsible for the behaviour of clinicians". While Medsafe forwards inappropriately directed coronial recommendations to the correct organisation, they emphasise that this system is flawed and it "undermines the credibility of the Coronial Services". Although Medsafe is currently operating as a "convenient post box for coroners", there is a risk that they will become a "disinterested post box", in keeping with findings from Australian research.[250]

As Medsafe points out, untargeted or inappropriately directed recommendations undermine organisations' "willingness to implement". These findings are consistent with Australian research, which found that the "more targeted and specific a recommendation, the more likely it was to be implemented."[251]

Whereas some coroners make the final decision about to whom to direct recommendations, others leave the decision to their coordinators. Some coroners direct a recommendation to a specific organisation, but the coordinators will identify the appropriate person within that organisation. Sometimes "minimal research to determine the agency" responsible will be required.[252] However, targeting recommendations appropriately can be challenging, particularly given the evolutionary flux of some government organisations. As one coroner explained, organisational changes mean that coroners should spend time ensuring that their recommendations are appropriately targeted:[253]

> If you can see that something has been an issue for a long time, you can think about what else could be done, and check whether the recommendations were made to the right organisation. Recommendations need to be made to an organisation that can actually do something about it. You really have to target the recommendation to the most appropriate person who can do something about it. Sometimes I have seen that a recommendation has gone to

---

[250] Boronia Halstead "Implementing Coroners' Deaths in Custody Recommendations: A Victorian Case Study" (1995–1996) 7 Current Issues in Criminal Justice 340 at 348.

[251] Law Reform Commission of Western Australia and Hands, above n 28, at 45; Rebecca Scott Bray "Coronial Law Reform" (2010) 35 AltLJ 232 at 232.

[252] Tidbury, above n 24, at 22.

[253] Interview with Coroner Aitken (Jennifer Moore, 22 January 2013).

an organisation, but there is now a new organisation that might be able to do something about the recommendation.

3.7 CONCLUSION

As I have outlined in this chapter, coronial recommendations have an extensive history. While there have been improvements in the quality of coronial recommendations, some historical problems, such as untargeted recommendations, persist.

While the *Recommendations Recap* contains summaries of recommendations, the CSNZ provides limited public descriptive statistics about the frequency and nature of coronial recommendations. Subject to the availability of resources, it would be useful for the CSNZ to produce reports modelled on jurisdictions such as Ontario, Canada and Victoria, Australia, in which descriptive statistics about coronial investigations, recommendations and comments are compiled.

My study aimed to assess accurately the number and nature of recommendations over a five-year period. An important research observation is that the difficulty of accessing full coroners' findings hinders researchers from undertaking this type of work. Given these difficulties, an important contribution of this study was quantifying the number of recommendations in my study period.

My key findings were that there were 607 coronial inquiries from 1 July 2007 – 30 June 2012 that resulted in 1644 recommendations, 1320 of which were unique recommendations. Two thousand and forty recommendations were sent to recipients. There were 309 recipients of recommendations during the study period. Seventy-two recommendations were untargeted and, unsurprisingly, many recommendations were directed to government organisations. Although there is no standardised structure for coronial recommendations, I found that they are typically shaped according to one of four overarching categories.

In the next chapter, I undertake a qualitative analysis of coroners' recommendations. In particular, I explore the extent to which coroners' recommendations are implemented.

4. Do coroners' recommendations "disappear into a black hole"?[1]

4.1 INTRODUCTION

Part of me says that generally our recommendations are being implemented. But I think that until you've done your analysis, we won't know for sure. It will be the first time that we will have any sort of handle on the extent that coroners' recommendations are implemented. I don't hear why our recommendations are implemented when they are. I don't often hear why they are not implemented either. Sometimes we will get a blunt letter back saying that the agency has the recommendation, but in polite language, they think that it is daft and they say that the coroners have not seen the broader picture because we have just focused on one particular case. . . . Other than that we don't hear anything about why recommendations are not implemented. That is, until the same thing happens another time. Then questions get asked like "well what did happen? Coroner X recommended this to you. What did you do? I see seven other coroners said the same thing and the Department still has not done anything. Why is that?" A classic example of that is prisoners hanging themselves. We asked why nothing had been done and the Department said that they knew the building was going to be demolished so there was not much point doing anything. But in the meantime half a dozen prisoners hanged themselves.[2]

This is one of only two studies in the world to examine organisations' responses to, and implementation of, coroners' recommendations. As the former NZ Chief Coroner points out, this research is "the first time that we will have any sort of handle on the extent that coroners' recommendations are implemented". Coroners receive limited feedback about organisations' responses to their recommendations. Apart from occasional "blunt letters", the extent of implementation of coronial recommendations is suggested when repeat fatalities occur, such as prisoners hanging themselves. Since October 2011, any responses that the CSNZ

[1] Mike Watson "Plea not to let coroners' rulings wither" *Stuff* (New Zealand, 22 March 2013).

[2] Interview with the Chief Coroner (Jennifer Moore, 12 September 2012).

receives from organisations have been published in *Recommendations Recap*.[3]

Exploring responses to coroners' recommendations is important for several reasons. First, the "practical and policy impact of coroners' recommendations will depend upon the extent of their implementation", which is currently not known.[4] Secondly, agencies ignoring coronial recommendations have been the subject of considerable criticism. Thirdly, commentary about the coronial jurisdiction has focused on organisational responses. The most prevalent concern is that coroners' recommendations are ineffective because the organisations to which they are directed ignore them. As one commentator put it, coroners' recommendations are "cast adrift with no distress beacon and a sleepy coastguard, into a sea of uncertainty".[5]

This concern has been voiced in public inquiries in Australia, England and NZ,[6] the scholarly literature,[7] by coroners,[8] families[9] and the media.[10]

---

[3] For example, see the Auckland District Health Board's response to coroners' recommendations about a healthcare-related death: Office of the Chief Coroner of New Zealand *Recommendations Recap Edition 1* (2011) at 5.

[4] Boronia Halstead "Coroners' Recommendations Following Deaths in Custody" in Hugh Selby (ed.) *The Inquest Handbook* (Federation Press, Sydney, 1998) 186 at 187.

[5] Boronia Halstead "Implementing Coroners' Deaths in Custody Recommendations: A Victorian Case Study" (1995–1996) 7 Current Issues in Criminal Justice 340 at 355.

[6] Deborah Coles and Helen Shaw *Learning from Death in Custody Inquests: A New Framework for Action and Accountability* (2012); Commonwealth of Australia *Royal Commission into Aboriginal Deaths in Custody National Report* (1991); Queensland Ombudsman *The Coronial Recommendations Project: An Investigation into the Administrative Practice of Queensland Public Sector Agencies in Assisting Coronial Inquiries and Responding to Coronial Recommendations* (2006); New Zealand Law Commission *Coroners* (NZLC R62 2000).

[7] For example, see Justin Malbon "Institutional Responses to Coronial Recommendations" (1998) 6 JLM 35; Ian Freckelton and David Ranson *Death Investigation and the Coroner's Inquest* (Oxford University Press, Melbourne, 2006).

[8] "Clear and Present Danger Ignored" *The New Zealand Herald* (Auckland, 17–18 October 1998); "Give Coroners a Break" *The New Zealand Herald* (Auckland, 15 September 1998).

[9] Editor The New Zealand Herald "Coroners must not be Ignored" *The New Zealand Herald* (Auckland, 11 March 2013); Joanne Carroll "Victim's Partner: Listen to Coroner" (Auckland, 25 March 2012).

[10] "Department Rejects Coroner's Quad Bike Call" *Stuff* (Auckland, 11 January 2011); Vaimoana Tapaleao "Findings by Coroners Fall on Deaf Ears" *The New Zealand Herald* (Auckland, 18 July 2014); Watson, above n 1.

Journalists who interviewed me at the start of this research were adamant that few, if any, coronial recommendations are implemented, despite my argument that I did not yet have the data to confirm or deny their assertions.[11] The substantial commentary about responses to coroners' recommendations is largely speculative, contradictory and based on "experience".[12] For example, two eminent coronial law scholars claim that it is rare for recommendations to be "ignored or snubbed" by agencies because of "media and political pressure".[13] In the same textbook, however, the authors lament the limited implementation of coronial recommendations, claiming that "most recommendations by coroners make their way into a void that relieves those to whom the recommendations were directed of responsibility to be responsive".[14]

Despite this abundant speculative commentary on coroners' recommendation powers and organisational responses to coroners, there is a paucity of empirical research on the topic.[15] A sociologist was one of the first researchers to trace the "fate of coronial recommendations".[16] The research concerned the early 1990s Australian controversy about the deaths of children which were caused by Mistral fans which overheated, ignited fires and killed the children. The research included analysis of documents from the coronial investigation and interviews with interested parties. It found a relatively high rate of implementation when the coroner endorsed remedial action already being undertaken by companies: 17/23 coroners' recommendations were fully or partially implemented. By contrast, the uptake of recommendations was lower for "coroner initiated"

---

11 For example, on 15 May 2012, during an interview about this research for "Checkpoint" on national radio, Mary Wilson argued that "we suspect that a lot of coroners' recommendations are ignored".

12 For example, Malbon claims that "experience suggests that many organisations fail to take coronial recommendations seriously." Malbon, above n 7, at 35.

13 Freckelton and Ranson, above n 7, at 678.

14 At 741.

15 The three main empirical projects on responses to coroners' recommendations are: Georgina Sutherland and others "What Happens to Coroners' Recommendations for Improving Public Health and Safety? Organisational Responses under a Mandatory Response Regime in Victoria, Australia" (2014) 14 BMC Public Health 732; Queensland Ombudsman, above n 6; Ray Watterson, Penny Brown and John McKenzie "Coronial Recommendations and The Prevention of Indigenous Death" (2008) 12 Special Edition 2 Australian Indigenous Law Review 4.

16 Fiona Haines "Innocent Deaths and Regulatory Failure: A Case Study of Change in the Absence of Punishment" (1999) 27 International Journal of the Sociology of Law 23 at 25.

recommendations: 8/26 coroners' recommendations were fully or partially implemented.[17]

In 2006, Queensland undertook a review of organisational responses, focusing on recommendations made to government agencies (hereafter "the Queensland study"). The review found a relatively high rate of implementation (68% fully or partially implemented).[18] However, the review did not distinguish between action taken before or after recommendations were issued. The study found that the main reasons for non-implementation of coroners' recommendations were that they were too costly, inappropriate or unrealistic, or not within the organisation's power to implement.

In 2008, Watterson et al. sent letters to several hundred organisations located in every Australian jurisdiction except Queensland, following their receipt of coroners' recommendations, to inquire how they had responded (hereafter "the Watterson et al. study").[19] The researchers found that the proportion of coronial recommendations implemented varied across jurisdictions as follows:[20]

- 27% in VIS
- 41% in TAS
- 48% in NSW
- 50% in WA
- 52% in SA
- 65% in NT
- 70% in ACT.

The researchers classified a large proportion of organisational responses as unknown (18% nationally). Key aspects of Watterson et al.'s methodology were not reported, including the number and type of organisations surveyed and the way in which determinations were made about implementation of coronial recommendations.

In her 2011 thesis about the determinants of coroners' recommendations in Victoria, Australia, Bugeja found that of the 380 organisations sent coroners' recommendations during her five-year study period, 44 (11.6%) responded. Of the 1278 recommendations sent to organisations, responses were received for 144 (11.3%).[21]

---

17 At 37.

18 Queensland Ombudsman, above n 6.

19 Watterson, Brown and McKenzie, above n 15.

20 At 9.

21 Lyndal Bugeja "Determinants of Coroners' Recommendations on External Cause Deaths in Victoria, Australia" (PhD, Monash University, 2011) at 269.

The most recent study was published in 2014 by the University of Melbourne's public health law group (hereafter "the Sutherland et al. study"), who surveyed 90 organisations that had received coroners' recommendations over a 33-month period.[22] The researchers asked recipient organisations what action, if any, they took, and what factors influenced their decision. The study found that a third of coroners' recommendations were implemented by the organisations to which they were directed. In contrast to the Queensland study, the Sutherland et al. project distinguished between action taken before and after recommendations were issued, which is a distinction that I adopt in this NZ study. The researchers also distinguished between "rejected" recommendations and "supplanted" recommendations; a distinction that I adopt. "Supplanted" recommendations are those which were not implemented because the organisation had already taken remedial action. As the authors emphasise, "supplanted recommendations focus attention on the adequacy of consultation between coroners and affected organisation and the length of time it takes for recommendations to be issued."[23]

Recognised limitations of the Sutherland et al. study include: (1) acceptance levels and attitudes among recipient organisations that did not respond to the survey may be different from those of respondents; and (2) a population-based survey with close-ended responses has limited scope for probing the nature of, and motivations for, organisational behaviour.[24]

This NZ study shares the first limitation of the Sutherland et al. study. I sent recruitment letters to all 232 organisations that received coroners' recommendations during my five-year study period, but only 79 agreed to be interviewed. While 79 interviews with organisations is a robust sample, it is possible that those organisations who did not agree to be interviewed respond differently to coroners' recommendations. Despite this limitation, my study makes an important contribution to the literature. Unlike the Sutherland et al. study, my research provides an in-depth qualitative study of action taken and views held within recipient organisations, and coroners' views, which, as Sutherland et al. highlight, "would be a valuable complement to our findings".[25]

Like the previous empirical studies, my main goal was to shed light on what, if any, action organisations had taken in response to coroners' recommendations. I was also interested in organisations' views about the recommendations they had received, and the response process.

---

22 Sutherland and others, above n 15.
23 At 733.
24 At 738.
25 At 738.

Direct comparisons between these studies and my research will not be possible because of the different research methods applied and variations in coronial legislation. Importantly, the Victorian Coroners Act includes a mandatory response regime, which means that the Sutherland et al. results may report a "best case scenario".[26]

Despite journalists' insistence on categorising organisations' responses to coronial recommendations as either "implemented"/"accepted" or "rejected"/"ignored", this study (like the three previous empirical projects) found that this reductive binary is not applicable. In the Watterson et al. study, organisations' responses were categorised as:[27]

- implemented
- partially implemented
- not implemented
- already in place at the time of the recommendation
- not referred to in the response
- insufficient information provided in the response.

The Sutherland et al. categorisation of organisations' responses is as follows:[28]

- "before the response"[29] (during the coronial inquiry)
- response to recommendations
    - implemented/accepted
    - supplanted (action had already been taken)
    - rejected.

I prefer this categorisation because my research found that "during the coronial inquiry" is pivotal to organisations' responses to, and implementation of, coroners' recommendations. I also found that supplanted recommendations were an important category.

My categorisation of organisations' responses is as follows:

- during the coronial inquiry
- response to recommendations
    - supplanted

---

26 At 738.
27 Watterson, Brown and McKenzie, above n 15, at 9.
28 Sutherland and others, above n 15, at 732.
29 At 738.

- rejected
- implemented/accepted
- partially implemented
- recommendation not received.

This chapter is organised according to this categorisation of responses to coroners' recommendations. In the first section, I discuss the "during the coronial inquiry" phase. Next, I analyse responses to recommendations. I focus on supplanted recommendations because this was the main reason for rejection of recommendations. In the next section, I discuss the other reasons that organisations reject coroners' recommendations. Finally, I explore the main action that organisations take for recommendations that are accepted/implemented or partially implemented.

In contrast to media speculation that all, or almost all, coroners' recommendations are rejected, my research found that organisations' responses are more nuanced. While 20% (86/426) of the recommendations in my sample were rejected, the number of implemented/accepted recommendations (133/426, 31%) is greater than some commentators might expect, and almost half (207/426, 49%) were supplanted (that is, organisations had already taken remedial and preventive action). In addition, all organisations reported that they "consider coroners' recommendations and take them seriously".[30] None of the organisations that I interviewed reported that they ignore coroners' recommendations. In addition, organisations' reasons for rejecting coroners' recommendations did not always accord with those purported by the media.

4.2 DURING THE CORONIAL INQUIRY

While organisations reported that a strength of the coronial jurisdiction is the independence of the inquiries, they also emphasised the importance of coroners consulting with them during the inquiry. Organisations did not believe that consultation with them would compromise judicial independence. Instead, they felt that coroners could consult and maintain their independence because parties' views could be considered, but rejected, if necessary. For instance, Pharmac described their understanding as follows:[31]

---

[30] For example, Interview with Electricity Engineers' Association (Jennifer Moore, 7 February 2013).

[31] Interview with Pharmac (Jennifer Moore, 27 November 2012).

> We know that they make independent recommendations. We are not trying to influence them to change their decision. We are just saying that we would like to be *consulted.* We would like to be given an opportunity to comment before the recommendation and adverse comment is made.

Similarly, a government organisation stated that they "would be happy to advise the coroner, but [they] would not be happy if the coroner thought that [they] were telling him or her what to do".[32]

In the 2009 Canadian Superior Court of Justice case, *Nishnawbe Aski Nation v Eden*, the proposed recommendations are discussed.[33] The organisation who would be asked to implement the coronial recommendations commented on the likelihood of implementation.[34] Their comments were considered by the Court.

As discussed earlier in this chapter, this research and the Sutherland et al. study found that the "during the coronial inquiry" phase is correlated to the uptake of coroners' recommendations. Organisations' responses to coronial recommendations, which are published in *Recommendations Recap*, highlight that organisations value consultation during the inquiry. For example, in response to coronial recommendations about a death involving a refrigerant which caused a fatal explosion, the Institute of Refrigeration, Heating and Air Conditioning Engineers of NZ (IRHACE) commented that they were "pleased that the Coroner's findings are congruent with the HVAC+R industry submissions to the inquest".[35] The IRHACE's response also outlines what action they had taken to implement the coroner's recommendations.[36]

One government organisation interviewed for this study noted that if "the recommendation does not indicate that they have considered our evidence, it does make us look at the recommendation differently . . . it does make us a bit jaded."[37] Likewise, according to Pharmac:[38]

> The coroners are saying that people ignore their recommendations, but they are not necessarily giving people an opportunity to comment before the

---

32 Interview with GovtOrg08 (Jennifer Moore, February 2013).

33 *Nishnawbe Aski Nation v Eden*, No 2009 CarswellOnt 3404, [2009] 3 C.N.L.R. 233, 97 O.R. (3d) 382, 254 O.A.C. 224, 178 A.C.W.S. (3d) 359 (Ontario Superior Court 29 May 2009).

34 *Nishnawbe Aski Nation v Eden*, above n 33 at para 26.

35 Office of the Chief Coroner of NZ *Recommendations Recap – Issue 2* (2012) at 45.

36 At 46.

37 Interview with GovtOrg11 (Jennifer Moore, 19 February 2013).

38 Pharmac, above n 31.

> recommendation is made. If they haven't given people a fair chance to respond during the inquiry then that may be a reason why people can't implement their recommendations.

Similarly, the NZ College of Midwives explained that:[39]

> There was a coroner who said recently, "I wonder why we make recommendations because nobody listens." Yeah, well you didn't listen to anybody, so this is what you reap. . . . I guess they think they have this watchdog role . . . and yes I understand that, but I think they've taken that too much at face value, and actually we can all work collaboratively, and they should be a part of that.

Many health sector organisations (19/26) remarked that the HDC provides interested parties with a preliminary report to comment on before making a final decision and that this approach should be adopted by coroners.[40]

In the Sutherland et al. study, 59% (53/90) of recipient organisations reported having had an opportunity to provide information to the coroner during the investigation.[41] Seventy-five per cent (40/53) felt their views had been taken into account in formulation of the recommendations.

Forty-two per cent (33/79) of the NZ recipient organisations that were interviewed for this research reported having had an opportunity to provide information to the coroner during the investigation. The majority of organisations felt (75/79) that the experience differed depending on coroners' varying approaches to input from organisations. Organisations also reported that their experience sometimes differed from case to case even when the same coroner presided. For instance, the Midwifery Council remarked that:[42]

> It's interesting how the coroner consulted with us on the Tairawhiti case, but didn't consult us on the other case, yet there was an adverse finding against the midwife in that one.

The reported rate of input by NZ organisations is lower than in Victoria, Australia. As I emphasised earlier, a direct comparison between the two studies is not possible. But the NZ findings show that a sizeable proportion of organisations (58%) felt that they were not sufficiently consulted. In Queensland, this percentage is higher. In the Queensland Ombudsman's

---

39 Interview with NZ College of Midwives (Jennifer Moore, 22 January 2013).

40 Interview with HealthCareOrganisation02 (Jennifer Moore, 12 February 2013).

41 Sutherland and others, above n 15, at 739.

42 Interview with Midwifery Council (Jennifer Moore, 17 December 2012).

2006 investigation into public sector agencies' perceptions of whether the coroner provided them with opportunities for input, 69.5% reported that they were *not* provided with such opportunity.[43]

These figures are important because, as I have pointed out in this chapter (and will also discuss in detail in Chapter 5), NZ recipient organisations reported that lack of consultation and input during the coronial inquiry was likely to discourage them from responding to, or implementing, the coroners' recommendations. A government organisation explained that:[44]

> There have been occasions in the past where we have had virtually no opportunity to provide input or comment or to challenge the recommendation. If that happens it is less likely that the recommendation will be implemented. So it's a lose–lose scenario.

Coroners that engage with organisations about proposed recommendations are more likely to achieve "buy-in", thereby increasing the likelihood that the recommendations will be implemented. In Ontario, Canada, the Coroner's Office developed an innovative system for encouraging consultation and "buy-in". The Ontario coroners can elect to hold informal conferences with organisations and families. Former Ontario coroner, Dr Young, describes the system as follows:[45]

> When a meeting with an institution goes well, there is frank discussion about the cause of death; the institution outlines where they consider things went wrong and their recommendations to prevent the same thing occurring again; and the institution and the coroner agree on the measures to overcome a similar death occurring.

In the Ontario system, once the coroner and organisation agree on preventive action, the recommendations are made available to the deceased's family and public.[46] If similar deaths occur after an agreement, the coroner can hold an inquest at which the organisation will be required to explain why deaths were not prevented. Although informal meetings are private, the agreement is made public. Malbon argues that the Ontario model demonstrates an understanding of organisational theory, which is essential if coroners wish to increase the uptake of their recommendations.[47]

---

43 Queensland Ombudsman, above n 6, at 14.
44 Interview with GovtOrg06 (Jennifer Moore, 22 February 2013).
45 Cited in Malbon, above n 7, at 47.
46 At 47–8.
47 At 49.

In NZ, all organisations interviewed, apart from three, appreciated having the opportunity to provide information to the coroner during the investigation. The organisations that preferred not to provide information stated that to do so would be too resource-intensive for small organisations.[48]

The organisations that prefer enhanced engagement argued that it does not have to involve time-consuming, extensive consultation. Many organisations highlighted the value of brief telephone calls to seek feedback.[49] However, a few coroners questioned whether it is appropriate for coroners to adopt such a practice.[50]

For those organisations that would like enhanced engagement with coroners, they felt that consultation is important because they have access to information that is not readily available to coroners. Such information may inform, and possibly change, coroners' formulation of recommendations. DHBs frequently commented that the delays in issuing coronial recommendations mean that remedial processes have already been put in place. If coroners do not consult with organisations, they risk issuing "superfluous" recommendations that do not take account of changes to clinical practice.[51]

Organisations that were supportive of consultation during coronial inquiries also pointed out that coroners should engage with organisations because agencies are able to undertake regulatory assessments.[52] Organisations have "access to all sorts of information that could be useful to the coroners and that they would not be able to access any other way".[53]

Organisations also emphasised that coroners should access a range of views. However, consultation with interested parties and organisations should not become a "trial, a campaign, a roving commission or a public platform for an interest group".[54] Consultation with organisations

---

[48] Interview with Law Commission (Jennifer Moore, 13 February 2013); Interview with HealthCareOrganisation03 (Jennifer Moore, 5 February 2013); Interview with Medsafe (Jennifer Moore, 8 February 2013).

[49] For example, Interview with GovtOrg12 (Jennifer Moore, 4 February 2013); Interview with St John (Jennifer Moore, 14 February 2013).

[50] Interview with Coroner Oldfield (Jennifer Moore, 12 October 2012).

[51] Interview with Greg Brogden (Canterbury DHB) (Jennifer Moore, 21 January 2013).

[52] GovtOrg06, above n 44.

[53] Interview with GovtOrg01 (Jennifer Moore, 28 February 2013).

[54] *Inquest into the Death of Tyler Cassidy: Rulings on Applications to be Granted Leave to Participate as Interested Parties Pursuant to s 56 Coroners Act 2008* [4 March 2010] Coroner's Court Victoria (Coroner's Court Victoria) at 41.

should identify people to drive the implementation of the recommended countermeasures. Research demonstrates that consultation with stakeholders is an important factor in the successful translation of research into practice.[55] Coroners need to maintain their independence. The consultation with organisations could be undertaken by coroners and/or researchers and specialists assisting with death investigations. In Victoria, Australia, the CPU undertakes consultation with stakeholders.

In 2006, the Queensland Ombudsman recommended amendment to the Coroners Act 2003 (QLD) to require that sufficient notice be given to, and input sought from, interested parties, particularly about preventive issues.[56] The QLD review of coronial recommendations had found that the coronial system does not ensure that relevant public sector agencies are sufficiently informed of the issues to be canvassed at coronial inquiries to enable them to provide appropriate input.[57]

In NZ, many organisations' complaints echoed the experiences in Queensland. For example, one healthcare organisation described their experience as follows:[58]

> We knew very little about the inquest until a week before it happened and we were asked if we could provide our local Southland manager to give a copy of the support plan. . . . I would like some advance letters of the issues so I could actually research and address them. . . . So I suppose my greatest concern here is that we need more involvement during the investigative stages of the coronial process, because that's when most of the work is actually done . . . consult earlier and allow sufficient time as well for the organisation to do the work.

Two-thirds of the organisations interviewed (52/79) suggested amendment of the Coroners Act 2006 (NZ) to require coroners to consult with organisations about proposed recommendations. For example, a healthcare organisation explained that:[59]

> Although coroners have to provide information where there is an adverse comment, there does not seem to be any requirement for them to provide a

---

[55] George A. Conway and others "Alaska's Model Program for Surveillance and Prevention of Occupation Injury Deaths" (1999) 114 Public Health Reports 550.

[56] Queensland Ombudsman, above n 6, at xiv.

[57] At xiii.

[58] Interview with HealthCareOrganisation399 (Jennifer Moore, 14 February 2013).

[59] Interview with HealthCareOrganisation199 (Jennifer Moore, 15 February 2013).

> draft copy of their recommendations to an organisation that may be asked to implement a recommendation. It would be useful – I would have thought – to do so because by providing that opportunity, the coroner may be presented with further information that they may not otherwise have had the opportunity to consider and that may make a better-quality decision. So we have to ask why there isn't that obligation in statute. The coroner could end up with a better-quality decision by consulting and that is the name of the game. We want coroners to be able to consider all of the information so that we ensure the recommendations have a level of rigour and balance that ensures that there will be limited opportunity to debate whether the course of action proposed is an appropriate one.

In keeping with this empirical finding, section 57B of the Coroners Amendment Bill 2014 provides that coroners must notify certain persons before making a recommendation or comment, and give those persons a reasonable time to comment on the proposed recommendation or comment.

Many NZ coroners interviewed (9/15) seek feedback from organisations about proposed recommendations without a statutory requirement to do so. There is variable practice across coroners about the method for seeking such feedback.[60] Several coroners noted that the "Chief Coroner does not like the idea of sending out findings in draft form", but that they nevertheless "frequently send recommendations out for information and comment". Coroner Atwood explained that consultation achieves "buy-in", avoids mistakes, and sometimes leads to redrafting of proposed recommendations:[61]

> In the *McNelis* case I sent the recommendations in provisional form and got useful feedback and made some changes. You get buy-in. And you also avoid making mistakes and getting it so that someone says publicly "a coroner has recommended that, but we are not doing it". . . . In the *McNelis* case, I made recommendations based on the evidence and they were given to Landcorp in provisional form and adjusted as a result of their input.

Likewise, Coroner Clarke commented that:[62]

> It's not good if an organisation suddenly gets faced with a recommendation that they have no knowledge of, because they might have had very valuable input which would have enhanced the utility of the recommendation. . . . It

---

60 One organisation asserted that coroners are "a law unto themselves". Interview with GovtOrg06 (Jennifer Moore, 22 February 2013).

61 Interview with Coroner Atwood (Jennifer Moore, 11 December 2012).

62 Interview with Coroner Clarke (Jennifer Moore, 29 October 2012).

> would not be unhelpful if the coroner sent the provisional form of the recommendations to the body concerned. But I don't do that because there is no need. There is no need because in inquest I tease this all out with the experts. I ask whether there is a need for a recommendation, what they think of the proposed recommendation. If they all agree, that is the end of the matter. If it's a chambers finding, then the recommendations should be sent out, unless there could be no argument because the recommendation is so obvious. But if the recommendations are contentious then you should send them out for comment. I agree that the sensible course would be to send the recommendations to the recipient and ask the organisations for responses. The law doesn't require it, but good practice dictates it.

If a recommendation contains adverse comment, it is a statutory requirement in NZ, and other jurisdictions, to notify the parties. As the Supreme Court of South Australia pointed out in 2011:[63]

> There is no doubt that a Coroner is subject to the rules of natural justice and procedural fairness. Those principles require that any party likely to be affected, either directly or indirectly, by a decision is to be given the opportunity to be heard and to make submissions before any decision is made.

Even if there is doubt about whether a comment is adverse, a consultative approach should be preferred.[64] The entire draft findings (including the adverse comment and recommendation) should be provided to the interested parties. Coroner Atwood, and a small number of other coroners, consider that the entire findings (rather than the adverse comment/recommendation alone) should be disclosed to interested parties. This practice provides context and conveys meaning.

This process may delay the coronial inquiry. The NZ ministerial review is focused on reducing delays in the coronial system.[65] My suggestion, although possibly less efficient, is consistent with natural justice and may ensure that comments (adverse or not) are more rigorous. My suggested approach is also consistent with Winkelmann J's comment in *Carroll v Coroner's Court* that "although the provision of draft findings is not a statutory requirement", she was "satisfied that would have been the

---

[63] *Onuma v Coroner's Court of South Australia* South Australia Supreme Court [2011] SASC 218, 9 December 2011 at para 95.

[64] Jennifer Moore "An Empirical Approach to the New Zealand Government's Review of the Coronial Jurisdiction" (2014) 21 JLM 602 at 622.

[65] Cabinet Paper *Coroners Act Review: Proposals for Reform – Paper 1* (2013) at 28–36.

appropriate step in this case".[66] As one coroner explained, it is "high risk" not to notify and consult, even if one is unsure about whether a comment is adverse.[67]

A coroner's failure to notify and consult the affected party about an adverse comment can have unfavourable consequences. The affected party may pursue judicial review of the coronial inquest and comments if s/he feels aggrieved by the procedure. This is what happened in *Onuma v Coroner's Court of South Australia*.[68] The appellant, a doctor, appealed from findings of the Coroner's Court after an inquest into the deaths of two women, each of which occurred after surgical procedures undertaken by the appellant. In the coroner's findings, two comments expressed doubt about the competence of the appellant. The appellant argued that there had been no evidence before the Court to justify those comments. During the inquest, the Coroner gave no indication of what his findings, comments or recommendations might be.[69] There was no notification or consultation. However, counsel was given the opportunity to make submissions about the appellant's competence. The Court considered that this opportunity afforded procedural fairness to the appellant. The Supreme Court of South Australia held that there was nothing in the material before the Coroner's Court to justify the two adverse comments which expressed doubt about the competence of the appellant doctor.

Several NZ coroners who I interviewed argued that although notification and consultation is important, only the adverse comment (and occasionally other selected material) should be disclosed to parties. These coroners assert that natural justice, and the specific requirements of the Act, can be achieved using this method. In addition, this approach avoids "the real danger that circulating the entire provisional decision, results in adverse comment about person A, and which adverse comment might be subsequently adjusted, being sent to person B."[70]

Several coroners (5/15) provided examples of cases where they did not consult. For example, Coroner Stewart described the following case:[71]

> Recently I made a recommendation about driveway deaths in children. Housing NZ is over-represented in driveway deaths. There has been a lot of research done on how to prevent children dying on driveways. The Child and

66 *Carroll & Woodhouse v Coroner's Court & Police* [2013] NZHC 906 at 73.
67 Interview with Coroner Fitzpatrick (Jennifer Moore, 25 September 2012).
68 *Onuma v Coroner's Court of South Australia*, above n 63.
69 *Onuma v Coroner's Court of South Australia*, above n 63, at para 97.
70 Interview with Coroner Reid (Jennifer Moore, 30 October 2012).
71 Interview with Coroner Stewart (Jennifer Moore, 12 October 2012).

> Youth Mortality Review Committee (CYMRC) has done reports on this. I had read the report and I had also read the articles about how we should separate play areas from driveways. So I endorsed the findings of the CYMRC. I recommended that Housing NZ give consideration to their shared driveways. I didn't give Housing NZ the opportunity to comment on that. It hit the media. The Chief got a letter asking for the opportunity to comment on it. Fair process is important. But we may be opening the floodgates giving everyone an opportunity to comment. I also think that they had already heard the recommendation. It was just from someone else. The CYMRC had already made the recommendation. I was simply endorsing it.

Coroner Stewart's concern about opening the floodgates if there is consultation with too many people was explored in Minister Borrow's review of the Coroners Act 2006 (NZ). The review proposes amending the Coroners Act 2006 (NZ) by inserting a definition of "interested parties" in the Act to refer to persons required to be notified under sections 23 and 81 of the Act.[72] A key challenge facing the Government will be deciding how to draft the provision, including who should be listed in the definition "interested parties". Coroners who participated in the study explained that deciding which people and organisations have an interest in the death can present challenges. Coroners "can't encapsulate everyone" in an inquiry.[73] The "floodgates" may be opened to a potentially unmanageable number if too many people and organisations are deemed as having an interest in a death.[74] Determining those who have an interest can be tantamount to deciphering "how long is a piece of string?"[75]

The Coroners Act 2006 (NZ) states that the coroner must give notice of the date, time and place of an inquest to the family, family representative and certain "other people or organisations the coroner considers have an interest in the death".[76] The Coroners Act 1988 provides some guidance. Under that legislation, those considered to have an interest in the death and who were entitled to notice were:[77]

- relatives
- any doctor who attended the person before death or during illness
- life insurance companies
- the Life Offices Association of New Zealand

---

72 Cabinet Paper, above n 65, at 27.4.
73 Atwood, above n 61.
74 Stewart, above n 71.
75 Atwood, above n 61.
76 Coroners Act 2006 (NZ), ss 81, 23.
77 Coroners Act 1988 (NZ), s 23(1), (2).

- every person whose conduct, in the opinion of the senior member of the police in the place where the inquest is to be held or the coroner, seems likely to be called into question
- the Secretary of Labour where the death arose during employment
- inspector of mines, coal mines or tunnels, if relevant.

"Interested parties" could include any of the people or organisations who, under the 1988 legislation, were entitled to receive notice of the inquest. This could also potentially include others not specified in the 1988 Act. The phrase has been given a liberal interpretation.[78] Public interest organisations such as the Human Rights Commission and legal aid bodies are increasingly granted standing.[79] A person will typically be considered to have an interest if there is a reasonable chance that the coroner may make an adverse comment about him/her:[80]

> The 2006 provision provides coroners with discretion to notify those who they consider to have an interest in the death. In exercising their discretion, coroners: balance the need to avoid repetition and unduly prolonged processes against the degree of knowledge or expertise demonstrated by the applicant for standing and the degree to which they and their counsel can assist by providing a point of view that might not otherwise emerge in the course of the inquest.

Appellate litigation has explored the procedural requirements for standing of interested parties. For example, in a leading Canadian decision on standing (*Black Action Defence Committee v Coroner*) a key issue was whether the two applicants (both community organisations) should have been granted standing at a coroner's inquest into the death of a black man who was shot by police.[81] Both applicants sought standing in order to explore whether race or cross-cultural issues were relevant. The coroner denied both applications for standing. Both applicants applied for judicial review to set aside the decisions denying them standing. The Court held that the coroner had made an error in not granting standing to the second applicant. This applicant should have been granted standing because the organisation could have provided valuable expertise to the jury. In particular, the second applicant could provide important information to the jury which may assist them to make recommendations about whether

---

78 Freckelton and Ranson, above n 7, at 566.

79 Megan Prictor "The Sideshow or the Circus? The Role for Public Interest Organisations at Inquests" (2012) 20 JLM 320.

80 Freckelton and Ranson, above n 7, at 567.

81 *Black Action Defence Committee v Huxter, Coroner* (1992) 11 OR (3d) 641.

the police required cross-cultural training. The Court also held that it is consistent with the preventive purpose of coronial legislation to recognise standing for those with a direct interest in the inquest.[82]

Given that standing is granted at coroners' discretion, it is perhaps unsurprising that decision-making varies between NZ coroners.[83] Most coroners (12/15) were concerned about granting a burdensome number of people and organisations standing. Coroners who took an inclusive approach, preferring to grant standing where possible, did so primarily because of the perception that rigorous, evidence-based findings were more likely to be generated. The former NZ Chief Coroner described the decision-making as follows:[84]

> A classic example from the other day was where the College of Midwives said "we are aggrieved that the coroner has made comments about midwifery practice and we have only learnt about them afterwards." The trouble was that the midwife concerned was not a member of the College. They were not party to it. But we have given that feedback to the coroner and we will cover it in training. When we are looking at who we might tell about an upcoming inquest, we think about who might have an interest. That may well be the relevant professional association or Royal College, who won't necessarily be able to give evidence, but who will be impacted by what you are saying and they may think "that is not fair. There's another side to this and we weren't given an opportunity to comment."

The interview with the College of Midwives confirmed the Chief Coroner's comments.[85] Other agencies, such as Pharmac, also expressed concern about their exclusion from coronial inquiries.[86] According to Coroner Atwood, "sometimes those interest groups escape through the middle. Child, Youth and Family Services is another one."[87] The overall tenor of interviews with organisations was that they would prefer an approach whereby they are consulted, even if there is doubt about whether the comment is adverse. Given the organisations' views, the coroners' fear of opening the floodgates to an onerous number of interested parties may not be unwarranted.

---

[82] See also the discussion about standing for public interest intervenors in *People First of Ontario v Porter, Regional Coroner Niagara* (1991) 85 DLR (4th) 174; (1991) 5 OR (3d) 609; [1991] OJ No. 3389 (Div Ct) at paras 54–6.

[83] Prictor, above n 79, at 326.

[84] Interview with Chief Coroner (Jennifer Moore, 12 September 2012).

[85] NZ College of Midwives, above n 39.

[86] Pharmac, above n 31.

[87] Atwood, above n 61.

The data has encouraged several coroners that I interviewed to change their practice. For example, Coroner Dymond commented that:[88]

> One of the things I'm taking from your visit to me is that I should consult more with people to whom I'm making recommendations, and . . . after being beaten up by the Chief Medical Officer, I don't think that I'll make any more to the hospital board without talking to them first.

Several participants suggested additional changes to coronial practice. For example, a lawyer argued that all coroners should ensure that "more evidence is directed to the recommendation component of the inquiry".[89] Organisations stressed that coroners should ensure that appropriate individuals are consulted. Large government organisations emphasised that a senior representative who can provide a national perspective should be consulted.[90] The consultation must be genuine.[91] Many organisations (49/79) offered to provide presentations or information to the CSNZ to assist coroners to understand their roles and organisational structures, which they believed will improve coroners' recommendations. As I highlight later in this chapter, failure to appreciate organisations' roles is one reason that coroners' recommendations are rejected.

A few organisations (4/79) explained that they have proactively contacted coroners to offer information during inquiries. For instance, Pharmac described their approach as follows:[92]

> We were aware from media discussion that there is potential for the coroner to instigate an investigation into a particular medicine – dabigatran. That's an anti-coagulant. We changed the funding from warfarin to dabigatran. There was a lot of media coverage about that. When we heard that the coroner might open an investigation about that, we contacted the coroner and said that we would like to participate in the investigation. We said that if the coroner had questions, he was welcome to come to us. The Chief Coroner contacted us and sought information from us. We decided to proactively contact the coroner because of our experiences with the other two recommendations. In those cases, recommendations had been made, but we had not been consulted or involved. We wanted to get in prior to recommendations being made. . . . But we can only do that when someone, like the media, has published. Otherwise we wouldn't know. Generally with suicide you wouldn't see the method of suicide so you

88 Interview with Coroner Dymond (Jennifer Moore, 16 October 2012).

89 For example, Interview with Lawyer02 (Jennifer Moore, 10 September 2012); Interview with Lawyer04 (Jennifer Moore, 5 February 2013).

90 Interview with GovtOrg07 (Jennifer Moore, 20 February 2013).

91 For example, Robert Barlow was disappointed that the coroner did not make substantive changes, but only changed the wording of his decision.

92 Pharmac, above n 31.

> wouldn't know that there was a medicine component to it. If we find out about a death or potential inquiry through the media, it might be hard for us to know which coroner to contact.

Pharmac's account spotlights that this approach is not ideal because organisations may not be aware of coronial investigations until after the matter has been closed. On that occasion, Pharmac had a positive engagement with the CSNZ.

Several organisations discussed positive consultation experiences that they have had with coroners and explained how those experiences encouraged them to implement the coronial recommendations. Organisations mentioned that they particularly appreciate site visits from coroners,[93] telephone calls,[94] and formal meetings with the Chief Coroner to discuss emerging trends and patterns in coronial findings.[95]

4.3 RESPONSES TO RECOMMENDATIONS

Since October 2011, the CSNZ *Recommendations Recaps* publications include summaries of responses received from organisations. The CSNZ does not produce annual reports with statistics about the frequency of NZ coroners' recommendations or responses received.

By contrast, several coronial jurisdictions overseas produce reports about organisations' responses to coroners' recommendations. For example, the UK Ministry of Justice produces summaries of reports and responses under Rule 43 of the Coroners Rules.[96] The annual reports for the Coroner's Court in Victoria, Australia include tables with the total number of recommendations and responses received during the reporting period.[97]

Similarly, the Office of the Chief Coroner for Ontario, Canada produces reports with statistics on the frequency of inquests, resulting

---

93 Interview with GovtOrg04 (Jennifer Moore).

94 Interview with HealthCareOrganisation299 (Jennifer Moore, 23 January 2013).

95 HealthCareOrganisation199, above n 59.

96 For example, see Ministry of Justice *Summary of Reports and Responses Under Rule 43 of the Coroners Rules: Eight Report* (2013); Ministry of Justice *Summary of Reports and Responses Under Rule 43 of the Coroners Rules: Sixth Report* (2012); Ministry of Justice *Summary of Reports and Responses Under Rule 43 of the Coroners Rules: Seventh Report* (2012).

97 Coroner's Court of Victoria *2012–13 Annual Report of the Coroner's Court of Victoria* (2013) at 43.

recommendations, responses from organisations, and the extent of implementation. For instance, the 2010 report documents that 282 recommendations were issued; 83% of organisations responded. In Ontario, organisations are under no legal obligation to respond to, or implement, coroners' recommendations. However, the 2010 report notes that most organisations "recognise the valuable and important contribution of jury-suggested recommendations and as a result, the majority of recommendations receive some manner of formal acknowledgment or response. The high response rate to recommendations is a credit to the integrity and effectiveness of the inquest jury process."[98] The Office of the Chief Coroner for Ontario reports also document that 9% of recommendations "had been implemented", 5% "will be implemented", 4% "had alternates implemented", 1% "will have alternates implemented", and 13% were "under consideration".[99]

In Australia, the Queensland Attorney General produces annual reports which outline the Government's responses to coroners' recommendations which were directed to government organisations in the reporting year.[100] In NSW, a Memorandum issued by the Department of Premier and Cabinet sets out the process for responding to coroners' recommendations directed at Ministers and NSW government agencies.[101] The purpose of the Memorandum is to ensure that there is a consistent process across government for responding to coronial recommendations, and that there is increased accountability and transparency in responding to such recommendations. The Memorandum states that the organisation has 21 days to acknowledge receipt of the recommendation and, if necessary, refer the recommendation to the appropriate agency.[102] Within six months of receiving a coronial recommendation, a Minister or NSW government agency should write to the Attorney General outlining any action being taken to implement the recommendation.[103] The Memorandum states that

---

98 Office of the Chief Coroner Ontario *Office of the Chief Coroner of Ontario 2010 Report on Inquests* (2012) at 7.

99 At 3.

100 For example, see Attorney-General and Minister for Industrial Relations, Queensland Government *The Queensland Government's Response to Coronial Recommendations 2008* (2009); Department of Justice and Attorney General, Queensland Government *The Queensland Government's Response to Coronial Recommendations 2009* (2011); Department of Justice and Attorney General, Queensland Government *The Queensland Government's Response to Coronial Recommendations 2010* (2011).

101 Department of Premier and Cabinet, NSW Government *M2009–12 Responding to Coronial Recommendations* (2009).

102 Department of Premier and Cabinet, NSW Government, above n 101.

103 Department of Premier and Cabinet, NSW Government, above n 101.

the Attorney General will maintain a record of all coronial recommendations made, together with the responses received from Ministers and NSW government agencies.[104]

The Western Australian Law Reform Commission undertook a review of coronial recommendations for WA inquests performed in 2007.[105] In that year there were 88 recommendations issued. The review found that medical care and mental health recommendations had a high rate of implementation.[106] The Department of Corrective Services and Police also provided a high level of responsiveness to recommendations. Recommendations directed to private entities received poor or no responses.[107]

In NZ, half of the organisations that I interviewed (39/79) have developed formal systems for cataloguing and responding to coroners' recommendations. For instance, one government organisation described their system:[108]

> We set up a system so when a recommendation comes in, we have one person who records it and keeps a full database of all the coroners' recommendations and if there's a recommendation in there directed to the Ministry of Transport then we have a special spreadsheet and we put a coversheet on it and we'll send that to the relevant manager in the Ministry and we put a 20 day turn around on that so that we can get back to the coroners or that on any of their recommendations. We will always respond to a recommendation from a coroner.

As I explained in Chapter 1, 79 of the 232 NZ organisations that were sent coroners' recommendations in my study period agreed to be interviewed. One thousand three hundred and twenty unique recommendations were directed to the 232 organisations. Four hundred and twenty-six recommendations were directed to the 79 organisations that I interviewed for this study.

Prior to every interview, I re-read the recommendations that were directed to that organisation. During interviews, I asked organisations to discuss the recommendations that they had received, whether they had responded to those recommendations, and the action, if any, that

---

104 Department of Premier and Cabinet, NSW Government, above n 101.

105 Law Reform Commission of Western Australia and Tatum L. Hands *Review of Coronial Practice in Western Australia: Background Paper Project 100* (2010) at 21–2.

106 At 22.

107 At 22.

108 GovtOrg12, above n 49.

they had taken. All organisations reported that they give coroners' recommendations serious consideration.

Organisations reported that a total of 31% (133/426) of the recommendations were accepted and implemented (fully or partially implemented). A total of 20% (86/426) of the recommendations were rejected. For 49% (207/426), the recommendations were supplanted, that is, remedial or preventive action had already been taken. These figures are based on organisations' self-reported response and implementation rates.

In the Sutherland et al. research, 36% (59/164) of the recommendations were supplanted, 37% were implemented and 27% were rejected.[109] As I stated earlier in this chapter, a direct comparison between the NZ study and Sutherland research is not possible, but it is noteworthy that in both studies significant numbers of recommendations were supplanted and, in NZ, almost half the recommendations were supplanted. This finding suggests that this is an area for improvement. As I explained in the previous section of this chapter, the number of supplanted recommendations could be reduced by enhanced engagement with organisations and interested parties during the coronial inquiry. In the next section I discuss supplanted recommendations in detail.

4.4 SUPPLANTED RECOMMENDATIONS

As I outlined earlier in this chapter, almost half (207/426, 49%) of the coroners' recommendations in my study period were supplanted. Recommendations were supplanted because organisations had already taken remedial action. There were more supplanted (49%) than rejected (20%) coronial recommendations in my study period.

In the 2012 Canadian Supreme Court of Yukon case, *Silverfox v Chief Coroner*, Veale J commented on the jury charge, which included:[110]

> A paragraph about recommendations, indicating that the fewer there were, the more likely they were to be implemented, and saying that they should not include changes already in effect.

This observation is consistent with the NZ empirical data. NZ organisations reported that the main reason for supplanted recommendations was internal investigations into the death, which were undertaken by

---

109 Sutherland and others, above n 15, at 733.

110 *Silverfox v Yukon (Chief Coroner)* Yukon Territory Court of Appeal Vancouver 2011 YKCA 9, 14 October 2011 at para 99.

the recipient organisations. The delay in issuing coroners' recommendations meant that their internal investigations, and remedial action, were completed before the coroners' recommendations were handed down. Likewise, in the Sutherland et al. study, in nearly half of supplanted recommendations, an investigation into the death by the recipient organisation was cited as the reason for having taken the action prior to the coroner's recommendation.[111]

Supplanted recommendations highlight the length of time it takes for recommendations to be issued. The potential for these delays to undermine the effectiveness of coroners' recommendation powers is well recognised.[112] It is hoped that any vital preventive action will be implemented expeditiously.

Health sector organisations were more likely to supplant coronial recommendations because of the internal reviews that are undertaken shortly after adverse events.[113] A lawyer captured other participants' sentiments as follows:[114]

> Timing for recommendations is important. Two years after the event, any changes have usually happened. Recommendations, if you want to call them that, are simply endorsing changes that have already been put in place. The internal root cause analysis will make recommendations for changes. The coroners come to it much later down the track.

Organisations frequently stated that coroners' recommendations often "endorse" or "formalise"[115] the remedial and preventive action that was taken after the organisation's internal review. In the Sutherland et al. study, the researchers wondered why coroners issue recommendations for action that has already been undertaken.[116] They conclude that there are three explanations: (1) coroners do not undertake adequate consultation and therefore have incomplete information to inform recommendations; (2) organisations act in anticipation of coronial findings; and (3) delays in the coronial process.[117] The NZ findings are consistent with the first and third explanations.

---

111 Sutherland and others, above n 15, at 739.

112 Parliament of Victoria Law Reform Committee *Coroners Act 1985 Review Final Report* (2006); Sutherland and others, above n 15.

113 For example, St John, above n 49; Interview with Waikato Hospital (Jennifer Moore, 12 December 2012); Midwifery Council, above n 42.

114 Lawyer04, above n 89.

115 HealthCareOrganisation299, above n 94.

116 Sutherland and others, above n 15, at 743.

117 At 743.

NZ organisations also pointed out that coroners sometimes endorse the internal reviews *and also* issue recommendations. The following description by a DHB reflects other organisations' experiences:[118]

> I guess the thing that we find is that we will often have done our own review first. So if we've got a significant event, we'd have often done what used to be called a sentinel event review, now called a root cause analysis that would have identified a number of steps. And often we'll find that coroners recognise "Okay, we've had these guys look at it themselves, they've spent a bit of time, they've made some changes or are implementing some changes," and they will often simply say "We commend that, and we recommend that the DHB implement those recommendations that they've adopted themselves, or identified themselves." From time to time there will be additional recommendations on top of that, or we might not have done a review ourselves for whatever reason, and the coroner will identify some issues. I think one of the first I had was back in 2002. A man who had fallen in the shower, an elderly man, had a subdural haemorrhage and died from that. We'd done some steps, but the coroner had identified environmental issues, and non-slip flooring, and that we needed to speed up our programme. We picked that up and ran with that. But in the majority of cases, the coroners are going to say "We'll adopt the DHB's recommendations." And I think that's what most DHBs would hopefully find.

Organisations outside the health sector also reported that they undertake their own internal investigations which are frequently endorsed by coroners.[119] For example, many prevention and safety-focused organisations, such as Surf Life Saving NZ (SLNZ), are proactive and undertake their own risk assessments of locations before fatalities occur.[120] They analyse the risk of drownings or injuries and explore ways to reduce those risks.

Similarly, another organisation explained that they continually review safety procedures and undertake internal investigations for all accidents, even if there are no fatalities:[121]

> We do our own internal investigation and when it is an accident, whether it involves a death or not, we always carry out an investigation. At every race meeting or every event there is somebody there who can fill out an accident investigation report and photograph the scene and the cars concerned and the information comes to us and we look at our rules, particularly our safety rules, around what actually happened in an accident situation. There are risks in motorsport. That's part of racing. But we do like to put rules in place to avoid future occurrences. The coroners are also interested in avoiding future occurrences.

---

118 Brogden (Canterbury DHB), above n 51.

119 For example, GovtOrg06, above n 44; GovtOrg07, above n 90; Interview with GovtOrg10 (Jennifer Moore, 1 May 2013).

120 Interview with Surf Life Saving NZ (Jennifer Moore, 11 February 2013).

121 Interview with Org1 (Jennifer Moore, 18 February 2013).

> Sometimes we've already done our own investigation. . . . We log every accident, and we can see a trend around circuits where there are disproportionate numbers of accidents occurring and also since under the circuit we might have more accidents and that maybe is a result of the surface of the tarmac. . . . We have safety walls and barriers in place. So we're always reviewing safety.

Organisations emphasised that it is important for coroners to consult with them about proposed recommendations to avoid "redundant recommendations", that is, recommendations that suggest work which organisations have already undertaken.[122] According to one organisation, "it's not often when there are new things that the coroner will come up with that we are not already doing."[123] On the one hand, supplanted recommendations highlight the inadequacy of consultation between coroners and organisations.[124] On the other hand, supplanted recommendations "imply a shared view of what preventive action ought to have been taken in the aftermath of an unexpected death".[125] As the NZ participants' comments demonstrate, often coroners and organisations agree on the appropriate remedial action. In the next section, I discuss examples where organisations and coroners do not agree on the remedial action that is required to prevent further fatalities.

4.5 REASONS FOR REJECTION OF RECOMMENDATIONS

The most frequent complaint in the literature is that coronial recommendations are ineffective because the organisations to which they are directed ignore or reject them. For example, Australian research has focused on the repeated coronial recommendations about aboriginal deaths in custody which have not been implemented.[126]

As I stated earlier in this chapter, 86/426 (20%) of coroners' recommendations in my study period were rejected. My finding resonates with overseas research.[127] Organisations reported that the main reasons for rejection were that the recommendations were:

---

[122] Interview with GovtOrg03 (Jennifer Moore, 1 March 2013).

[123] GovtOrg07, above n 90.

[124] Sutherland and others, above n 15.

[125] At 743.

[126] Jennifer Corrin and Heather Douglas "Another Aboriginal Death in Custody: Uneasy Alliances and Tensions in the Mulrunji Case" (2008) 28 Legal Studies 531 at 545.

[127] Malbon, above n 7; Watterson, Brown and McKenzie, above n 15; Sutherland and others, above n 15.

- never received
- incorrectly targeted
- non-evidence-based
- not logistically and/or economically viable
- unclear
- adverse comments
- erroneous law
- already in place at the organisation
- a response is not required by law.

These reasons are consistent with previous research. For example, Sutherland et al. found that the leading reasons for rejection were that the recommendation was not logistically viable, or relevant to the recipient organisation's business.[128] The NZ organisations cited additional reasons for rejection that have not been explored in previous research. For example, organisations reported that they are less likely to implement coronial recommendations that contain adverse comment.

Rejected recommendations arguably raise questions about the quality of recommendations and/or inappropriate organisational responses to sound recommendations. As Sutherland et al. argue, "the true picture is likely to be more complicated than ascribing 'fault' to one side or the other. Discord between what coroners believe organisations should do to protect health and safety and what organisations can, or are willing to do may be attributable to a misalignment of perspectives."[129] Organisations typically take a private perspective on the cost-effectiveness of preventive measures. Research has not evaluated the economic viability of coroners' recommendations. However, it is well known that the cost of implementation is a key reason for the rejection of coronial recommendations.[130] Without such information, it is difficult to assess the extent to which rejection of coronial recommendations is due to low-quality recommendations as opposed to economically unviable recommendations or poor choices by recipient organisations.[131]

4.5.1 Recommendations not Received

Empirical research about the implementation of Australian coroners' recommendations has found that in a significant number of cases, the

---

128 Sutherland and others, above n 15.
129 At 742.
130 Haines, above n 16, at 40.
131 Sutherland and others, above n 15, at 742.

recipient organisations had not received copies of the recommendations that were directed to them and, in some instances, were unaware of such recommendations.[132]

In NZ, 14/79 (18%) organisations interviewed reported that they were unaware of and/or had never received recommendations directed to them. One organisation had not received any recommendations directed to them.[133] One recommendation had been directed to this organisation in 2011:[134]

> That they review their patient information literature on Abdominal Aortic Aneurysm, to consider whether adequate and clear information is given regarding the risk of Deep Vein Thrombosis/pulmonary thromboembolism, and the steps that need to be taken to manage that risk. The literature review should also consider whether to outline within the brochures, the specific signs and symptoms of deep vein thrombosis/pulmonary thromboembolism and what steps (for example, medical review) should be taken in the event that such symptoms are experienced.

This recommendation was directed to the Auckland District Health Board's Vascular Services, and the Royal Australasian College of Surgeons. Therefore, it is possible that the CSNZ administrative staff only sent the coroner's findings to the Auckland DHB. Alternatively, the coroner's finding may have been misplaced upon its arrival at the Royal Australasian College of Surgeons.

The former NZ Chief Coroner is aware that occasionally there have been "process issues" within the CSNZ:[135]

> I accept that we have let ourselves down in the past by not targeting properly or not even sending them. That was a process issue at our end because our staff did not understand that it was their responsibility. Sometimes we uncovered that Coroner X made a recommendation, and that coroner got a response from the agency, but that Coroner X never passed that information on to me. Again, we have been working on that. . . . We now say that coroners must send out recommendations to the Research Counsel so that we can post it on the website and put it in the *Recap*. But also we want coroners to let us know if they get a response from agencies. So there are some gaps there that we are working on.

---

132 Queensland Ombudsman, above n 6, at xi.

133 Email from Allan Panting (Royal Australasian College of Surgeons) to Jennifer Moore regarding receipt of coroners' recommendations (3 December 2012).

134 *Cutfield* [2011] NZCorC 35.

135 Coroner, above n 84.

More often, organisations had received a few, but not all, of the recommendations directed to them. My 2014 article in the *NZ Medical Journal* included a table with the coroners' recommendations directed to health sector organisations. That article prompted several organisations to email me requesting copies of recommendations that they had not received. For example, the Health Quality and Safety Commission's (HQSC) email stated:[136]

> I noted in your [*NZ Medical Journal*] article that it was highlighted that HQSC has received coroner's recommendations, yet we have not been aware of any recommendations directed to us. We are highly motivated to implement any recommendations that we can.

On 21 July 2014, I emailed all the coroners' recommendations that were directed to the HQSC to them. I also forwarded the correspondence to the former NZ Chief Coroner, who replied:[137]

> Important to note that we were referred to the relevant MRC (Mortality Review Committee) who come under HQSC now but the lack of cross communication appears to be at their end, not ours.

The research findings demonstrate that the administrative processing systems for coroners' recommendations could be improved by both the CSNZ and some organisations.

4.5.2 Incorrectly Targeted and Inapplicable Recommendations

Many organisations (53/79) reported that they rejected coroners' recommendations because they were not directed to the correct organisation. For instance, recommendations have been directed to the Ministry of Transport that should have gone to the NZ Transport Agency, and recommendations have been directed to the Midwifery Council when the NZ College of Midwives should have been the recipient.[138]

Several responses from organisations which are recorded in the *Recommendations Recap* highlight the issue. For example, a response from the Ministry of Youth Development (MYD) stated that a 2011

---

136 Email from Shelley Hanifan to Jennifer Moore regarding recommendations directed to HQSC (18 July 2014).

137 Email from Chief Coroner to Jennifer Moore regarding recommendations directed to HQSC (22 July 2014).

138 GovtOrg12, above n 49; Midwifery Council, above n 42.

coroner's recommendation "largely falls outside of MYD's responsibility, and would be more usefully addressed to other agencies".[139] Similarly, the Families Commission referred a coroner's recommendation to the Ministry for Social Development (MSD) because the MSD has "oversight of matters relating to the protection of children, and preventative education of parents, family and whānau" and was, therefore, the most appropriate organisation at which to direct the recommendation.[140]

This is a different problem from untargeted recommendations, which I discussed in Chapter 3. Untargeted recommendations do not specify an identifiable organisation. Incorrectly targeted recommendations do identify a specific organisation, but the organisation is inappropriate. All organisations reported that they are unlikely to implement untargeted or incorrectly targeted recommendations. Organisations did not appreciate being a "convenient PO box" for misdirected coroners' recommendations.[141] The "credibility" of the CSNZ was called into question by organisations because "if a coroner is directing the recommendation to the wrong place, then one wonders how valid the actual recommendation is."[142]

Although identifying which organisation to direct an adverse comment and/or recommendation to will often be easy, more than half the interviewed organisations commented that they had received adverse comments or recommendations that should not have been directed to their organisation. For instance, one health care sector organisation received a coroner's recommendation that could not be implemented because it was not directed to the correct organisation:[143]

> The comments weren't really within our ambit. We did have discussions with the College. They agreed with us. We were going to jointly refer the coroners on to the Ministry of Health who we felt were best placed to deal with the recommendations. . . . None of the recommendations were things that we could pick up. . . . If the coroner had consulted with us, we would have told them that we weren't the appropriate organisation.

The organisation would have preferred consultation. Engagement may have ensured that the coroner's comment was directed to the appropriate organisation which, in turn, increases the likelihood that the comment will

---

139 Office of the Chief Coroner of NZ, above n 35, at 6.
140 At 16.
141 Medsafe, above n 48.
142 Interview with David Cliff (Police) (Jennifer Moore, 22 April 2013).
143 Interview with HealthCareOrganisation377 (Jennifer Moore, 13 December 2012).

be implemented. Although the organisation is not required to re-direct the coroner's comment, it did so. Standards New Zealand has also taken the liberty of re-directing coroners' comments that were incorrectly sent to it. Standards New Zealand faces additional challenges. It described its experiences as follows:[144]

> Every coronial recommendation creates pressure on us to do something. But we have no ability to do so unilaterally . . . our policy settings don't necessarily allow us to. So it's a bit more complex for us. . . . A coroner in good faith, and using good judgement, makes a recommendation involving a standard, that standard may or may not be a NZ standard. If it's a Trans-Tasman standard, it has Trans-Tasman implications. Our ability in NZ to change an Australian-NZ standard is limited because we need to bring our Australian colleagues on board.

When a coroner recommends changes to a standard, Standards New Zealand often has to undertake consultation and engagement with its Australian counterparts and stakeholders. The Ministry of Consumer Affairs described similar experiences. Aspects of the product safety regime might require buy-in from Australia and cannot be changed easily by simply directing a comment to the Ministry.

Another common complaint was that some coroners appear to have little understanding that organisations have different arms – operational and policy. A well-intentioned, but misdirected, coroner's comment cannot be acted upon if it is received by the wrong arm of the organisation. For instance, Maritime NZ explained that:[145]

> We are not the policy body. So in those cases, we actually draw that to the attention of the coroner by writing to them, or counsel will make that submission on our behalf. We will inform the Ministry as well. We can often see by the questions that the coroner is asking that they are going down a policy not an operational path. . . . Maritime is operational. If you want transport policy, you have to go to the Ministry of Transport.

Coronial comments could be improved by enhancing coroners' understanding of specific regimes, such as standards and product safety and, in general, the "machinery of government":[146]

> I believe our coroners don't fully understand the machinery of government. . . . I've talked to the State Services Commission about this too. I've advocated for

144 Interview with Standards NZ (Jennifer Moore, 26 October 2012).
145 Interview with Maritime NZ (Jennifer Moore, 19 February 2013).
146 Standards NZ, above n 144.

what I call "the map". The map should be a state sector map: who does what, where are the centres of excellence for certain things, who has the statutory responsibilities to do certain things. It is incredibly confusing, especially with all these restructures and mergers and acronyms. It's hard enough when you are on The Terrace, let alone when you are a coroner based in Invercargill, to understand which agency is responsible for certain things. The map is a listing of all public sector departments, crown entities with a small descriptor around what legislative and regulatory regimes everyone is responsible for. But even that alone is not really enough. Understanding the interface between agencies is also important; for example, the interface between Standards and Consumer Affairs.

Interviews with organisations confirm Standards New Zealand's observation. However, the coroners' relatively new electronic Bench Book does now contain a lot of updated information about organisations.[147]

Some coroners misunderstand an organisation's empowering legislation. For example, it was not uncommon for organisations to complain that their empowering legislation does not enable them to make the changes advocated by the coroner.

These problems are not restricted to NZ. Australian research found that 40% of coroners' recommendations in Victoria involved organisations directing the recommendation to another organisation.[148] NZ organisations suggested that CSNZ researchers could investigate the most appropriate organisation to which to direct coronial recommendations.[149]

4.5.3 Non-Evidence-based Recommendations

In Chapter 5, I define "evidence", discuss evidence-based recommendations and coroners' statutory preventive function in detail. The purpose of this section is to emphasise that the findings highlight that organisations were more likely to reject recommendations that were not evidence-based. In interviews, all coroners recognised that non-evidence-based recommendations are likely to be rejected. For example, when asked for her view about why organisations reject recommendations, Coroner Stewart remarked:[150]

because they are ridiculous and not based on evidence! If a recommendation is generalised, who is going to implement it. For example, if a Coroner

---

[147] Email from Chief Coroner to Jennifer Moore regarding the draft of JLM article (19 July 2013).

[148] Bugeja, above n 21, at 277.

[149] Interview with GovtOrg09 (Jennifer Moore, 12 February 2013).

[150] Stewart, above n 71.

> recommends that thou shall chew your food twenty times, who is going to implement that? Who does that get sent to? Or you should hide guns from mentally disabled people. That recommendation is wrong on so many levels.

Organisations reported that recommendations that were not informed by the evidence about effective preventive measures were unlikely to be implemented. For example, the following example from a government organisation captures other organisations' concerns:[151]

> It was broadly the same picture with the nail gun suicide. The coroner recommended that there should be a licensing scheme so that only people who are registered can hire these things. But the fact that someone is registered is not necessarily going to stop them from taking their own life. The recommendation did not have any regard for the cost that would be involved in setting up a licensing regime. . . . How effective would it be to negate the risks that are involved? Where was the evidence?

Organisations commented that they are likely to reject recommendations if there is evidence from overseas which indicates the proposals would be ineffective. For example, the National Poisons Centre stated that:[152]

> The coroner also recommended that an audio telephone recording system be installed to automatically record and hold the conversation, which we haven't done. We decided not to go down that path, mainly because there are other poison centres overseas which had enormous problems with that.

As I pointed out in Chapter 1, if recommendations are not reasonably open on the evidence, there may be a power to quash them. Numerous cases highlight the importance of coroners' basing their decision-making, findings and recommendations on "reliable and comprehensive evidence".[153] Cases also emphasise the importance of expert evidence to assist the coroner and/or jury to decide whether recommendations should be made and, if so, their content.[154] The empirical data and cases suggest that

---

[151] GovtOrg01, above n 53.

[152] Interview with Wayne Temple (National Poisons Centre) (Jennifer Moore, 13 February 2013).

[153] *Montréal (Ville de) c Perreault*, 1667 (QCCS 22 April 2013) at para 29.

[154] *Picha v British Columbia (Presiding Coroner)*, No 2008 CarswellBC 1292, 2008 BCSC 818, [2008] B.C.W.L.D. 5326, [2008] B.C.W.L.D. 5304, [2009] B.C.W.L.D. 1375, 87 Admin. L.R. (4th) 161, 170 A.C.W.S. (3d) 783, 78 W.C.B. (2d) 332 (British Columbia Supreme Court 24 June 2008); *R (on the application of Sreedharan) v HM Coroner for the County of Greater Manchester and Ors* Court of Appeal London [2013] EWCA Civ 181, 26 March 2013.

non-evidence-based recommendations are unlikely to be implemented and/or may be quashed by the courts.

4.5.4 Not Logistically and/or Economically Feasible

Consistent with previous research about the implementation of coronial recommendations, these findings reveal that one of the main reasons for the rejection of coronial recommendations is that they are not logistically feasible and/or economically viable. For example, Standards NZ explained that they have been unable to implement some coroners' recommendations because the logistics of doing so would require amendment of Trans-Tasman standards.[155]

Many organisations explained that they rejected coroners' recommendations after undertaking cost–benefit analyses. According to one government organisation:[156]

> There might have been competing policy issues, or it was not sufficiently evidence-based, or we did a cost–benefit analysis and it was not feasible. An example is that if a coroner makes a recommendation for people to wear seatbelts on quad bikes, it is difficult because quad bikes are not fitted with suitable equipment. As the regulator, we are talking about overseas manufacturers and a whole raft of inter-agency considerations about safety. There are overseas trade agreements. It becomes complicated. In addition to whether this is a good idea, there are all those other complications.

Similarly, a government organisation described a case where it was not logistically feasible to implement the coroners' recommendations:[157]

> There will be a number that we don't implement for sound reasons. There may be practical or resourcing issues. I'll read one out to you. It's one that we ignored. It is from 1998. The recommendation was that "The [organisation] consider establishing a protocol for regular safety investigations of all huts and camping sites in respect to trees . . . and also issue safety brochures about the dangers of climatic conditions." There was a storm and a tree fell over and crushed someone in a hut. We have 950 huts and all of them have trees around them. We have more than 1500 camping sites which all have trees around them. We are not going to check all of those sites and huts to see whether there is a tree that might fall over in a storm. It would be nice to have known that the tree would be affected by a storm. But equally if we go in with chainsaws and clear all the trees, we will be criticised for that. People like trees. There are different

155 Standards NZ, above n 144.
156 GovtOrg06, above n 44.
157 GovtOrg07, above n 90.

> values and clashes. We generally follow the line that people expect some risk in the outdoors. So that was a recommendation that was not practical to implement. It was an unfortunate act of god, but it would be too resource-intensive to implement.

Many government organisations reported that they did not implement recommendations because implementation would "be too costly for the ratepayers".[158]

Despite these concerns about economic feasibility, a 2013 Canadian case noted that coroners should not be prevented from making recommendations because of the cost associated with the implementation of those recommendations.[159] The case concerned a death that was caused during a police operation. The City of Montreal and the Police asked the Court to quash a coroner's decision authorising a public hearing into the safety mechanisms on the gun holsters used by the police officers who shot the deceased. The application was dismissed.

4.5.5 Unclear Recommendations

In Chapter 5, I describe participants' statements that unclear recommendations, and poorly structured findings, limit the preventive potential of coronial recommendations. The purpose of this section is to highlight that organisations reported that unclear recommendations will often be rejected. Unclear recommendations include:

- poorly worded recommendations
- findings which do not explicitly state whether there are recommendations
- poorly structured findings which hinder identification of the recommendations.

For example, one organisation described their experience as follows:[160]

> The format of the report is half a dozen pages. 1, 2, 3 pages of background, it then has a section called "inquest". There are no actual recommendations. There's not a heading "Recommendations". When I read it at the time and just re-read it now, I would identify at least two statements which may be recommendations. . . . There's a statement that "The view of the court, that

158 Interview with Wellington City Council (Jennifer Moore, 31 January 2013).

159 *Montréal (Ville de) c Perreault*, above n 153, at para 34.

160 Interview with Sean Goddard (Department of Conservation) (Jennifer Moore, 14 May 2013).

> where there is any evidence of seismic activity, on or near Raoul Island, staff should immediately be withdrawn from the crater area" and that "observations of volcanic activity within that area should be conducted remotely for a period which needs to be conservatively assessed following the conclusion of such activity".

Ten out of 79 organisations reported rejection of coroners' recommendations because they were unsure whether the findings included recommendations. Fifteen out of 79 organisations reported rejection of recommendations because the word choice did not provide sufficiently clear instructions about the action required. Organisations suggested that coronial findings should follow a standardised structure, including a heading "recommendations". In their view, coroners should always state whether or not there were any recommendations. If no recommendations were issued, the findings should state this.

4.5.6 Adverse Comments in Recommendations

Adverse comments in recommendations have not been cited as a reason for rejecting coroners' recommendations in previous research about the implementation of coronial recommendations. The qualitative approach of this study may have elicited this additional reason for non-implementation of recommendations.

Pharmac's experience with coroners' adverse comments is illustrative. Two coroners made recommendations to Pharmac which Pharmac considered were adverse comments. On neither occasion was Pharmac notified or given an opportunity to comment before those recommendations/adverse comments were published. The only notice was through media reports.[161] One case involved a real estate agent who had a high level of zopiclone in her system when she took her own life.[162] In the inquest into her death, the coroner made adverse comments about Pharmac's management of zopiclone, a sedative:[163]

> The Court has a real concern about the prescribing of these type of medications given what it heard at this finding and recommends that Pharmac revisit this amendment to fall in line with the recommendation now made.

---

[161] "High level of sleeping pills in estate agent's body". *Stuff* (New Zealand, 28 September 2010).

[162] *McAuley* [2010] NZCorC 100.

[163] *McAuley*, above n 162.

Pharmac can set rules about the quantity of a medicine that can be funded. Pharmac can restrict the amount that gets dispensed. Pharmac had placed controls on zopiclone so that it had to be dispensed monthly. When the price of the product was reduced, Pharmac determined that it did not matter whether a large quantity of zopiclone was dispensed at once or not. Therefore, Pharmac removed the *funding* restriction. According to Pharmac, there is misunderstanding about the difference between funding restrictions and prescribing restrictions:[164]

> People call it a *prescribing* restriction, but it is not; it's a *funding* restriction. When we make those changes, we do public consultation. So we put together a proposal to make the change, we consult on it, then we make a decision. We had been through this process. . . . This method is controlling expenditure. We may do that on medicines that we find are dispensed all at once and they aren't all used, so that wastes money. Or we might put prescribing restrictions on medicines so that they target only the group that will most benefit from it.

When the coroner recommended that Pharmac change the restriction, Pharmac had two concerns:[165]

> (1) We had already heard from this person [the expert medical practitioner who appeared at the inquest] and considered that view when we made our decision; and (2) the *funding restriction was in place when the deceased died.* So that was irrelevant to the death of the person who the inquest was about. *Therefore, why was a recommendation made about a decision that we made subsequent to the death of the patient?* Arguably, the prescribing restriction did not assist, because the patient still died. So we thought the recommendation was ridiculous. . . . We felt that there was an adverse comment made about Pharmac.

These recommendations directed to Pharmac were not implemented. Pharmac's experience illustrates the negative impact that coronial adverse comments can have on organisations' reputations, even though

---

[164] Pharmac, above n 31. Reproduced with permission of Thomson Reuters (Professional) Australia Limited, www.thomsonreuters.com.au. This article was first published by Thomson Reuters in the *Journal of Law and Medicine* as Jennifer Moore "An Empirical Approach to the New Zealand Government's Review of the Coronial Jurisdiction" (2014) 21 JLM 602. For all subscription inquiries please phone, from Australia: 1300 304 195, from Overseas: +61 2 8587 7980 or online at www.thomsonreuters.com.au/catalogue. The official PDF version of this article can also be purchased separately from Thomson Reuters.

[165] Pharmac, above n 31.

the Coroner's Court does not find fault. Appellate litigation has also emphasised this point:[166]

> Although there is no finding of liability or blameworthiness, the findings of fact and the conclusions of the inquest judge may well have an adverse impact upon the reputation of a witness or a party to the inquest.

4.5.7 Erroneous Law in Recommendations

Five organisations interviewed reported that they rejected recommendations because the proposals contained erroneous law. For instance, one government organisation stated that they "have had occasions where the coroners make mistakes, where coroners have referred to redundant provisions in the law".[167] Another government organisation explained that they rejected a coroner's recommendation because it recommended unnecessary amendment to the law:[168]

> Sometimes recommendations get thrown in the filing cabinet because we cannot implement them for very good reasons. A good reason might be because of the current law and if the coroner had bothered to look it up, he might not have made the recommendation. The coroner should not recommend to change the law to do that because the law already says that.

A DHB reported that a coroner's recommendation could not be implemented because it "didn't reflect the obligations we've got under the Land Transport legislation and some other consent processes".[169] The coroner's recommendation was that the Southern DHB institute a protocol that, wherever possible, a blood sample is taken from patients who have been involved in a road crash as soon as they are admitted to hospital.[170] The formal response from the DHB to the coroner stated:[171]

> Section 73 of the Land Transport Act 1998 permits the taking of blood samples in road traffic crashes and provides immunity from civil or criminal action where such samples are taken. However, while this Act does mandate the patient submit to the taking of a sample it does not mandate the medical

---

166 *Silverfox v Yukon (Chief Coroner)*, above n 110, at para 29; *Forestell v Regional Health Authority*, No 2014 CarswellNB 457, 2014 NBCA 40, 244 A.C.W.S. (3d) 337 (New Brunswick Court of Appeal) at para 13.

167 GovtOrg12, above n 49.

168 GovtOrg03, above n 122.

169 Brogden (Canterbury DHB), above n 51.

170 *Smith* [2012] NZCorC 11.

171 Office of the Chief Coroner of NZ, above n 35, at 38.

> practitioner to take such samples. In clinical practice such evidential samples are taken pursuant to specific requests to medical staff by the police for them.

In an inquiry into the death of a pedestrian, the Christchurch City Council rejected recommendations because implementation of the proposal would have been illegal:[172]

> It is illegal for us to install a green left arrow unless there are no other movements permitted to enter this same section of the intersection. With the current operation of the intersection, this is not possible for us to do.

This reason for rejecting coroners' recommendations has not been cited in previous research about the implementation of coronial recommendations. The qualitative approach of this study may have elicited this additional reason for non-implementation of recommendations.

4.5.8 Recommended Change already Exists

Some organisations (32/79) complained that coroners' failure to consult with them during the inquiry meant that coronial recommendations suggested changes that were already in place within organisations. This reinforces the importance of the consultation theme that runs throughout this book. According to the College of Midwives:[173]

> They recommend that we do what we already do because they don't know, they've got no clue. They don't know. And because their doctor expert hasn't got a clue what midwifery education is, so the doctor experts says "Oh these midwives, they need to learn this in midwifery school." Of course they learn it in midwifery school. So he recommends that they learn this, and then everybody goes "Oh for God's sake. We already do that."

The case law also reveals that it is unnecessary to make coronial recommendations to an organisation that has already implemented the proposed change. For example, in the 2013 English case *R (Shaw) v HM Coroner*, the daughter of the deceased claimed that the coroner should have made a Rule 43 report.[174] Her father died shortly after surgery to treat a defective heart valve. Dismissing the daughter's claim, the Court commented

---

[172] At 39.

[173] NZ College of Midwives, above n 39.

[174] *R (on the application of Mrs Gabriele Shaw) v HM Coroner, Assistant Deputy Coroner for Leicester*, No [2013] EWHC 386 (Admin) (High Court (Administrative Court) 27 February 2013).

that it was not surprising that the coroner did not make recommendations because there was evidence that remedial action was already being undertaken.[175] If the coroner had made recommendations, it is highly likely that they would have been supplanted because the recommended change already existed.

4.5.9 Response not Required by Law

A small number of organisations (14/79) stated that they rarely, or never, respond to coroners' recommendations because there is no statutory mandatory response requirement. These organisations pointed out that coroners are *functus officio*, unable to engage with organisations' responses, and therefore, they felt that writing formal responses would be ineffective. These findings are consistent with Australian research, which also found that a reason for non-implementation by relevant authorities was that the authorities were not required by law to respond.[176]

4.6 IMPLEMENTED RECOMMENDATIONS

The figures that I outlined earlier in this chapter demonstrate that some coroners' recommendations are accepted and implemented by organisations. For example, in Victoria, Australia, the Transport Industry Safety Group (TISG) was established in 1996 following a coroner's recommendations about the death of a 14-year-old male pedestrian in a truck-related road crash.[177] The incident occurred as a result of the failure of the truck driver's employer, a transport company, to provide the driver with proper training and supervision.[178] The Victorian TISG comprises senior executives from a number of organisations, including the Transport Workers Union (Victoria/Tasmania), the Victorian Transport Association, VicRoads, Victoria Police, WorkSafe Victoria, the Transport Accident Commission, the Bus Association (Victoria), the Victorian Waste Management Association and Monash University Accident Research Centre.[179] The TISG meets regularly with the State

---

[175] *R (on the application of Mrs Gabriele Shaw) v HM Coroner, Assistant Deputy Coroner for Leicester*, above n 174, at para 90.

[176] Watterson, Brown and McKenzie, above n 15.

[177] Transport Safety Group *A Guide to Occupational Health and Safety Transport Industry* (2006).

[178] At preface.

[179] At preface.

Coroner to develop proactive strategies to reduce the incidence of death and serious injury within the transport industry.[180]

In NZ, there are many examples of coroners' recommendations that have been accepted and implemented. For instance, in his autobiography, Stewart (who was a coroner in Nelson from 1965 to 1978), describes his experiences.[181] In particular, Stewart gives examples of recommendations which were initially ignored, but eventually implemented. In an inquest into the death of a driver, Stewart recommended that seatbelts should comprise diagonal belts and waist belts. Stewart writes that "several years later, the combination of a diagonal plus waist seat belt was made universal in all new cars".[182]

The CSNZ *Recommendations Recaps* outline examples of the action taken by organisations to implement coronial recommendations. For instance, the NZ Transport Agency (NZTA) launched a drug-driving advertising campaign in response to a coroner's recommendation that "further publicity be given by [NZTA] to the dangers of driving while affected by cannabis".[183] In the inquiry, the coroner found that the deceased died from injuries sustained in a motor vehicle crash.[184] After smoking cannabis, the deceased lost control of his vehicle.

As I outlined earlier in this chapter, in interviews, organisations reported that they accepted 133/426 (31%) of coroners' recommendations. Organisations do not always implement recommendations in precisely the way that is prescribed by the coroner. I coded these responses as "partially implemented". For example, one DHB described their experience as follows:[185]

> They may need to be implemented with a twist. It is not as straightforward as it may appear. Part of making a recommendation is you need to work through the spin-off issues that might flow from implementation. . . . You'd think that a recommendation about producing information for young people would be relatively straightforward to implement. That just involved a leaflet. That was producing leaflets on certain types of medication for young people. Trying to get consensus on the content of the leaflet was exceptionally difficult. There were all sorts of challenges. . . . So even producing a leaflet, a recommendation that might appear simple, has enormous complications.

---

180 At preface.

181 G.P. Stewart *The Rough and the Smooth: An Autobiography by G.P. Stewart* (The Heritage Press, Waikanae, 1994).

182 At 252–3.

183 Office of the Chief Coroner of NZ *Recommendations Recap – Issue 3* (2012) at 32.

184 *Stevenson* [2012] NZCorC 78.

185 Interview with HealthCareOrganisation01 (Jennifer Moore, 4 December 2012).

Organisations reported that they were more likely to implement coronial recommendations if there was consultation during the coronial inquiry, and the recommendations were clear, evidence-based, logistically and financially viable, appropriately directed, fell within the organisations' roles, and prevention-focused. Many organisations reported (47/79) that they sometimes implemented recommendations that did not meet these criteria if they felt that non-implementation posed a reputational risk, particularly because of media pressure.

These findings are similar to the Sutherland et al. study results. Their research found that prevention of future death or injury was cited as the most important reason for taking action.[186] The reputational implications of not acting on recommendations were also rated as an important reason for implementation. Forty-two per cent of respondents rated the legal implications of not acting on coroners' recommendations as an important reason to implement. Commentators in the UK have also observed that the legal implications of non-implementation often encourage organisations to accept coronial recommendations.[187] If recommendations are not heeded by individuals, corporations and industries, future similar events may have an adverse impact on them. The successful prosecution of a company under the UK Corporate Manslaughter Act may herald the launch of more prosecutions and dissuade organisations from rejecting coronial recommendations.[188]

In NZ, 23/79 organisations interviewed stated that the legal implications prompted them to implement coroners' recommendations. Two coroners interviewed mentioned that there is "bite back" in the form of potential "criminal nuisance charges or something like that".[189] As one coroner explained:[190]

---

186 Sutherland and others, above n 15, at 738.

187 Gerard Forlin and Louise Smail "Come in Number 43: The Impact of Rule 43" [2011] March New Law Journal 306 at 36.

188 At 36.

189 Atwood, above n 61. Reproduced with permission of Thomson Reuters (Professional) Australia Limited, www.thomsonreuters.com.au.

This article was first published by Thomson Reuters in the *Journal of Law and Medicine* as Jennifer Moore "An Empirical Approach to the New Zealand Government's Review of the Coronial Jurisdiction" (2014) 21 JLM 602. For all subscription inquiries please phone, from Australia: 1300 304 195, from Overseas: +61 2 8587 7980 or online at www.thomsonreuters.com.au/catalogue. The official PDF version of this article can also be purchased separately from Thomson Reuters.

190 Atwood, above n 61. Reproduced with permission of Thomson Reuters (Professional) Australia Limited, www.thomsonreuters.com.au.

> If the same thing happens again in the same place, then you could be facing criminal charges because it has been brought to your attention, you knew about it and you did nothing. . . . The roading authorities; they do respond, and they do take notice because they think, "Ah, if someone's crashed into the end of this bridge because it hasn't got Armco rails up, if we have another one, are we criminally negligent?" The answer would be yes.

During interviews, the most commonly cited example of a successful response to, and implementation of, coronial recommendations was the Auditor General's 2008 report *Responses to the Coroner's Recommendations on the June 2003 Air Adventures Crash*.[191] On 6 June 2003, an aircraft crashed on approach to the Christchurch International Airport, killing the pilot and seven passengers. The coroner's May 2006 findings raised concerns about the regulation of the general aviation sector (smaller planes, agricultural operators and helicopters). The findings included 31 recommendations. Twenty-four were directed to the Civil Aviation Authority (CAA). Six were directed to the Ministry of Transport and one to the NZ Institute for Crop and Food Research.

At the Minister of Transport's request, the Auditor General assessed whether the CAA and the Ministry had properly considered the coroner's recommendations. The Minister "put in place a monitoring system to ensure that all the recommendations in the report were acted upon".[192] The review concluded that overall the CAA and Ministry "responded systematically to the coroner's recommendations".[193] The Auditor General found that the CAA's process for monitoring its response to each of the coroner's recommendations was robust. By contrast, the review found that the Ministry's process "should have been more comprehensive".[194]

Of the 24 recommendations directed to the CAA, 11 were accepted and implemented, nine were supplanted, and four were rejected because alternative action had been undertaken.[195] Of the six recommendations

---

This article was first published by Thomson Reuters in the *Journal of Law and Medicine* as Jennifer Moore "An Empirical Approach to the New Zealand Government's Review of the Coronial Jurisdiction" (2014) 21 JLM 602. For all subscription inquiries please phone, from Australia: 1300 304 195, from Overseas: +61 2 8587 7980 or online at www.thomsonreuters.com.au/catalogue. The official PDF version of this article can also be purchased separately from Thomson Reuters.

191 New Zealand Office of the Auditor-General *Responses to the Coroner's Recommendations on the June 2003 Air Adventures Crash* (2008).

192 Michael Cullen "Urgent Reports Sought on Christchurch Crash Finding" (Wellington, 30 May 2006) <www.beehive.govt.nz>.

193 New Zealand Office of the Auditor-General, above n 191, at 5.

194 At 6.

195 At 6.

directed to the Ministry, two were accepted and implemented, four were rejected. One recommendation was rejected because it was already covered by the existing legislation.[196]

For-profit organisations that I interviewed had also implemented coroners' recommendations. For example, Telecom installed a public telephone landline at Bethells Beach in accordance with a coroner's recommendation.[197] The recommendation was issued after an inquiry into the death of two men who drowned after they were swept from rocks while fishing.[198] At the time of the interview, Telecom noted that the telephone had not been used and, therefore, doubted whether the action was fulfilling its preventive aim.[199]

During interviews, organisations reported that the most common type of action taken to implement coronial recommendations was the adoption or modification of policies and practices, or the introduction of educational programmes. Similarly, the Sutherland et al. study found that among accepted recommendations, the most common types of action taken were implementation of education programmes or training (36/60) and adoption of policies, procedures or standards (28/60).[200] For nine accepted recommendations, the organisation had resolved to implement the recommendation, but the precise type of action was undecided.[201]

4.7 CONCLUSION

This chapter has revealed that in contrast to media speculation that all, or almost all, coroners' recommendations are rejected, organisations' responses are more nuanced. While I found a significant proportion of organisations in my sample did not respond to, or implement, coroners' recommendations, the number of implemented/accepted recommendations is greater than some commentators might expect and all organisations reported that they give coroners' recommendations serious consideration.

While quantification of implementation rates is useful, it is important to remember the broader picture. In her analysis of the Australian coroners' recommendations about the Mistral fan controversy, Haines reminds us that:[202]

---

196 At 6.
197 Interview with Telecom (Jennifer Moore, 13 February 2013).
198 *Michael* [2009] NZCorC 108.
199 Telecom, above n 197.
200 Sutherland and others, above n 15, at 739.
201 At 739.
202 Haines, above n 16, at 47.

> The Coronial recommendations may have been imperfect, and certainly met a mixed fate, but to focus purely on the quantifiable influence of such suggestions may be to miss the quintessential importance of institutions such as these, namely their role as guardian (however imperfect) of social values.

My mixed methods qualitative and quantitative approach to the investigation of coroners' recommendations has attempted to heed Haines' warning. The qualitative techniques used in my study may account for some of the differences between the findings of this study and previous research. NZ organisations' reasons for rejecting coroners' recommendations are remarkably similar to those documented in the Australian empirical studies. However, my research elicited two reasons for rejection of coronial recommendations that were not documented in the Australian studies: (1) adverse comments in recommendations; and (2) erroneous law in recommendations.

Comparisons between the implementation rates of NZ coroners' recommendations and Australian coroners' recommendations should be made with trepidation because of the different coronial legislation. As Sutherland et al. observed, their results may be a "best case scenario" because of the Victorian mandatory response regime.[203] My findings are not generalisable to other jurisdictions because of such differences.

This chapter highlights that there are two particularly important areas for improvement: (1) consultation with organisations before recommendations are issued; and (2) directing recommendations to the appropriate organisations. Consultation also emerges as an important theme in the next chapter. The high number of supplanted recommendations highlights the importance of consultation processes and the considerable length of time it takes for coroners to issue recommendations. It is important to separate the rejected from supplanted recommendations.[204] These two forms of inaction spotlight different policy considerations.

Although the inclusion of some organisations' responses to coroners' recommendations in the *Recommendations Recaps* is an improvement, there is little publicly available information about the extent of implementation of recommendations in NZ. It is, therefore, difficult for the Government, coroners and the community to assess the preventive impact of coroners' recommendations. The results outlined in this chapter are a first step to address this gap. As Freckelton has observed, it is important for the community to know which recommendations are

---

203 Sutherland and others, above n 15, at 738.

204 At 732.

rejected and why. The reasons may be sound, or they may not be, but the families of the deceased and the community should be informed.[205] In Chapter 6, I explore how a mandatory response regime, and associated monitoring system, would facilitate this information-gathering and enable accountability of organisations.

---

205 Ian Freckelton "The Myers Oration 2005: Untimely Death, Law and Suicidality" (2005) 12 Psychiatry, Psychology and Law 265.

5. The promise of saved lives: coroners' preventive function

5.1 INTRODUCTION

In the previous chapter I outlined the argument that the preventive potential of coronial recommendations is undermined when recommendations are not implemented by organisations. This chapter explores coroners' preventive function in detail and, in particular, the following questions:

- Do coroners' recommendations save lives?
- What counts as a "successful" coroner's recommendation? Is success measured by the number of lives saved and/or evidence of the uptake of recommendations by organisations?
- How can we maximise the preventive potential of coroners' recommendations?

NZ coroners have been described as "public health officials" because of their statutory preventive functions.[1] The principal role of coroners is to investigate and determine causes of deaths that occur in sudden, unexpected or unnatural circumstances. This work advances public health indirectly, not least by enhancing the quality of vital statistics and public health surveillance.[2] Some coronial data is shared with other injury and death prevention agencies in NZ and overseas.[3] In some jurisdictions,

[1] Ian Freckelton "Death Investigation, the Coroner and Therapeutic Jurisprudence" (2007) 15 JLM 242.

[2] Georgina Sutherland and others "What Happens to Coroners' Recommendations for Improving Public Health and Safety? Organisational Responses under a Mandatory Response Regime in Victoria, Australia" (2014) 14 BMC Public Health 732.

[3] George A. Conway and others "Alaska's Model Program for Surveillance and Prevention of Occupation Injury Deaths" (1999) 114 Public Health Reports 550; Deon York "Learning from Tragedy: New Zealand's National Mortality Review Programme" (Health Services Research Centre Victoria University Seminar Series, Wellington, 5 September 2012); Carol Conroy and Julie Russell "Medical Examiner/Coroner Records: Uses and Limitations in Occupational

such as NZ, Australia, Ireland, the UK and most Canadian provinces, coroners are also vested with authority to play a more direct role in advancing public health. As part of their findings, they may issue recommendations aimed at reducing risk and improving health and safety in the community.

While the prophylactic function of coroners has been adopted by many jurisdictions, controversies remain about the limits to be imposed on coroners to ensure that their inquiries are not unduly "discursive"[4] or "wide-ranging".[5] One aspect is whether coroners should be confined to making findings about the circumstances, cause of death and identity of the deceased, or whether coroners should also make preventive recommendations. The most commonly asserted advantage of coronial inquiries is that they are undertaken in public, with input from relevant interests, in order to fulfil the public interest in recommending mechanisms for the prevention of similar deaths in the future.[6]

Few studies have systematically examined coroners' recommendations and little is known about how effectively this function is exercised. My research findings are consistent with the limited previous research results. Coroners' findings and recommendations are "extremely important to injury prevention, but there are improvements that could be and should be made".[7]

There have been improvements in NZ since the introduction of the Coroners Act 2006 (NZ). For example, in 2013, Coroner Matenga released his findings about 13 cycling deaths in 2010 which also took into account 94 other cycling deaths since 2007.[8] However, coroners typically investigate a single death during an inquiry and this is the most commonly cited weakness of coronial investigations. Research has found that coronial

---

Injury Epidemiologic Research" (1990) 35 *JFSCA* 932; Randy Hanzlick "The Centres for Disease Control and Prevention's Medical Examiner/Coroner Information Sharing Program (MecISP)" (1997) 42(3) Journal of Forensic Science 531.

[4] *Harmsworth v State Coroner* [1989] 989 VR at 995 (Nathan J).

[5] *Re Doogan; Ex parte Lucas-Smith* (2005) 193 FLR 239 at 249–50.

[6] Ian Freckelton "Coronership under Challenge: The Evolving Institution of the Modern Coroner" (The Greek Legal and Medical Conference, Corfu, Greece, 2009).

[7] Lyndal Bugeja *Farm-related Fatalities in Victoria July 2000–June 2003* (2004) at 60.

[8] Tessa Johnstone and Alex Fensome "Cycling views 'must change'" *Stuff* (New Zealand, 15 November 2013). I have referenced a newspaper report instead of coroner's findings because the full findings are not available on the CSNZ website or NZLII. Coroner Matenga did not make recommendations. Therefore, there are no recommendations available on NZLII. The findings are not on the CSNZ website under "findings of public interest".

inquiries which only focus on the case under inquiry (without consideration of previous similar inquiries) generate inconsistencies across coronial investigations into the same cause of death. For instance, research which examined 20 British Columbia coronial investigations into suicide by oxygen deprivation with helium found that there were inconsistencies across the findings which could not be explained by differences in the facts or scientific evidence.[9] Epidemiologists/public health researchers have argued that coroners should gather previous similar cases in order to identify trends and patterns amongst groups of cases.[10] By understanding how and why deaths occur, appropriate steps can be taken to prevent similar incidents occurring. Coronial findings should note the relevant contributing factors to the death and comment on prevention issues. Currently, the "variations in the . . . approach to the investigation process and the presence, content and quality of findings and recommendations suggest that there is scope for improvement in the coronial system of each [Australian] State and Territory" and, I would add, NZ.[11]

This study's findings are consistent with the literature. While there have been improvements since the introduction of the Coroners Act 2006 (NZ), interview participants reported that the prophylactic potential of recommendations is not being maximised. This chapter explores the factors that foster and impede the preventive potential of coronial recommendations. The chapter begins by outlining coroners' statutory power to make recommendations, and examples of recommendations which have had a positive public health impact.

5.2 STATUTORY PROPHYLACTIC FUNCTION

In 1907, Dr Brend, a doctor and barrister, highlighted the potential preventive purpose of coronial inquiries when he wrote:[12]

---

9 Russel D. Ogden and Shereen Hassan "Suicide by Oxygen Deprivation with Helium: A Preliminary Study of British Columbia Coroner Investigations" (2011) 35 Death Studies 338.

10 Timothy Robert Driscoll and others "Coverage of Work Related Fatalities in Australia by Compensation and Occupational Health and Safety Agencies" (2003) 60 Occupational Environmental Medicine 195; Bugeja, above n 7.

11 Driscoll and others, above n 10.

12 Graeme Johnstone "An Avenue for Death and Injury Prevention" in Hugh Selby (ed.) *The Aftermath of Death* (Leichhardt Federation Press, New South Wales, 1992) 140 at 140.

> [The] value of the [coroner's] statistics is diminished by absence of coordination. Hence we have the anomaly that while full inquiry is conducted into deaths from violent and unnatural causes, practically no subsequent use is made of the information for public health purposes.

Death prevention was emphasised as the main purpose of coronial inquiries as early as 1915 when Brend declared that "if prevention of deaths is not now regarded as the main purpose to be served by inquests, the inquiry becomes of relatively little value."[13]

It was the Ontario Law Reform Commission's (OLRC) 1971 report on the coronial system and the 1980 Norris Review into the Victorian coronial system that placed the preventive function at centre stage. The OLRC stated that an inquest has two primary preventive purposes. First, an inquest is a means for "formally focusing community attention and initiating community response to preventable deaths"[14] and, secondly, an inquest is a way of satisfying a community that the circumstances surrounding a death of one of its members will not be ignored, concealed or overlooked.[15] Endorsing the Norris Review, the OLRC agreed that coronial systems should aim to preserve human life.[16]

By contrast, the Brodrick Committee's 1971 review of the coronial system in England and Wales recommended the removal of the right to attach riders to findings. This recommendation was adopted in the Coroners Act 1980 (UK).[17] This position has been maintained in the recent Coroners and Criminal Justice Act 2009 (UK). Freckelton has observed that this means there is no explicit preventive role for coroners in England and Wales.[18]

Australia has distanced itself from the English position, providing its coroners with preventive functions. The Parliamentary debates about the Victorian, Australian Coroners Bill 2008 highlight the importance of the preventive work of the Coroner's Court. During its second reading, the Attorney General pointed out that:[19]

---

13 At 140.

14 Ontario Law Reform Commission *Report on the Coroner System in Ontario* (1971) at 142.

15 At 142.

16 John Norris *The Coroners Act 1958 – A General Review* (1981) at 4.

17 Ian Freckelton and David Ranson *Death Investigation and the Coroner's Inquest* (Oxford University Press, Melbourne, 2006) at 23 and 655.

18 Ian Freckelton "Anglo-Australian Coronial Law Reform: The Widening Gap" (2010) 17 JLM 471 at 474.

19 (9 October 2008) Australian (Victoria) Parliamentary Debates 4033 at 4035.

> There was a need to strengthen the prevention role of the coroner. Whilst the Victorian coronial system has an impressive history in the area of prevention, including recommendations regarding tractor rollover protection structures, safety barriers for swimming pools, suicide prevention in prison cell design, and mistral fans, the committee recognised that the role could be further supported. The bill addresses this issue and is supported by the establishment of the first coroner's prevention unit, which will assist the coroner in relation to the formulation of appropriate prevention recommendations as well as help monitor and evaluate the effectiveness of those recommendations.

Similarly, NZ has also distanced itself from the English position, adopting the broader preventive role for its coroners. This is evident in the Law Commission's report on coroners, which states that an inquest should not be a mere formality, but should be socially and statistically significant in a modern community, recognising that substantial community benefit can result from a forward-looking preventive role.[20]

The importance of the coronial prevention role was also evident in the 2006 NZ Parliamentary debates about the Coroners Bill:[21]

> There was strong feeling that we as a community need to learn as much as possible from those unexplained deaths, and to use that knowledge to help avoid future deaths. Families often mention that they want something good to come out of such wasteful deaths. To that end, the chief coroner is charged with setting up and maintaining a register of coroners' specified recommendations and comments, in order to have a permanent record of information from coroners' findings that can be used to prevent further fatalities.

The Law Commission's commitment to a preventive role for coroners is expressed in the purpose of the Coroners Act 2006 (NZ). Section 3(1) states:

> The purpose of this Act is to help to prevent deaths and to promote justice through—
> (a) investigations, and the identification of the causes and circumstances, of sudden or unexplained deaths, or deaths in special circumstances; and
> (b) the making of specified recommendations or comments (as defined in section 9) that, if drawn to public attention, may reduce the chances of the occurrence of other deaths in circumstances similar to those in which those deaths occurred.

The Act takes an explicitly prophylactic approach, with its primary aim being to prevent deaths and promote justice.[22] Section 3(1)(b) provides

---

20 New Zealand Law Commission *Coroners* (NZLC R62 2000) at 8.

21 (9 May 2006) 631 *New Zealand Parliamentary Debates* 2866.

22 Ian Freckelton "Reforming Coronership: International Perspectives and Contemporary Developments" (2008) 16 JLM 379 at 382.

that the preventive aim will be achieved by making recommendations. This connection between prevention principles and the recommendatory power of coroners is well recognised. Halstead has summarised the relationship:[23]

> Coroners' recommendations are the distillation of the preventive potential of the coronial process. Actions taken in response to recommendations carry the promise of lives saved and injury averted. Proactive strategy has the potential to avert deaths but also alleviate risks to health and safety more generally.

In NZ, this "promise of lives saved and injury averted" is further expressed in section 9 of the Coroners Act 2006 (NZ), which defines "specified recommendations or comments" as "recommendations or comments about the avoidance of circumstances similar to those in which the death occurred or the way in which any people should act in circumstances of that kind". This definition allows coroners to consider a wide range of factors relating to a death. However, the section 9 definition contains two limiting clauses: "in circumstances similar to those in which the death occurred", also found in sections 4 and 57, and "in circumstances of that kind". Recommendations should relate to the circumstances in which the particular death occurred, preventing a coroner from viewing the death too broadly.

NZ coroners are independent judicial officers. Their ability to describe the facts as they see them is not impeded by political motivation. The Coroner's Court, unlike other NZ courts and tribunals, is an inquisitorial jurisdiction; coroners are not concerned with blame but instead with a "search for truth by investigative inquiry".[24]

The inquisitorial nature of the Coroner's Court is supported by the wide investigatory powers that the Coroners Act 2006 (NZ) accords coroners.[25] This allows for an inquest to assemble a wider range of experts and information than would have been considered necessary in the criminal jurisdiction. In addition, inquests are not subject to the strict rules of evidence used elsewhere in the law.[26] Freckelton and Ranson argue that:[27]

> This freedom to conduct an inquest in a manner most likely to reveal the true facts surrounding a death is one of the great strengths of the coroner's

---

23 Boronia Halstead "Coroners' Recommendations Following Deaths in Custody" in Hugh Selby (ed.) *The Inquest Handbook* (Federation Press, Sydney, 1998) 186 at 187.

24 Freckelton and Ranson, above n 17, at 725.

25 Coroners Act 2006 (NZ) s 119–31.

26 Coroners Act 2006 (NZ) s 79(1).

27 Freckelton and Ranson, above n 17, at 727.

> investigation process. It is assisted by the testing of witnesses under oath, thereby providing an element of quality assurance with respect to evidence of both fact and opinion, which may be missing in internal inquiries held by other organisations involved in the death.

As I pointed out in the introduction of this chapter, these wide investigatory powers should not be deployed as an opportunity to undertake a "roving Royal Commission".[28] Many organisations interviewed for this study (69/79) preferred coroners' recommendations to highlight issues that should be investigated further by the appropriate entities. The lawyer for a health care organisation captured the sentiment of many organisations when she explained that:[29]

> If the mandate is to identify a series of questions or issues arising out of a death that require further attention, then that sits comfortably with a fact-finding objective. Coroners determine what happened, this raises a series of questions and coroners refer it on to authorities to reach determinations or investigate. . . . And the best coroners do exactly that. They recognise their own limitations, but also put weight behind looking at the issues further.

The organisations that advocated this approach reported that the statutory preventive function would be fulfilled in this manner without becoming unduly wide. These participants argued that this approach allows coroners to take a systems perspective while also including organisations in the preventive process.

All the coroners interviewed for this study reported that their statutory preventive function is appropriate and important. Almost all coroners (14/15) described the Act's prophylactic purpose as "an opportunity to learn . . . to help prevent it happening again".[30] Most coroners (13/15) conceptualised the preventive purpose, and their recommendatory powers, as the "pivotal",[31] "primary"[32] and "main limb of the Act".[33]

Although coroners recognised the importance of their preventive function, most (12/15) described the challenges of undertaking this function. The following comments reflect other coroners' concerns:[34]

---

28 *Re Doogan; Ex parte Lucas-Smith*, above n 5, at 28.
29 Interview with Lawyer04 (Jennifer Moore, 5 February 2013).
30 Interview with Coroner Armstrong (Jennifer Moore, 11 October 2012).
31 Interview with Coroner Price (Jennifer Moore, 12 October 2012).
32 Interview with Coroner Woodward (Jennifer Moore, 10 November 2012).
33 Interview with Coroner Atwood (Jennifer Moore, 11 December 2012).
34 Interview with Coroner Fitzpatrick (Jennifer Moore, 25 September 2012).

> I know the Act says that we have a prevention role. But I don't think the system is well set up to support that objective. . . . I don't think that it is well understood by coroners.

These concerns were shared by most organisations interviewed (65/79). A small number of organisations (9/79) questioned whether coroners should be vested with a statutory preventive function. The following comment from a government organisation captures other organisations' views:[35]

> I wonder whether they should have a statutory preventive function. In other countries coroners are confined to cause of death. We have so many investigations going on. There are so many different investigative authorities that I wonder whether we are ending up with repeat investigations. I wonder whether investigations done by the experts would result in a better preventive message, than those done by coroners.

By contrast, the preventive role of coroners appears to be one that is supported by NZ families. Coroners assist families through grieving by helping them to understand the circumstances in which their loved ones died. Many families also express the desire that the death of their relative not be in vain. Nicky Wagner MP commented on this point in the second reading of the Coroners Bill: "Families often mention that they want something good to come out of such wasteful deaths."[36] Families want the coronial process to ensure that no other family will have to endure their loss.

Unfortunately, not all unexpected deaths are preventable. According to one organisation:[37]

> Sometimes even with the best systems in the world you can't prevent death. If we look at mental health, we are concerned about the suicide rates in NZ. But there are a group of people who, no matter what any family or health profession does, there is a certain inevitability about an eventual outcome of suicide because mental illness has, as one of its fatal outcomes, suicide. I have knowledge of situations where everyone did everything right, but there was still a suicide. Usually under these circumstances, the coroner will say that the person received good care and nothing more could have been done. That is part of the challenge of having that in the legislation, that sometimes people who are distressed by the death assume that someone or something could have prevented the death. But sometimes it could not have been prevented. That is hard to hear. I don't envy the coroner's challenge under those circumstances.

---

35 Interview with GovtOrg07 (Jennifer Moore, 20 February 2013).

36 (9 May 2006), above n 21.

37 Interview with Ministry of Health (Jennifer Moore, 15 February 2013).

Overall, this study's participants were supportive of the statutory preventive function. However, there was recognition that the "challenge of having that in the legislation" is that some families assume that all unexpected deaths are preventable. Sometimes "nothing more could have been done" to save the deceased. In the next section, I discuss examples of preventable deaths, where more could have been done, and the coronial recommendations did have a positive impact on future prevention strategies.

5.2.1 Coronial Recommendations Prevention Success Stories

This study's findings demonstrate that the effectiveness of recommendations is limited by various factors such as untargeted recommendations, under-resourcing, poor access to full coronial findings, and the absence of a requirement to respond to recommendations. While almost all organisations interviewed for this study (77/79) were "supportive of the coroner's role in preventing future deaths through recommendations",[38] they often felt that "recommendations would not have prevented deaths".[39] Some organisations (61/79) that were interviewed reported that "the vast majority [of coroners' recommendations] don't have a positive impact".[40] The majority of these organisations (72/79) emphasised that "without data [they] couldn't say for sure", but that they "were not convinced that recommendations do have much public health impact".[41]

However, there are examples of recommendations that have had a positive public health impact. Analysis of coroners' recommendations in England has found that "some good and valuable recommendations have been made".[42] Coroners in England have sometimes identified problems with health care that standard mortality data collection within the health care organisation had missed.[43] For example, preventable neonatal

---

38 Interview with Pharmac (Jennifer Moore, 27 November 2012).

39 Pharmac, above n 38.

40 Interview with HealthCareOrganisation399 (Jennifer Moore, 14 February 2013).

41 Interview with HealthCareOrganisation299 (Jennifer Moore, 23 January 2013).

42 Gerard Forlin and Louise Smail "Come in Number 43: The Impact of Rule 43" [2011] New Law Journal 306 at 306.

43 Jennifer Moore "Coroners' Recommendations about Healthcare-related Deaths as a Potential Tool for Improving Patient Safety and Quality of Care" (2014) 127(1398) NZ Medical Journal 35; Tanya Claridge, Gary Cook and Richard Hale "Organizational Learning and Patient Safety in the NHS: An Exploration of the Organizational Learning that Occurs Following a Coroner's Report under Rule 43" (2008) 14 Clinical Risk 8.

deaths following insertion of long lines was documented by coroners, but missed by the health care organisation.[44]

In NZ, some health care organisations interviewed (11/26) for this research gave examples of coroners' recommendations that had a positive impact on clinical practice.[45] For instance, one health care organisation explained that:[46]

> We had a lady who stopped taking her anticoagulation meds after she went on IVF. When she went back on the meds she got blood clots in her heart and passed away. The coroner looked at the case and found that there was poor communication between the GP and the IVF specialist. Recommendations were made about communication, monitoring and responsibility. We took those recommendations on board and we believe that patients in that lady's situation are safer as a result.

Research about coronial recommendations in Victoria, Australia has identified child drownings in domestic swimming pools, tractor-related deaths, scuba-diving deaths and railway level-crossing-related deaths as success stories.[47]

An often cited success of coronial recommendations is the advent of legislation requiring fencing of swimming pools. Such legislation in Victoria "largely resulted from coronial recommendations made in the 1990s".[48] This was recognised in the parliamentary debates on the Building Act 1993 (Vic), which contains requirements in regards to the fencing of swimming pools:[49]

> The coroners' reports have noted that: the majority of toddlers drown in their own family pool or are invited guests — so perimeter fencing is of little assistance — because toddlers are usually already within the property. A four-sided isolation fence which separates the pool from the house is the best single measure to address the risk of a child drowning. The coroners' reports demonstrate that this is a serious matter.

---

44 Moore, above n 43; Claridge, Cook and Hale, above n 43.

45 Moore, above n 43, at 48.

46 Interview with HealthCareOrganisation214 (pseudonym) (Jennifer Moore, 13 March 2013).

47 Stephen Cordner and B. Loff "800 Years of Coroners: Have They a Future?" (1994) 344 The Lancet 799 at 800.

48 Lyndal Bugeja and David Ranson "Coroners' Recommendations: Do They Lead to Positive Public Health Outcomes?" (2003) 10 JLM 399 at 400.

49 (1 December 1993) Victoria Parliamentary Debates Legislative Council 1495.

The legislation, in conjunction with public awareness campaigns about the dangers of young children around private swimming pools, has been successful in bringing about a significant decrease in the number of children under five years of age who drown each year in private pools.[50]

In NZ, Coroner Evans' recommendations to change the layout of Centennial Highway were commonly cited by this study's research participants (82/123) as an example of recommendations which prompted positive change. Centennial Highway is a notoriously dangerous stretch of road north of Wellington. In 2000, Coroner Evans investigated eight deaths that occurred within a year of each other on the coastal route. In his April 2001 findings, he recommended that a median barrier be constructed along Centennial Highway to reduce the risk of head-on collisions.[51] A 700m-long median barrier was constructed in 2004.[52] The barrier was subsequently extended to a length of 3.4km after Coroner Evans found that three subsequent crashes on the road in 2004 could have been prevented if there was a median barrier in place.[53] Newspapers reported that "since the Centennial Highway median barrier was installed, it [has] been hit more than 20 times, potentially saving 50 or more people from head-on crashes".[54] Coroner Evans "will be forever remembered as the coroner who recommended the Centennial Highway barriers".[55]

Another example of coronial recommendations that have contributed towards avoidance of preventable transport accidents is the systematic lowering of the speed limit in the Wellington central city. At the inquest of Corinne Bongiovanni, a woman who was killed as she crossed Lambton Quay, it was observed that there were a number of international studies showing the extent of injuries suffered by pedestrians is proportionate to the speed of the vehicle they were struck by.[56] The coroner recommended the reduction of the speed limit on Lambton Quay from 50km/h to 30km/h. Wellington City Council adopted this recommendation in 2005. Since then, the Wellington City Council has taken the initiative

---

50 Terry Nolan and Ian Scott "Update on Pool Drownings and Isolation Fences" (1991) 7 Hazard 6; Bugeja and Ranson, above n 48.

51 Interview with Coroner Clarke (Jennifer Moore, 29 October 2012).

52 "Barrier on Notorious Road" *The New Zealand Herald* (Auckland, 24 November 2004).

53 NZPA "Doctor Calls for Action on Barrier" (New Zealand, 29 September 2005).

54 Alastair Stewart "Centennial Highway Barrier Delay" *Kapiti Observer* (Kapiti Coast, 14 January 2010).

55 Interview with Mr Dawson (lawyer) (Jennifer Moore, 10 September 2012).

56 Clarke, above n 51.

and a more wide-scale project is under way to lower the speed limit in 21 suburban centres around Wellington.[57]

The coroners who were interviewed for this research reported that they often encourage publicity of a public health issue in order to generate positive change. Increasing the profile of an issue, hopefully leading to a reduction in deaths, is the outcome that coroners have been trying to achieve with sudden unexpected death in infants (SUDI). The former NZ Chief Coroner explained that:[58]

> . . .a consistent message coming from the coroners for some time has been that people should be aware of the safe sleeping messages such as put baby on back, not on tummy, keep baby's head clear, keep baby in a separate cot with no cracks or things they can fall down, and don't co-sleep, or have baby close by when you are drunk or stoned. We have seen the SUDI death rate plummet. That is a very good example of how the constant drum beat of coroners' recommendations had a small role in that.

There are approximately 60–70 SUDI deaths each year, all of which are investigated by a coroner.[59] Many of these children die as a result of bed-sharing or from being placed in inappropriate sleeping positions. In 2008 Coroner Evans conducted successive inquests into the deaths of seven babies. Coroner Evans' findings asked the Director-General of Health to issue stronger warnings on the risks of bed-sharing, recommending:[60]

> 1. That the public health advice in relation to safe infant care practices and safe sleeping environments be strengthened and broadened as to make clear that:
>   (i) bed-sharing by adults and siblings with infants under six months exposes the infant to the risk of death and should be avoided.
>   (ii) the safest place for babies to sleep for the first six months of life is in a cot beside the parental bed.
> 2. That steps be taken by the Ministry to ensure that the same advice is given by public health educators and health professionals in those public health sectors over which the Ministry has influence.
> 3. That the Moe Ora scheme, referred to in the findings, and similar schemes, be encouraged by Government and lent every possible support, with a view

---

57 Wellington City Council *Lower Speed Limits in Suburban Shopping Areas – Overview* (2011).

58 Interview with the Chief Coroner (Jennifer Moore, 12 September 2012).

59 Plunket "Sudden Unexpected Death of an Infant (SUDI) – Plunket" <http://plunket.org.nz/your-child/welcome-to-parenting/sudden-unexpected-death-in-infancy-sudi/>.

60 *Tito-George* [2009] NZCorC 183.

> to ensuring that every new mother and mother-to-be is provided with a cot if she is unable to afford the cost of purchase.

The decision to conduct the seven inquests as a group lifted the public profile of SUDI. Coroner Evans' recommendations have been restated or referred to in a number of subsequent inquests into SUDI, and in media reports.[61] Organisations, such as Plunket, have adopted Coroner Evans' recommendations.[62] Much of the media coverage now includes advice from Plunket on the factors known to prevent sudden death.[63] Culturally appropriate methods of co-sleeping have also been developed and publicised. Two examples are the wahakura, a small bassinet-like structure woven from flax,[64] and the Pepi Pod.[65] Both allow babies to sleep in the parental bed in their own separate and safe sleeping environment. SUDI is an example of coroners' recommendations contributing to positive changes.

NZ parliamentary debates sometimes reflect concerns expressed by coroners in their recommendations. For example, Coroner Smith's recommendations about the death of Cedric Joyce in 2005 were cited in the parliamentary debates about the Private Security Personnel and Private Investigators Bill.[66] Joyce died of restraint asphyxia while being restrained by two bouncers outside a Blenheim bar.[67] The bouncers were later found not guilty of manslaughter in October 2006. At the inquest, Coroner Smith called for compulsory training for security staff and for the proposed Private Security Personnel and Private Investigators Bill, drafted partly in response to the incident, to be fast-tracked through Parliament.[68]

---

61 *Baby R* [2012] NZCorC 199; *Hemi-Tango* [2011] NZCorC 50; *Joseph* [2011] NZCorC 188; *Purcell* [2010] NZCorC 109; *Tuake* [2011] NZCorC 97; Lane Nichols "Infant Died in Bed with Sibling" *The Dominion Post* (Wellington, 22 July 2011).

62 Plunket, above n 59.

63 For example, see "People Not Keeping to Cot Death Advice" *Sunday Star Times* (New Zealand, 16 November 2010).

64 David Tipene-Leach "Sudden Infant Death and Co-sleeping: A Better Message" (2010) 123(1309) NZMJ 137.

65 Jamie Morton "Group Latches onto Quake Idea to Cut Baby Deaths" *The New Zealand Herald* (Auckland, 29 June 2011).

66 (7 September 2010) 666 *New Zealand Parliamentary Debates* 13705.

67 "Coroner's Plea after Man Dies While Held by Bouncer" *The Marlborough Express* (Marlborough, 16 September 2008).

68 Blair Ensor "Calls to Fast-track Bouncer Bill" *The Marlborough Express* (Marlborough, 30 October 2009); "Coroner's Plea after Man Dies While Held by Bouncer", above n 67.

Although the Bill was not fast-tracked, the debate on the Bill reflects some of Coroner Smith's concerns:[69]

> The bill seeks to address the risks associated with untrained security personnel becoming involved in physical confrontation. In 2008 the Wellington regional coroner, Ian Smith, called for compulsory training following the tragic death of Cedric Joyce in Blenheim in 2005 after he was restrained by bouncers outside a pub.

According to five coroners interviewed for this research, successful outcomes can also be prompted by the coronial *process*. For instance, one coroner explained that:[70]

> With safety-focused organisations, the involvement of the coroner is sometimes useful for them in making safety changes and really putting the microscope on something. So it might not be the recommendation, but the process itself. Sometimes the organisation itself has moved to make changes. Even though DHBs are quality- and safety-focused, sometimes they don't identify quite serious things until the coroner becomes involved. [Lawyers] have said once or twice that it is the coroner's process that is quite often where change comes for them.

These examples suggest that coroners' recommendations can be effective catalysts for change or contribute towards preventive measures. The coronial investigation can be important for achieving the first policy process required for successful research–practice translation: public recognition that there is a policy problem that needs to be addressed.

This study has contributed to the dearth of empirical information available about the effectiveness of NZ coroners' recommendations by examining the extent to which they are implemented. As participants pointed out, the coronial process (even without recommendations), and publicity about inquests, can also generate positive change towards prevention strategies. In this section I have also described examples of coroners' recommendations that have improved quality of patient care.

Despite these success stories, the experience and perception of many organisations interviewed (61/79) was that the preventive potential of coroners' recommendations is not being realised. This finding is consistent with recent Australian research which reported that 45/90 organisations sent coroners' recommendations believed that the recommendations were unlikely to be effective in preventing death and injury.[71] In the next section

69 (7 September 2010), above n 66.
70 Interview with Coroner Oldfield (Jennifer Moore, 12 October 2012).
71 Sutherland and others, above n 2.

I explain why the preventive potential of coroners' recommendations is not being maximised and discuss strategies for improvement.

5.3 MAXIMISING THE PREVENTIVE POTENTIAL OF CORONIAL RECOMMENDATIONS

5.3.1 Law Reports and Un/targeted Recommendations

In Chapter 1 I explained that under-reporting in the coronial jurisdiction and untargeted recommendations undermine the preventive potential of coroners' recommendations. In this section, I briefly reiterate these points in order to emphasise that these deficiencies in the coronial system hinder the coronial prophylactic function.

Without official law reports or easy access to full coronial findings online, coroners are unable to fulfil their preventive function. Without adequate reporting systems, coroners are hindered from gathering previous cases which would help them to discern patterns. These shortcomings impact the quality, consistency and rigour of coroners' recommendations.

As I have pointed out elsewhere, NZ is not the only jurisdiction with inadequate coronial reporting systems.[72] For example, the recent review of Scottish fatal accident investigations found that the database of recommendations was "not up to date"[73] and that mechanisms should be put in place to ensure that "determinations be more readily available for sheriffs in later FAIs [fatal accident investigations] to consider for their relevance to them". Analysis of a single case in isolation, with no reference to previous cases or deaths of a similar nature, has limited preventive impact. It is difficult for coroners to consider previous cases without easy access to full coronial findings. In order to maximise the preventive potential of coronial recommendations, my research supports the introduction of *Coroner's Court Law Reports* and online access to *full* coronial findings on a system such as NZLII.

As I discussed in Chapter 3, untargeted recommendations (which do not identify a specific organisation or person) have little or no preventive impact. Australian research has demonstrated that vaguely directed recommendations receive poor or no responses and have little or no preventive

---

72 Jennifer Moore and Mark Henaghan *New Zealand Coroners' Recommendations, 2007–2012 (final report)* (2014).

73 Legal System Division, Scottish Government *Review of Fatal Accident Inquiry Legislation: A Consultation Paper* (2008) at 24.

impact.[74] Organisations can argue that the recommendation was not directed at them and therefore does not require any action which, in turn, limits the effectiveness and preventive potential of recommendations.[75] If a recommendation is inappropriately directed, its preventive potential is undermined because it does not reach the organisation that can consider and/or implement it.[76] In order to maximise the preventive potential of their recommendations, coroners need to ensure that recommendations are targeted at a specific organisation and/or person.

Some coroners do target their recommendations. However, this research found that 23% of recommendations were untargeted. The former NZ Chief Coroner has recognised the importance of targeted recommendations. Coroners "are trying to ensure that a recommendation is targeted and that it says *who* it is to go to".[77] Improvements to coronial practice in this area are under way. In response to the media's questions about untargeted recommendations in July 2014, the then Chief Coroner stated that "we took that on board and the coroners have really got that message".[78] The Chief Coroner explained that coroners "need to take the trouble to say 'where's the best person to send this recommendation to?' so they can respond, and we know it's not disappearing out into the ether and nobody reads it".[79]

5.3.2 Resources, Support and Training

As I outlined earlier in this chapter, many coroners do not feel able to fulfil their preventive function because of under-resourcing, inadequate support, time pressures and inadequate training. Coroners described the challenges of undertaking their preventive role. The following comments reflect other coroners' concerns:[80]

---

[74] Law Reform Commission of Western Australia and Tatum L. Hands *Review of Coronial Practice in Western Australia: Background Paper Project 100* (2010).

[75] Moore, above n 43, at 50.

[76] At 50.

[77] Interview with Chief Coroner (Jennifer Moore, 12 September 2012).

[78] David Loughrey "Chief Coroner Welcomes Study" *Otago Daily Times* (Dunedin, 18 July 2014).

[79] Loughrey, above n 78.

[80] Fitzpatrick, above n 34. Reproduced with permission of Thomson Reuters (Professional) Australia Limited, www.thomsonreuters.com.au.

This article was first published by Thomson Reuters in the *Journal of Law and Medicine* as Jennifer Moore "An Empirical Approach to the New Zealand Government's Review of the Coronial Jurisdiction" (2014) 21 JLM 602. For all subscription inquiries please phone, from Australia: 1300 304 195, from Overseas:

> I know preventing deaths is often touted as an important aspect of the coronial system, but when I look at our system, it is under-resourced for us to do that effectively. Also, I don't think that we are trained to do that well. . . . I think we would need dedicated research staff. We only have two researchers for 16 coroners. They help us with the legal research. But we'd want to have something like in Victoria [Australia], where they have a team who helps coroners to decide whether recommendations need to be made. We don't get that.

The NZ Government's current review is concerned with increasing efficiency, but there is little acknowledgment that the drive to reduce delays may negatively impact upon coroners' ability to fulfil their preventive function. These findings are consistent with similar overseas studies.[81]

Most coroners appreciated the need for their investigations and recommendations to be informed by evidence. All coroners defined "evidence" as information tested in court. Such "evidence" may include research and scientific evidence. However, coroners reported that they were often unable to draw on this information because of financial constraints and staff shortages.

An Australian study found that coroners felt their full potential to contribute to death and injury prevention was not being achieved because of the absence of training, lack of resources and lack of feedback regarding the implementation of their recommendations.[82] Most New Zealand coroners are not trained in the disciplines (such as epidemiology or statistics) that would be required to undertake comparative health and safety assessments. Ready access to epidemiological advice would enable the facts to be interpreted in light of the wider context and specific populations, enabling the formulation of robust recommendations.

The appropriateness and accuracy of coroners' recommendations is affected by the quality of information and advice available to coroners. The need for a multi-disciplinary research team to assist coroners has been recognised.[83] The Coroner's Court in Victoria, Australia, includes a specialised service for coroners – the Coroners Prevention Unit (CPU) – created to strengthen their prevention role and provide them with expert assistance by undertaking tasks such as assisting coroners in the develop-

---

+61 2 8587 7980 or online at www.thomsonreuters.com.au/catalogue. The official PDF version of this article can also be purchased separately from Thomson Reuters.

81 Lyndal Bugeja "Determinants of Coroners' Recommendations on External Cause Deaths in Victoria, Australia" (PhD, Monash University, 2011).

82 At 315.

83 Boronia Halstead *Coroners' Recommendations and the Prevention of Deaths in Custody: A Victorian Case Study* (1995).

ment of prevention-focused coronial recommendations, and collecting and analysing data relating to reportable deaths.[84] The CPU comprises a multidisciplinary team trained in medicine, law, public health and the social sciences that assists coroners with their prevention role. Information is drawn from the scientific research literature, an assessment of policy is undertaken, and stakeholder consultation is conducted to generate evidence-based recommendations.

The State Coroner's Office in Victoria also has a Clinical Liaison Service (CLS) which provides coroners with assistance from practising clinicians for the investigation of healthcare-related deaths.[85] Evaluation research found that this service contributes towards improving patient safety.[86]

Coroners in Queensland, Australia are assisted by the clinical expertise provided by the Clinical Forensic Medicine Unit (CFMU). Government medical officers (GMOs) are available on an "as needed" basis to assist the coroner's preliminary assessment of a reported death, particularly those that occur in clinical settings.[87] GMOs from the CFMU review the report of the death and the deceased person's medical records, and then alert the coroner to any clinical issues requiring further follow-up or independent clinical expert opinion. GMOs are available to assist regional coroners on request.[88]

The CSNZ utilises the Health and Disability Commissioner expert clinical adviser list to identify health professionals who are competent to provide advice on the quality of clinical care. This is useful for assessing an individual clinician. However, formulating a recommendation to change systems should draw from a broader skillset. Extrapolating generic clinical care recommendations based on an individual case can result in recommendations that are difficult to implement. Although there is statutory authority for the coroners to seek additional advice, the former NZ

---

84 "Coroners Prevention Unit – Coroners Court of Victoria" <http://www.coronerscourt.vic.gov.au/home/coronial+investigation+process/whos+involved/coroners+prevention+unit/>.

85 Victorian Institute of Forensic Medicine and the Coroner's Court of Victoria "Clinical Liaison Service, State Coroner's Office and the Victorian Institute of Forensic Medicine, Victoria, Australia" Clinical Liaison Service <http://www.health.vic.gov.au/cls/>.

86 Joseph Elias Ibrahim and others "The Impact of a Clinical Team Assisting a Coroner's Investigation of Healthcare-related Deaths: Reflections on Six-years of Service" (2010) 12 Legal Medicine 28.

87 Queensland Office of the State Coroner *Office of the State Coroner Annual Report 2011–2012* (2012).

88 Queensland Office of the State Coroner, above n 87.

Chief Coroner has stated that there is limited funding for this and that the service is not resourced for more complex analysis.[89]

The Minister's review is concerned with improving the efficiency of coronial services. Research has found that the coronial process was delayed and limited because of a lack of readily available clinical expertise.[90] The Victorian CLS was established to remedy this problem. If the NZ Government is serious about "improving processes within the coronial system to ensure they are timely",[91] the research evidence and the Victorian model should be considered. An evaluative study of the CLS concluded that the "model should be considered throughout Australia and in other countries with similar judicial arrangements".[92] All research participants felt that the Victorian model could be usefully adapted to the CSNZ to improve the quality of coronial recommendations and processes. The former NZ Chief Coroner would like access to in-house trained investigators including medical, legal and forensic expertise.[93] The introduction of a service similar to the Victorian CPU could assist NZ coroners to accurately identify preventable deaths and formulate recommendations that are consistent with public health principles, thereby enhancing the prophylactic potential of recommendations. The introduction of a service similar to the Victorian CPU to assist coroners in Western Australia has been recommended by the Western Australian Law Reform Commission.[94]

The empirical evidence demonstrates that although most coroners state

---

89 Coroner, above n 77.

90 Parliament of Victoria Law Reform Committee *Coroners Act 1985 Review Final Report* (2006); United Kingdom *Death Certification and Investigation in England, Wales and Northern Ireland: The Report of a Fundamental Review ('The Luce Report')* (Cmnd 5831 2003); Joseph Elias Ibrahim and others *The Role of the Coronial Process in Initiatives for Improving Patient Safety and Quality of Health Care: Final Report of a Consultancy into the Coronial Death Investigation Process in Australia* (Report Submitted to the Australian Council for Safety and Quality in Healthcare 2003).

91 Cabinet Paper *Coroners Act Review: Proposals for Reform – Paper 1* (2013) at 5.

92 Ibrahim and others, above n 86, at 33.

93 "Ask Me Anything: Chief Coroner Judge Neil MacLean" *The National Business Review* (New Zealand, 14 December 2012) 31.

94 Tatum L. Hands "Under the Microscope: Reforming Western Australia's Coronial System" (2012) 39 Brief: Journal of the Law Society of Western Australia 12 at 4; Law Reform Commission of Western Australia and Tatum L. Hands *Review of Coronial Practice in Western Australia: Discussion Paper Project 100* (2011) at 164.

that recognising a preventable death is "obvious",[95] their recommendations are not systematically consistent with public health principles. Consistent with overseas research, NZ coroners' recommendations rarely identify the population at risk or whether the proposed countermeasure[96] addresses an identified risk factor.[97] Given that most NZ coroners are not trained in public health, or related disciplines, it is not surprising that there was little awareness of the need to recommend interventions that identify risk factors and target the population at risk. Access to specialised multidisciplinary teams within the CSNZ could remedy this problem and produce improved recommendations.

Many coroners who were interviewed also suggested further training opportunities where they could assess and critique their recommendations. At present, coroners meet twice per year. Although coroners are judicial officers, they are excluded from the training opportunities available to other members of the judiciary. The "Institute of Judicial Studies does not consider it part of its mandate to provide training for coroners".[98] All of this study's participants support training for coroners through the Institute of Judicial Studies.

The Law Commission's 2000 report found that coroners felt undervalued. The report made recommendations to improve the status of coroners.[99] The majority of coroners interviewed still feel that they "struggle to get proper recognition".[100] The government review should include provision for adequate *in-house* training. Coroners felt that external training, alone, was insufficient. They also need to meet as a group to discuss

---

[95] During interviews, eight NZ coroners stated that preventable deaths were "obvious" or they used similar phrases to indicate that such deaths are easy to identify. Australian research has also found that coroners consider preventable deaths easy to identify. See Bugeja, above n 81, at 309.

[96] A "countermeasure" is any intervention that addresses a specific risk factor for injury.

[97] Bugeja, above n 81, at 320.

[98] Judge MacLean "Coronial Reform and the Role of the Chief Coroner" [2012] NZLJ 207 at 210.

[99] New Zealand Law Commission, above n 20, at 5.

[100] Armstrong, above n 30. Reproduced with permission of Thomson Reuters (Professional) Australia Limited, www.thomsonreuters.com.au.

This article was first published by Thomson Reuters in the *Journal of Law and Medicine* as Jennifer Moore "An Empirical Approach to the New Zealand Government's Review of the Coronial Jurisdiction" (2014) 21 JLM 602. For all subscription inquiries please phone, from Australia: 1300 304 195, from Overseas: +61 2 8587 7980 or online at www.thomsonreuters.com.au/catalogue. The official PDF version of this article can also be purchased separately from Thomson Reuters.

quality improvement measures. Without sufficient training opportunities, it is unlikely that recommendations will be improved or will achieve their preventive potential.

Coroners spend time making recommendations, and considerable financial resources are spent on public inquests and the administration of the Act. The Ministry of Justice spent NZ$16.57 million to administer the Coroner's Act in 2010–11.[101] The outlay of cash is justified, partly, on the basis that coroners' recommendations contribute to preventive public health and safety goals. Yet it is difficult for coroners to fulfil their preventive function. To successfully fulfil their statutory prophylactic function, it is vital that coroners are sufficiently resourced. Coroners need assistance in applying a preventive framework to their recommendations.[102] National and international reviews of coronial services report that the public expects high-quality death investigations.[103] This expectation cannot be adequately fulfilled by the current CSNZ because of the high caseloads, understaffing, under-resourcing and lack of access to specialised expertise. Although the government review cites the importance of the coroners' prevention functions, it includes few proposals to address the problems discussed in this section. To achieve the prophylactic potential of coroners' recommendations, the NZ Government's current review of the coronial jurisdiction should include proper resourcing for the CSNZ and consideration of Victorian and Queensland models.

5.3.3 Individual Cases and Comparative Risks

Coroners should "be able to detect trends over time", which is "in marked distinction to their historical concern with individual cases".[104] Despite improvements such as inquiries into clusters of deaths, the coronial jurisdiction's focus on individual cases persists today. Australian research about deaths in custody found that coroners' "consideration of each case in isolation" meant that they did not "regard any other cases which might have involved similar systemic risks factors".[105] In Victoria, Australia in 1990, five people died in custody following arrests for drunkenness. Research into the coroners' findings about these deaths concluded that:[106]

---

101 Email from CSNZ to Jennifer Moore "regarding figures" (2 August 2011).

102 Bugeja, above n 81.

103 For example, see the discussion about international reviews of coronial services in Freckelton and Ranson, above n 17.

104 Cordner and Loff, above n 47, at 800.

105 Halstead, above n 83, at 16.

106 At 16.

> The increase should arguably have been noticed by coroners and responded to, at least to the extent of noting any emerging patterns. There is no evidence that there was any awareness on the part of the coroners of the links between these cases or the legislative position in Victoria in relation to the decriminalisation of public drunkenness. The fact that the eight cases in this study were heard by five different coroners may have contributed to the lack of awareness of the magnitude of the problem or any developing trend.

The organisations interviewed for this study also reported that many coronial findings do not discuss "developing trend[s]" or "emerging patterns". The National Poisons Centre, which has reviewed large datasets of coronial information, observed that "there didn't seem to be any kind of pattern in the recommendations".[107] The coroners I interviewed were aware of this issue. Coroner Atwood commented that they "should be looking at other coroners' findings".[108] Another coroner remarked that they should not "be too contradictory or divided in [their] recommendations".[109] In keeping with the Australian research findings above, such inconsistencies are more common when multiple cases about the same cause of death are heard by different coroners. The former NZ Chief Coroner has encouraged inquiries into clusters of deaths because he is aware of the limitations of an investigation into an isolated case.[110] The Chief Coroner has also assigned the same coroner to investigate several cases over time about a particular cause of death.[111]

Although the community can learn from one death, when a greater number of deaths with common circumstances are identified, the potential to learn is greater. This is why I have argued that it is essential that coroners and others interested in prevention (for example public health researchers) have access to previous coronial findings. It is also important that a minimum dataset for all external cause deaths be developed in consultation with key stakeholders. Researchers have found that it is not possible to derive an accurate estimate of the number of work-related deaths in NZ each year by merging administrative data files from the

---

107 Interview with Wayne Temple (National Poisons Centre) (Jennifer Moore, 13 February 2013).

108 Atwood, above n 33.

109 Armstrong, above n 30.

110 Coroner, above n 77.

111 Interview with Coroner Aitken (Jennifer Moore, 22 January 2013); Coroner, above n 77.

CSNZ, ACC or OSH.[112] The most effective and accurate way to determine whether a death is work-related would be through coronial investigations.

Coroners should consult previous findings because, when a similar incident has already been investigated, it may provide important guidance on avenues to be explored in the inquiry. Such ongoing analysis will identify patterns of concern which would not normally be detected by separate coroners in single investigations.

The government review proposes amending the Act to "ensure coroners' recommendations or comments are specific to the case and evidence before the Coroner".[113] The two limiting clauses in section 9 should encourage coroners to make recommendations that are specific to the case. Will statutory amendment remedy the problem? A potential undesirable, unintended consequence of requiring coroners to focus on the *particular* death in the *specific* case may be that they do not look at patterns or comparative risks. How many similar deaths have occurred in the last 20 years? How do the health and safety risks correlated with that type of death compare with the risks associated with different types of death? For example, what is the comparative risk assessment for deaths related to drinking Coca-Cola versus deaths attributed to alcohol?[114] By not systematically addressing areas where the greatest morbidity or mortality burdens exist, coroners limit their ability to reduce illness, disease and injury at the population level.

A commonly cited weakness of coroners' recommendations is that they focus on an isolated case.[115] The Law Commission commented on this limitation as follows:[116]

> The fundamental problem is that coroners' recommendations are usually about a unique set of facts associated with one individual death. . . . What I've never seen is somebody going through to say, "Here are the themes from five years of coroners' reports," and to then make that a much larger issue. . . . It needs some back-office analyst to put all this stuff together, all the themes and threads. Because at the moment, the reports . . . are based on a sample of one.

---

[112] Injury Prevention Research Unit, Department of Preventive and Social Medicine, University of Otago, John D. Langley and Colin Cryer *Submission to the Justice and Electoral Select Committee on the Coroners Bill* (2005) at 4.

[113] Cabinet Paper, above n 91, at 271.

[114] A coroner recently correlated Coca-Cola consumption with a woman's death. See Sam Boyer "Coca-cola Addiction Linked to Death" *Stuff* (New Zealand, 12 February 2013).

[115] Interviews with organisations, legal and medical professionals.

[116] Interview with Law Commission (Jennifer Moore, 13 February 2013).

Similarly, other organisations I interviewed commented on the weakness of coronial inquiries "based on a sample of one":[117]

> I think that coroners, or anyone, should be very cautious about extrapolating policy recommendations pertaining to single case studies. . . . Policy direction has to come from a wider set of data around national, international research, local audits, evaluations, reviews, performance data. You see some patterns and trends in what's happening. . . . So that would be a recommendation – that the coroner's court has a research resource that is independent of the coroner and provides some research data and aggregate data to set in context what they're thinking . . . we're casting into doubt the efficacy of the validity of a single case to inform national policy. . . . I think that coroners have to work in the context of a range of public servants trying to make sense of what's happening for these children. To do that on the basis of sound research evidence and patterns and trends, rather than the drama of a single case which may be horrific, capture the public attention and puts them under pressure to do something meaningful with that, but actually it may not provide a sustainable solution for future problems and it could potentially add to the future problem.

According to this organisation, the "drama of a single case" should not be the sole basis for policy change. This organisation's view was shared by almost all the organisations that participated in this research (78/79). In keeping with my argument about resources for the CSNZ, organisations argued that coroners need "research resource" to assist them to identify patterns, trends and "aggregate data" in order to realise the preventive potential of their recommendations.

Research participants suggested that recommendations could be improved by requiring coroners to consider similar cases, undertaking analysis of patterns and comparative risks.[118] The following observation by the Ministry of Transport captures the participants' sentiments about comparative risks and patterns:[119]

---

[117] Interview with Chief Social Worker, Child Youth and Family, Ministry of Social Development (Jennifer Moore, 29 May 2013).

[118] Interviews with organisations, legal and medical professionals.

[119] Interview with Ministry of Transport (Jennifer Moore, 4 February 2014). Reproduced with permission of Thomson Reuters (Professional) Australia Limited, www.thomsonreuters.com.au. This article was first published by Thomson Reuters in the *Journal of Law and Medicine* as Jennifer Moore "An Empirical Approach to the New Zealand Government's Review of the Coronial Jurisdiction" (2014) 21 JLM 602. For all subscription inquiries please phone, from Australia: 1300 304 195, from Overseas: +61 2 8587 7980 or online at www.thomsonreuters.com.au/catalogue. The official PDF version of this article can also be purchased separately from Thomson Reuters.

> There's no requirement for skateboard riders to have a helmet, a mandatory helmet like a cyclist. And so Coroners are saying that this should be mandated. We've gone back and said, "No, because mandating that requirement on everybody, when, if we looked back over the last nine years there've only been two deaths. We can't justify mandating a rule that covers everybody over two deaths. And when you consider that only one of those deaths happened on a road, then it's not reasonable for us to mandate something." . . . We provided the statistics to justify our position.

The statistics enabled the Ministry of Transport to argue that the introduction of a requirement for helmets was not justified. I make no assessment about whether helmets should be required for skateboarders. Rather, the point is that an assessment of like cases over an extended period of time may improve the quality of recommendations. Investigating a single death in isolation may exaggerate the risks.[120] Recommendations based on a statistical analysis of contributory and/or causal factors common to a number of cases could have more of a preventive impact than those related to single, specific cases.

Currently, the extent to which New Zealand coroners utilise large datasets or refer to previous coronial findings to inform their recommendations is variable. Many coroners "work in silos",[121] discovering previous similar coronial cases by chance, often by listening to media reports:[122]

---

[120] Reproduced with permission of Thomson Reuters (Professional) Australia Limited, www.thomsonreuters.com.au. This article was first published by Thomson Reuters in the *Journal of Law and Medicine* as Jennifer Moore "An Empirical Approach to the New Zealand Government's Review of the Coronial Jurisdiction" (2014) 21 JLM 602. For all subscription inquiries please phone, from Australia: 1300 304 195, from Overseas: +61 2 8587 7980 or online at www.thomsonreuters.com.au/catalogue. The official PDF version of this article can also be purchased separately from Thomson Reuters.

[121] Interview with Electricity Engineers' Association (Jennifer Moore, 7 February 2013); Woodward, above n 32.

[122] Interview with Coroner Frank (Jennifer Moore, 10 October 2012). Reproduced with permission of Thomson Reuters (Professional) Australia Limited, www.thomsonreuters.com.au.

This article was first published by Thomson Reuters in the *Journal of Law and Medicine* as Jennifer Moore "An Empirical Approach to the New Zealand Government's Review of the Coronial Jurisdiction" (2014) 21 JLM 602. For all subscription inquiries please phone, from Australia: 1300 304 195, from Overseas: +61 2 8587 7980 or online at www.thomsonreuters.com.au/catalogue. The official PDF version of this article can also be purchased separately from Thomson Reuters.

> [A] coroner heard on the news that there had been an accident. He phoned me to tell me that he had done a similar one. So that was how I found out. I shouldn't have to find about it like that. . . . It's amateur at the moment. I should be able to get that information elsewhere.

Given these challenges, it is perhaps unsurprising that some coronial findings refer to previous similar cases, whereas others do not. As one organisation put it, "sometimes coroners refer to like cases and sometimes they don't".[123] According to one participant, this inconsistency "reflects the limitations of the jurisdiction rather than being a criticism of the coroners" because coroners:[124]

> do not have the resource to undertake a full commission of inquiry. . . . The resource they have (one particular death) does not fit comfortably with the ultimate objective. So you have coroners making recommendations that are in some cases ill-informed, incomplete or simply out of context. That is not a criticism of the coroners. I feel dreadfully sorry for them when they have to make public interest recommendations on the basis of a handful of parties giving evidence in relation to one particular death. It's difficult for coroners to draw in the broader context. I think the other jurisdictions like HDC recognise their limitations. . . . HDC is looking at the rights of the patient involved. The coroners are looking at the broader public interest. . . . Where the coronial jurisdiction can come into its own is by drawing data from related deaths. That can be in the form of a post-inquest process, pulling together, collecting over time, information from a number of different cases and consolidating. Or, in fact, hearing inquests into related deaths together. That's where there can be the benefit of the coronial process.

Many health sector organisations that I interviewed (19/26) reported that coroners' recommendations about clinical practice which are based on "one case do not necessarily make a good protocol"[125] and are of limited value. Analysis of "one case" in isolation, with no reference to previous cases or deaths of a similar nature, has limited preventive impact. A psychiatrist, Professor Werry, expressed concern about coroners' understanding of health risks:[126]

> The coroner issued a recommendation about huffing. I tried to get hold of the report because I wanted to know what the true frequency and age distribution of huffing actually is. This would give me an idea of what the size of the

---

[123] Interview with HealthCareOrganisation199 (Jennifer Moore, 15 February 2013).

[124] Lawyer04, above n 29.

[125] HealthCareOrganisation299, above n 41.

[126] Interview with Professor Werry (Jennifer Moore, 12 November 2012).

> risk is. I am not in favour of huffing. But before you tell the Government it should do this or that, you need to have a good idea of what the risks really are. In my view, the risks associated with huffing are inconsequential to young people compared with the risks associated with alcohol. They are not in the same universe. I get concerned about coroners' pronouncements about topics like huffing because they distort what the real risks actually are. . . . Coroners should consult with actuarial risk assessors so that they are aware of the actual risk. The risk might be 1 in 5000. Those figures should be appended to the coroners' recommendation so that the group that gets the recommendation, like the Government, knows what the risk is.

Although Werry expresses concern about coroners' understanding of the risks, it is important to note that the CSNZ devoted an issue of *Recommendations Recap* to huffing.[127] The discussion included input from the Child and Youth Mortality Review Committee and the Drug Foundation.[128] According to the then NZ Chief Coroner, there was a positive response, including from a number of major retailers who adopted a voluntary restriction on sale policy.[129] Echoing other participants' comments, the psychiatrist, as noted in the quote above, had trouble accessing the coroner's report. If a single huffing death is examined in isolation, it is difficult for the coroner to accurately assess the comparative risks related to other unhealthy, and potentially life-threatening, behaviours. I am not arguing that a single death is not a tragedy. Rather, I am illustrating why it is important for coroners to be able to access previous similar cases. Without adequate reporting systems, coroners are hindered from gathering previous cases which would help them to discern patterns. These shortcomings impact the quality and rigour of coroners' recommendations.

The quality of coroners' recommendations can be improved by taking account of previous similar findings. During an investigation into deaths caused by school buses, the coroner "researched what other coroners said first before making recommendations" because this approach "gives more credit to what you are saying if you can point to other examples of similar recommendations".[130]

Coroners who consulted previous findings were able to discern limita-

127 Email from Chief Coroner to Jennifer Moore "regarding the draft of JLM article" (19 July 2013).

128 Coroner, above n 127.

129 Coroner, above n 127.

130 Interview with Coroner Pennell (Jennifer Moore, 13 October 2012).

tions in interventions which had been used to try to prevent similar deaths. The following example is illustrative:[131]

> There is a case about a young girl who was jet skiing and who died. There were recommendations in that case. Anyone can get a high-powered speed boat without licences. I called for that to be looked at. The next day or the day after, a boy about 19, who was representing the Coast Guard, said that the coroner didn't get it right, only education was required. My response was that there have been a number of deaths like this so where has the educative value been? I used [another coroner's] findings in there. I also used [another case about] a school boy on jet skis. So I used the same information again. I've got another one coming up and I can repeat other coroners' recommendations and my own previous recommendations.

The majority of organisations interviewed stated that they were more likely to implement coroners' recommendations if the findings referred to previous similar cases. For example, a coroner's recommendations about a hunting death, which refer to earlier inquests into hunting, were implemented.[132] Several months after the release of the coroner's recommendations, the *Arms Code* was amended to incorporate the coroner's recommendations about hunting.[133]

Sudden unexpected death in infancy (SUDI) was often cited by coroners and organisations as an example where robust recommendations have been made. Participants explained that recommendations for SUDI deaths have been effective because they have involved collaboration with experts and they have also been examined for patterns. For example, Coroner Fitzpatrick stated:[134]

---

[131] Frank, above n 122. Reproduced with permission of Thomson Reuters (Professional) Australia Limited, www.thomsonreuters.com.au.

This article was first published by Thomson Reuters in the *Journal of Law and Medicine* as Jennifer Moore "An Empirical Approach to the New Zealand Government's Review of the Coronial Jurisdiction" (2014) 21 JLM 602. For all subscription inquiries please phone, from Australia: 1300 304 195, from Overseas: +61 2 8587 7980 or online at www.thomsonreuters.com.au/catalogue. The official PDF version of this article can also be purchased separately from Thomson Reuters.

[132] *Dodds* [2013] NZCorC 308.

[133] Email from Coroner Frank to Jennifer Moore regarding the draft of the JLM article (22 July 2013).

[134] Fitzpatrick, above n 34. Reproduced with permission of Thomson Reuters (Professional) Australia Limited, www.thomsonreuters.com.au.

This article was first published by Thomson Reuters in the *Journal of Law and Medicine* as Jennifer Moore "An Empirical Approach to the New Zealand Government's Review of the Coronial Jurisdiction" (2014) 21 JLM 602. For all

> In terms of our prevention role, I like the work we have done on SUDI, where there is an alliance and collaboration with researchers who know what they are doing and we are assisting that process. It is informing our understanding of the issue and it increases our chances of commenting usefully. I would hope that eventually we would be able to do a similar thing about suicide . . . we could do similar work with appropriate academics and researchers and contribute that way because I don't think that our value is in making recommendations on a case-by-case basis.

Coroners' recommendations about SUDI are useful not only because they focus on the health and safety messages about safe sleeping for babies, but also because they draw from evidence from a number of cases. Coroners referred to the "patterns" in SUDI cases.[135] Many coroners (10/15) stated that in SUDI cases they "reiterate Coroner Evans' previous findings about SUDI".[136] In my study period, there were 47 repeated coroners' recommendations about SUDI.[137]

Several organisations (4/79) cited examples of particular types of death where coroners' recommendations had identified emerging patterns and trends. For example, organisations specified cyberbullying as an example where coroners "added value" because "they noticed the trends recurring before anyone else did".[138]

While this study and previous research highlights the limitations of an evidence base that any one death is likely to present, there may be occasions where it is acceptable to focus on a specific case. For example, it may be appropriate for the coroner to focus on an isolated case in inquiries where the issues are "narrowly concentrated on local conditions – such as local road design and traffic management arrangements" or in cases involving "particular institutions – hospitals, prisons, and care homes".[139]

However, for the coroners who do consult previous coronial findings and analyse patterns, it is of concern that some of their colleagues make recommendations on a "case-by-case basis":[140]

---

subscription inquiries please phone, from Australia: 1300 304 195, from Overseas: +61 2 8587 7980 or online at www.thomsonreuters.com.au/catalogue. The official PDF version of this article can also be purchased separately from Thomson Reuters.

135 Frank, above n 122.

136 Atwood, above n 33.

137 Moore, above n 43, at 40.

138 Interview with Wellington City Council (Jennifer Moore, 31 January 2013).

139 United Kingdom, above n 90, at 96.

140 Interview with Coroner Stewart (Jennifer Moore, 12 October 2012). Reproduced with permission of Thomson Reuters (Professional) Australia Limited, www.thomsonreuters.com.au.

> I always get one of the researchers to see if she can find similar cases to check what other coroners have done. This is another important point. The worst situation is when you have two coroners making two completely different recommendations about the same thing. Credibility goes out the window. This is what worries me about the recommendations that aren't evidence-based because I don't want to be bound by those recommendations.

Inconsistent recommendations undermine "credibility" and "devalue the coronial process".[141] Organisations pointed out that this issue may "not be the coroner's fault. It might be the people who provide the information to the coroners who are not looking at other cases."[142] Organisations reported that recommendations that do not reflect "the right advice, the right input" from experts and/or organisations are considered less evidence-based, "valid",[143] and prevention-focused.[144] These organisations pointed out that when coroners do not "consult the people who really can make a difference in terms of the impact of coroners' recommendations, then the ability to get that finality for the family is somewhat reduced".[145]

Some coroners reported (8/15) that it is their standard practice to consult with organisations that may be able to inform their recommendations. Coroner Stewart described a bunk bed case which involved analysis of previous similar cases and consultation with an organisation:[146]

> I did a bunk bed case and I remember getting researchers to check whether there had been any other bunk bed cases. That was interesting because none of the findings made recommendations about bunk beds. Then I talked to Standards NZ and realised that there were standards associated with railings. I had used Standards NZ before where a baby died in a stroller. I wanted to know what warnings were put on strollers for using them as sleeping spaces for babies.

This article was first published by Thomson Reuters in the *Journal of Law and Medicine* as Jennifer Moore "An Empirical Approach to the New Zealand Government's Review of the Coronial Jurisdiction" (2014) 21 JLM 602. For all subscription inquiries please phone, from Australia: 1300 304 195, from Overseas: +61 2 8587 7980 or online at www.thomsonreuters.com.au/catalogue. The official PDF version of this article can also be purchased separately from Thomson Reuters.

[141] Interview with Mountain Safety Council (Jennifer Moore, 15 February 2013).

[142] Interview with GovtOrg08 (Jennifer Moore, 5 February 2013).

[143] Interview with Police (Jennifer Moore, 22 April 2013).

[144] Electricity Engineers' Association, above n 121.

[145] Electricity Engineers' Association, above n 121.

[146] Stewart, above n 140.

Some organisations (44/79) stated that they have provided the CSNZ with data to assist with their inquiries. This data can include statistics and information about patterns. For instance, the NZ Transport Agency has provided coroners with:[147]

> data about crash trends and crash patterns. International practice says crashes are rarely random events, so you might have a pattern of risks along a stretch of road where a crash happens. . . . Any recommendation at some point should be based on those overall patterns.

Similarly, the Police also provided coroners with information when they:[148]

> did a review of the suicides that had occurred over a 12-month period. We provided information about the patterns. We gave this to Neil [Chief Coroner]. They thought it was fantastic. But they relied on an outside agency to provide that information to them.

As the Police point out, the CSNZ "relied on an outside agency to provide" vital information to them. As I outlined earlier in this chapter, a service similar to the Victorian CPU should be introduced in NZ. This would enable consultation with stakeholders. Information about patterns could be gathered which would improve the preventive potential of coronial recommendations. The Police noted that approaches within the CSNZ have improved. However, their view is that coronial practice is overly focused on outcomes for family, rather than prevention initiatives for the community:[149]

> The risk with coroners (probably mainly a few years ago), is that they would tend to deal with a death as a single event, rather than putting it into the context of a whole lot of similar things happening. Since we've had the Chief Coroner, we've noticed that they have improved because they've looked at themed reviews, for example all the pedestrians or cyclists that have been killed and looking at what went wrong in general. That's a good approach. . . . If there was something in the Act that required coroners to look at groups of events rather than single deaths, that would be helpful. . . . Put the death into a database. What are the themes? What are the patterns? At the moment the focus seems to be on cause of death for the information of families, rather than for the community, or for people trying to prevent things from happening.

---

147 Interview with NZ Transport Agency (Jennifer Moore, 12 February 2013).
148 Police, above n 143.
149 Police, above n 143.

Like the Police, 35/79 organisations also suggested that the Coroners Act 2006 (NZ) should be amended to require coroners to consider patterns, trends and comparative risks instead of "single deaths". These organisations argued that consideration of a "wider number of cases makes the recommendations more evidence-based".[150] In the next section, I discuss how evidence-based recommendations can increase their preventive potential.

5.3.4 Evidence-based Recommendations

After the release of the NZ Law Commission's seminal 2000 report on coroners, Coroner Evans posed "practice problems" questions, several of which pertained to recommendations:[151]

> In what kinds of circumstances should we make recommendations and comments pursuant to section 15(1)(b) of the Act? To whom should such recommendations be addressed? Do they require to be supportable upon the evidence heard at inquest? Should the making of recommendations be reserved for the most serious cases? Do we water down the value attached to such recommendations by making too many?

This study's participants' response to Coroner Evans' third question was a resounding "yes". All coroners, organisations and interested parties reported that coroners' recommendations must be "evidence-based". When asked to define "evidence-based", all coroners stated that it meant information tested in court or, as Coroner Evans said in 2000, "supportable upon the evidence heard at inquest". Such evidence may include research or scientific evidence.

According to the former NZ Chief Coroner, recommendations must be "concise, precise, targeted and evidence-based".[152] As I have discussed in this chapter and in Chapter 3, my findings support his observation that recommendations must be targeted towards an identifiable person and/or organisation. The following comment from Coroner Stewart captures the sentiments of some coroners:[153]

> Recommendations have to be evidence-based. Just because you are a coroner does not mean that you are a god and that you can pluck recommendations out

---

[150] GovtOrg08, above n 142.

[151] Coroner Evans "The New Zealand Law Commission Report on Coroners 2000: Coronership in New Zealand in the New Millennium" (Australasian Coroners' Society Conference, Brisbane, 2000) at 14.

[152] Coroner, above n 77.

[153] Stewart, above n 140.

> of the air. They have got to be meaningful and evidence-based. This is why I make very few of them. . . . Evidence is about having a foundation upon which to base your recommendation rather than plucking it out of thin air or stating the obvious. That foundation could be witnesses, or research.

As I outlined in Chapter 3, the number of recommendations made varies depending on the coroner. Like Coroner Stewart, some coroners "make very few" recommendations, partly to avoid "water[ing] down the value" of recommendations. As one coroner put it, "one would not think of making a recommendation unless the evidence shows a need for it".[154]

The NZ Government's current review of the coronial jurisdiction proposes amending the Act to ensure that coroners' recommendations are specific to the evidence before the coroner.[155] This study's findings are consistent with that proposal. Coroners' recommendations have been quashed and set aside upon judicial review on the grounds that they were not supported by the evidence.[156] For example, in *Suckling v Malcolm*, the High Court quashed the coronial recommendations, holding that they improperly contained "expressions of personal opinion on matters not within the proper ambit of the Coroner's investigation".[157]

The organisations that I interviewed also commented that recommendations that are based on "personal perspectives" are unlikely to be implemented. Organisations were wary of coronial comments that recommendations were a "no-brainer" because they believed that such recommendations were not "justifiable" according to the evidence.[158] The recommendation that cyclists should wear high-visibility clothing was frequently cited by organisations (48/79) as an example of a non-evidence-based and non-justifiable recommendation.[159]

In order to avoid unfavourable judicial reviews and non-evidence-based recommendations, several coroners suggested that the structure of coroners' findings should be standardised to ensure that the evidence is clearly linked to the conclusions and recommendations. In the section on

---

154 Clarke, above n 51.

155 Cabinet Paper, above n 91, at para 271.

156 *Suckling v Malcolm* High Court Timaru CP 6/87, 13 September 1989.

157 *Suckling v Malcolm*, above n 156.

158 Interview with GovtOrg06 (Jennifer Moore, 22 February 2013).

159 *Fitzgerald* [2013] NZCorC 6. The coroner made four recommendations to the Minister of Transport, one of which was: "That just in the same manner that it is compulsory for a cyclist to wear a safety helmet when cycling on public roads, all cyclists (with the exception of those partaking in a controlled event, such as a road race) should wear high-vis clothing."

practice notes and Coroner's Court Rules, which is later in this chapter, I discuss the importance of standardisation in coronial findings. In this section, I am emphasising that coronial findings must be written so that the connections between recommendations and evidence are clear. The following examples from Coroner Reid demonstrate how to achieve such connections between the evidence and recommendations:[160]

> There needs to be a correlation between the evidence and the recommendation. The reader should not be left wondering how and why the coroner made the recommendation. It should be evident from reading the expert opinion and evidence in the finding. In the *Piper Chieftain* case[161] in the recommendations, I did a preamble for each recommendation, drawing from the evidence, so that it was clear. We need to get consistency in drafting. It is more than the template. The template is the setting, but there is an art to extracting comments and recommendations from the evidence. If you look at the *Timothy Stone* case[162] and go to the second to last page with the recommendations, then go to the last page "the above recommendations are directed to skiers generally. . .". I ran these recommendations past the expert witness and he came back with useful suggestions relating to the NZ ski instructors' alliance so that came in as a result of his suggestion. These recommendations are very clearly based on the evidence. If you look back at the evidence, you will see where they come from. The protective helmets recommendation was based on evidence on that point. The Mt Cheeseman Ski Club recommendations were related to terrain management evidence. So all the recommendations are evidence-based.

This coroner's description highlights that "consistency in drafting" is necessary. It also points out the importance of consulting with expert witnesses about proposed recommendations. In the *Timothy Stone* case, the coroner redrafted his recommendations on the basis of the experts' input. Other NZ coroners also follow this practice. After the research interviews, two coroners commented that they had altered their practice on the basis of my preliminary findings on this point. For instance, Coroner Dymond noted that he had "taken up your suggestion that you don't make a recommendation to somebody until you tell the person what you're recommending and make sure it's workable or in the right language and so on".[163]

The organisations that I interviewed overwhelmingly preferred coroners to consult with them about proposed recommendations. In section 5.3.8 "Evaluation and Feedback", which is later in this chapter, I highlight

---

160 Interview with Coroner Reid (Jennifer Moore, 30 October 2012).

161 New Zealand Office of the Auditor-General *Responses to the Coroner's Recommendations on the June 2003 Air Adventures Crash* (2008).

162 Stone [2012] NZCorC 187.

163 Interview with Coroner Dymond (Jennifer Moore, 16 October 2012).

that organisations prefer to provide feedback during the coronial process. Organisations want to provide coroners with evidence to inform their recommendations. The National Poisons Centre provided an illustrative example:[164]

> The most recent work we did with the coroner in Wellington over the helium death. There was some very good research that had come out of Australia and some other countries. I was able to give them the figures on deaths in Australia and northern Europe. . . . So that was really spot on.

Similarly, many organisations want to provide coroners with research evidence to inform their recommendations:[165]

> Instead of having a sound research base to recommendations, they can come up with a bright idea that might sound right, but according to the research, is wrong. An example is the blood alcohol level for driving in NZ. The level in NZ is stupidly high. We end up with hundreds of unnecessary deaths and injuries on the road because of our unusually high level and because of the current legislation. Coroners could look at international research. Every international study says the same thing. The ability to look at the commonalities of deaths and injuries relating to the blood alcohol level could provide coroners with powerful recommendations. But this sort of powerful recommendation that could be made, hasn't been done.

Organisations argued that research evidence can be used to formulate "powerful" recommendations. Some coroners worried that their colleagues "do not think about research-based evidence".[166] This concern reinforces the importance of consultation with organisations to discuss the evidence. The following example demonstrates how the coroner's proposed recommendation was reformulated on the basis of consultation and expert input:[167]

> **Coroner:** I think evidence can be in the form of witnesses and in the form of research. When I feel that there is a sufficient academic base that is publicly available. The research has been done. I didn't need an expert. In other areas, I think that we should be calling evidence on recommendations. Whether it's a medical or engineering report, we should call the evidence. An example is the case of the fishermen who were being swept off a rock by the beach because they were accessing the rocks by a cable. It was a big thick wire that had been erected over a cave. It was difficult for rescuers to access. The cable had been

---

164 Temple (National Poisons Centre), above n 107.
165 Interview with David Cliff (Police) (Jennifer Moore, 22 April 2013).
166 Aitken, above n 111.
167 Stewart, above n 140.

taken down several times by the local council. We went out to the beach to look at it. We had about three deaths there. I went to the inquest thinking that we could fix it by getting rid of the cable. We called the harbour master and Surf Life Saving NZ. In the course of the inquest there was discussion about whether it would be safe to remove the cable and the wire. There was the comment that if the wire and cable were removed it might increase the risk because then the fishermen would try to access the fishing spot by going over the headland and that was even more dangerous. So that complicated matters!
Jennifer: Gosh! What did you do?
Coroner: I said someone needs to analyse this properly. I made a recommendation that there should be liaison between the parties with a view to assessing the risks involved in removing the cable. I felt that there was more evidence and information that needed to be gathered before I could make a recommendation.

This coroner recommended that the organisations gather further evidence in order to decide how to remedy the situation. This consultation, and approach to the evidence, increases the likelihood that the outcome will prevent future similar deaths. The following description from Maritime NZ captures organisations' preferred consultative approach:[168]

> We want to provide input and we want to provide evidence to assist the coroner. Agencies like us will spend lots of time analysing accident data to prove whether or not different types of interventions work. This can help the coroner to make evidence-based recommendations.

The *Queensland State Coroner's Guidelines* are consistent with the research participants' preferences. These guidelines encourage coroners to "seek input from agencies who will be required to consider whether and if so how the recommendation can be implemented".[169] Obtaining such evidence from organisations has the additional advantage that recommendations will be based on patterns and trends and, therefore, prevention-focused.

However, several coroners (4/15) pointed out that their decision-making about whether to call experts and, if so, how many, and gathering the right evidence is not always easy. Coroner Oldfield's description of evidence and experts captures the complexity of this decision-making:[170]

> I think there are times when you do not require expert evidence to make an evidence-based recommendation. For example, with the scrum machine case I had evidence about what happened on the day. I had evidence from the school and OH&S. It was enough evidence for me to say that the machine was unstable

168 Interview with Maritime NZ (Jennifer Moore, 19 February 2013).
169 *Queensland State Coroner's Guidelines* (2013) at chapter 9, p 21.
170 Oldfield, above n 70.

and potentially dangerous. But I had trawled through every word of what I had to get there.

On the other hand, I would never have considered making recommendations in that health care case, if I had not had careful and skilled evidence from experts about the medicine and the guidelines.

And then there are other cases where I either would or wouldn't make a recommendation without expert evidence. For example, I dealt with the death of a man who hit a wire rope barrier on the road and there is a lobby against the danger of wire rope barriers. I got expert evidence in relation to the issues because if I were to make recommendations about wire rope barriers, I needed to be sure and, in fact, in that case I did not make recommendations in relation to wire rope barriers because I was satisfied on the basis of the evidence that it would not be warranted. I decided that on the basis of the expert evidence and the facts.

The evidence has to be based on the facts of the case and the coroner needs to decide how much evidence she or he needs to make the recommendation. . . . Sometimes it is hard. At what point do you move from one level of evidence to another? When do you need expert evidence? When do you need to pin your recommendation on that expert evidence? When do you need more expert evidence? For example, I have a case that has haunted me. I can't do it any better, but it was a suicide of a young teenager and everything had failed her. The ultimate failure, possibly, was at the school. I am not necessarily satisfied it was an ultimate failure. She was seen by a school counsellor. The counsellor assessed the risk of further self-harm as low. The counsellor arranged to see her the next day, but the child hanged herself overnight. The counsellor acted in accordance with the guidelines. I did get some expert advice. It was around all the things that had failed the child. I did make comment in the end, but it was hinged on the expert advice – that a school counsellor cannot, on their own, observe a child all the time. I could go on and on and get more expert advice, but sometimes you need to go with your gut and say that someone needed to keep that child safe. I have thought about it so much that I am probably not a safe driver anymore. When should I stop?

Some coronial recommendations did not appear to be based on evidence. For example, in a transport accident case, the coroner makes a "generalised recommendation because [he had] no evidence before" him:[171]

I recommend that the police consider formalising their policy and produce guidelines for officers to follow when stopping drivers who are in breach of restricted licences. This is a somewhat generalised recommendation because I have no evidence before me which would enable me to make a more specific recommendation. But I have confidence that the police will consider whether it is necessary to make a formal policy and produce guidelines or whether, as stated by Inspector Wallace, police have already addressed the issue by increas-

[171] *Kingi* [2011] NZCorC 90.

ing expectations that drivers who are stopped while in breach of the terms of their restricted licence should be prevented from driving on.

Health sector organisations emphasised that their calls for input and consultation did not mean that they were not supportive of external independent scrutiny of their practices which could provide insight into the operation of health care systems.[172] Some organisations (53/79) also emphasised that their input is intended to facilitate discussion during the coronial process. They did not expect that coronial findings or recommendations would always accord with organisations' input. The following exchange between the researcher and an organisation demonstrates the distinction:[173]

> **Jennifer:** Does this mean that coroners' recommendations should be *based* on industry expertise?
> **EEA:** Well I think to me that sounds almost a bit arrogant, because in a sense, I don't have a problem with third parties looking at what we do and saying you need to improve. *It needs to be considered and discussed with the industry, rather than saying it's got to be based on industry outcomes.* Because if the coroner looks at it and he says, "Well actually I know you guys do a lot of good work but I think you're short here," then we might just have to put our hand up and say, "Well actually you're right."

Organisations also pointed out that their input may differ from the views of other experts and/or interested parties. The coroner will hear evidence about the events in question and their relationship to the death. S/he can hear evidence about the problems in the case and the pros and cons of various solutions to the problem. Such evidence can inform the coroner's decision-making about whether recommendations are necessary and, if so, how to formulate those recommendations. However, different parties may place greater emphasis on specific aspects of evidence.

Deaths at nursing homes sometimes generate this situation.[174] The family, nursing home, health professionals and Ministry of Health may all have different views about the relevance and importance of evidence. The family may wish to comment on all aspects of the care given to their relative, including medical, recreational and dietary for the entire time that the deceased lived in the home. The organisation (for example the nursing home) may wish to provide clinical evidence and data about adverse events to assist the coroner. However, the organisations interviewed

---

172 Moore, above n 43, at 48.
173 Electricity Engineers' Association, above n 121.
174 Franklin Moskoff and James Young "The Roles of Coroner and Counsel in Coroner's Court" (1987–1988) 30 Crim LQ 190.

accepted that the coroner will, and should, reach his/her own decision about the weight to be placed upon the different parties' evidence.

Interestingly, while many health sector organisations interviewed approved of external coronial scrutiny, they also noted that recommendations which were inconsistent with clinical evidence and practice were less likely to be implemented. The following example was typical of many health sector organisations' views:[175]

> This has been discussed at the National Chief Medical Officer meetings. We've sometimes discussed some of the recommendations in other parts of New Zealand, especially when we've not agreed with the recommendations that the coroners make because we feel from a medical point of view, they're not evidence-based and not really in keeping with what we can do in practice. It's hard to action those ones.

These concerns were foreshadowed in the health sector submissions on the Coroners Bill 2006. For example, the NZ Chief Medical Officers' and Health and Disability Commissioner's submissions argued that coroners must have easy access to clinical expertise and use a robust selection process for obtaining experts.[176] As I pointed out earlier in this chapter, the quality of information available to coroners correlates with the quality of their recommendations. Health sector submitters prefer coroners to invoke section 83 of the Coroners Act (NZ) to use specialist clinical advisers to sit with, and help, the coroner.[177] However, the coroners interviewed explained that financial constraints often prevent them from fully utilising this option. In addition, advice given by a specialist adviser may be given any weight the coroner thinks fit.[178] These issues provide further weight to my proposal to introduce a service similar to the Victorian CLS.

During interviews with health sector organisations, one recommendation was almost universally cited as an example of a recommendation that

---

[175] Interview with HealthCareOrganisation599 (Jennifer Moore, 10 December 2012).

[176] NZ Chief Medical Officers and Colin McArthur *Submission to the Justice and Electoral Select Committee on the Coroners Bill* (2005) at 1; Helena Strange and Health and Disability Commissioner *Submission to the Justice and Electoral Select Committee on the Coroners Bill* (2005) at 1.

[177] Coroners Act 2006 (NZ) s 83; (2 August 2006) 633 *New Zealand Parliamentary Debates* 4666. Section 83(1) of the Act states that: "If satisfied that it is desirable to do so, the chief coroner may, on the recommendation of a coroner, appoint a cultural, legal, medical, or other specialist adviser to sit with and help the coroner at an inquest by giving advice."

[178] Coroners Act 2006 (NZ) s 83(5).

was inconsistent with clinical evidence and unlikely to be implemented. The recommendation was made after an 80-year-old woman died of a subdural haematoma caused by an accidental fall:[179]

> To: All District Health Boards and to the Medical Council of New Zealand, for dissemination to all hospitals and doctors in private practice.
> 1. That all clinicians should adopt a very low threshold in deciding whether to request a CT scan for elderly patients presenting a head injury.

A DHB made the following comments about this recommendation:[180]

> There was one in particular that agitated nearly all of us. It was about clinical practice about CT scanning after head injury. It was a recommendation that basically said that everybody who falls over, well, I'm exaggerating, but, everyone who falls over gets a CT scan. We thought, "Hang on guys, we've got pretty good protocols in place from the College of Emergency Medicine." That recommendation stands out as being one where the coroner was really firm about our threshold for CT scans in elderly head injuries. We thought, "Well, actually, on the basis of one case, does not necessarily make a good protocol." . . . There has to be communication between DHBs and coroners, otherwise the recommendations can be misguided.

Like this DHB, many health sector organisations (20/26) reported that they were not adequately consulted about clinical evidence during the coronial process, which was particularly problematic if the coroner made recommendations about clinical practice. Improved communication between coroners and clinicians, and ease of access to clinical expertise for the CSNZ, could enhance the preventive potential of coroners' recommendations and also improve quality of care and patient safety.[181]

In aviation, commentators have similarly complained when coroners' recommendations have not reflected aviation best practice, evidence or adequate consultation with industry experts. In an inquiry about a Tiger Moth aircraft crash,[182] an interested party commented:[183]

> This strikes me as the coroner making comments in an area in which he has no expertise at all. The comment "recovery from a spin, once encountered, was highly unlikely" shows his ignorance. Spins are not "encountered", they must

---

179 *Rippey* [2011] NZCorC 10.
180 HealthCareOrganisation299, above n 41.
181 Moore, above n 43, at 48.
182 *Copland* [2011] NZCorC 192.
183 Interview with InterestedParty1 (Jennifer Moore, 14 January 2013).

> be induced by mishandling the controls, either intentionally or unintentionally. In this case, I suspect it was unintentional because regulations require any aerobatics to be performed above a minimum altitude and in an area clear of other traffic. In the circuit at an airfield is not permitted. Did the pilot have a reputation for ignoring the rules? If not, this was probably unintentional. The question now is why? I would want to know the wind direction and strength at the time and where in the circuit this happened. A Tiger Moth is a slow aircraft and is greatly affected by the wind. There are well-known visual illusions caused by the wind taught to every student pilot. Flying downwind can give the impression of adequate speed, but this is from looking at the ground going by; the actual aircraft airspeed might be very low.
>
> The other well-known trap is when turning from base leg onto final. If the centre line is being overshot, the tendency is to apply rudder in order to increase the turn rate. This is exactly the way to enter an intentional spin – slow down, apply "g" and apply some rudder so one wing stalls before the other. I expect the NZ Accident Investigation Department were involved. They would have looked at other factors apart from those above like the pilot's history, medical reports, recent experience, whether dual controls were fitted and could the passenger interfere. More needs to be said about this in the coroner's report. There is a lot more to this than just "encountering a spin".

By contrast, in a coronial inquiry involving an Airborne Windsports Edge XT-912 microlight aircraft which crashed on Gibbs Hill, Tasman District while on a commercial scenic flight,[184] the industry perception was that the coroner "had done his homework, consulted with experts, and studied the accident report in detail".[185]

Recommendations that are evidence-based are more likely to achieve greater preventive impact because organisations reported that they will typically implement evidence-based recommendations. For example, the Midwifery Council noted that if recommendations "are well-founded, well-communicated, well-evidenced, and they're feasible within the context of practice, then I would do everything I can to implement them".[186]

Producing "well-evidenced" recommendations, though, is not always easy. Despite the cultural depictions of forensic scientists and medical examiners as objective mediators of scientific truth in television shows such as *CSI*, *Body of Proof* and *Crossing Jordan*, there is uncertainty in medical science.[187] There are also different types of medical evidence

---

[184] *Charles* [2012] NZCorC 40.

[185] InterestedParty1, above n 183.

[186] Interview with Midwifery Council (Jennifer Moore, 17 December 2012).

[187] Jennifer Moore "Handling Uncertainty: Standard and Local Practices in the Case of Libido and Contraception in Evidence-based Decision-making" (2005) 14 Health Sociology Review 174.

(accorded differing levels of weight), with the randomised controlled trial typically considered the gold standard in the evidentiary hierarchy. Likewise, various types of legal evidence are given different probative value. According to Professor Werry, there is a difference between the legal and scientific definitions of "evidence". The former refers to "factoids collected by the police for court", while the latter is "governed by a set of rules which determine its probable degree of accuracy. The gold standard is that of the Cochrane collaboration."[188]

Several health sector organisations complained that their evidence is weighted unfavourably by the Coroner's Court. For example, the Midwifery Council pointed out that the value placed on midwifery evidence varies across coroners. They described their experience as follows:[189]

> We have such trouble in the Coroner's Court because they really do think that when the doctor says a pregnant woman shouldn't go more than five days, that's the evidence. There's no evidence for that! So we would then have to get up and say this expert witness is not evidence-based. But our evidence base, which is midwifery, isn't valued in the same way as them.

The Midwifery Council's experience arguably reflects the "boundary work" that has been undertaken to demarcate "science" from "non-science".[190] Their description suggests what theorists call "the medicalisation of labour".[191] Their experience may also be a reflection of the privileged positioning of gold standard scientific evidence in medical decision-making. "Experience" is not privileged in the "evidence–experience" binary. In analyses of how residents "learn to doctor", sociologists of medicine have shown that pure distinctions between informal experience and formal experience do not really exist.[192] "Evidence" and "experience" are complementary resources.

However, the issue of whether "experience" counts as "evidence" persists in medicine and law. I discuss standardisation in law later in this chapter. The standardisation movement in medicine emerged in health

---

188 Werry, above n 126.

189 Midwifery Council, above n 186.

190 Thomas F. Gieryn "Boundary Work and the Demarcation of Science from Non-science: Strains and Interests in Professional Identities of Scientists" (1983) 48 American Sociological Review 781.

191 J.M. Usher *Body Talk: The Material and Discursive Regulation of Sexuality, Madness and Reproduction* (Routledge, London and New York, 1997).

192 Stefan Timmermans and Alison Angell "Evidence-based Medicine, Clinical Uncertainty, and Learning to Doctor" (2001) 42 Journal of Health and Social Behaviour 342.

care in the late 1980s.[193] Its guidelines, decision tools and recommendations for health practitioners on how to practise medicine are based on a systematic evaluation of scientific evidence. The key objective of guidelines and decision tools is to standardise decision-making across practitioners and time. Proponents of evidence-based medicine tend to be critical of basing clinical decisions on experience.[194] A small number of coroners (4/15) defined "evidence" in the Coroner's Court as including experience. For example, Coroner Pennell defined "evidence" as follows:[195]

> Empirical evidence or scientific backing. Genuine, long-term experience, or a combination of both. Case law, evidence heard in court.

Social scientists and philosophers of science have long questioned whether experience can ever be disentangled from what counts as "evidence".[196] Calling the artificial distinction between "experience" and "evidence" into question, two Australian doctors provide an amusing parody in the *British Medical Journal*.[197] The authors offer seven alternative grounds for standardised decision-making: eminence-based medicine (base your decisions on seniority), vehemence-based medicine (substituting browbeating your colleagues for evidence), eloquence-based medicine, providence-based medicine (letting God decide), diffidence-based medicine (do nothing from a sense of despair), nervousness-based medicine and confidence-based medicine (restricted to surgeons).[198] This parody suggests that evidence-based medicine interacts, and competes, with other elements and factors in medical decision-making. Likewise, evidence-based coroners' recommendations and coronial decision-making interacts with other elements such as "genuine, long-term experience".

Sometimes there is conflicting scientific evidence. Occasionally there is no gold standard evidence, or any scientific evidence. Very few health sector organisations (2/26) commented on these limitations. The two health sector organisations that did recognise the uncertainties in evidence,

---

[193] D. Sackett and others *Evidence-based Medicine: How to Practice and Teach EBM* (Churchill Livingstone, New York, 1997); Moore, above n 187.

[194] Sackett and others, above n 193.

[195] Pennell, above n 130.

[196] Patricia Benner and Christine Tanner "Clinical Judgment: How Expert Nurses Use Intuition" (1987) 87 American Journal of Nursing 23; Timmermans and Angell, above n 192; P. Atkinson *Medical Talk and Medical Work: The Liturgy of the Clinic* (Thousand Oaks, London, 1995).

[197] David Isaacs and Dominic Fitzgerald "Seven Alternatives to Evidence-based Medicine" (1999) 319 British Medical Journal 1618.

[198] Isaacs and Fitzgerald, above n 197.

reframed "evidence-based" as "evidence-based *opinion*" or "evidence-informed" because "80% of maternity practice doesn't have good evidence for it".[199] Likewise, a DHB explained that "most of the population believes that medical opinion is set in stone; whereas, in fact, the evidence base for 40% of what we do is zero".[200]

Despite these challenges with evidence, all participants noted that when gold standard evidence is available, it should inform coronial recommendations. Participants observed that non-evidence-based recommendations reduce the validity and impact of quality recommendations. Coroner Dymond described an illustrative example:[201]

> A coroner called for snow tyres to be abolished. . . . He might want them outlawed in his jurisdiction, but, in the far South, they're almost compulsory. There are hundreds if not thousands of vehicles in Central Otago in the winter equipped with snow tyres, including things like emergency vehicles. So you put out a comment like that and it reduces the impact of valid recommendations. People say, "Here's another stupid coroner."

What should be considered the gold standard coroner's recommendation? There are various options, such as: (1) the recommendation is robust and evidence-based; (2) the recommendation is internally consistent; (3) the recommendation stimulates action towards prevention; (4) the recommendation reduces deaths and injury.[202] My view (supported by the empirical evidence) is that coronial recommendations should be evidence-based and prevention-focused. In particular, the principles for recommendation formulation should include:[203]

1. targeting an identifiable organisation and/or person
2. providing a prevention solution
3. outlining the level of regulation that the recommendation is directed towards, for example legislation, policy, standards, guidelines, advocacy, and so on

---

199 Midwifery Council, above n 186.
200 HealthCareOrganisation299, above n 41.
201 Dymond, above n 163.
202 Bugeja, above n 81, at 253.
203 Samantha Hauge and Lyndal Bugeja "Enabling Public Health and Safety through the Coroners' Death Investigation System: The Principles and Practice of the Coroners Prevention Unit" (Asia Pacific Coroners Conference, Australia, 2011).

4. outlining the strategy for how the recommendation could be implemented, for example environment, product and/or design change, education or training, behaviour modification
5. identifying the priority population at risk
6. identifying the risk or contributing factors that the intervention will mitigate.

The following example does not apply the above injury prevention principles: "Lastly, in stating the obvious, chewing one's food properly before swallowing goes without saying."[204] By contrast, a theoretical example of a coroner's recommendation which applies public health/prevention principles is:

> Surf Life Saving NZ amend section 11 of the Guidelines for the Safe Pool Operation 2001 to require the installation of non-slip surfaces on all diving boards and towers to prevent incidents of slips, trips and falls amongst patrons and staff of public swimming pools.

This recommendation targets an appropriate organisation (Surf Life Saving NZ), which is the primary drowning prevention agency. It provides a prevention solution: the installation of non-slip surfaces. It outlines the level of regulation: policy reform. Modification to the environment is identified as the strategy for implementation. The patrons and staff of public swimming pools are identified as the priority populations at risk. The recommendation identifies risk or contributing factors as falls and drownings. Surf Life Saving NZ could be consulted by the coroner and provide evidence to assist in the formulation of such a recommendation.

The consultation with experts and organisations required to formulate evidence-based recommendations may delay the coronial process. Delays are costly and may be undesirable and stressful for parties, particularly families. Therefore, there must be a balance between consultation and efficiency. I discuss delays in the next section.

5.3.5 Delays

A significant number of organisations (51/79) and interested parties (5/8) reported that delays in the coronial process prevent recommendations from achieving their preventive potential. The following comments from a lawyer illustrate many participants' concerns:[205]

---

204 *Erepeta* [2008] NZCorC 43.
205 Interview with Lawyer02 (Jennifer Moore, 10 September 2012).

> At the moment, the coroner's role is problematic because of delays. By the time coroners have heard cases and issued recommendations, often organisations and health professionals have already identified changes that need to be implemented to reduce the chances of future deaths. For example, if HDC is investigating, the coroner may await the HDC outcome. The organisation will think about how the death occurred and what to do to prevent future deaths. This will often happen before the coroner makes recommendations. Delays are inhibiting coroners from achieving the Act's purpose.

Many health sector organisations' (24/26) comments were consistent with the lawyer's observations. For example, a senior clinician explained that because "the coronial stuff comes out a long time after we're done, we've almost always done our own analysis and put measures in place to ensure there are no similar adverse events in the future".[206] As I explained earlier in this chapter, access to clinical expertise was introduced to the Victorian, Australian Coroner's Court in order to improve procedural delays, and evaluative research has found this strategy has been successful. This provides further support for my recommendation that a similar service should be introduced in the CSNZ.

The participants who did not agree that delays impact the preventive potential of recommendations were concerned about the tension between quality and timeliness. As Child, Youth and Family stated, "if you do a lot of things quickly, you'll most certainly sacrifice quality."[207]

Coroners specified various factors that contributed to delays:

- the time-consuming nature of inquests (compared with chambers inquiries)
- waiting for other organisations such as HDC to complete their investigations into deaths
- inequitable coronial case loads in different parts of NZ
- the Ministry of Justice's counting methodologies for open versus closed cases.

Several coroners emphasised the importance of holding inquests despite their time-consuming nature. For example, Coroner Dymond described the process as follows:[208]

---

206 Interview with Waikato Hospital (Jennifer Moore, 12 December 2012).

207 Chief Social Worker, Child, Youth and Family, Ministry of Social Development, above n 117.

208 Dymond, above n 163.

> We take justice out to the people and hold inquest hearings in the centre of a population for the benefit of families. . . . So although Auckland have a greater body count, they've got no idea of the mileage that we do. . . . I don't think anybody would doubt that the ideal for a coroner is to conduct an inquest in open court. . . . I won't say they [families] enjoy the experience, but they actually benefit from the experience, and I don't think I've ever found anybody in the previous 25 years who has ever regretted coming to an inquest. It's a closure, it's a catharsis. . . . It's very easy to convince the family that they don't want an inquest in open court – they want a hearing on the papers. Therefore life is a lot easier for us. We don't have to travel. . . . I can sit here, get the information in, dictate a finding, and flick it out. That's what effectively we're being forced to do by the constraints on resources and time. When we go to inquest, even if we drive in our own time early in the morning or late at night, we're still away. We try to do the routine work as best as we can, but it takes time and it's not easy.

The "constraints on resources and time" adversely impact on coronial processes. The NZ public demands, and deserves, a high-performing coronial system. This study's findings demonstrate that providing adequate resources and access to expertise (such as clinical advice) would reduce delays in the coronial system. Introduction of a service similar to the CPU would mean that the CSNZ had staff dedicated to consultation with stakeholders. In Victoria, Australia, this consultation has improved the preventive potential of coroners' recommendations. Some organisations conceptualise their preventive goals as aligned with coroners' prophylactic function. I explore this topic in the next section.

5.3.6 Alignment of Prevention Goals

Some organisations interviewed for this study reported that their organisational prevention policies were aligned with the coronial statutory prophylactic function. For instance, a government organisation commented that "the Coroners Act and our Act have similar focuses which include safety. We are both in the business of improving safety."[209] Similarly, the Department of Conservation observed that the coroners' "prevention focus is entirely consistent with our national approach . . . our whole focus . . . is around prevention".[210]

Organisations hoped that the coronial process would foster relationships with coroners which would focus on prevention strategies. For example, some health care organisations (14/26) reported that it is useful

209 GovtOrg08, above n 142.

210 Interview with Sean Goddard (Department of Conservation) (Jennifer Moore, 14 May 2013).

to work with coroners to produce preventive recommendations and outcomes:[211]

> It's a question of joining forces. If you're talking about deaths that occur as the result of a kid not being immunised, then the coroner's office should join hands with the paediatricians and get it out on a broad front. And if you're talking about wearing helmets, again contact those of us who deal with the emergency situations that result from not wearing helmets and say, "Look, let's get this out there and take preventive action." And so as opposed to just the coroner saying it, the coroner should potentially approach involved stakeholders and say, "I'm going to make this recommendation, do you agree with it and would you be happy to endorse it?" Share the learning to prevent deaths and publicise the potential risks.

Similarly, Maritime NZ stated that their "goals are aligned with the coroners'. We both want to prevent similar deaths from occurring."[212] They "actively monitor and use coroners' inquiries to assist with what we are doing". Maritime NZ "sees coroners as another body that helps advance [their] cause which is to help avoid people getting killed on boats". Organisations such as Surf Life Saving NZ, the Mountain Safety Council and the Department of Conservation also conceptualised their prevention roles as dovetailing with the coronial prophylactic function.

Surf Life Saving NZ is developing a website, CodeBlue, which is dedicated to prevention and targets "higher-level bodies like coroners, territorial authorities and councils".[213] CodeBlue is a web-based information management system, which stores all the data and recommendations from aquatic risk assessments conducted throughout NZ.[214] The website allows stakeholders to review completed risk assessments and collaborate to implement the recommendations to reduce the risk of drowning and injury in NZ.[215] Surf Life Saving NZ want to work with the CSNZ to prevent morbidity and mortality:[216]

> We don't just want coroners making recommendations when someone drowns. We want to try to involve coroners to prevent people from drowning. I guess that depends on how they see their role too in terms of providing some support

---

211 Waikato Hospital, above n 206.
212 Maritime NZ, above n 168.
213 Surf Life Saving NZ "CodeBlue" Code/Blue Aquatic Risk Management <http://www.codeblue.org.nz/>; Interview with Surf Life Saving NZ (Jennifer Moore, 11 February 2013).
214 Surf Life Saving NZ, above n 213.
215 Surf Life Saving NZ, above n 213.
216 Surf Life Saving NZ, above n 213.

> for that prior to deaths actually occurring. There will always be drownings. It's not zero risk, but we do our best to try to stop drownings.

Surf Life Saving NZ's comments are similar to other organisations who want to "involve coroners" in their prevention endeavours. Many such organisations referred to coroners as "partners" in prevention.[217] The NZ Transport Agency, for example, argued that coroners can maintain their judicial independence while working in a partnership.[218] Likewise, the Department of Conservation developed the Outdoor Safety Code: five simple safety messages for the outdoors which aim to reduce incidents.[219] The Department of Conservation's view was that if coroners cited this Code in their recommendations, it would be "an incredibly powerful mechanism for getting the prevention message across".[220] Throughout the research process, I introduced senior representatives from organisations to the Chief Coroner to foster these collaborative prevention-focused strategies.

Many organisations view coroners as "a mechanism to get action" for their prevention goals.[221] This often involves using coroners' recommendations as an opportunity to lobby the Government for resources and funding.[222]

Many organisations (41/79) reported that they analyse coroners' findings and recommendations in order to further their organisational prevention goals. The *Dive Magazine NZ* and website include full coronial findings about diving-related deaths.[223] The editor of *Dive Magazine NZ* explained that they include coroners' recommendations because "divers want to read this stuff. They want to know what went wrong on dives so that hopefully they don't make the same mistake."[224] *Dive Magazine* editorials have discussed what can be learned from coroners' recommendations. Likewise, the Ministry of Health read coronial findings to "look

---

217 NZ Transport Agency, above n 147.

218 NZ Transport Agency, above n 147.

219 Goddard (Department of Conservation), above n 210.

220 Goddard (Department of Conservation), above n 210.

221 Surf Life Saving NZ, above n 213.

222 For example, Goddard (Department of Conservation), above n 210; Temple (National Poisons Centre), above n 107.

223 *Dive Magazine NZ* "Dive New Zealand : Coroners and Accident reports" Dive NZ <http://www.divenewzealand.com/index.asp?s1=safety&s2=Coroner%27s+and+Accident+Reports>.

224 Interview with Editor, *Dive Magazine* (Jennifer Moore, 5 February 2013).

for patterns . . . common issues that are emerging, so that for the benefit of future patients, we can make changes".[225]

Some organisations remarked that changes could only be made for the benefit of the community if coroners and organisations formulate "consistent safety messages".[226] Several organisations, such as the NZ Transport Agency, provided us with reports outlining their safety messages, which they would like coroners to consider when formulating recommendations. Organisations would prefer "strategic alignment" between their safety messages and coroners', particularly "when coroners comment on health and safety in the media".[227] This approach will increase the preventive potential of coroners' recommendations because the safety messages communicated to the public are consistent.

However, organisations emphasised that these consistent safety messages must be based on prevention principles. Although most coroners (11/15) stated that recognising a preventable death is "obvious", their recommendations were not systematically consistent with public health principles. Coroners' recommendations rarely identify the population at risk or whether the proposed countermeasure addresses an identified risk factor. Practice notes which encourage coroners to consult with interested parties may assist coroners to develop recommendations based on prevention principles. I discuss this issue in the next section.

5.3.7 Practice Notes, Rules, Guidelines and Standardisation

Coroners are not required to observe the rules of procedure and evidence which apply in other courts of record.[228] However, the 2008 Ontario Goudge report is an important reminder of the unacceptability of death investigations that are not rigorous and that are the product of inadequately evaluated expert evidence.[229]

On the one hand, research participants were generally positive about the inquisitorial nature of coronial inquiries. On the other hand, there was overwhelming support from organisations (75/79) and interested parties (7/8) for coroners to observe procedural rules to foster consistency and standardisation in coronial practice.

---

225 Ministry of Health, above n 37.

226 Goddard (Department of Conservation), above n 210; Mountain Safety Council, above n 141; NZ Transport Agency, above n 147.

227 NZ Transport Agency, above n 147.

228 Freckelton and Ranson, above n 17, at 570.

229 Stephen Goudge *Inquiry into Paediatric Forensic Pathology in Ontario* (2008).

The NZ coronial jurisdiction does not have official guidelines or Coroner's Court Rules. The former NZ Chief Coroner explained that there is the Bench Book, which provides suggestions about coronial practice.[230] There is also a newsletter in which he includes "suggestions about what to think about when [coroners] are doing Y, or to be aware that there has been a new development in a certain area".[231] In addition, there is facility in the Act for the Chief Coroner to issue practice notes. The then NZ Chief Coroner stated that he has:[232]

> only ever issued one, which was about the role of the coroner in after-hours mode. I have steered clear, for better or worse, of issuing any other practice notes or guidelines, other than through regular newsletters and training.

Subsequent to the interview, the Chief Coroner has issued further practice notes. Organisations (75/79) and interested parties (7/8) were supportive of the Chief Coroner issuing more practice notes and/or the introduction of Coroner's Court Rules or guidelines to promote consistency and standardisation. However, only 6/15 coroners supported the Chief Coroner issuing more practice notes.

Inconsistency in coronial practice has been highlighted by commentators.[233] Debates about the Coroners Bill 2006 reveal that an important purpose of the proposed legislation was to assure families that:[234]

> They will be subject to a standardised process that is the same the length and breadth of the country. This legislation will set down guidelines for professional standards to which coroners will adhere . . . the terms under which coroners currently operate and what may be called their practice guidelines have never really been established.

The intended purpose of the Chief Coroner's practice notes was to "get consistent processes and protocols that will help get consistency across the country".[235] The rationale for the Justice and Electoral Committee's recommendation to introduce a provision into the Coroners Bill 2006 requiring coroners to have regard to practice notes was to "inform and promote

230 Coroner, above n 77.
231 Coroner, above n 77.
232 Coroner, above n 77.
233 New Zealand Law Commission, above n 20; Department of Justice and Community Safety *Review of the Coroners Act 1997 – Discussion Paper* (2008).
234 (25 July 2006) 632 *New Zealand Parliamentary Debates* 4394.
235 (10 May 2006) 631 *New Zealand Parliamentary Debates* 2972.

consistency of coronial practice".[236] In the current review of the coronial jurisdiction, the Minister for Courts also proposes introducing practice notes to achieve consistency in coronial practice. There was consensus among the lawyers and organisations that I interviewed that the Coroner's Court procedures lacked transparency and that coronial practices were ad hoc and inconsistent.

An important issue is whether there is a need for procedural rules or whether the power of the Chief Coroner to issue practice directions is sufficient. Organisations (70/75) and interested parties (5/7) preferred the introduction of procedural rules. Participants were concerned that coroners need only "have regard to" practice notes issued by the Chief Coroner.[237]

My view is that the introduction of Coroner's Court Rules would provide greater certainty to participants and improve efficiency by codifying procedural aspects of coronial proceedings. The coroners I interviewed had differing opinions about this issue. The main argument of those coroners who oppose the introduction of Coroner's Court Rules was that this would fetter their judicial independence. However, procedural rules should not interfere with substantive matters. A practice note is focused on process, procedure and practice, not on policy or the content of coronial findings. The then NZ Chief Coroner has stressed that:[238]

> no Head of Bench can direct his individual judicial officers about policy or direction as to what sort of findings coroners should make. For example, I can't say to coroners that I think they are being unnecessarily coy about suicide and direct them about what they should say in their findings. I have publicly discussed my view about suicide. But I cannot make individual coroners adopt a certain position about that. It is up to the individual coroner as to how they will implement the sections of the Act.

Several coroners, who support the introduction of Coroner's Court Rules, apply the High Court Rules for specific procedural matters. Coroner Aitken provided the following example:[239]

> I always apply the High Court Rules for expert witnesses in my Coroner's Court. I let my experts know that I am doing that. I get them to read and sign

---

[236] Justice and Electoral Committee *Coroners Bill: Report from the Justice and Electoral Committee* (2004) at 4.

[237] Coroners Act 2006 (NZ) s 6.

[238] Coroner, above n 58.

[239] Aitken, above n 111.

> the forms. The Coroner's Court Bench Book says that is what you should do and the appendices have examples. It is helpful for the expert too. If you want to do some "hot-tubbing", they are not surprised.
>
> I think we should be applying the same procedural rules. I think the Chief should decide what the rules are because one of his roles is to try to achieve consistency. I think it would help if we had the Coroner's Court Rules. It would be so much easier. It is easier for new coroners and it would be much better for consistency. Or we could say that the High Court Rules apply in so far as x, y and z. Procedure is in every court. I was surprised that it wasn't in the Coroner's Court.

In the recent parliamentary debates about the Judicature (High Court Rules) Amendment Bill, Russell Fairbrother MP commented on the importance of procedural rules and advocated for the introduction of rules for the Coroner's Court:[240]

> My experience in the Family Court, which is now some time ago; my experience in the Coroner's Court, which was just two months ago, under the new Act; and my recent experience in the Privileges Committee, show that no matter how well a tribunal endeavours to work through the inquisitorial process, if there is a lack of clarity of rules, then intuition is not always the best guide to procedure. . . . In concluding, I must say these rules are long overdue. They will be welcome by the Bar. I do hope that our other tribunals—particularly the Coroner's Court and the Family Court—can receive the same attention as to the rules that guide their processes. The rules of a court are the rules that determine that justice is in fact delivered.

The Western Australian Law Reform Commission recently recommended the introduction of Coroner's Court Rules in Western Australia.[241] Several jurisdictions, such as the UK, some Canadian provinces (for example Ontario) and Australian states (for example Victoria) have Coroner's Court Rules.[242] The UK Coroner's Court Rules or the Australian States' Coroner's Court Rules could be used, with appropriate modifications, as models for the proposed NZ Coroner's Court Rules.

Several of the coroners I interviewed, who opposed the introduction of Coroner's Court Rules, were supportive of practice notes to guide coronial practice. However, they also commented that practice notes should be made in consultation with coroners. Given that many coroners still feel

---

240 (26 August 2008) 650 *New Zealand Parliamentary Debates* 18846.

241 Hands, above n 94, at 4.

242 Coroners (Inquest) Rules 2013 (UK); Coroners Rules 2009 (Vic); Coroners Act RSO 1990 (Ont.). Clause 15, section 25 of the Coroners Act RSO 1990 (Ont) provides that the Chief Coroner may make additional rules of procedure for inquests.

undervalued, and they need only "have regard to" practice notes, it is important that coroners have input.[243]

The Minister's current review of the coronial jurisdiction proposes amendments which will require the Chief Coroner to produce further practice notes. Legal commentators who have been "crying 'Practice Notes!!'" will no doubt welcome this news.[244] The Chief Coroner is aware that many practitioners and commentators have been calling for practice notes. He realises that it is currently "difficult to find out what the practice is".[245]

The procedure for adverse comments is an area where there is variable coronial practice. In the course of an inquiry, or as part of the findings, a coroner may comment on the conduct of any person in relation to the circumstances of the death.[246] The coroner must not comment adversely on a person without notifying the person and giving the person an opportunity to be heard.[247] A coroner's recommendation could be interpreted as including adverse comment.

This study's empirical evidence highlights that coroners hold differing views about what constitutes an adverse comment. There are also divergent opinions about the notification procedure. Should the adverse comment alone, or the entire findings, be disclosed to the person/s subject to the adverse comment? Australian research has also identified variable and problematic coronial procedure for adverse comments.[248] I have discussed these issues elsewhere.[249] My focus in this chapter is to highlight that the notification procedure for adverse comments could be the subject of a practice note or a provision in the proposed Coroner's Court Rules.

The practice note or rule should advocate a conservative approach, as I have discussed elsewhere.[250] Even if there is doubt about whether a comment is adverse, a consultative approach should be preferred. The entire draft findings (including the adverse comment and recommenda-

---

243 Coroners Act 2006 (NZ) s 6.

244 Matthew Lark "Chief Coroner comments on another round of change" (12 July 2013) ADLSI Independent Voice of Law <http://www.adls.org.nz/for-the-profession/news-and-opinion/2013/7/12/chief-coroner-comments-on-another-round-of-change/>.

245 Lark, above n 244.

246 Coroners Act 2006 (NZ) s 58(1).

247 Coroners Act 2006 (NZ) s 58(3)(a), (b).

248 Hands, above n 94, at 13.

249 Jennifer Moore "An Empirical Approach to the New Zealand Government's Review of the Coronial Jurisdiction" (2014) 21 JLM at 620–25.

250 At 622.

tion) should be provided to the interested parties. Coroner Atwood, and a small number of other coroners, consider that the entire findings (rather than the adverse comment/recommendation alone) should be disclosed to interested parties. This practice provides context and conveys meaning. The introduction of a Coroner's Court Rule about this area of practice would require all coroners to adopt a standard approach which is consistent with this study's empirical evidence.

The *Queensland State Coroner's Guidelines* outline provisions for procedural fairness, including adverse comment. The Guidelines provide that:[251]

> Care should be taken to ensure any person or organisation that is the subject of adverse comment in the narrative findings has been given an opportunity to respond to the allegations.

This study's findings also support the introduction of a practice note, guideline or rule which requires enhanced engagement with organisations and interested parties during the coronial inquiry and, in particular, during the formulation of recommendations. As I have outlined elsewhere in this chapter, organisations prefer a consultative approach and want to provide feedback on proposed recommendations during the coronial inquiry.[252]

The *Queensland State Coroner's Guidelines* could be used, with appropriate modifications, as a model for the proposed NZ coronial practice note, guideline or rule on this topic. Chapter 7 of the *Queensland State Coroner's Guidelines* describes the procedure for obtaining expert reports during coronial inquiries. The Guidelines also encourage coroners to seek feedback from experts, interested parties and stakeholders on proposed recommendations.[253] Healthcare-related deaths are highlighted as an area where it is particularly important for coroners to obtain expert input into draft recommendations.[254] The Guidelines provide that:[255]

> Once the coroner decides to hold an inquest, it is recommended that early consideration be given to possible recommendations, with a view to inviting input from relevant health care sector stakeholders for examination during the inquest.

---

251 *Queensland State Coroner's Guidelines*, above n 169, at chapter 8, p 15.

252 See section 5.3.8 "Evaluation and Feedback" and section 5.3.6 "Alignment Prevention Goals".

253 *Queensland State Coroner's Guidelines*, above n 169, at chapter 7, p 21.

254 At chapter 7, p 21.

255 At chapter 7, p 21.

Depending on the circumstances of the death, the coroner may consider approaching the following entities for their views on possible recommendations:

- relevant medical specialist colleges
- relevant regulatory authority e.g. health practitioner registration board or the Therapeutic Goods Administration
- relevant health industry representative bodies e.g. Australian Medical Association
- Patient Safety and Clinical Improvement Service, Queensland Health
- Office of the Chief Psychiatrist, Queensland Health
- Drugs of Dependency Unit, Queensland Health
- Private Health Regulatory Unit, Office of the Chief Health Officer, Queensland Health
- Queensland Maternal and Perinatal Quality Council
- Australian Commission on Safety and Quality in Health Care.

It is preferable that this response gathering process is commenced prior to the inquest to allow sufficient time for all parties to consider the responses, and for arrangements to be made for relevant witnesses to give evidence.

As I have pointed out, the purpose of these guidelines, practice notes and rules is to foster standardisation in coronial practice. Researchers have also called for coroners to use a standard structure or template for their findings. For example, in their analysis of toddlers' drownings, Blum and Shield argue that:[256]

The coroner could develop a standard reporting format for drowning fatalities to ensure uniform reporting, particularly details concerning the means of entry and compliance status.

The UK *Guidance for Coroners on Changes to Rule 43* provides coroners with suggestions about the structure and content of Rule 43 reports.[257] As I pointed out in Chapter 1, there is a template structure for NZ coronial findings, but it is used infrequently.

Some of the coroners I interviewed (7/15) recognised the importance of the structure of coronial findings. One coroner suggested that it may be preferable to "put the recommendations at the start of [their] findings" because this is "more reader friendly".[258] All organisations and interested parties would prefer a standard structure for coronial findings and

---

[256] C. Blum and J. Shield "Toddler Drowning in Domestic Swimming Pools" (2000) 6 Injury Prevention 288.

[257] UK Ministry of Justice *Guidance for Coroners on Changes to Rule 43: Coroner Reports to Prevent Future Deaths* (2008) at 8.

[258] Aitken, above n 111.

recommendations. For instance, a health sector organisation provided the following reasoning:[259]

> There is definitely a difference between High Court decisions and coroners' findings. But that's partly because High Court decisions are written mostly for lawyers. Whereas a broader range of people read coroners' findings. Bearing that in mind, we would like to see a better structure. We would also like to see them restricting themselves to their jurisdiction – cause of death and so on. Some findings are more clear and precise than others. Some findings are all over the place. There needs to be structure. If recommendations are made, the coroners need to say why they came to that conclusion. There is sometimes no logical explanation for a recommendation. There is sometimes a leap in logic. Sometimes we have to guess how the coroner reached his/her conclusion.

Another organisation advocated for a "standard template that [all coroners] use" because their experience is that it was sometimes unclear whether there were any recommendations. This organisation described their experience as follows:[260]

> It would be helpful for people if [coroners] at least say, "In this case I don't have any recommendations." Just say it in a sentence at the end so that it's really clear because otherwise people might hunt through thinking, "Oh, this is a recommendation", when it's not. If there are no recommendations, state there are none. There should be a standard template that everyone uses. Make it clear what the recommendations are. Don't bury them. Use a heading. It might be just a case of a template if the reports are consistently written to provide even a clearer opportunity to respond. Because in the report [findings] I have here, there is nothing in here to say even who it's being addressed to.

The preventive potential of coronial recommendations is undermined when they are "buried" in the findings, forcing organisations to "hunt" for them. Commentators have also argued that coroners' recommendations would be more prevention-focused if the content for specific categories of death was standardised. Findings on occupational health and safety research on suicide should always include the following information:[261]

- uniform classification of occupations
- record deceased's work history

---

259 Interview with HealthCareOrganisation499 (Jennifer Moore, 23 October 2012).

260 Goddard (Department of Conservation), above n 210.

261 J. Bottomley, E. Dalziel and M. Neith *Work Factors in Suicide: Evidence for a New Commitment in Occupational Health and Safety Research, Policy and Practice* (Urban Ministry Network, Victoria, Australia, 2002).

- identify socio-demographic information
- specific presence or absence of family relationship problems
- uniformly report blood alcohol concentration results
- record work injury information
- systematically record and classify health problems
- report mental health status (clinical versus lay diagnosis), particularly in relation to depression, and
- classify nature of work issues.

In NZ, the Injury Prevention Research Unit's submission on the Coroners Bill 2006 also identified information that should be routinely reported in coronial findings to facilitate prevention strategies.[262]

A more consistent and detailed approach to coronial findings would not only greatly facilitate research, but also benefit the coroners themselves. Identification of patterns and trends in previous similar cases could be undertaken quickly. In order to identify trends and patterns amongst these groups of cases, it is important that coroners include in their finding the relevant contributing factors to the death and comment on prevention issues.[263] The *Queensland State Coroner's Guidelines* provide information about how to write prevention-focused recommendations and encourage coroners to use NCIS to analyse previous similar cases for patterns and trends.[264] In the next section, I explore how coroners should receive feedback about the extent to which their recommendations have had a positive public health impact.

5.3.8 Evaluation and Feedback

Australian commentators have pointed out that the preventive coronial process would benefit from feedback about the quality and implementation of coroners' recommendations.[265] An important question is when should such feedback occur? Is feedback through a mandatory

---

262 Injury Prevention Research Unit, Department of Preventive and Social Medicine, University of Otago, Langley and Cryer, above n 112.

263 Bugeja, above n 7, at 60.

264 *Queensland State Coroner's Guidelines*, above n 169, at chapter 9, pp 19–21.

265 Boronia Halstead "Implementing Coroners' Deaths in Custody Recommendations: A Victorian Case Study" (1995–1996) 7 Current Issues in Criminal Justice 340 at 353; Ian Freckelton "Death Investigation and the Evolving Role of the Coroner" (2008) 11 Otago LR 565; United Kingdom, above n 90.

response regime for coroners' recommendations sufficient? Under this regime, feedback would occur *after* the recommendations have been released in coroners' findings. Would feedback *during* the coronial inquiry increase the likelihood that recommendations are evidence-based and prevention-focused?

All organisations interviewed for this research preferred the idea of early feedback, which would occur during the coronial investigation process. For example, the following comments from a health care sector organisation are representative of other organisations' views:[266]

> A mandatory response regime is a good idea, but it definitely cannot be a replacement for having early involvement and participation and establishing the facts and all the information which needs to be presented at the hearing. . . . Far more important is actually getting involvement earlier and making sure that sufficient information is presented to the coroner.

Similarly, the following exchange between the researcher and Coroner Fitzpatrick describes the advantages of early feedback:[267]

> **Jennifer:** What do you think of other jurisdictions where there are mandatory response regimes?
> **Coroner Fitzpatrick:** I think it would be helpful because it would help us understand the reasons why things aren't being done. If there are things that we could do differently, that would improve the quality of our recommendations. It should not be mandatory that agencies do what we say. There are lots of good reasons why agencies can't do what we recommend. But telling us why they have not would be helpful.

---

[266] HealthCareOrganisation399, above n 40. Reproduced with permission of Thomson Reuters (Professional) Australia Limited, www.thomsonreuters.com.au.

This article was first published by Thomson Reuters in the *Journal of Law and Medicine* as Jennifer Moore "An Empirical Approach to the New Zealand Government's Review of the Coronial Jurisdiction" (2014) 21 JLM 602. For all subscription inquiries please phone, from Australia: 1300 304 195, from Overseas: +61 2 8587 7980 or online at www.thomsonreuters.com.au/catalogue. The official PDF version of this article can also be purchased separately from Thomson Reuters.

[267] Fitzpatrick, above n 34. Reproduced with permission of Thomson Reuters (Professional) Australia Limited, www.thomsonreuters.com.au.

This article was first published by Thomson Reuters in the *Journal of Law and Medicine* as Jennifer Moore "An Empirical Approach to the New Zealand Government's Review of the Coronial Jurisdiction" (2014) 21 JLM 602. For all subscription inquiries please phone, from Australia: 1300 304 195, from Overseas: +61 2 8587 7980 or online at www.thomsonreuters.com.au/catalogue. The official PDF version of this article can also be purchased separately from Thomson Reuters.

Jennifer: Could the process be different? Could the process happen further upstream, instead of waiting until the recommendation has been made?
Coroner Fitzpatrick: Yes, ideally it would be good if we knew why a recommendation wouldn't be useful before we made the recommendation. If the agency has bought into the idea and then they don't implement it, they could be held to account.

Likewise, the former NZ Chief Coroner recognises the importance of early feedback and has stated that the CSNZ could be improved by "encouraging further cooperation between coroners, government agencies, other investigating agencies and stakeholders in order to help coroners discharge their preventative role".[268]

In addition to improving the quality of recommendations, early feedback may mean that an organisation "has bought into the idea". Public health research demonstrates that such "buy-in" is vital for the translation of principles into practice and, therefore, could increase the uptake of evidence-based recommendations.[269] The relationship between the coroner and target organisation does not fit neatly into conventional implementation models: bottom–up versus top–down. As an outsider, the coroner is unlikely to have an in-depth understanding of the full policy context of the organisation to which his/her recommendations are expected to fit. Coroners may also have limited understanding of organisations' resource constraints. It is unsurprising, therefore, that some organisations interviewed for this project described coroners' recommendations as "ideals"[270] or "unrealistic gold standards".[271] Likewise, research has described some coroners' recommendations are "detached good ideas".[272]

This study's findings demonstrate that coroners should be provided with feedback about their proposed recommendations, both during and after the coronial inquiry. Early feedback from organisations will increase the likelihood that sufficient input to formulate recommendations is received. Early consultation with organisations may also improve the rate of implementation of recommendations. Feedback after the coronial inquiry (through a mandatory response system) provides monitoring of implementation rates.

The preventive potential of coroners' recommendations could also be improved by judicial reviews. A few coroners (3/15) raised this idea. For

---

268 Judge MacLean, above n 98, at 5.
269 Conway and others, above n 3.
270 GovtOrg07, above n 35.
271 Interview with GovtOrg09 (Jennifer Moore, 12 February 2013).
272 Halstead, above n 265, at 354.

example, Coroner Fitzpatrick explained the benefits of judicial reviews as follows:[273]

> It's a shame that we are not judicially reviewed more often. It would help because we are in such a vacuum. There was a judicial review application recently, but it was withdrawn. I was disappointed because I was looking forward to seeing what it said. It would give us some guidance. I would be pleased to be judicially reviewed. It would be nice to know what a judge thinks about the parameters of our work. Without that we are left making it up as we go along. A judicial review would be good for oversight and rigour in the Coroner's Court.

These research findings, and a 2013 judicial review of coronial procedure, had a positive impact on coronial practice. During interviews, I asked coroners to discuss their approach to adverse comments. I explained that the preliminary research findings supported a consultative approach whereby the entire draft findings (including proposed recommendations) should be provided to the interested parties.[274] I also explained that organisations I interviewed preferred to be notified by coroners about adverse comments, rather than being surprised by the media. My suggestion is consistent with natural justice and should improve the quality and preventive potential of recommendations. The judicial review of Coroner Ryan's adverse comments during the inquest into the death of Iraena Asher is consistent with this study's findings.[275] One coroner was prompted to change his approach, stating:[276]

> Since the interview, Justice Winkelman's decision of *Carroll* has been released. That has put natural justice principles fairly and squarely into the limelight in the Coroner's Court. Accordingly, I have changed both my view and practice regarding the sending out of recommendations (and I suspect this may the case for a number of us on the bench). Specifically, I have now started to consider whether I should send my proposed recommendation to the affected party before the release of the final finding (so as to make the process fair and to potentially improve the recommendation by getting comment in advance). It has the advantage also that the affected party is forewarned in the event the finding is picked up by the media.

---

273 Fitzpatrick, above n 34.

274 Moore, above n 249, at 622.

275 *Carroll & Woodhouse v Coroner's Court & Police* [2013] NZHC 906.

276 Email from Coroner Stewart to Jennifer Moore regarding Carroll and adverse comments (18 June 2013).

Consultation with parties/organisations about adverse comments also provides opportunities for early feedback. The organisations that I interviewed supported judicial review as an evaluative feedback tool, in theory. However, in practice, many organisations had considered, but rejected, judicial review as an option because it would damage their relationship with coroners. According to one organisation that was "upset" about the coroner's recommendations, they decided against judicial review because they "didn't want a war with coroners" with whom they have ongoing relationships.[277]

In *Carroll*, adverse comments were not made about an organisation. The adverse comments concerned Ms Carroll, Ms Woodhouse and Mr Woodhouse, who had cared for the deceased in the hours preceding her death. The judicial review application was filed by them. Organisations that receive coroners' recommendations and coroners have arguably benefited from Winkelmann's judgment in *Carroll*. The preventive potential of at least one coroner's recommendations will potentially be improved by the comments that he will receive on his draft recommendations as a result of the judicial review.

5.4 CONCLUSION

This chapter highlighted that the majority of research participants are supportive of the statutory preventive function. While there have been improvements since the introduction of the Coroners Act 2006 (NZ), the findings suggest that the prophylactic potential of coroners' recommendations has not yet been fully realised in NZ. I have presented a number of factors that posed difficulties for capitalising on the lifesaving opportunities that coroners' recommendations provide.

All participants reported that coroners' recommendations have the potential to contribute to the prevention of injury and death. All participants understood that coroners have a statutory preventive function. However, coroners (11/15), interested parties (7/8) and health care organisations (24/26) questioned whether this function was being maximised. Interested parties (7/8), health care organisations (25/26) and coroners (13/15) suggested that recommendations could be improved by encouraging coroners to consider similar cases, undertaking analysis of patterns and comparative risks.

The preventive role is sometimes marginalised because the coronial

277 HealthCareOrganisation399, above n 40.

process is concerned with unpacking the facts of individual cases, rather than the systematic identification of patterns of morbidity and mortality. This focus reflects the legal profession's case-by-case approach. A preventive approach requires the identification of patterns and remedial responses.

This study's findings highlight strategies for improving coronial recommendations and are important for death investigation systems that wish to strengthen their preventive function. This study confirms the barriers to maximising the preventive potential of recommendations which have been identified by previous research.[278] These barriers mean that some NZ coroners' recommendations have failed to have a significant impact on preventing adverse events.[279]

I have outlined the main strategies which would enable coroners to effectively fulfil their statutory preventive role. In particular, my findings demonstrate the importance of appropriately targeted recommendations. In addition, the results highlight that early feedback from interested parties and organisations is crucial for "buy-in" from participants and prevention-focused recommendations. Another important strategy is the introduction of a mandatory response regime for coroners' recommendations. This could improve the preventive potential of recommendations by ensuring that recommendations are considered by the organisations that can implement them. I explore mandatory response regimes for coroners' recommendations in the next chapter.

278 Carol Grech "Coronial Inquiries into Fatal Adverse Events in South Australian Hospitals: From Inquest to Practice" (PhD, The University of Adelaide, 2004); Ray Watterson, Penny Brown and John McKenzie "Coronial Recommendations and the Prevention of Indigenous Death" (2008) 12 Special Edition 2 Australian Indigenous Law Review 4; Halstead, above n 83.

279 Grech, above n 278.

6. Mandatory responses to coroners' recommendations

6.1 INTRODUCTION

The former NZ Chief Coroner has expressed the view that a mandatory statutory regime for follow-up to coroners' recommendations should be introduced.[1] Such a mandatory response regime requires meaningful responses from those entities to which coroners have made recommendations. Those entities need to indicate either how they would implement recommendations, or the reasons why implementation would not take place.

Many NZ coroners feel a deep sense of frustration that their preventive recommendations are not being heeded, contributing to otherwise preventable deaths.[2] Family members of deceased persons also feel frustration that their loved ones' deaths are not making as great a difference in saving lives as they could.[3] The preventive potential of coroners' recommendations could be maximised during and after the death investigation process. In Chapter 5, I considered how consultation with agencies and experts during the death investigation could improve coroners' recommendations and, thereby, strengthen the preventive potential of coroners' recommendations.

This chapter explores how that preventive potential can be strengthened once the investigation is complete. In particular, it considers whether a statutory mandatory response regime for coroners' recommendations should be introduced. New Zealand's coronial regime does not require organisations to which coroners direct recommendations to respond to them. On the basis of the empirical evidence, I argue that the Coroners Act 2006 (NZ) should be amended to include a mandatory response

---

1 For example, see Frank Neill "Give Coronial Recommendations Some Teeth" (2012) 806 LawTalk 8.

2 Editorial "Coroners wisdom unheeded" *Stuff* (New Zealand, 12 January 2013).

3 For example, see Cliff Taylor "Toxic gas death inquiry" *The New Zealand Herald* (Auckland, 15 June 2008).

regime. This change should only occur alongside the additional reforms which I have discussed in the preceding chapters, such as the introduction of Coroner's Court Law Reports and electronic access to full coronial findings.

6.2 NZ GOVERNMENT'S REVIEW

The former NZ Chief Coroner is "comfortable with the thrust of the reforms",[4] but he has expressed disappointment that the current government review does not include consideration of a mandatory statutory regime for follow-up to coroners' recommendations.[5] The first Cabinet paper only mentions the issue once:[6]

> A number of overseas jurisdictions (such as Australia and the UK) have grappled with similar issues and how to respond to them. They have implemented a variety of measures with mixed success. Some jurisdictions have taken the approach of requiring mandatory responses, (rather than mandatory implementation) to ensure coroners' recommendations are considered and implemented where appropriate. In some instances, these governments have provided resources to assist with the formulation of recommendations. While this may achieve improved recommendations, it would come at a cost to the government.

The second Cabinet paper contains one paragraph about the public discussion on whether legislation should be introduced to require agencies to respond to coroners' recommendations.[7] However, the paper does not commit to the introduction of such reform because "reasonable coronial recommendations will voluntarily get a response from government agencies".[8]

Although there is acknowledgment that such reform could improve recommendations, the topic is excluded from the review because of the cost. The 2000 Law Commission report recommended introduction of a system

---

[4] Cabinet Paper *Coroners Act Review: Proposals for Reform – Paper 1* (2013) at 9.

[5] Radio NZ "Changes to Coroners' Inquests proposed" <http://www.radionz.co.nz/national/programmes/morningreport>.

[6] Cabinet Paper, above n 4, para 21.

[7] NZ Ministry of Justice *Coroners Act Review: Proposal for Reform – Cabinet Paper 2* (2013) para 34.

[8] NZ Ministry of Justice, above n 7 para 34.

to make responses to recommendations mandatory.[9] Parliament did not adopt the Commission's suggestions in the new legislation. Specifically, Parliament did not incorporate the Law Commission's Recommendation 14, which states:[10]

> We recommend that where a coronial recommendation concerns a government agency, a Chief Coroner must give notice of that recommendation to the agency concerned, the Minister responsible for that agency, the Attorney General, and any other agency or individual affected by the recommendation. The government agency must, within three months, report to its Minister the steps it intends to take in relation to the coronial recommendation and a copy of that report must be provided to the Chief Coroner. The Chief Coroner must include particulars of the government agency's response in the annual report from the Office of the Chief Coroner.

It is disappointing that the current government does not wish to give adequate consideration to whether the lack of mandatory follow-up to coronial recommendations limits coroners' ability to put preventive principles into practice. At the very least, the review should consider the extent to which coroners' recommendations are implemented because the rate of implementation is related to the degree of health and safety impact of recommendations.

6.3 JURISDICTIONS' APPROACHES

This section explores several jurisdictions' approaches to responses to coroners' recommendations. Several overseas jurisdictions have statutory mandatory response regimes (Table 6.1).

6.3.1 New Zealand

The Coroners Act 2006 (NZ) governs NZ's coronial law. Following the result of a NZ Law Commission report and an 18-month legislative gestation period, the Act revitalised the coronial jurisdiction, updating the previous 1988 statute, which was considered well overdue for reform. Mandatory responses to recommendations were not mentioned in the parliamentary debates about the Coroners Bill 2006.

The current Act features an "overtly prophylactic" focus.[11] Despite its

---

9 New Zealand Law Commission *Coroners* (NZLC R62 2000) at 60.

10 At 60.

11 Ian Freckelton "Reforming Coronership: International Perspectives and Contemporary Developments" (2008) 16 JLM 379.

Table 6.1 Jurisdictions' approaches to mandatory responses

Jurisdiction	Coroners' Training	Statutory Mandatory Response
NZ	Legal	No
England	Legal*	Yes
Scotland	Legal	No
VIC, Australia	Legal	Yes
SA, Australia	Legal	Yes (Limited)
QLD, Australia	Legal	Yes
NSW, Australia	Legal	Yes
NT, Australia	Legal	Yes
WA, Australia	Legal	No
ACT, Australia	Legal	Yes (Limited)
TAS, Australia	Legal	No
Ontario, Canada	Medical	No**

Notes:

* Since 2013 newly appointed coroners must have the five year judicial eligibility qualification (like all judges) which requires five years of legal practice or part-time judicial practice. Coroners appointed before 2013 could be lawyers or doctors.

** Ontario has a unique system which typically garners responses from organisations.

emphasis on preventing deaths, NZ's coronial regime does not require organisations to which coroners direct preventive recommendations to respond to such recommendations. The Ministry of Justice eschewed a mandatory response regime in drafting the legislation, despite the Law Commission's support for such a regime in its 2000 report.[12]

Once coroners' recommendations or comments are finalised, the Act merely requires that coroners send a certificate of findings, together with any specified recommendations or comments, to the chief executive of the Ministry of Justice.[13]

As I explained in Chapter 2, on 31 July 2012, the New Zealand Courts Minister, the Hon Chester Borrows, announced a targeted review of the coronial system and the Coroners Act.[14] At the time of writing, there is no indication that any statutory response regime will be included as part of the legislative reform.

The Hon Shane Jones, an Opposition MP, proposed a Coroners

[12] New Zealand Law Commission, above n 9, recommendation 14.

[13] Coroners Act 2006 (NZ), s 94(4)(d).

[14] Chester Borrows "beehive.govt.nz – Coronial system to be reviewed" (31 July 2012) <http://www.beehive.govt.nz/release/coronial-system-be-reviewed>.

Amendment Bill, which was introduced in November 2012.[15] This Bill would require the Minister of Justice, within 90 days of the making of a coroner's recommendations or comments, to report to the House of Representatives setting out the Government's response to those recommendations or comments.[16] While this is a Private Member's Bill and as such it may not progress, the benefits and limitations of such a parliamentary follow-up regime will be discussed later in this chapter.

6.3.2 Australia

Unlike NZ, Australia has no national coronial regime.[17] Rather, each state or territory has its own regime controlling coronial processes, including the making of recommendations to prevent deaths and whether responding to those recommendations is mandatory.

(a) Victoria

Victorian coronial law is contained in the Coroners Act 2008 (Vic). Like NZ's legislation, a central purpose of the Act is to contribute to a reduction in the number of preventable deaths.[18] A Victorian coroner may make recommendations to any Minister, public statutory authority or entity, including recommendations relating to public health and safety or the administration of justice.[19] Once a recommendation is made, an entity must respond in writing within three months of receiving a recommendation, specifying the statement of action (if any) that it has taken, is taking, or will be taking, in relation to a coroner's recommendation.[20] There has been confusion as to whether private entities fall within the purview of this mandatory response requirement. Under Victoria's Interpretation Act, "entity" is defined as including a person and an unincorporated body, and so includes private bodies.[21] Additionally, a solicitor working within

---

15 Hon Shane Jones. "Coroners Amendment Bill, Proposed Bill – member" (20 November 2012) New Zealand Parliament <http://www.parliament.nz/>.

16 Hon Shane Jones. "Coroners Amendment Bill, Proposed Bill – member, explanatory note" (20 November 2012) New Zealand Parliament <http://www.parliament.nz/>.

17 Although some systems related to coroners do function at the national level; for example, the National Coronial Information Service (NCIS), an Internet-based data storage and retrieval system for Australian coronial cases. See the National Coronial Information Service website: <http://www.ncis.org.au>.

18 Coroners Act 2008 (VIC), s 1(c).

19 Coroners Act 2008 (VIC), s 72(2).

20 Coroners Act 2008 (VIC), s 72(2); Coroners Act 2008 (VIC), s 72(3).

21 Interpretation of Legislation Act 1984 (VIC), s 38.

the Coroner's Court of Victoria has confirmed that private bodies are obligated to respond to recommendations directed at them.[22]

On receiving a response from an entity, the coroner must publish the response on the Internet, and provide a copy to certain interested persons.[23] In practice, both written findings (including recommendations) and their responses are published within a database on the Coroner's Court of Victoria website. This database is searchable by subject term, and all recommendations and responses from 1 November 2009 onwards are included in the database (with some earlier findings included at the request of coroners).[24]

The coronial investigation process in Victoria is supported by a number of specialist services. In particular, the CPU is a non-statutory body that was established in 2009 to strengthen the coroners' prevention role. A key function is monitoring and collecting information on responses to and implementation of those recommendations.[25] Anecdotal evidence suggests that coroners who engage the CPU in this capacity produce evidence-based recommendations which are more likely to be implemented.[26]

(b) New South Wales and Queensland

Both NSW and QLD adopted new coronial legislation in the last decade. The Coroners Act 2003 (QLD) has death prevention as a focus through the making of coroners' recommendations as a primary object, while the Coroners Act 2009 (NSW) has an object enabling coroners' recommendations on matters including public health, implying that the prevention of deaths is also important.[27] Both Acts allow coroners to make recommendations directed at relevant entities for these purposes.[28]

---

22 Email from Sarah Gebert, senior in-house solicitor, Coroner's Court Victoria, to Catey Boyce regarding whether for-profit and non-government not-for-profit organisations are required to respond to coroners' recommendations (12 August 2013).

23 Coroners Act 2008 (VIC), s 72(5).

24 Victorian coronial findings (including recommendations and responses) from 1 November 2009 can be accessed from the Coroner's Court of Victoria website. See <http://www.coronerscourt.vic.gov.au/home/coroners+written+findings/>.

25 CPU, Coroner's Court of Victoria "Brochure – Coroners Prevention Unit – Coroners Court of Victoria" (August 2013) Coroner's Court of Victoria <http://www.coronerscourt.vic.gov.au/home/coronial+investigation+process/brochure+-+coroners+prevention+unit>.

26 Email from Georgina Sutherland, Melbourne University, to Jennifer Moore regarding the Melbourne University coronial research (14 July 2014).

27 Coroners Act 2009 (NSW), s 3(e); Coroners Act 2003 (QLD), s 3(d).

28 Coroners Act 2009 (NSW), s 82; Coroners Act 2003 (QLD), s 46.

The Queensland Parliament rejected an Opposition Member's Bill which would have required government bodies to inform the coroner as to actions taken or not taken pursuant to recommendations; if not satisfied with the reports, the coroner would then have forwarded them to the Attorney General to be tabled in Parliament.[29] The Bill failed to reach its second reading.[30] While agreeing with the thrust of the Bill's provisions that agencies should report on responses to coroners' recommendations, the Government rejected the Bill on two grounds. Firstly, it considered it was constitutionally unsound to require the executive to report to coroners – judicial officers – on matters of policy, and even more inappropriate for coroners to advise on their satisfaction as to policy. This would muddy the separation of powers and politicise the judiciary.[31] Secondly, it considered the coronial regime did not have the administrative capacity to undertake such an extensive role.[32]

Both QLD and NSW have now implemented mandatory response regimes through executive orders directed at government entities. New South Wales has achieved this through a Ministerial Memorandum. In 2009, the New South Wales Department of Premier and Cabinet set out a process "to ensure that there is a consistent process across government for responding to coronial recommendations, and that there is increased accountability and transparency in responding to such recommendations".[33] Under the Memorandum, a Minister or NSW government agency should, within 21 days of receiving a coroner's recommendation, acknowledge receipt of the recommendation and, within six months of receipt, write to the Attorney General outlining any action being taken to implement the recommendation. If implementing a recommendation is not proposed, reasons should be given. The Attorney General is to collate these responses. Every six months, the Attorney General will arrange for a report to be published on the Internet summarising recommendations and government responses to them.[34] In Queensland, a Cabinet request to the Attorney General has established

---

29 Coroners (Reporting Arrangements) Amendment Bill 2007, cl 3.

30 Queensland Hansard, Record of Proceedings Wednesday, 4 June 2008 at 1942.

31 The Hon DM Wells speaks to this in depth; Queensland Hansard, Record of Proceedings Wednesday, 30 April 2008 at 1381–2.

32 At 1376.

33 Department of Premier and Cabinet, NSW Government *M2009–12 Responding to Coronial Recommendations* (2009).

34 To access these reports summarising government responses, see the Attorney General and Justice Department's website: <http://www.lsb.lawlink.nsw.gov.au/lsb/coronialrecommendations.html>.

a similar system in that state, with collations of government responses to coroners' recommendations accessible from the Queensland Department of Justice and Attorney General's website.[35]

(c) Northern Territory

The Northern Territory, like Victoria, has a legislative regime requiring government responses to coroners' recommendations. The Coroners Act 1993 (NT) allows coroners to make recommendations to the Attorney General on any matter connected with an investigated death or disaster, including public health or safety or the administration of justice.[36] Since 2002, if the Attorney General receives a recommendation that contains comments relating to a government agency, he or she must, without delay, give the recommendation to the Chief Executive Officer of the agency.[37] The particular Chief Executive Officer must, within three months of receipt, give the Attorney General a written response to the recommendation, including a statement of the action that the agency is taking, has taken, or will take, with respect to the recommendation.[38] The Attorney General must then, without delay, report on the recommendation and the response, and lay a copy of this report before the Legislative Council within three days of completing the report.[39] The same procedure applies more specifically to any report or recommendation made in relation to a death of a person held in custody.[40]

(d) Southern Australia and the Australian Capital Territory

In Southern Australia and the Australian Capital Territory, government need only respond to coroners' recommendations when they relate to deaths that have occurred in custody, or deaths which were contributed to by injuries sustained while being held in custody. This is a result of the recommendations of the Australian Royal Commission into Aboriginal Deaths in Custody (RCADC), which found that "thoroughly conducted coronial inquiries hold the potential to identify systemic failures in custodial practices and procedures which may, if acted on, prevent future deaths in similar circumstances. In the final analysis adequate post

---

[35] Queensland Government "Response to Coronial Recommendations" Queensland Government, Australia <https://publications.qld.gov.au>.

[36] Coroners Act 1993 (NT) 1993, s 35(2).

[37] Coroners Act 1993 (NT), s 46A(1).

[38] Coroners Act 1993 (NT), s 46B(1); Coroners Act 1993 (NT), s 46B(2).

[39] Coroners Act 1993 (NT), s 46B(3).

[40] Coroners Act 1993 (NT); Coroners Act 1993 (NT), s 27.

death investigations have the potential to save lives."[41] The narrowed focus of these jurisdictions stems from the widely recognised view that a person in custody is owed a special responsibility by the state while in its control.[42]

In Southern Australia, the coroner must send recommendations to a public agency in relation to a death in custody to that agency, and the Minister responsible for that agency must, within around six months of receiving the recommendations, lay a report before each House of Parliament giving details of any action taken or proposed to be taken in consequence of those recommendations.[43]

In the ACT, a response to coronial findings, including recommendations, must be given by the specific custodial agency in whose care the person died to the Minister responsible for the agency within three months of receiving coronial recommendations. The relevant Minister must give a copy of the response to the coroner, who then disseminates the responses more widely.[44]

(e) Western Australia and Tasmania

Neither Western Australia nor Tasmania has a mandatory response regime. While Western Australia's current Act permits the Governor to make regulations giving effect to the RCADC's recommendations relating to the investigation of the death of a person held in custody,[45] no such regulations have been made.[46] The state is currently undergoing an overhaul of its coronial legislation. Given its Law Commission's support for mandatory response regimes, it seems likely that Western Australia will implement such a regime in the near future.[47]

The Tasmanian legislation includes in the coroner's functions both discretionary and mandatory powers. There is a discretion to comment upon any matter connected with the death, including public health or

---

41 Commonwealth of Australia *Royal Commission into Aboriginal Deaths in Custody National Report* (1991).

42 R. Brazil "The Coroner's Recommendation: Fulfilling its Potential? A Perspective from the Aboriginal Legal Service" (2010) 15 Australian Indigenous Law Review 94 at 96.

43 Coroners Act 2003 (SA), s 25(4); Coroners Act 2003 (SA), s 25(5).

44 Coroners Act 1997 (ACT) 199, s 75; Coroners Act 1997 (ACT), s 76.

45 Coroners Act 1996 (WA), s 59(2)(d).

46 Coroners Regulations 1997 (WA).

47 See recommendation 87 in Law Reform Commission of Western Australia *Review of Coronial Practice in Western Australia: Final Report* (Law Reform Commission of Western Australia, Perth, January 2012).

safety or the administration of justice,[48] and a duty to make recommendations in order to prevent further deaths: "A coroner *must*, whenever appropriate, make recommendations with respect to ways of preventing further deaths and on any other matter that the coroner considers appropriate."[49] Tasmanian coroners are thus compelled to make preventive recommendations, where appropriate, unlike in most other jurisdictions, where the legislation is framed in terms of a discretionary power to make recommendations or comment in respect of preventable deaths. Unlike Western Australia, there are as yet no indications that Tasmania's legislative scheme will evolve to require responses from organisations to coroners' recommendations.

6.3.3 Canada

(a) Ontario

The Ontario Office of the Chief Coroner's focus on death prevention is clear from its motto: "We speak for the dead to protect the living."[50] As I outlined in Chapter 2, the Ontario coronial regime nevertheless differs substantially from its Australasian counterparts. While a NZ coroner must have held a practising certificate as a barrister or solicitor for more than five years,[51] the Ontario Coroners Act specifies that a coroner must be a qualified medical practitioner.[52] This gives the Ontario coronial regime a public health orientation.[53]

The Ontario coronial system is also unique in that it features an informal, alternative process for conducting reviews of deaths: the Regional Coroner's Review system.[54] Its function is a combination of fact-finding and mediation, used instead of, or before, a public inquest. After an initial investigation, a coroner may hold informal meetings with family members of the deceased and institutions involved in the death, for example, hospitals, in order to discuss the circumstances of the death (usually in the presence of independent experts) and also any recommendations which

---

48 Coroners Act 1995 (TAS), s 28(3).

49 Coroners Act 1995 (TAS), s 28(2).

50 See the Office of the Chief Coroner's website: <http://www.mcscs.jus.gov.on.ca/english/DeathInvestigations/office_coroner/coroner.html>

51 Coroners Act 2006 (NZ), s 103(2).

52 Coroners Act RSO 1990 (ca;on), s 3(1).

53 See Ministry of Community Safety and Correctional Services' website: <http://www.mcscs.jus.gov.on.ca/english/DeathInvestigations/AboutDeathInvestigationsinOntario/DI_intro.html>.

54 Ontario Law Reform Commission *Report on the Law of Coroners* (1995).

would prevent similar deaths.[55] This method of avoiding cumbersome formal processes and finding effective ways of preventing future deaths is not a statutory function, but the power to hold the process derives from the coroner's ability to obtain assistance or the use of experts at any point of an investigation or inquest.[56]

Attendance at review meetings is not compulsory, although institutions (particularly hospitals, where reviews are used most often) tend to prefer informal meetings in lieu of formal inquests.[57] This is because such meetings enable Ontario coroners to consider, for example, medical adverse events without having to put complex medical evidence before a jury – a jury being a requirement in Ontario at a public inquest.[58] Discussions between regional coroners and institutions are closed to the public and off the record, which allows for "frank, collegial exchanges"[59] of information relating to the circumstances surrounding a particular death. Generally the jointly reached recommendations are not publicised, although those relating to systemic issues across many institutions may be issued in press releases.[60]

After a meeting, the coroner sends a formal copy of the recommendations to the institution, requesting a response. In turn, the coroner sends copies of both the formal recommendations and institutional response to the deceased's family. While responding to the recommendations is not mandatory, a response can generally be expected given the institution's participation in their creation. Where an institution ignores the recommendations or otherwise does not comply with the review process, the coroner can open an inquest into the matter. This is especially likely to occur where a similar death occurs after an agreement on recommendations has been reached, where the institution will be asked to explain why the agreed recommendations did not prevent the death.[61] The threat of a future inquest perhaps acts as an effective incentive to promote responses

---

55 Office of the Chief Coroner, Ontario *Guidelines for Regional Coroner Reviews* (2002).

56 Coroners Act RSO 1990, s 15(4).

57 Parliament of Victoria Law Reform Committee *Coroners Act 1985 Review Final Report* (2006) at 412.

58 At 418.

59 Stanley Myles MacKenzie Leslie "Speaking for the Dead: Coroners, Institutional Structures and Risk Management" (Doctor of Philosophy, University of Toronto, 2011) at 75.

60 At 411.

61 Justin Malbon "Institutional Responses to Coronial Recommendations" (1998) 6 JLM 35 at 47.

to recommendations in Ontario compared with Australasian jurisdictions. As the Victorian Parliamentary Law Commission report noted:[62]

> Because inquests are held less frequently, they tend to attract a greater amount of public interest and media attention, and so they are something to be feared by an organisation that failed to comply with its agreement with a coroner.

As the Office of the Chief Coroner does not keep a record of the cases it considers in alternative, private forums, it is difficult to quantify the exact number of regional reviews held each year.[63] However, it is noteworthy that the number of public inquests held in Ontario (excluding inquests mandated by the legislation, such as those relating to deaths in police or prison custody or deaths in the course of their employment) has decreased in recent decades:[64]

> In sum, coroner's inquests aimed at producing public safety recommendations are rare events in Ontario. The rate at which they are convened has been reduced by around 60 per cent when data from the mid 2000s are compared to those from the mid 1980s. While inquests mandated by the Act continue at approximately the same rate in the two periods, concerns about efficiency and costs have played a role in the reduction of discretionary inquests.

It appears that the ability to investigate death informally in Ontario saves the time and expense public inquests otherwise entail, leading to "a more flexible, efficient and effective coronial system".[65]

Finally, like Victoria, the Ontario coronial system also provides support services to strengthen the corner's prevention role. In particular, the Office of the Chief Coroner oversees expert death review committees, the membership of which includes experts from a range of relevant fields including medicine, law, and social sciences.[66] These committees provide advice and expertise for investigations and reviews conducted by the Office of the Chief Coroner.[67] Key functions in relation to death investigation

---

[62] Parliament of Victoria Law Reform Committee, above n 57, at 413.

[63] Leslie, above n 59, at 72.

[64] At 55.

[65] Parliament of Victoria Law Reform Committee, above n 57, at 417–18.

[66] The committees comprise the Domestic Violence Death Review Committee; Maternal and Perinatal Death Review Committee; Geriatric and Long-Term Care Review Committee; Paediatric Death Review Committee; and Deaths under Five Committee.

[67] Office of the Chief Coroner Annual Report 2009–2011, website: <http://www.mcscs.jus.gov.on.ca/english/DeathInvestigations/office_coroner/

and the formulation of recommendations include identifying the presence or absence of systemic issues which may require follow-up by the Investigating, Regional or Chief Coroner, and advising the Chief Coroner of cases that may further public safety if examined through the inquest process.[68]

(b) Alberta

Death investigations in Alberta are performed by medical examiners (physicians) with the assistance of medical examiners' investigators.[69] When a death occurs suddenly or cannot be explained, the Office of the Chief Medical Examiner investigates in order to determine the circumstances of the death.[70] In certain cases, the Chief Medical Examiner may give notice of certain deaths to the Fatality Review Board. In turn, the Board must recommend to the Minister of Justice that a public fatality inquiry be held in some cases. All deaths caused by an on-duty police officer must be recommended for a public fatality inquiry. Additionally, all deaths of patients under the Mental Health Act 2000 (Alberta), children in government custody, and individuals in custody or in jail automatically are recommended for a public fatality inquiry unless the death was due to natural causes, was not preventable, and the Board determines that an inquiry would not serve the public interest.[71] The Minister may then order that a Provincial Court judge conduct a public fatality inquiry.[72] The judge then presides over a public fatality inquiry, determining the circumstances of death and making recommendations to prevent future deaths in a written report, which is delivered to the Minister.[73] After this, however, the formal process finishes and no requirements mandating responses to recommendations follow.

(c) Quebec

One of the Quebecois coronial system's main goals is to help prevent avoidable deaths by compiling, publishing and providing access to

---

PublicationsandReports/AnnualReports/AnnualReport0911/OCC_annual_report_0911.html>.

[68] Office of the Chief Coroner Annual Report 2009–2011.

[69] Fatality Inquiries Act 2000 (Alberta) 2000, s 6; Fatality Inquiries Act 2000 (Alberta), s 7; Fatality Inquiries Act 2000 (Alberta), s 9.

[70] Fatality Inquiries Act 2000 (Alberta), s 19(1).

[71] Fatality Inquiries Act 2000 (Alberta), s 32; Fatality Inquiries Act 2000 (Alberta), s 33.

[72] Fatality Inquiries Act 2000 (Alberta), s 35(1).

[73] Fatality Inquiries Act 2000 (Alberta), s 53.

complete information on the causes and circumstances surrounding any violent or mysterious death in Quebec.[74] One function of the coroner at an inquest or investigation is to make any pertinent recommendation directed towards better protection of human life.[75] Following death investigations, Quebecois coroners must write reports including, where applicable, such recommendations.[76] Coroners may, if appropriate, transmit the recommendations appearing in these reports to any concerned persons, associations, departments or agencies.[77] Regulations require permanent coroners to have eight years of experience as a physician, barrister or notary.[78] Investigative coroners, who are usually doctors, carry out most death investigations, but legally trained coroners carry out around twenty public inquests each year, where it is necessary and useful to obtain information from witnesses in public and under oath.[79]

The Quebec coroner's website includes a catalogue of all coroners' recommendations categorised by relevant topic.[80] The Chief Coroner must make an annual report to the Minister of Public Security of the coroners' activities, which may include a summary of recommendations made following death investigations, and in turn the Minister must publicise this report by tabling it in the National Assembly.[81] However, as Freckelton notes, no mandatory response regime is involved whereby government must respond to such recommendations: "[t]here is no legal obligation to adopt the coroner's recommendations, and any action taken along those lines depends on the institution's moral authority and credibility."[82]

---

74 Ian Freckelton and David Ranson *Death Investigation and the Coroner's Inquest* (Oxford University Press, Melbourne, 2006) at 76.

75 An Act Respecting the Determination of the Causes and Circumstances of Death 2011 (Quebec) 2011, ch R–02.

76 An Act Respecting the Determination of the Causes and Circumstances of Death 2011 (Quebec), ch R–0.2, s 91 and s 92(5).

77 An Act Respecting the Determination of the Causes and Circumstances of Death 2011 (Quebec), ch R–0.2, s 98.

78 Regulation respecting criteria and procedures for selecting persons fit for the post of coroner, RRQ, c R-0.2, Division 111 r5.

79 Freckelton and Ranson, above n 74, at 76.

80 Bureau de Coroner Quebec "Recommandations – Bureau du coroner" (2007) Bureau du Coroner <http://www.coroner.gouv.qc.ca>.

81 An Act Respecting the Determination of the Causes and Circumstances of Death 2011 (Quebec), ch R–0.2, s 29.

82 Freckelton and Ranson, above n 74, at 77.

6.3.4 England

As outlined in Chapter 2, Rule 43 of the Coroners Rules 1984 (UK) created the power for a coroner to report a matter to a relevant authority where a coroner believed that action should be taken to prevent the recurrence of fatalities similar to the one under inquest.[83] While strictly speaking this power to report is not a power to make particular recommendations, such recommendations may be informally made within official reports.[84] This delegated legislation was updated in 2008 in order to give greater prominence and importance to coroner reports to improve public health and safety.[85] For example, coroners were given wider remit to make reports to prevent future deaths; it did not have to be related to a similar death.[86]

The 2008 rules also established a mandatory written response requirement, a change that arose primarily because of the consistent failure by many agencies to respond to Rule 43 reports.[87] Entities to which coroners made Rule 43 reports consequently had 56 days to send a written response to the report, which the Lord Chancellor would in turn publish.[88]

This coronial response regime has since been enshrined in primary legislation in the Coroners and Justice Act 2009 (UK). Under this new Act, the coroner must report matters to the newly established Chief Coroner and all "interested persons" where there is a risk that other, similar deaths may occur and the coroner believes action should be taken to prevent such an occurrence.[89] The Chief Coroner acts as a centralised figure for the coronial system, with functions that include ensuring that reports and responses made in relation to deaths in one coronial district are not overlooked in another, so that preventable deaths are less likely to occur.[90]

---

83 See Coroners (Amendment) Rules 2008 (England and Wales) Rule 43A.

84 Christopher Dorries *Coroners' Court: A Guide to Law and Practice* (2nd ed., Oxford University Press, Oxford, 2004).

85 *Guidance for Coroners on Changes to Rule 43: Coroner Reports to Prevent Future Deaths*. Suggested that this was necessary in order to meet obligations under the Convention, Art 2.

86 UK Ministry of Justice *Guidance for Coroners on Changes to Rule 43: Coroner Reports to Prevent Future Deaths* (2008) at 3.

87 At 14.

88 Coroners (Amendment) Rules 2008 (England and Wales) Rule 43A.

89 Coroners and Justice Act 2009 (England and Wales) 2009, Sch 5, s 7; See also reg 28(4) of: *Coroners (Investigations) Regulations 2013 (UK)*, which came into effect on 25 July 2013. Note, the Coroner may also send a copy of the report to any other person who the coroner believes may find it useful or interesting.

90 UK Ministry of Justice, above n 86.

This is to be achieved through the publication of six-monthly summaries of Rule 43 reports (which are renamed as "Reports on Action to Prevent Future Deaths")[91] and their corresponding responses on the Ministry of Justice website and also in the Chief Coroner's annual report.

The summaries include trends, reports with wider implications, and annexes giving details of the number of reports issued by each coroner district, and organisations which have not responded to the coroner and all reports received.[92] While it has been remarked that the English coroner has no explicit preventive role,[93] the implicit importance of death prevention to the regime is perhaps borne out in this legislative mandatory response requirement.[94]

It should be noted that implementation of many of the changes introduced by the 2009 Act has been an ongoing process as at the time of writing, although the majority of provisions relating to coronial investigations and inquests (including those relating to Rule 43 reports) commenced on 25 July 2013.[95] Summarising the changes that came into force on that date, the Chief Coroner stated:[96]

> Inquests will be heard earlier, usually within six months. Families will receive information earlier and will have greater access to documents and evidence. Bodies will be released earlier for burial or cremation. Fewer inquests will be needed as a result of early investigation. And there will be a special emphasis upon coroners reporting to prevent future deaths.

---

91 Office of the Chief Coroner *Guidance No. 5: Reports to Prevent Future Deaths*. For simplicity, this chapter will continue to use the term "Rule 43 reports" to refer to Reports on Action to Prevent Future Deaths.

92 These summaries can be accessed from the Ministry of Justice's website, at <http://www.justice.gov.uk/coroners-burial-cremation/coroners/rule-43>.

93 Ian Freckelton "Anglo-Australian Coronial Law Reform: The Widening Gap" (2010) 17 JLM 471 at 474.

94 Note, however, that the newly published guidelines on Rule 43 reports state that while such reports are important, they are "ancillary to the inquest procedure and not its mainspring" (citing *Re Kelly (deceased)* (1996) 161 JP 417). See Office of the Chief Coroner *Rule 43 Reports* at para 6.

95 Coroners and Justice Act 2009 (England and Wales) 2009, s 182; the new regime applies to any inquest not completed prior to 25 July 2013. The response requirement is now specified in Sch 5, s 7(2) of the Act, and also in reg 29 of Coroners (Investigations) Regulations 2013 (UK), above n 89.

96 Judiciary of England and Wales "Judges, Tribunals and Magistrates Chief Coroner: Implementation of relevant parts of Coroners and Justice Act 2009" (25 July 2013) Judiciary of England and Wales <http://www.judiciary.gov.uk/media/media-releases/2013/ChiefCoronerImplementationOfRelevantPartsOfCoronersAndJusticeAct2009>.

Further review of the practice of issuing Rule 43 reports is anticipated. On 21 September 2012, the Chief Coroner indicated that the process of issuing and responding to these reports will be reviewed as part of a "ten point plan" to address problems within the existing coronial system.[97] This review will be aimed at ensuring greater consistency in the number and quality of reports issued, as there has been significant regional variation in the content of, and frequency in which coroners issue, Rule 43 reports (with some coroners issuing no such reports at all).[98]

6.3.5 Scotland

As I outlined in Chapter 2, death investigation in Scotland is carried out by the Office of the Procurator Fiscal and the Sheriff Courts. The relevant legislation provides sheriffs conducting fatal accident inquiries with no explicit preventive purpose or power. However, sheriffs make recommendations in around one-third of cases,[99] and this power may be implied in the sheriff's duty to make determinations on any reasonable precautions whereby death might have been avoided and any systemic defects which contributed to the death.[100] Upon making a determination, a sheriff must send a copy of the determinations reached to the Lord Advocate,[101] and to the parties to the proceeding,[102] and the Government maintains a website where some recommendations are published in brief.[103]

However, no response to any recommendations made within a sheriff's determinations is currently required. A Scottish Government commissioned review of fatal accident inquiries was published in late 2009, promoting an explicit preventive purpose achieved through a recommendatory power, and the creation of a mandatory response regime similar to

---

97 See Chief Coroner's Speech to the Annual Conference of the Coroners' Society of England and Wales (21 September 2012) at <http://www.judiciary.gov.uk/Resources/JCO/Documents/Speeches/chief-coroner-speech-coroners-society-conference.pdf>.

98 Chief Coroner's Speech to the Annual Conference of the Coroners' Society of England and Wales (21 September 2012) at para 63.

99 "Review of Fatal Accident Inquiry Legislation" The Scottish Government <http://www.scotland.gov.uk/About/Review/fatal-accident-review>.

100 Fatal Accidents and Sudden Deaths Inquiry (Scotland) Act 1976, s 6(1)(c) and (d).

101 Fatal Accidents and Sudden Deaths Inquiry (Scotland) Act 1976, s 6(4)(a).

102 Fatal Accidents and Sudden Deaths Inquiry Procedure (Scotland) Rules 1977, Rule 11(3).

103 See the Scottish Government's website at <http://www.scotland.gov.uk/Topics/Justice/law/fatalaccidentinquiries/Recommend>.

Victoria's system.[104] The Scottish Parliament has not yet made a legislative response to this report.

6.4 THE DEBATE

Although the benefits to the community of a coronial system which has a prophylactic function are well recognised,[105] there is ongoing debate about whether mandatory response regimes should be included in coronial legislation. Opponents of such regimes argue that this expansion of coroners' powers would mean that every coroner would assume the role of a far-reaching Royal Commissioner, without the restraint of appropriate terms of reference for the inquiry.[106] Supporters of mandatory regimes contend that the absence of sanction for non-compliance with coroners' recommendations means that the ability of recommendations to achieve their purpose is limited. Agencies ignoring coronial recommendations have been the subject of considerable criticism. The lack of a compliance requirement causes difficulties in determining the degree to which coroners' recommendations are implemented and to which coroners receive feedback on the effectiveness of their recommendations.

The Victoria Law Reform Committee found that "almost all of the witnesses to this inquiry who gave evidence on this issue supported the view that there should be mandatory responses to coronial recommendations".[107]

Key questions are:

- Do coroners, agencies and interested parties believe that a mandatory response regime should be introduced?
- Should mandatory statutory regimes for follow-up to coronial recommendations be part of New Zealand law and considered in the current government review?
- *When* in the coronial process should feedback about coroners' recommendations occur?

---

104 "Review of Fatal Accident Inquiry Legislation", above n 99.
105 New Zealand Law Commission, above n 9, at 19.
106 Parliament of Victoria Law Reform Committee, above n 57, at 367.
107 At 396.

6.5 EMPIRICAL EVIDENCE

What does the NZ empirical evidence reveal about coroners', agencies' and interested parties' views? Only two organisations did not support such law reform. All coroners interviewed were in favour of the introduction of a mandatory response regime. Coroners do not wish to rely on publicity in order to receive responses from organisations.[108] Several coroners also mentioned that such a regime would be advantageous for the system because having responses to recommendations on public record could "allow people to view how the government has responded to issues over time".[109]

Five coroners pointed out that a mandatory response regime should only be introduced alongside other changes aimed at improving the quality of recommendations. For instance, Coroner Stewart's remarks are reflective of this perspective:[110]

> I think it [mandatory response regime] would be a good idea. I think it would mean that organisations would take recommendations seriously. It may have a positive impact on coroners too. Their recommendations could be more robust, knowing the organisations would have to respond. . . . But you would want the recommendations to be good first.

As I discussed in Chapter 5, one option for enhancing the quality of coroners' recommendations "first" is to ensure that coroners receive feedback about their recommendations *before* they are finalised. A disadvantage of a statutory mandatory response regime is that coroners receive responses/feedback from organisations about recommendations at the conclusion of the investigation.

Like coroners, all organisations (apart from two) were supportive of the introduction of a mandatory response regime. All but three (39/42, 93%)

---

108 Interview with Coroner Armstrong (Jennifer Moore, 11 October 2012).

109 Liam Hyslop "Action, Not Words, Prevent Tragic Deaths" *The Dominion Post* (Wellington, 13 July 2013) A19.

110 Interview with Coroner Stewart (Jennifer Moore, 12 October 2012). Reproduced with permission of Thomson Reuters (Professional) Australia Limited, www.thomsonreuters.com.au.

This article was first published by Thomson Reuters in the *Journal of Law and Medicine* as Jennifer Moore "An Empirical Approach to the New Zealand Government's Review of the Coronial Jurisdiction" (2014) 21 JLM 602. For all subscription inquiries please phone, from Australia: 1300 304 195, from Overseas: +61 2 8587 7980 or online at www.thomsonreuters.com.au/catalogue. The official PDF version of this article can also be purchased separately from Thomson Reuters.

of the questionnaire respondents were supportive of the introduction of a mandatory response system. Their reasons for supporting such a regime were the same as those expressed by coroners. Organisations also favoured a mandatory response regime because it would be useful for their internal processes:[111]

> It'd be useful for us as an organisation to write a formal response. That way we know that everything has been covered off. Managers want to know whether the coroner's recommendations from the last event had been implemented. It's a formal closing of the loop that protects agencies as well.

Media reports and interviews with interested parties such as families demonstrate that they favour the introduction of a mandatory response regime. The main reason for their support is that there is a perception that organisations can too easily ignore coroners' recommendations. As Coroner Atwood pointed out, the "old perennial question from the public is do they [organisations] have to take any notice of your decisions?"[112]

A mandatory response regime would not, and should not, guarantee implementation of coroners' recommendations. As I explained in Chapter 4, sometimes organisations have valid reasons for not implementing coroners' recommendations. For example, the organisation's empowering legislation may not enable it to implement the coroner's recommendations, the recommendation may not be within the organisation's business, or it may be directed at the wrong organisation. Introduction

---

[111] Interview with Sean Goddard (Department of Conservation) (Jennifer Moore, 14 May 2013). Reproduced with permission of Thomson Reuters (Professional) Australia Limited, www.thomsonreuters.com.au.

This article was first published by Thomson Reuters in the *Journal of Law and Medicine* as Jennifer Moore "An Empirical Approach to the New Zealand Government's Review of the Coronial Jurisdiction" (2014) 21 JLM 602. For all subscription inquiries please phone, from Australia: 1300 304 195, from Overseas: +61 2 8587 7980 or online at www.thomsonreuters.com.au/catalogue. The official PDF version of this article can also be purchased separately from Thomson Reuters.

[112] Interview with Coroner Atwood (Jennifer Moore, 11 December 2012). Reproduced with permission of Thomson Reuters (Professional) Australia Limited, www.thomsonreuters.com.au. This article was first published by Thomson Reuters in the *Journal of Law and Medicine* as Jennifer Moore "An Empirical Approach to the New Zealand Government's Review of the Coronial Jurisdiction" (2014) 21 JLM 602. For all subscription inquiries please phone, from Australia: 1300 304 195, from Overseas: +61 2 8587 7980 or online at www.thomsonreuters.com.au/catalogue. The official PDF version of this article can also be purchased separately from Thomson Reuters.

of a mandatory response regime may not solve this problem. Instead, providing coroners with feedback about proposed recommendations early in the investigation process may ensure that this problem is solved and, therefore, result in an improved rate of implementation.

In a climate of austerity, there may be insufficient resources to ensure that organisations make meaningful, considered responses that are then also carefully followed up by coroners or their support staff. As Federated Farmers explained:[113]

> It's not practical to have a [mandatory response] regime like that, especially if coroners are going to send us stuff that is not relevant and should not have been sent to Farmers.

Federated Farmers' comments were echoed by the small number of other participants who were not supportive of the introduction of a mandatory response regime. The recurring reasons were:

- the variable quality of coroners' recommendations
- incorrectly targeted recommendations
- poor consultation by some coroners
- organisational structures, and
- the low likelihood of meaningful consideration and responses from organisations and coroners.

6.5.1 Mandatory Recommendations

One choice that legislatures must make is whether the power for coroners to make recommendations should be discretionary or mandatory. There is jurisdictional variance as to whether, and when, a coroner is required to make a recommendation. For example, in the English and Tasmanian systems, if a coroner opines that a recommendation could be made that may prevent deaths, the legislation specifies that the coroner must make the recommendation; that is, the coroner has a legal duty in such a situation to make the recommendation if appropriate.

By contrast, legislation in Victoria and Ontario, among others,[114] provides that a coroner may make recommendations in such situations, but imposes no legal duty as such. Other jurisdictions adopt a middle-ground approach: the power to make recommendations can be either

---

[113] Interview with Federated Farmers (Jennifer Moore, 18 December 2012).

[114] For example, the other Australian states where a general discretion to recommend is provided are Queensland, New South Wales and the ACT.

discretionary or mandatory, depending on the category of death. In Western Australia, for example, a coroner must comment on the quality of the supervision, treatment and care of a person who died while in care, but in relation to other categories of death, a coroner has a discretionary power to comment.[115] Similarly in the Northern Territory, where a person has died in custody, a coroner is required to make such recommendations with respect to the prevention of future deaths in similar circumstances as the coroner considers to be relevant,[116] but for all other kinds of death, a coroner has a general discretion to comment.[117]

In the case of a mandatory duty, when the recommendation-making power is conditional upon whether a particular coroner believes a recommendation is "appropriate" in the circumstances, the distinction between a discretionary or a mandatory power may not be significant. In other words, the inclusion of language such as "whenever appropriate" or similar may mean that, in effect, the recommendation-making function is discretionary and coroners can therefore decide whether or not to make recommendations.

However, in part because of an apparent reluctance of some coroners to issue recommendations despite circumstances in some cases suggesting a preventive recommendation would have been appropriate and beneficial, a number of commentators and law reform committees consider that imposing a positive duty on coroners to make recommendations would improve the preventive potential of coroners' recommendations. Both the National Report of the Royal Commission into Aboriginal Deaths in Custody and the Report of the Law Reform Committee of the Victorian Parliament considered that coronial legislation should impose an express duty on coroners to make recommendations in appropriate cases.[118]

There are several benefits in mandating coroners to make recommendations. Firstly, a legal duty could ensure greater frequency in the making of recommendations. This latter aspect is supported by the experience in England. Since the introduction of a legislative duty on coroners to issue

---

115 Coroners Act 1996 (WA), s 25(2) and (3).

116 Coroners Act 1993 (NT) 1993, s 26(2).

117 Coroners Act 1993 (NT), s 34(2).

118 See for example recommendation 13 of Commonwealth of Australia, above n 41, at 4589: "It is important that coroners should make such recommendations and that governments should give consideration to imposing a more positive duty on coroners in this respect." See also Parliament of Victoria Law Reform Committee, above n 57, at 383: "the committee also considers that the Act should impose a positive duty on coroners to make recommendations in appropriate cases."

Rule 43 reports in 2008, there has been a year-on-year increase in the number of such reports issued.[119] Secondly, a legal duty may also better allow aggrieved relatives and interested advocacy groups to use legal means to compel coroners to make formal recommendations regarding the prevention of further deaths. These groups could challenge a coroner's decision not to issue recommendations despite appropriateness, or a coroner's making mistakes of fact or law in deciding whether a recommendation would be appropriate. If government entities had to respond to recommendations, incentive might exist for families and other advocates to seek formal recommendations in order to have lessons learned from preventable deaths. Thirdly, compelling coroners to make recommendations could also help shift the aspirations of the coronial position to recognise the modern importance of death prevention, not just death investigation. As Baroness Butler-Sloss notes, it seems an "odd mix" to have a strong purpose of death prevention followed by the weak conclusion of a discretion to carry out this purpose; one would expect a coroner to have a duty to make reports or recommendations aimed at death prevention.[120]

It is possible that coroners who issue recommendations less frequently risk failing to fulfil their moral duties relating to death prevention and public health. A mandatory recommendation-making requirement could avoid this. While obliging coroners to make recommendations may appear to stray into an area of judicial independence,[121] it is not unusual for a judicial officer to face procedural obligation. There should be no constitutional qualms with controlling coronial procedure to promote the purpose of the coronial regime, so long as the substance of the coroners' recommendations is not affected. Despite this, it is significant that many participants who were interviewed expressed a number of concerns, tending to suggest that a legal duty may reduce the usefulness and credibility of coroners' recommendations in practice.

Several coroners agreed that recommendations will not be required in all cases. As one coroner remarked in relation to drink-driving deaths: "I don't think that there is anything else that I can recommend. I can only say that this is, tragically, another case."[122] Similar remarks were made with respect to co-sleeping: "[I]t saddens me that we seem to be still struggling with co-sleeping and it's clearly not a recommended practice. And I'm

---

[119] Ministry of Justice *Summary of Reports and Responses under Rule 43 of the Coroners Rules: Ninth Report: For period 1 October 2012 – 31 March 2013* (2013) at 25.

[120] (23 June 2009) 178 GBPD HL 1562.

[121] Interview with Coroner Owen (Jennifer Moore, 3 October 2012).

[122] Interview with Coroner Frank (Jennifer Moore, 10 October 2012).

not going to make a recommendation because I'd only be repeating the wheel."[123] Reflecting these concerns, one coroner stated:[124]

> My view about recommendations is that because of the way the system is, coroners feel they should recommend every five minutes. I think that dilutes the value of what we can say. So when I make recommendations I hope people will take it more seriously because I don't make recommendations all the time. I don't need to hear the sound of my voice for the sake of it and I don't need to reinvent the wheel, but if I think there is something genuinely of interest or will make a difference, I will make a recommendation.

Other participants also indicated that, in some cases, it will be unhelpful to make recommendations. A lawyer with NZ Coroner's Court experience stated that sometimes coroners issue recommendations simply "to be seen to be doing something. They make recommendations that don't or would not have causally changed the outcome."[125] A danger in such an approach is that it could potentially lead to unnecessary and ill-conceived recommendations. According to Child, Youth and Family Services, caution is therefore needed in taking such an approach:[126]

> It is a mistake, I think, to want to do something as a result of the tragedy and to show some benefit coming from the review, without thinking about the long-term consequences of that decision. . . . [W]hen you're making a determination about what should be done it may make the reviewers themselves feel better that they've done something because they've encountered the tragedy of this child in that situation, where they feel a need to make a recommendation but they'll always think about the systemic implications of what that means and the impact on the service. So we just need to be careful about that really.

One problem inherent in the process of formulating recommendations is that "they arise piecemeal, and inevitably in a way that is coloured by and responsive to the dilemmas posed by particular cases."[127] Mandating the recommendatory power will not address this problem; in fact, it may exacerbate it. This concern was reflected in the comments of research participants. For example, many organisations highlighted difficulties in responding to recommendations based on isolated cases of death. Child, Youth and Family Services commented that "coroners, or anyone, should

---

123 Atwood, above n 112.

124 Interview with Coroner Walsh (Jennifer Moore, 13 October 2012).

125 Interview with Lawyer02 (Jennifer Moore, 10 September 2012).

126 Interview with Child, Youth and Family Services (Jennifer Moore, 29 May 2013).

127 Freckelton and Ranson, above n 74, at 738.

be very cautious about extrapolating policy recommendations pertaining to single case studies."[128]

Another problem identified by agencies is that there can often be a "scattergun"[129] of different recommendations relating to one particular issue or policy: "Instead of one recommendation which relates to half a dozen events, each one makes his or her own recommendation. Police can't keep amending policies on the hoof every six to eight weeks as a coroner comes up with a different recommendation."[130] Echoing these concerns, Child, Youth and Family Services commented that:[131]

> If you repeatedly add in additional procedures, regulations, systems over the top of what you've already got, you run the risk of designing or developing a system that is so elaborate that it actually gets in the way of your ultimate outcome, which is improving the lives of vulnerable children across the community. So, the temptation, I think, of a review is to do something, to make some kind of recommendation, spot some deficiency in the system or in the practice and portfolio recommendation, but you need to be cautious about that because you could then add in additional complexity to the task if that problem isn't a risk of occurring again in a number of different contexts in the future. So that is a risk.

Many participants were also concerned that coroners at times make conflicting recommendations regarding the same issue or policy. Such conflicting recommendations significantly reduce the likelihood of implementation and undermine the credibility of the coronial system in general. As one coroner noted:[132]

> Being able to comment meaningfully on how to prevent deaths in the future is really difficult and frustrating. I know that agencies get criticised for not following recommendations, but many times I think that I don't blame them. We make conflicting recommendations. One coroner recommends one thing, another something else, the exact opposite. I have had cases where that has happened. I've specifically not made a recommendation on the basis that the Department and industry had made indications that meant there was no need to make a recommendation. Then a few weeks later another coroner had made recommendations about the same type of death and those recommendations were contrary to what I had said. So of course people won't take us seriously.

---

[128] Interview with Child, Youth and Family Services (Jennifer Moore, 29 May 2013).

[129] Interview with David Cliff (Police) (Jennifer Moore, 22 April 2013).

[130] See for example Cliff (Police), above n 129.

[131] Interview with Child, Youth and Family Services (Jennifer Moore, 29 May 2013).

[132] Interview with Coroner Fitzpatrick (Jennifer Moore, 25 September 2012).

The participants' comments above demonstrate that the potential of coroners' recommendations to contribute to death prevention depends not on the frequency of recommendations made, but rather on the quality of those recommendations and the approach followed by coroners in deciding whether or not to make recommendations. Mandating coroners to make recommendations is thus unlikely to improve the quality or preventive potential of recommendations. Neither the prophylactic objective of the recommendatory power nor the interests of families are best served when coroners make unnecessary, impractical or ill-conceived recommendations simply because they are required to do so. Instead, changes upstream, such as providing coroners with increased support and improving access to previous coronial findings and other resources, may be more effective in terms of increasing consistency in practice across coroners and improving the preventive potential of recommendations.

6.5.2 Regimes for Responses to Coroners' Recommendations

(a) Mandatory responses, not mandatory implementation

As I stated earlier in this chapter, in NZ at present, there is no obligation on agencies or individuals to whom coroners' recommendations are made to respond to those recommendations. This is despite the NZ Law Commission's support for imposing such an obligation in its 2000 report:[133]

> [W]here a coronial recommendation concerns a government agency, a Chief Coroner must give notice of that recommendation to the agency concerned, the Minister responsible for that agency, the Attorney General, and any other agency or individual affected by the recommendation. The government agency must, within three months, report to its Minister the steps it intends to take in relation to the coronial recommendation and a copy of that report must be provided to the Chief Coroner. The Chief Coroner must include particulars of the government agency's response in the annual report from the Office of the Chief Coroner.

Before discussing in detail the arguments surrounding mandating responses to coronial recommendations, it is important to be clear about what such a regime would not entail. The distinction between mandatory implementation and mandatory response requirements is trite. The former obliges entities to put coroners' recommendations into action, irrespective of the recommendations' value, while the latter merely

---

[133] New Zealand Law Commission, above n 9, recommendation 14.

requires entities to give a considered response to recommendations directed to them; a considered rejection would suffice this requirement. Despite this, the literature conflates the two concepts too often. As Chief Coroner Neil MacLean notes, "sometimes government misunderstands and thinks that we want mandatory implementation introduced. . . . That would be the judiciary intruding into the realm of the executive . . . I am not saying that."[134]

Such an implementation regime would fundamentally change the role of the Coroner's Court into a "general administrative appeal tribunal" and "create duplication with the court's judicial review role".[135] In addition, the New Zealand Law Commission rightly noted that a mandatory implementation requirement would be dangerous, as a coroner who made a recommendation "may not have had all the available information and options in front of him or her".[136] Empowering coroners – judicial officers on par with District Court judges – to dictate policy to government or even private entities would inevitably invite bad policy. As such, no jurisdiction has a mandatory implementation requirement. Despite this, and despite receiving no submissions advocating such a requirement, the Ministry of Justice rejected both mandatory response and mandatory implementation requirements by conflating the two together:[137]

> Requiring agencies to implement or respond to coroners' recommendations would have significant compliance costs for government agencies, and it is not clear that there would be significant benefits from *this* approach. *It* would also impinge upon the separation of powers by making the executive accountable to judicial officers on matters of public policy. (emphasis added)

---

[134] Interview with the Chief Coroner (Jennifer Moore, 12 September 2012). Reproduced with permission of Thomson Reuters (Professional) Australia Limited, www.thomsonreuters.com.au.

This article was first published by Thomson Reuters in the *Journal of Law and Medicine* as Jennifer Moore "An Empirical Approach to the New Zealand Government's Review of the Coronial Jurisdiction" (2014) 21 JLM 602. For all subscription inquiries please phone, from Australia: 1300 304 195, from Overseas: +61 2 8587 7980 or online at www.thomsonreuters.com.au/catalogue. The official PDF version of this article can also be purchased separately from Thomson Reuters."

[135] Mai Chen "New Zealand's Ombudsman Legislation: The need for amendments after almost 50 years" (2010) 41 VUWLR 723 at 737, discussed in relation to conferring similar binding recommendatory powers on Ombudsmen in New Zealand.

[136] New Zealand Law Commission *Coroners A Review: A Discussion Paper* (NZLC PP36 1999) at 31–133.

[137] *Ministry of Justice Departmental Report* (2006) at 7.

With reform of NZ's existing coronial legislation pending, there is an opportunity for the NZ Government to consider whether some form of mandatory statutory response regime to coroners' recommendations should be included in the reforms. It is significant that almost all of the participants interviewed during this research were in favour of introducing such a regime. Somewhat disappointingly, however, the Ministry of Justice's current review of the Act has yet to include consideration of whether such a response regime should be introduced as part of the legislative reforms. This is despite the Ministry noting in its Cabinet Paper that:[138]

> A number of overseas jurisdictions (such as Australia and the UK) have grappled with similar issues and how to respond to them. They have implemented a variety of measures with mixed success. Some jurisdictions have taken the approach of requiring mandatory response, (rather than mandatory implementation) to ensure coroners' recommendations are considered and implemented where appropriate. In some instances, these governments have provided resources to assist with the formulation of recommendations. While this may achieve improved recommendations, it would come at a cost to the government.

It is true that a proposal mandating entities affected by coroners' recommendations to take consequential action would be a "significant and revolutionary step, transforming coroners from traditional examples of judicial officers into risk managers working in part within a complex public health regulatory context".[139] Indeed, opponents of mandatory response regimes have argued that this expansion of coroners' powers would mean that every coroner would assume the role of a far-reaching royal commissioner, without the restraint of appropriate terms of reference for the inquiry.[140] However, while mandating responses may change the place of coroners within both a legal and public health context, "it may well be that it would transform coroners into entities of real, ongoing relevance".[141] Further, despite the Ministry's concern as to cost, a formal response requirement would arguably be a modest and proportionate provision for monitoring, and assessment of, considered proposals arising from preventable deaths.

---

[138] Cabinet Paper, above n 4, at 21.

[139] Ian Freckelton "F.W. Guest Memorial Lecture: July 12 2007: Death Investigation and the Evolving Role of the Coroner" (2008) 11 Otago LR 565 at 581.

[140] See the Victorian Bar's comments in the Parliament of Victoria Law Reform Committee, above n 57, at 367.

[141] Ian Freckelton "The Myers Oration 2005: Untimely Death, Law and Suicidality" (2005) 12 Psychiatry, Psychology and Law 265 at 275.

This is particularly true given that the NZ community already expends considerable resources on public inquests.[142]

There are certainly a number of potential benefits that follow from the introduction of such a regime. As the Victorian Parliamentary Law Reform Committee noted in its 2006 review of Victoria's Coroners Act 1985, the ability of agencies to ignore coroners' recommendations with impunity and without public scrutiny "has been the subject of considerable criticism and a source of frustration for the families of people who have died in circumstances giving rise to coronial recommendations which are not acted upon".[143] The Committee was particularly concerned that expending considerable resources in the process of death investigation and the making of recommendations arising from such investigations is a "wasteful exercise if the recommendations can be ignored by those to whom they are directed".[144] While a mandatory response requirement would not compel compliance, it would mandate responsiveness in the public interest and on the public record.[145] This "public interest" component has been defined by one commentator as "the open scrutiny of and accountability for deaths and the accountability of the coronial system itself".[146]

Many participants who were interviewed highlighted the advantages of a response regime in terms of increasing accountability. Coroners commented that a response regime would be advantageous for "the system"[147] because having responses on the "public record"[148] could "allow people to view how the government has responded to issues over time".[149] Several organisations also supported a mandatory response regime as a means to ensure accountability in the public sphere. For example, one organisation commented that "for coroners to effect systemic change . . . and if the coroner is there to make things better for those who are left behind, then they need more bite and power."[150] Even if there is good reason for not

---

142 Ian Freckelton "F.W. Guest Memorial Lecture: July 12 2007: Death Investigation and the Evolving Role of the Coroner" (2008) 11 Otago LR 565 at 583.

143 Parliament of Victoria Law Reform Committee, above n 57, at 369.

144 At 406.

145 Freckelton, above n 139, at 583.

146 Rebecca Scott Bray "Death Scene Jurisprudence: The Social Life of Coronial Facts" (2010) 19 Griffith Law Review 567 at 586.

147 For examples, see Coroner, above n 134; Atwood, above n 112; Frank, above n 122.

148 Coroner, above n 134; Frank, above n 122.

149 Atwood, above n 112.

150 Interview with Standards NZ (Jennifer Moore, 26 October 2012).

implementing a particular recommendation, several organisations noted that "we should be required to publicly state that. . . . If we don't want to implement the recommendations, we can just give good reasons and be accountable to the public about whether those reasons are enough."[151] The Police similarly commented "[t]hey should respond. If there is a whole process and there is a valid recommendation, and it is ignored, that is not acceptable in my view."[152]

A mandatory response regime could also enhance the therapeutic potential of the coronial jurisdiction by putting in place a mechanism by which family members of a deceased can be informed of the steps an agency will (or will not) take in order to prevent future deaths. As one organisation noted:[153]

> A lot of energy is put into coronial inquiries. The families of the deceased want to know what happened and why, but most also want change. "I don't want this happening to anyone else's son or daughter." So to give the coroners some more bite in terms of requiring responses could be useful.

The potential therapeutic benefits of a mandatory response regime have been highlighted by several other commentators. For example, during the second reading of New Zealand's Coroners Bill, Nicky Wagner MP commented that "[f]amilies often mention that they want something good to come out of such wasteful deaths."[154] Barbara Stone MP also noted in relation to Queensland's Coroners Bill 2002 that:[155]

> Often media reports show families wanting more done to ensure that the same tragic circumstances that resulted in the death of their loved one are not repeated. They want to know that their loved one did not die in vain. This bill will go a long way to ensuring recommendations to reduce the risk of similar tragedies are heard and acted upon.

Other advantages may flow from a mandatory response regime. Research participants considered that a response requirement would provide a valuable means by which coroners can receive feedback about the effectiveness of recommendations they make. As Standards New Zealand explained:[156]

---

151 Goddard (Department of Conservation), above n 111.
152 Cliff (Police), above n 129.
153 Interview with Standards NZ (Jennifer Moore, 26 October 2012).
154 (9 May 2006) 631 *New Zealand Parliamentary Debates* 2866.
155 (27 March 2003) Australian Parliamentary Debates 903.
156 Interview with Standards NZ (Jennifer Moore, 26 October 2012).

> In some ways it's just a "please explain tool". You might make a cost–benefit decision not to implement a coroner's recommendation, but if so, then say so. It'd be a very useful level of transparency. Also it'd be great to have that information going back to the coroner because then they can take it on board for the next recommendation. If coroners don't get feedback from organisations about why they think a coroner's recommendation could not be implemented, they can't take it on board or use it to feed into future recommendations, which means there may not be improvements going forward.

Many coroners recognised the role of feedback in improving the quality of their recommendations. For example, one coroner noted:[157]

> I think it would be helpful because it would help us understand the reasons why things aren't being done. If there are things that we could do differently, that would improve the quality of our recommendations. It should not be mandatory that agencies do what we say. There are lots of good reasons why agencies can't do what we recommend. But telling us why they have not would be helpful.

Another important advantage of a response regime is that it may enable "data-based evaluation of the extent to which coroners' recommendations are implemented".[158] The current lack of a comprehensive reporting mechanism, which records the agencies that are the subject of recommendations, their responses, and what actions have been taken, causes difficulties in collating empirical information relating to the degree to which coroners' recommendations can be implemented and therefore contribute to preventing further deaths in practice.[159]

(b) Alternative statutory models to a mandatory response regime

Rather than introducing a mandatory response regime applicable to all entities to which coroners' recommendations are directed, an alternative option is to extend the statutory tools currently available to coroners to include a discretionary power to request responses to recommendations. This may be a more cost-effective means to ensure coroners' recommendations are adequately considered.

In NZ, such statutory powers already exist within the jurisdictions of both the Office of the Health and Disability Commissioner and the Office of the Ombudsman. For example, the HDC noted:[160]

---

157 Interview with Coroner Fitzpatrick (Jennifer Moore, 25 September 2012).

158 Freckelton and Ranson, above n 74, at 20.

159 Submission of David Ranson, Parliament of Victoria Law Reform Committee, above n 57, at 374.

160 Interview with the HDC (Jennifer Moore, 22 February 2013).

> It is interesting that there is no requirement to respond in the Coronial jurisdiction and yet in the HDC they can request the organisation to report on how they responded to their recommendations. So there is a bit more teeth around how the HDC processes work [sic].

The HDC is an independent Crown entity created under the Health and Disability Commissioner Act 1994. It is charged with promoting and protecting the rights of health and disability services consumers, and facilitating the fair, simple, speedy and efficient resolution of complaints.[161] Part of this role includes the making of recommendations to "any appropriate person or authority in relation to the means by which complaints involving alleged breaches might be resolved and further breaches avoided".[162] Importantly, the HDC can request any person to whom such a recommendation is made to "notify the Commissioner, within a specified time, of the steps (if any) that the person proposes to take to give effect to the recommendation".[163] If the Commissioner opines that the person has failed to take "adequate and appropriate" action within a reasonable timeframe, the Commissioner has power to progress matters by referring the matter to the relevant oversight body or to the Minister of Health.[164]

Under the Ombudsman Act 1975, the Ombudsman may make similar recommendations to organisations and can require those organisations to report within a specified timeframe what steps they intend to undertake to implement the recommendations.[165] Materially, where an organisation fails to adequately respond to a recommendation, the Ombudsman can escalate the matter further by sending the recommendation and the organisation's report to Parliament.[166] Ombudsmen have sent one such report to Parliament.[167] The Act also confers a power on the Ombudsman to require local authorities and specified organisations to publish a summary of the report and recommendation and make it available for inspection and copying by members of the public.[168] In addition, the Ombudsman can inform the complainant of his or her recommendation and whether

---

161 Health and Disability Commissioner Act 1994, s 6.

162 Health and Disability Commissioner Act 1994, s 14(g).

163 Health and Disability Commissioner Act 1994, s 46(1).

164 Health and Disability Commissioner Act 1994, s 46(2)(a). In addition, the Commissioner may comment on the matter: s 46(2)(b).

165 Ombudsman Act 1975, s 22(3).

166 Ombudsman Act 1975, s 22(4).

167 Chen, above n 135, at 733.

168 Ombudsman Act 1975, s 23; see also Part 3 Sch 1 for a list of organisations. A public notice that the report and recommendations are available for public inspection shall be put in whatever media the Ombudsman requires.

appropriate or adequate action has been taken by the department or organisation within a reasonable time.[169]

Importantly, while neither jurisdiction confers power to make binding recommendations,[170] the common feature of both regimes is the ability to progress matters where an agency fails to take appropriate action in response to a recommendation. Such referral mechanisms may be effective in securing high compliance rates with response requirements. Indeed, this may even explain why the majority of recommendations issued by Ombudsmen and the HDC are not only responded to, but also complied with.[171]

Given the "perennial"[172] issue in coronial regimes is the ability of agencies to ignore coroners' recommendations, a statutory follow-up model similar to that of the HDC or Ombudsman could be usefully adapted to increase the accountability of agencies to which recommendations are directed. However, conferring statutory power on coroners to refer matters to Parliament or some other oversight body in circumstances where an agency fails to take action in response to a recommendation invites concern. Such referral powers effectively confer power on coroners to comment on the appropriateness, or adequacy, of an agency's response; as already discussed, this invites attendant problems relating to the separation of powers. It is possible that the use of referral powers could be restricted to where an agency simply *fails* to respond to a recommendation following a coroner's request.

However, this would largely resemble a mandatory response requirement in practice. This is primarily because even under this alternative statutory model, coroners would be encouraged to request responses from agencies, as a matter of course, in order to secure key benefits of improved recommendations and increased accountability, among others. For this reason, the remainder of this chapter considers coronial reform only in terms of whether a mandatory response requirement should be introduced and the changes necessary to ensure that such a regime is effective. The monitoring regime and referral powers similar to those of Ombudsmen and the HDC will, however, be discussed later in this chapter in the context of monitoring responses and securing compliance with any mandatory response requirement.

---

169 Ombudsman Act 1975, s 24.

170 Note however the Ombudsman does have binding recommendatory powers with respect to official information requests: Official Information Act 1987 (NZ), s 32(1)(a).

171 In relation to Ombudsmen, see Mai Chen "New Zealand's Ombudsman Legislation: The need for amendments after almost 50 years′ (2010) 41 VUWLR 723. See also HDC, above n 160.

172 Atwood, above n 112.

(c) Summary

An important issue in respect of coronial investigations is what ensues once the investigation process is complete and following the making of recommendations. At present, the absence of any regime mandating responses to coroners' recommendations "leaves as the only 'weapon'/ power possessed by coroners the potential criticisms generated of relevant bodies by the media. This is manifestly unsatisfactory."[173] While several models for follow-up to coroners' recommendations are available, empirical evidence and available literature demonstrates that introducing a mandatory response regime could improve the preventive potential of coroners' recommendations. There is wide support among those interviewed for the introduction of a mandatory response requirement in combination with other reforms. Perceived advantages of such a regime include that it will increase accountability of agencies and of the coronial system in general; provide a means by which families can draw comfort that something good may follow from the death of their loved one; provide much needed feedback on the effectiveness and practicality of coroners' recommendations; and provide a means by which empirical data relating to the implementation of recommendations by agencies can be collected and analysed, in order to effectively assess the degree to which coroners' recommendations contribute to death prevention in practice.

Notably, the participants' broad support for mandatory response regimes is consistent with views expressed during Victoria's recent coronial reforms that culminated in the introduction of a mandatory response regime. Specifically, the Parliament of Victoria Law Reform Committee found that "almost all of the witnesses to this inquiry who gave evidence on this issue supported the view that there should be mandatory responses to coronial recommendations."[174] Recent findings reported by researchers from Melbourne University demonstrate that Victorian stakeholders remain supportive of a mandatory response requirement.[175] Summarising these findings, it was reported that:[176]

---

[173] Freckelton, above n 139, at 581.

[174] Parliament of Victoria Law Reform Committee, above n 57, at 396.

[175] Details about the project can be found at: University of Melbourne "David Studdert, Jane Pirkis and Graham Sewell – ARC Linkage Project: Learning from Preventable Deaths" University of Melbourne <http://www.law.unimelb.edu.au/index.cfm?objectId=54E887B0-E775-11E0-9E6D0050568D0140>.

[176] Email from Georgina Sutherland to Jennifer Moore regarding Melbourne University research (18 July 2014).

> In short, we found broad support for the mandatory response regime from those recipients who are required to respond under the new Act. This was clearly evident across both [quantitative] and [qualitative] results. There is some variation, of course, by the recommendation they received and whether they thought they were appropriate, relevant, effective etc. Not a surprising result, but interesting in that even among recipient entities who rejected the recommendations directed to them ([because] they couldn't or wouldn't implement them) were still supportive of the legal requirement to respond with a statement of action.

If NZ introduced a mandatory response system, how should it operate? The next section explores this question.

6.5.3 The Practical and Operational Concerns for a Mandatory Response Regime

A proposal for a mandatory response regime requires close consideration of several key areas of practical and operational concern. Important questions include: what is the appropriate timeframe that agencies should be mandated to respond to coroners' recommendations? Should private entities as well as public (that is, governmental and quasi-governmental) entities be required to respond? What form of monitoring system should be included as part of any response regime? Finally, should coroners have enforcement powers in relation to their recommendations, and/or should there be sanctions for agencies' non-compliance with a response requirement? The following section considers each of these questions in turn.

(a) Timeframe for responses

The first issue requiring consideration is whether agencies should be mandated to respond to coroners' recommendations within a specified timeframe, and if so, what length of time would be appropriate. Among jurisdictions with existing mandatory response regimes, all delimit some length of time in which an entity must respond. However, there is variation as to the length of time specified. For example, in Australia, legislation in Victoria, the Northern Territory and the ACT prescribes a three-month timeframe, while legislation in New South Wales, Queensland and South Australia prescribes a six-month timeframe. In England, agencies must currently respond to Rule 43 reports within 56 days, although there is now provision within the legislation to apply for an extension where appropriate, the length of which is to be specified at the discretion of the coroner.[177] It is worth noting that a recent proposal to decrease the 56-day

---

[177] See reg 29(5) of the Coroners (Investigations) Regulations 2013.

timeframe to one month was abandoned following consultation with key stakeholders. The general thrust of the submissions was that the proposed one-month time limit was insufficient and would have adversely impacted upon the quality of responses.[178]

The primary reason for specifying a timeframe within which agencies must respond rests largely on a desire to secure such responses in a timely manner and avoid further delays in coronial processes. Decreasing delay in the time between the making of a recommendation and action taken by an agency in response has important ramifications for the preventive and therapeutic potential of recommendations. With this in mind, a timeframe of six months, or longer, for responses is problematic. At the same time, however, there is a need to recognise that insufficient time to consider coroners' recommendations may impact on the quality of an entity's response.[179] The complexity of the dynamics in which government, and quasi-government agencies in particular, operate should be taken into account. It was this latter consideration that led the Victorian Parliament Law Reform Committee to favour a six-month timeframe for responses to recommendations, rejecting an earlier proposal for a timeframe of three months. The Committee envisaged that a six-month timeframe would "allow adequately for consideration of recommendations directed towards complex systemic problems".[180]

Notably, the NZ Law Commission recommended in its 2000 report that agencies should be required to respond to recommendations within three months, but gave no explicit justification for this position. The current impetus to reduce delay in NZ's coronial system would suggest that a three-month requirement may be more appropriate.[181] However, to provide a degree of flexibility for agencies situated within complex regulatory environments, provision could be made, as under the English approach, for extensions to the length of time within which a particular agency must respond to a recommendation. This would accommodate situations where, for example, significant or complex policy work is required to be undertaken before a response may be sent detailing the action the agency will undertake.

---

[178] Ministry of Justice (UK) *Implementing the Coroner Reforms in Part 1 of the Coroners and Justice Act 2009: Response to consultation on rules, regulations, coroner areas and statutory guidance* (2013) at 25.

[179] At 25.

[180] Parliament of Victoria Law Reform Committee, above n 57, at 408.

[181] Delay is primary consideration in Ministry's review: see Cabinet Paper, above n 4.

(b) The public/private divide

Another key issue in relation to introducing a mandatory response regime is whether the obligation to respond to coroners' recommendations should be confined to the public sector, or whether it should apply to private entities as well. When the Law Commission recommended a mandatory response regime be introduced in NZ, it opined that while coroners could issue recommendations to *any* entity, public or private, only government entities should be subject to a response requirement. Some organisations interviewed also questioned the efficacy of requiring private entities to respond to coroners' recommendations. For example, the Porirua City Council stated that:[182]

> We already work in that kind of environment and the private sector don't, necessarily. Private businesses wouldn't be used to that. The fact that a coroner is involved with your business, the way you're running your business; it's just a different thing.

The former NZ Chief Coroner similarly stated that restricting the requirement to government organisations was appropriate because "they are accountable to the public and more likely to be able to respond".[183]

However, if one of the primary goals of coronial investigations is death prevention, distinguishing between public and private entities does not seem particularly apposite, particularly since deaths clearly occur in the private sector as well. As one agency stated, a response requirement applicable to private entities is necessary because "[t]his is about broader community accountability and broader community interests and learning from deaths".[184] Private entities should also be required to respond because considerable resources are spent in the making of recommendations, the proposals are serious, and the recommendations are less likely to be aimed at private entities. Provided consideration is given to the nature

---

[182] Interview with GovtOrg04 (Jennifer Moore, 1 February 2013). Reproduced with permission of Thomson Reuters (Professional) Australia Limited, www.thomsonreuters.com.au.

This article was first published by Thomson Reuters in the *Journal of Law and Medicine* as Jennifer Moore "An Empirical Approach to the New Zealand Government's Review of the Coronial Jurisdiction" (2014) 21 JLM 602. For all subscription inquiries please phone, from Australia: 1300 304 195, from Overseas: +61 2 8587 7980 or online at www.thomsonreuters.com.au/catalogue. The official PDF version of this article can also be purchased separately from Thomson Reuters.

[183] Coroner, above n 134.

[184] Interview with Layer04 (Jennifer Moore, 5 February 2013).

and capabilities of the entity to which a recommendation is directed, it is reasonable to include private bodies within a response requirement. Moreover, the empirical data suggests that concerns relating to difficulties in requiring private entities to respond may be overstated. Most private organisations at which coroners' recommendations are directed already respond,[185] indicating that mandating the requirement would not be burdensome or inappropriate.

Other considerations to note include that private sector organisations have fewer entities to which they are accountable. This is significant for two reasons: firstly, these private bodies may have the capacity to respond to, and take action in response to, coroners' recommendations due to increased independence and flexibility; and secondly, a lack of accountability and oversight mechanisms within the private sphere may conceivably lead to industry failures that result in otherwise preventable deaths. There is also a practical consideration to note relating to an increased encroachment of private industry into roles traditionally executed by the state. An oft-cited example is the use of private security companies in the running of prisons. The involvement of these quasi-governmental bodies in the regulation and delivery of public services can blur the distinction between private and public. This may result in confusion at times as to who is obligated to respond and who is not. A requirement that *all* entities must respond, including both public and private bodies, could avoid this.

(c) Monitoring and adequacy of responses

A mandatory response regime will not be effective unless there is a monitoring process to ensure that responses to recommendations are made. Such a monitoring regime could also provide opportunities for critical evaluation of responses to specific recommendations and collation of information, allowing the effectiveness and impact of coronial recommendations to be measured.[186] However, there are a number of questions that arise in relation to a proposal for such follow-up. These include: who should be responsible for monitoring responses and the nature and scope of this role (that is, whether it should be limited only to monitoring whether responses are made, or whether it should also include monitoring the adequacy of those responses). Closely related is the question of whether, and if so, how, implementation of coroners' recommendations should be monitored.

---

185 Coroner, above n 134.

186 Parliament of Victoria Law Reform Committee, above n 57, at 405.

(d) Responsibility for monitoring responses

There are a number of overseas models available with respect to who should follow up to ensure responses are made. In Australia, for example, several different types of government organisations may follow up responses to recommendations, depending on the state jurisdiction.[187] In Victoria and (when applicable) the ACT, coroners themselves have the responsibility to ensure that responses are made and subsequently published on the Internet. In Victoria, the CPU assists coroners in carrying out this function. In Queensland, New South Wales and the Northern Territory, each Attorney General takes responsibility, collating and consolidating responses once they are made. In Southern Australia, Ministers with responsibility over government entities to which recommendations are directed must file a report containing details of any action taken or proposed to be taken to the legislature directly, although it is unclear who within the House of Parliament is responsible to ensure this does in fact take place.

There are problems involved with each of these methods of monitoring responses. Most coroners' recommendations tend to be aimed at government entities, so relying upon a government official, the Attorney General, to ensure government responses are made appears problematic. Ideally, an external watchdog would certify compliance rather than expecting the Government to hold itself accountable.

On the other hand, in New Zealand, the Attorney General fulfils a similar accountability role at times, for example, in notifying Parliament when proposed legislation contravenes the New Zealand Bill of Rights Act 1990.[188] One benefit of a governmental follow-up approach to coroners' recommendations, particularly where the Attorney General then tables agencies' responses, or summaries of these responses, in Parliament, is that "if coroners know that a recommendation and responses to it would be put before Parliament, they are going to be very careful how they would frame that recommendation."[189] Notably, some participants interviewed agreed that government departments "need to report to Parliament about what they are doing with recommendations".[190]

Relying upon coroners themselves to follow up the recommendations

---

[187] For a summary of the administrative requirements in each Australian jurisdiction with respect to monitoring response to coronial recommendations, see Standing Committee of Attorneys-General *Implementation of Coronial Decisions Across Australia*.

[188] New Zealand Bill of Rights Act 1990, s 7.

[189] Parliament of Victoria Law Reform Committee, above n 57, at 401.

[190] Goddard (Department of Conservation), above n 111.

they issue also invites attendant problems. The extra government expenditure this new coronial role would require must be taken into account, although given the potential of a monitoring regime to aid death prevention measures, funding this role may be justified. Additionally, coroners, as judicial officers, have a specialised role in terms of marshalling evidence and controlling a courtroom in the processes of death investigation and prevention. To require a coroner to monitor entities' compliance with recommendations even after those processes are complete would "change the coroner's role".[191] To this end, an issue commonly raised by coroners during the interviews was that many do not systematically read organisations' responses because they are *functus officio* once investigations are completed.

It is accepted that a coroner should not alter a formal recommendation once finalised, particularly in response to untested evidence provided by agencies following an investigation. However, there should be no *functus* concerns if coroners and/or their researchers are reviewing previous responses to recommendations in order to assess the feasibility of those recommendations. This is essential in enhancing the preventive potential of recommendations. Organisations' responses may contain important information which coroners should bear in mind when formulating a new recommendation. For example, if an organisation's response points out that the recommendation was not able to be implemented because the recommended policy change was already in existence or was not feasible for some reason, the coroner can use this knowledge when drafting the new recommendation. The coroner would not then make the same recommendations that, for reasons already stated by the particular agency, cannot be implemented. Additionally, as one organisation noted, information in organisations' responses could also be used to "better profile the organisations so that recommendations were better directed to the appropriate organisation".[192]

While it is preferable that information concerning coroners' recommendations be collected centrally within the coronial system, rather than independently through the Attorney General, there remain constitutional concerns if coroners are to monitor government responses.[193] As discussed above in relation to mandatory implementation regimes, it is for this reason that it is improper for coroners to determine whether government

191 Ministry of Justice *Coroners Bill: Departmental Report 27 February 2006* (2006) at 19.

192 Interview with HealthCareOrganisation377 (Jennifer Moore, 13 December 2012).

193 Cabinet Paper, above n 4, at 21.

responses are satisfactory. That being so, if coroners were merely requiring the agency's response to conform to specified requirements, and were not forming an opinion on a response's substance, such judicial encroachment concerns may be allayed. This appears to be the approach taken in Victoria, where coroners must ensure that responses specify "a statement of action (if any) that has, is, or will be, taken in relation to the recommendations made by the coroner".[194] Victorian coroners therefore monitor the process of response-making but not the substance of the responses made.

An alternative to either follow-up regime is to designate (or establish) a person within the CSNZ who is to assume responsibility for monitoring responses to recommendations. Such a role has been established within the HDC in New Zealand. As the HDC commented in relation to follow-up to and compliance with recommendations:[195]

> . . .we also make recommendations. We don't have any statutory power to enforce them. But we do follow up. I was discussing this with a colleague. We find that 99% of our recommendations are complied with. I think this is because when we make the recommendation we say, "Please report back to us on such and such date providing evidence about what you have done." We then write to them to ask what has happened. We follow up.

With respect to who is responsible for this follow-up process, the HDC further noted:

> . . .we have a person called the "recommendations liaison coordinator". She follows up on all sorts of things. Under our Act, if we conduct a formal investigation, we go to sections 45 and 46, which talk about the recommendations. But we often make recommendations in cases which were not investigated. We call these recommendations as well, but they are not statutory recommendations I suppose. So our recommendations liaison coordinator follows up on all those types of recommendations. She also follows up other things. For example, under our Act we might refer a complaint to a different body, or we might refer a complaint back to the provider to deal with. They will have to report back under our Act about what they have done. So the coordinator follows that up too. She has relationships with the registration authorities, the DHB patient liaison people and so on.

The HDC has thus designated a liaison officer whose position includes monitoring responses to, and implementation of, recommendations issued by the Commissioner. Creating a similar position within the CSNZ has a number of key advantages. It would avoid burdening resource-limited

---

194 Coroners Act 2008 (VIC), s 72(4).
195 Interview with the HDC (Jennifer Moore, 22 February 2013).

and time-constrained coroners with a follow-up role, while still facilitating a direct means by which coroners can receive feedback concerning their recommendations. This would ensure that issues relating to the quality and practicality of those recommendations can be identified and disseminated quickly to all coroners and researchers in order to improve the preventive potential of future recommendations. Without this feedback mechanism, important opportunities to save lives through the making of recommendations may potentially be lost.

(e) Storage and access to responses

As I stated in Chapter 1, in NZ at present, the CSNZ collates responses, where received, and summaries of these responses may then appear in the *Recommendations Recap* publication. This publication, as mentioned earlier, is disseminated to all coroners and is available to the general public.[196]

The English coronial regime adopts a similar approach; the Chief Coroner's six-monthly reports summarise Coroners' Rule 43 reports and associated responses. In addition, these summary reports record the agencies that have, or have not, responded to coroners' reports.

However, for both the NZ and English jurisdictions, full responses from agencies are not published in these summaries nor are they published on the Internet. This differs from the approach taken in Victoria, whereby agencies' responses are published in full alongside corresponding recommendations on the Coroner's Court of Victoria website.

If a mandatory regime is to improve the quality of coroners' recommendations and to confer the touted benefits of increased accountability and transparency, it is important that coroners and the public have full access to feedback in the form of agencies' responses. As one coroner noted, "there needs to be clear and correct information in the public domain. . . . A high level of transparency is required for people who die in the state's grip."[197] For this reason, any monitoring regime should ideally adopt Victoria's approach in publishing agencies' responses online in full, in addition to summarising these responses in summary or annual reports.

---

[196] These publications can be accessed from the Coronial Services' website at <http://www.justice.govt.nz/courts/coroners-court/publications/recommendations-recap>.

[197] Interview with Coroner Fitzpatrick (Jennifer Moore, 25 September 2012).

(f) Adequacy of responses

The next issue requiring consideration concerns the nature and scope of the monitoring regime. Again, for the reasons discussed above, permitting coroners to comment on the adequacy of government policy in the form of responses is constitutionally undesirable. On the other hand, however, the absence of such power may mean that the quality of organisations' responses is reduced.

In NZ at present, there is variation in the extent to which agencies provide considered responses to coroners' recommendations. Responses, where received, can range from pro forma, "tokenistic" responses that specify, for example, a vague commitment to consider the matter in some future forum; to comprehensive responses stating the reasons why further action will or will not be taken. As the then NZ Chief Coroner explained:[198]

> It ranges from being totally ignored, to a bland letter that says "The Ministry is giving active consideration to all the matters you raise," end of story. If you look at the release we have done on huffing, you can see a rather non-committal response from the Ministry of Youth Affairs to our recommendation about ways of reducing kids from huffing themselves to death. That will be coming out tomorrow. There is an increasing tendency for actual Ministers like Tony Ryall, Steven Joyce and some others, who will actually read the recommendation, absorb it and will write a detailed letter back saying that they have read the recommendations, considered them and are doing X and Y about it. And it is not just an official reply. It is the Minister taking a genuine interest. Many Ministers say that they find our recommendations interesting and they do respond.

It cannot be doubted that some form of review mechanism would serve a valuable role in terms of providing accountability and discouraging agencies from giving such "tokenistic" responses to coroners' recommendations. These responses, unaccompanied by meaningful consideration or action, will not advance the object of death prevention. In fact, they may hinder progress in public health by creating the appearance of progress in the implementation of public health principles when in fact there is none,

---

[198] Coroner, above n 134. Reproduced with permission of Thomson Reuters (Professional) Australia Limited, www.thomsonreuters.com.au. This article was first published by Thomson Reuters in the *Journal of Law and Medicine* as Jennifer Moore "An Empirical Approach to the New Zealand Government's Review of the Coronial Jurisdiction" (2014) 21 JLM 602. For all subscription inquiries please phone, from Australia: 1300 304 195, from Overseas: +61 2 8587 7980 or online at www.thomsonreuters.com.au/catalogue. The official PDF version of this article can also be purchased separately from Thomson Reuters.

and by failing to give coroners and public health researchers a sense of the worth of coronial recommendations.

However, it is difficult to see how legislation could be drafted to require truly meaningful responses to coroners' recommendations, particularly in an environment where some organisations may not regard coroners' recommendations as worthy of considered responses. Medsafe, for example, noted that "[m]eaningless responses to meaningless recommendations are much easier to manage from a purely bureaucratic and cynical perspective. It's easier to write a meaningless standard letter back to the coroner, but we haven't fixed the system."[199] Upstream changes to improve the quality of coroners' recommendations are therefore critical in ensuring that organisations feel that responding to recommendations is worthwhile. The quality of recommendations and responses needs to be improved, otherwise the system risks "getting rubbish in, and putting rubbish out".[200]

Beyond this, approaches taken in other mandatory response jurisdictions to ensure organisations respond adequately generally rely on guidelines, rather than legislating specific requirements to which agencies' responses must conform. In Victoria, for example, alongside a legislative requirement that agencies specify "a statement of action (if any) that has been, is being, or will be taken"[201] in response to coroners' recommendations, the Coroner's Court of Victoria has published a *Practice Handbook* containing guidance for legal practitioners. Included in this handbook is a table of possible categories of responses and the suggested information that ought to be included to assist entities in fulfilling their statutory obligations.[202] While these guidelines are not binding on entities, most organisations' response letters to coroners' recommendations appear to conform to the handbook's suggested approach.[203] One reason for this relates to the fact that all responses are then published online in their entirety, allowing for public scrutiny of the adequacy of the response. This provides a powerful incentive for agencies to comply with the handbook's recommendations in order to fulfil their statutory obligations and avoid any adverse publicity.[204]

Some jurisdictions also provide a review mechanism whereby the Chief Coroner or the State Coroner's Office may comment on the adequacy of

---

199 Interview with Medsafe (Jennifer Moore, 8 February 2013).

200 Medsafe, above n 199.

201 Coroners Act 2008 (VIC), s 72.

202 Coroner's Court of Victoria *Practice Handbook: A Legal Practitioner's Guide to the Coronial System in Victoria* (2011) at 60.

203 Telephone discussion with Georgina Sutherland, Melbourne, July 2014.

204 Informal interview with Lyndal Bugeja at CPU, 13 December 2013.

agencies' responses in summary reports and/or an annual report tabled in Parliament. In Ontario, for example, the Chief Coroner issues annual reports that contain detailed statistical analyses of coroners' recommendations and agencies' responses from all inquests held in a particular year. Ontario agencies responding to recommendations are also given the opportunity to evaluate their own responses according to a list of codes that represent different degrees of implementation or reasons for non-implementation, failing which staff at the Chief Coroner's Office will assign appropriate response codes.[205]

A combination of both these approaches may be effective in motivating agencies to provide considered responses to recommendations. At the very least, responses should be published in full to ensure organisations are accountable to the public. A review mechanism whereby the Chief Coroner can comment on the adequacy of responses in a published summary or annual report should also be included in tandem with any mandatory response regime, if introduced. This would not be an onerous task: while there is currently no legislative requirement in NZ to publish reports summarising recommendations and any responses received, this is done informally through quarterly publications of the *Recommendations Recap*. However, for any review mechanism to be worthwhile in terms of maximising the preventive potential of the coronial system, upstream improvements to the quality of recommendations must be made prior to introducing such a review function.

(g) Monitoring implementation

The final factor to consider with respect to monitoring responses is whether a monitoring regime should include measuring the extent to which agencies implement coroners' recommendations. As I explained in Chapter 4, currently there is sparse information concerning the implementation rate of recommendations in NZ. This has led to difficulties in evaluating the effectiveness of coroners' recommendations in terms of contribution to injury avoidance and death prevention. Introducing a monitoring regime that includes within its purview agencies' implementation of recommendations would indicate the health and safety impact of coronial investigations and enable "data-informed decision making about how to adjust and evolve the coroner's jurisdiction".[206]

Extending the level of monitoring beyond a mandatory response requirement and an assessment of the adequacy of responses through summary

---

[205] Parliament of Victoria Law Reform Committee, above n 57, at 399.
[206] At 404.

and/or annual reports is not without difficulty. Cognisant of the funding and time constraints such a follow-up role would entail, the Victorian Parliament Law Reform Committee acknowledged that "[i]t is likely that the only realistic monitoring which could be done beyond the receipt and assessment of a mandatory response would be dependent on the voluntary reporting by relevant agencies of their implementation progress."[207] As such, few jurisdictions have legislated towards monitoring implementation. In theory, the best approach involves a prevention team supporting the Coroner's Court in publishing, monitoring and evaluating responses to and implementation of coroners' recommendations.[208] In Victoria, for example, one of the functions of the CPU includes "monitoring and collecting information on the response to, and implementation of, coronial recommendations".[209]

However, the CPU is not a statutory body and there is no explicit legislative guidance concerning its role. Further, in practice, Victorian follow-up of recommendations consists of collecting responses and publishing them online. There does not usually appear to be capacity – and in any case, any funding made available – to systematically monitor the rate of implementation of recommendations, let alone to monitor how that subsequent implementation might be contributing to death prevention.[210]

Any coronial law reform should consider introducing some mechanism whereby the implementation rate of coroners' recommendations can be measured. This is important given that the "practical and policy impact of coroners' recommendations will depend upon the extent of their implementation".[211]

One option would be to designate or create a role within the CSNZ, similar to that of the recommendations liaison coordinator within the HDC, whose responsibilities include monitoring implementation. As the HDC has indicated, with respect to the role of the liaison officer, there is certainly scope to monitor the steps taken by health providers following

---

207 At 405.

208 Federation of Community Legal Centres, Victoria *Saving Lives by Joining up Justice: Why Australia Needs Coronial Reform and How to Achieve it* (2013) at 32.

209 Coroner's Court of Victoria Coroners Prevention Unit (11 October 2013) <http://www.coronerscourt.vic.gov.au/home/coronial+investigation+process/whos+involved/coroners+prevention+unit/>.

210 Federation of Community Legal Centres, Victoria, above n 208, at 33.

211 Boronia Halstead "Coroners' Recommendations Following Deaths in Custody" in Hugh Selby (ed.) *The Inquest Handbook* (Federation Press, Sydney, 1998) 186 at 187.

receipt of a recommendation.[212] The HDC's follow-up model could be adopted within NZ's coronial regime. Alternatively, if a research team equivalent to Victoria's CPU was established within the CSNZ, it would not be unreasonable to extend funding for this role to enable monitoring of implementation rates. There was support among several participants for provision to be made for this function. For example, one participant commented that:[213]

> Maybe the coroner could make recommendations and then the Coronial Services could do a review to check whether anything has changed. Has anything been learned? That would be useful for the victims to see too and to see whether anything has been learned.

It should be noted that there are also opportunities to monitor implementation outside the coronial regime itself, such as through the creation of dedicated public pressure groups like INQUEST in the United Kingdom.[214] These groups contribute to the follow-up of agencies' implementation of coroners' recommendations, for example, by identifying and publicising the names of agencies who fail to take appropriate action in response to coroners' recommendations. Thus, regardless of the form any monitoring regime ultimately takes, it is important that sufficient information is made publicly available (for example, by publishing responses in full) to enable members of the public and community groups to carry out these activities effectively.

(h) Enforcement and sanctions

A number of commentators in the literature have expressed the view that there should be some form of sanction for agencies who do not respond to coroners' recommendations. Significantly, no jurisdiction punishes failures to respond to recommendations with penal sanctions. Instead, these regimes rely primarily on potential adverse publicity brought about by the coroners' increasingly prominent community role; substantial media/public interest in coronial proceedings; and the pressure these bring to bear to "name and shame" parties into responding.[215] For many regimes, such "naming and shaming" involves publicising on coroners' websites, cases where the relevant entity has not responded within the mandatory time

---

212 Interview with the HDC (Jennifer Moore, 22 February 2013).

213 *Barlow* [2008] NZCorC 35.

214 The website for INQUEST can be accessed at <http://www.inquest.org.uk/>.

215 Parliament of Victoria Law Reform Committee, above n 57, at 397.

period. This process has proved extremely effective in Victoria: responses are usually provided within a very short time following publication of a failure to respond.[216] At the time of writing, the Victorian Coroner's Court website shows that of the 639 cases where findings are published, none have outstanding responses outside of the mandatory three-month limit provided by the Victorian legislation.[217] In England and Wales, the ability of the Chief Coroner to record the names of agencies that fail to respond to Rule 43 reports in the six-monthly summaries appears to have also been effective in generating a high rate of compliance with the mandatory response requirement.[218]

It is possible the negative publicity brought upon agencies that fail to respond to coroners' recommendations may be enough to secure compliance in NZ. Additional sanctions in the form of legislative penalties may therefore not be necessary. There is nothing new in legislation imposing obligations without any punitive consequences for non-compliance. The Resource Management Act 1991, for example, requires local authorities to process applications for resource consents "within 20 working days", but there are no penalties in the Act for failure to comply.[219]

The main pitfall of mandatory response legislation which imposes no sanctions for outstanding responses beyond "naming and shaming" is that entities might still fail to take coroners' recommendations seriously. While the experiences in other jurisdictions suggest that naming and shaming may be effective in securing at least formal compliance with response

---

[216] Law Reform Commission of Western Australia and Hands, above n 47, at 174.

[217] Coroner's Court of Victoria Case Findings <http://www.coronerscourt.vic.gov.au/home/coroners+written+findings/>.

[218] Ministry of Justice (UK) *Summary of Reports and Responses under Rule 43 of the Coroners Rules: Ninth Report: For period 1 October 2012 – 31 March 2013* (June 2013) at para 2.5. Since the mandatory response requirement was introduced in England and Wales, the number of agencies recorded in Rule 43 summary reports as having failed to respond to Rule 43 reports within the time limit are as follows: 2.5% for the period between 17 March 2008 to 31 March 2009; no outstanding response for the period between 1 April and 30 September 2009; 1.2% for the period between 1 October 2009 and 31 March 2010; 2.2% for the period between 1 October 2009 and 31 March 2010; 4.2% for the period between 1 October 2010 and 31 March 2011; 6.5% for the period between 1 April 2011 and 30 September 2011; 5.7% for the period between 1 October 2011 and 31 March 2012; 1.7% for the period between 1 April 2012 and 30 September 2012; and 0.6% for the period between 1 October 2012 and 31 March 2013. Summary Reports for these periods can be accessed from the Ministry of Justice's website, available at: <https://www.gov.uk/government/publications>.

[219] Resource Management Act 1991, s 115.

requirements, agencies could still theoretically write pro forma responses to recommendations. The political reality is that, faced with a controversial recommendation implying an entity could have done something to prevent a death, that entity is not going to publicly criticise the Coroner's Court.[220] Rather, they are more likely to formally acknowledge the recommendation and say, for example, they have created a working group to consider the issues raised.[221] Imposing further penalties or enforcement powers could arguably be justified if this would encourage substantive, and not merely formal, compliance with a response regime.

However, this is difficult to enforce given the current variable quality of coroners' recommendations. It would therefore be difficult to frame legislation in a way that will secure considered responses from agencies, let alone to impose legislative sanctions for agencies that fail to respond adequately. Thus until upstream changes are introduced to improve the quality of coroners' recommendations, problems relating to the quality of agencies' responses may not be adequately resolved.

That being said, effective monitoring regimes where follow-up to responses includes an ability to progress matters further where an entity fails to take appropriate action in response to a recommendation may increase the likelihood of substantive compliance with a response requirement. As discussed, an example of such a monitoring regime is that of the HDC. As the HDC noted:[222]

> If they [health providers] don't comply – and that is rare – we sometimes say that we will notify the health practitioner's registration authority that they have declined to follow our recommendations. This could become a professional misconduct issue, but of course that would be for the professional body to decide. They don't want to have something referred to their professional body. We would always let them know that we planned to do this. If we were dealing with an organisation, we would look at their funders. For example, if we were dealing with a rest home, we may let them know that we will notify their DHB that they have not complied with our recommendations. We may let their auditors know. So I think that is why we get compliance.

In Ontario, the ability of a coroner to progress matters from regional reviews to public inquests similarly provides a powerful incentive for entities to respond to and/or implement a coroner's recommendation.

There are difficulties in adopting the follow-up regimes used by Ontario Coroners and the HDC to secure substantive compliance with a response

---

220 See for example Interview with CYFS (Jennifer Moore, 29 May 2013).

221 Telephone discussion with Prof Ian Freckelton (12 December 2012).

222 Interview with the HDC (Jennifer Moore, 22 February 2013).

requirement. Such referral powers, whereby coroners refer organisations' responses if they are adjudged inadequate, arguably transform any mandatory response regime into a mandatory implementation regime. With respect to Ontario's approach, there are also important differences between Ontario and other jurisdictions' coronial systems, which make direct translation of the Ontario follow-up regime less straightforward.[223] As the Victorian Parliament Law Reform Committee noted, "coroners in Ontario are medical practitioners, not lawyers, and coronial inquests occur before a jury; both of these factors provide strong motivations for all parties to attend informal conferencing."[224] Finally, in relation to the HDC's follow-up model, whereas the HDC is a Crown entity with a narrow jurisdiction in the delivery of health and disability services and the rights of health consumers, the coroner is a judicial officer who must investigate deaths in variable circumstances and engage with a diverse range of entities. As such, a coroner may not have the knowledge, time and/or resources to determine whether action taken, or proposed to be taken, by an entity is appropriate.

These above considerations suggest that the introduction of a mandatory response regime need not, and indeed should not, be accompanied by the imposition of penalties or enforcement powers to secure substantive compliance with coroners' recommendations. The ability to publicly "name and shame" organisations that fail to respond adequately, together with a review mechanism whereby the Chief Coroner can comment on the adequacy of responses in summary reports, may suffice. There is existing power under the Coroners Act 2006 (NZ) to refer a death to other investigating authorities, such as the HDC. In certain circumstances, referral might be appropriate where an entity that is subject to professional oversight failed to take action in response to a death and that failure has contributed to another death.[225]

(i) Summary

It has been recognised that the introduction of a mandatory response regime would be a "significant and revolutionary step".[226] As such, a number of practical and operational considerations must be taken into account. The empirical evidence and available literature suggests that if such a regime were to be introduced in NZ, it should require both

223 Parliament of Victoria Law Reform Committee, above n 57, at xlix.
224 At xlix.
225 Coroners Act 2006 (NZ), s 119.
226 Freckelton, above n 139, at 581.

public and private organisations to which coroners' recommendations are directed to respond. There should be a three-month timeframe within which organisations must respond, although extensions should be available at the discretion of coroners to agencies where complex policy matters are involved. In addition, monitoring of agencies' responses should occur centrally within the coronial system, preferably through a recommendation liaison coordinator and/or a research unit affixed to the Coroner's Court. Responses should be published online in full on the Ministry of Justice website, and the Chief Coroner should collate and consolidate all agencies' responses in summary reports, commenting on the adequacy of these responses and/or identifying those agencies that fail to respond.

6.5.4 Changes during the Coronial Investigation to Improve the Quality of Coroners' Recommendations

While almost all organisations interviewed were supportive of the introduction of a mandatory response regime, the majority nonetheless considered that a response regime should only be introduced in combination with additional changes that are required during the coronial investigation. The small number of organisations who were not supportive of the introduction of mandatory responses were concerned that other reforms were more important. Medsafe, for example, observed that a response regime would not necessarily encourage meaningful consideration and responses from organisations:[227]

> If you make responses compulsory, you might get that sort of meaningless gesture. I would much rather see considered and appropriate recommendations coming out of the system, than meaningless responses to inappropriate recommendations.

Recurring reasons raised by those participants who were not supportive included the variable quality of coroners' recommendations, incorrectly targeted recommendations, poor consultation by some coroners, limits arising from organisational structures, and the low likelihood of meaningful consideration and response from organisations. As Federated Farmers explained:[228]

> We're a subscription-based organisation, and we are not flush with money. We run a lean machine. If we had to do it, we'd have to, but it'd be hard to

---

[227] Medsafe, above n 199.
[228] Interview with Federated Farmers (Jennifer Moore, 18 December 2012).

> increase the workload without extra cash. . . . If the job got filtered down to elected people like me, it'd be really hard. It'd be better to be done by paid, fully employed staff. Then it'd be part of their job, but it'd be much harder for elected members. Our organisation is structured differently. If the recommendation is grossly wrong and it requires a lot of work to make a bit of it feasible, it'd take heaps of time to write meaningful responses. It depends on the quality of the report, the relevance of it and it depends on how much time we have to make meaningful responses. It might be easier to have the coroners consult with the Federated Farmers earlier in the process, rather than writing a response after the fact. That would be less work. The bottom of the cliff is never as successful.

Another concern with the introduction of a mandatory response system is its potential to create further delays in a coronial system that is already burdened with time pressures. Requiring mandatory responses could further extend the inquest process if sufficient notice and consideration is required to be given to those entities at which recommendations are directed. Freckelton and Ranson describe the effects of delay on the coronial system as follows:[229]

> [Delay] reduces the immediacy of the coronial response, allows distress and anger to fester on the part of family and community members, and takes the sting out of recommendations by coroners for change, as these can be readily dismissed as dealing belatedly with different times and different factual scenarios than those currently obtaining.

Concerns about delay and the need to increase efficiency in New Zealand's coronial system have been a significant focus of the Ministry of Justice's current review of the Coroners Act.[230] One NZ practitioner already feels that "delays in the present system make recommendations pointless,"[231] serving only to reopen old wounds and delay closure. This is because by the time coroners have issued recommendations, organisations and health professionals have often already identified their own internal changes to minimise future deaths, making the recommendations redundant. Delays are therefore arguably inhibiting coroners from achieving the Act's purpose.

Introducing a mandatory response regime may not be worthwhile unless, and until, the atmosphere into which recommendations are released is improved and existing delays in the system are reduced. Despite broad support among the organisations interviewed for a mandatory response

---

229 Freckelton and Ranson, above n 74, at 741.

230 Cabinet Paper, above n 4, at 18.

231 Interview with lawyer02 (Jennifer Moore, 10 September 2012).

regime, it is significant that the need for such upstream reform was highlighted by almost every organisation interviewed. For example, Standards New Zealand commented, "[i]n principle, I would support a response regime, but it'd have to be part of something broader, rather than simply 'agency you must write letters to the Coroner.'"[232] Child, Youth and Family Services similarly commented:[233]

> It [mandatory response regime] may improve the whole quality of the process. So it would probably make the coroners think more carefully about the quality of their recommendation and it would make us pay more attention to what they are suggesting. *I think that would have to be set, within a wider set of changes we talked about earlier*. . . . So you'd probably want some training and guidance for coroners about making sensible recommendations. You probably want to back that up with some sort of external checks and balances on what their thinking is and if there is an evidence base to support their decisions. (emphasis added)

Detailed discussions of the changes that should be introduced alongside a mandatory response regime have been discussed in other chapters; for example, recommendations must be targeted (as discussed in Chapter 3) in order to ensure a mandatory response regime is worthwhile.

6.6 CONCLUSION

The best way forward may be to provide coroners with feedback upstream and focus on improving the atmosphere into which recommendations are released. This would involve enhancing the quality of coroners' recommendations in terms of sources of advice, practicality, adherence to prevention principles, timeliness and effectiveness. Once an environment of increased respect for coroners' recommendations is created, the cultural and political expectation could be that organisations make meaningful responses to coronial recommendations, rather than tokenistic replies, which are then given purposeful consideration by the CSNZ.

Recent research in Victoria, Australia (one of the jurisdictions with a mandatory response regime) found that three-quarters of respondents approved of this statutory system.[234] The NZ empirical evidence

---

232 Interview with Standards NZ (Jennifer Moore, 26 October 2012).

233 Interview with CYFS (Jennifer Moore, 29 May 2013).

234 Georgina Sutherland and others "What Happens to Coroners' Recommendations for Improving Public Health and Safety? Organisational Responses under a Mandatory Response Regime in Victoria, Australia" (2014) 14 BMC Public Health 732.

suggests that the Coroners Act 2006 (NZ) should be amended to include a mandatory response regime for coroners' recommendations. However, the introduction of a mandatory response regime, in isolation from the other necessary reforms discussed in this book, is unlikely to enhance the preventive potential of coroners' recommendations.

7. Dying for change

Judge: But we've got to verify it legally
To see. . .
Major: To see. . .
Judge: If she. . .
Major: If she. . .
Judge: Is morally, ethically
Munchkin 1: Spiritually, physically
Munchkin 2: Positively, absolutely
Munchkin 3: Undeniably and reliably dead
Coroner: As Coroner I must aver,
I thoroughly examined her. . .
and she's not merely dead,
But really most sincerely dead.[1]

7.1 INTRODUCTION

This scene from the movie *The Wizard of Oz* depicts the citizens of Oz appealing to coronial expertise. After examination of the crushed body of the Wicked Witch of the East, the coroner confirms for the public her untimely accidental death. The coroner officially declares her dead with the production of an oversized "Certificate of Death": "Ding dong, the Witch is dead. . ."

The duties of modern NZ, Australian or English coroners no longer include examination of the deceased. Despite their "shape-shifting" roles throughout history, the coroner continues to play an important role in investigating and certifying sudden, violent and unnatural deaths.[2] An important purpose of an inquest is to establish that a person has in fact died (or, is "spiritually, physically, positively, absolutely, undeniably and reliably dead"). The state is interested in ascertaining the causes of deaths in order to prevent similar deaths from occurring in the future.

At the centre of this book is the coronial preventive function. For this

1 *The Wizard of Oz* (Warner Bros, California, 1939).

2 Ian Freckelton and David Ranson *Death Investigation and the Coroner's Inquest* (Oxford University Press, Melbourne, 2006) at v.

statutory prophylactic purpose to be achieved, coronial inquiries should be of social and statistical significance in a modern community.[3] The coroners I interviewed for this study recognised the importance of their prevention role. The following comment resonated with many coroners:[4]

> Obviously first of all I'm looking for any avenues that would make a recommendation applicable. That's a key point of the Act in my view: to identify where a recommendation could properly be made. But at the same time I don't think we should be making recommendations where it's just self-evident. If there's someone who drinks and drives and smashes into a tree, it's ridiculous to say that people shouldn't be drinking and driving, because that's the law, and everybody knows it anyway. But if you can find specific areas where a comment, when brought to the public's attention, might prevent further deaths; or, an actual recommendation, then that's really what we've got to be doing.

Coroners may not make recommendations in their findings in cases where known risk factors are present and prevention strategies are in place. For example, as the above quotation demonstrates, legislation and enforcement of BAC limits for drivers of motor vehicles to deter drink driving are unlikely to generate coronial recommendations. In *Ippel* (a case about drinking and driving), Coroner McDowell declined to issue recommendations, explaining that "as the message about speed, and not drinking and driving is well known I do not propose to make any further comments or recommendations in this matter."[5]

The prevention role of the coroner was recognised as early as 1821. However, this role has evolved and strengthened over time to include the identification and promotion of prevention interventions via their capacity to make recommendations and comments. The information generated from the coroner's death investigation is important as a source to describe the injury burden and identify risk factors.

Although recommendations are the formal mechanism by which coroners can address death and injury prevention, coroners' findings that do *not* contain recommendations could also influence the development of prevention strategies. For example, the circumstances or facts stated in the coroner's finding, in the absence of a formal recommendation, may prompt changes to prevent a recurrence, particularly if the case receives media attention.

Given the NZ Ministry of Justice's expenditure on the coronial

---

3 *Re Hendrie* High Court Christchurch CP 445/87, 12 January 1988 Hardie Boys J.

4 Interview with Coroner Owen (Jennifer Moore, 3 October 2012).

5 *Ippel* [2011] NZCorC 170.

jurisdiction and the high public profile of NZ coroners, it is surprising that the main preventive tool (recommendations) has been under-researched. It is "remarkable that no empirical base" had been generated.[6] An important objective of this research was to fill these knowledge gaps for the benefit of the CSNZ and the public. A major strength of this project is that it was the first empirical study of NZ coroners' recommendations. It aimed to describe and investigate the nature, recipients and preventive potential of NZ coroners' recommendations from 1 July 2007 to 30 June 2012. A retrospective study of coroners' recommendations during the study period was undertaken. Interviews were conducted with coroners, recipients of recommendations and interested parties. Surveys were completed by recipients of recommendations to generate robust data to test whether the Coroners Act 2006 (NZ) should be amended to include a mandatory response regime for coroners' recommendations.

This research has informed coronial practice and organisations' policies. In addition, the findings have contributed to law reform, including the NZ Government's current review of the coronial jurisdiction.

An additional strength of the study was its mixed methods: legal, qualitative and quantitative. The advantages of mixed-methods research are acknowledged in the literature.[7] The response rates for coroner and organisation participants are strengths of the project.

The purpose of this chapter is to highlight the lessons from the empirical evidence about how the preventive potential of coroners' recommendations can be realised for the benefit of citizens in NZ and other jurisdictions. In the next section of this chapter I review the preceding chapters. Then I discuss the implications and limitations of my research. Finally, I make suggestions for further research.

7.2 REVIEW OF PRECEDING CHAPTERS

As I have highlighted throughout this book, there is a dearth of empirical data on coroners' recommendations, despite their preventive potential. Until my research in NZ, no empirical research had been undertaken about NZ coroners' recommendations. Internationally, there is only one empirical study about coroners' recommendations, which was undertaken

6 Freckelton and Ranson, above n 2, at 742.

7 J.E.M. Sale, L.H. Lohfeld and K. Brazil "Revisiting the Quantitative-Qualitative Debate: Implications for Mixed-methods Research" (2002) 36 Quality and Quantity 43.

by University of Melbourne researchers in Australia.[8] Despite these significant knowledge gaps, coroners worldwide spend time making recommendations and considerable financial resources are spent on public inquests and the administration of coronial legislation. The outlay of cash is justified, partly, on the basis that coroners' recommendations contribute to public health goals. Yet, until my study, no research had assessed the preventive impact of coroners' recommendations. I argued that the community has an interest in, and could benefit from, an efficient and effective coronial system.

This book explored NZ coroners' recommendations over the five-year study period: 2007–12. I have quantified, described and analysed these recommendations to assess their frequency, content, implementation and preventive potential. My research aimed to provide much-needed empirical data to inform the NZ Government's review of the coronial jurisdiction and the debate about whether law reform is required to enable coroners to fulfil their statutory prophylactic function.

Chapter 1 introduced the subject of the book, outlined the aims, pivotal agendas and significance of the research. One of the aims of this project has been to inform coroners' practice in light of the research findings. I have also provided information to inform the debate about the law reform required to enhance the coronial jurisdiction. In Chapter 2, I described the NZ coronial jurisdiction and compared it with overseas Coroner's Courts.

Chapter 3 described and quantified the coroners' recommendations in my study period. Given the limitations of the coronial information that I outlined in the previous chapter, an important contribution of this study was quantifying the number of recommendations from 2007 to 2012. The results and discussion in this chapter addressed my research objective to describe the nature, frequency and recipients of NZ coroners' recommendations, 1 July 2007 – 30 June 2012. An important finding was that 23% of recommendations in my study period were untargeted.

In the next chapter I analysed the organisations' responses to my interview questions about what action (if any) they took and what factors influenced their decision. I explained that little is known about whether, and how, organisations that receive recommendations act on them. But there is much speculation that most coronial recommendations are not

---

[8] Georgina Sutherland and others "What Happens to Coroners' Recommendations for Improving Public Health and Safety? Organisational Responses under a Mandatory Response Regime in Victoria, Australia" (2014) 14 *BMC Public Health* 732.

implemented. The most prevalent concern (expressed by coroners, public inquiries, the media and the public) is that coroners' recommendations are ineffective and have little or no preventive impact because the organisations to which they are directed ignore them. This chapter provided landmark data on the actual rate of implementation of NZ coronial recommendations.

Chapter 5 traced the origins of coroners' statutory prophylactic function. It also analysed the key barriers to maximising this function and strategies for improvement. This chapter highlighted that the research participants are supportive of the statutory preventive function. While there have been improvements since the introduction of the NZ Coroners Act 2006 (NZ), the findings suggest that the prophylactic potential of coroners' recommendations has not yet been fully realised in NZ. The empirical evidence in this chapter suggested that recommendations could be improved by encouraging more coroners to consider similar cases, undertaking analysis of patterns and comparative risks.

The preventive potential of coroners' recommendations could also be improved by the introduction of a mandatory response regime, which was the topic of Chapter 6. I analysed the debate about whether mandatory response regimes should be included in coronial legislation, drawing from overseas experiences. This chapter described the participants' overwhelming support for the introduction of such a regime. I highlighted that introduction of a mandatory response regime cannot be a replacement for early consultation with organisations and interested parties *during* the coronial process. I argued that the NZ Coroners Act 2006 (NZ) should be amended to include a mandatory response regime and that the Government's review (which excludes this proposal) is inconsistent with the empirical evidence.

7.3 IMPLICATIONS AND CONTRIBUTION OF RESEARCH

As this study was the first of its kind in NZ, and one of only two worldwide, the findings make an important contribution to the NZ and international literature and the CSNZ. Many participants (33) made positive comments about the potential contribution of this research. For instance, a lawyer remarked that "this piece of work is overdue and is really important".[9] Another health sector organisation stated that it "is

[9] Interview with Lawyer04 (Jennifer Moore, 5 February 2013).

heartening to know you're doing this research . . . because it is important that someone investigates the [coronial] process".[10]

A key finding was that there were 607 coronial inquiries that resulted in 1644 recommendations during my study period. There were 309 recipients of coroners' recommendations. These figures were previously unknown. Therefore, these figures, alone, are an important contribution to our understanding of the coronial jurisdiction.

NZ government organisations received the highest proportion of recommendations (121/309). Not-for-profit organisations received 67 recommendations, for-profit organisations received 44 recommendations and individuals received five recommendations. There were 72 recommendations that did not specify an identifiable organisation. The NZ Ministry of Health received the second-highest proportion of coroners' recommendations. Transport accidents, drowning, intentional self-harm and complications of medical or surgical care were the main underlying causes of death categories investigated by coroners. Fifty-eight of the 607 enquiries involved complications from medical or surgical care.

The 123 interview participants reported that there have been improvements in coronial recommendations since the introduction of the Coroners Act 2006 (NZ), but that the prophylactic and patient safety potential of recommendations is not being maximised.

This empirical study was also the first in NZ (and one of only two worldwide) to provide data on implementation rates for coroners' recommendations. The most prevalent concern is that coroners' recommendations are ineffective because the organisations to which they are directed ignore them. Therefore, this study's findings about implementation are an important contribution to the CSNZ and the public.

7.3.1 Informing Coronial Practice

I am focused on research–practice translation. Feedback to participants is a vital component of this endeavour. I sent all interested participants copies of the preliminary themes elicited from the interview transcripts and/or their interview transcripts. Interested participants were also asked to comment on the draft version of an article published on the findings of this research.[11] Their feedback was invaluable. The final research findings were presented to CSNZ in both written and oral formats.

---

10 Interview with HealthCareOrganisation699 (Jennifer Moore, 19 June 2013).

11 Jennifer Moore "An Empirical Approach to the New Zealand Government's Review of the Coronial Jurisdiction" (2014) 21 JLM 602.

Coroners reported that a positive outcome of this research was learning more about their colleagues' practices. As I outlined in this book, coroners sometimes work in "silos" and they only meet twice per year. Coroner Aitken explained:[12]

> We don't know what other coroners do. I only know because I have appeared as counsel. It will be helpful to know what other coroners do. . . . We hope your research can help us to do our job better. Just talking to you stimulated me to think of things to put in the Bench Book.

Organisations also commented that they were pleased to learn more about coronial procedures. Many organisations reported that they were glad to learn that they were "not a lone voice" and that other agencies had similar experiences during coronial inquiries. This government agency's description captured other organisations' views:[13]

> Sometimes we have wondered whether it is just us. It's useful to know that we are not alone.

Another important outcome for organisations was that the research provided the impetus to build or strengthen relationships with the CSNZ. Coroners were also pleased to develop such relationships with external bodies. One coroner asked me for the contact details of the participating organisations. With the permission of the organisations, I provided this information at the conclusion of the project. This result is invaluable because a key finding of the research was that consultation with, and input from, organisations is vital to quality coronial investigations and findings. During the research, I connected coroners with organisations, for example a coroner was connected with my contacts from Federated Farmers and the Chief Coroner with clinicians from a DHB.

My 2014 *NZ Medical Journal* article about coroners' recommendations and healthcare-related deaths generated lots of attention from health organisations and the media. Many organisations contacted me to request copies of coronial recommendations that my study identified as directed to them, but that had never been received. I supplied the requested information. For example, on 21 July, the NZ Health Quality and Safety Commission contacted me to request all the coroners' recommendations that had been directed to them during my study period. I included the CSNZ in the discussion and they provided further information. These

---

12 Interview with Coroner Aitken (Jennifer Moore, 22 January 2013).

13 Interview with GovtOrg08 (Jennifer Moore, 5 February 2013).

outcomes are important because it may increase the likelihood that the recommendations will be considered and implemented.

I have been in contact with the CSNZ, particularly the former Chief Coroner Judge MacLean, throughout the research process. The coroners' support, enthusiasm for the research and willingness to adopt recommendations stemming from the empirical evidence have been impressive. For example, since I discovered that 23% of coroners' recommendations are untargeted, the former Chief Coroner has announced publicly that the CSNZ has taken that "on board" and they have changed their practices accordingly to ensure that recommendations identify specific organisations.[14] In addition, in May 2015, I facilitated a workshop at the NZ Annual Coroner's Continuing Education Programme. We developed a checklist for the formulation of recommendations which is based on legal and public health principles.

7.3.2 Improving Preventive Potential of Recommendations

My objective to inform coronial practice, discussed in the section immediately above, should also improve the preventive potential of coroners' recommendations. In Chapter 5, I outlined numerous strategies to achieve this goal.

The findings of this study highlight the need for the establishment of protocols for coroners to identify the circumstances under which a recommendation is warranted and guidelines for their formulation. Ideally, recommendations should draw from the theoretical frameworks of injury prevention and public policymaking to ensure they are targeted, evidence-based and, preferably, acceptable. The introduction of coronial guidelines or Coroner's Court Rules would help to generate consistency in coronial procedures. Coroners should be consulted about the development of such documents.

Providing coroners with adequate support, resources and training, together with the introduction of *Coroner's Court Law Reports* and electronic access to full coronial findings, are key areas that need to be addressed if coroners are to be an effective public health and safety apparatus for the state.

There also need to be mechanisms for monitoring and evaluating coronial recommendations such as a mandatory response system and feedback about proposed recommendations during the coronial inquiry. This could

---

[14] David Loughrey "Chief Coroner Welcomes Study" *Otago Daily Times* (Dunedin, 18 July 2014).

include active engagement with the injury prevention workforce and the community, within the limits of coronial judicial independence.

Many of the organisations interviewed offered to provide assistance which may enhance the preventive potential of recommendations. For example, a DHB expressed "hope that this research creates a bit of change".[15] Another health sector organisation offered to present the research findings to Health Board meetings in order to encourage change. This participant stated:[16]

> So let's talk about how we can actually make sure that happens. If it's something that's related to health, you can give it to me and I'll make sure it's discussed by all of the Health Board Chairs, or we'll give it to the organisation that can facilitate that change for us.

7.3.3 Law Reform

Some of the changes suggested by the empirical evidence do not require law reform. Instead, many require operational changes. As a government organisation put it, the coronial system "is not so broken that we need everything fixed, but we could make some useful changes".[17]

However, my findings suggest that some amendments to the Coroners Act 2006 (NZ) are required to enhance the coronial preventive function. In particular, the Act should be amended to include a mandatory response system for coroners' recommendations. The participants overwhelmingly supported the introduction of such a regime. My findings provide robust empirical support for this law reform. Not only is my recommendation based on 123 interviews, but I also analysed over 40 responses to a survey to supplement the interview data. Australian research has evaluated the Victorian coronial jurisdiction, which has statutory mandatory responses, and the results were positive.[18] At the time of writing, the Minister for Courts had not acted on this suggestion because of the cost. However, commentators have pointed out that the cost is not unreasonable and the costs are borne primarily by organisations, not the Government.[19]

To increase the likelihood of my findings having an impact on law

---

[15] Interview with HealthCareOrganisation299 (Jennifer Moore, 23 January 2013).

[16] Interview with HealthCareOrganisation799 (Jennifer Moore, 12 November 2012).

[17] Interview with GovtOrg01 (Jennifer Moore, 28 February 2013).

[18] Sutherland and others, above n 8.

[19] Sutherland and others, above n 8.

reform, I published two articles about the findings of my research early in the research process and during the government review.[20] I have provided the Minister and his advisers with advance copies of these publications and I have given them oral explanations. Representatives from the Ministries of Health and Justice have also attended presentations about my research findings.

I continue to advocate for the introduction of mandatory responses, particularly in the media. There were 23 media items about the research findings on 18 July 2014.[21] I also advocate for this change in my role as a member of the NZ Law Society Health Law Committee. The committee discussed my submission on the Coroners Amendment Bill 2014 at its September 2014 meeting.

The Government announced their review in July 2012. Prior to that, in May 2012, one of the Minister's advisers contacted me about this project after reading about it in the media.[22] The original terms of reference for the Government's review did *not* include coroners' recommendations.[23] But, after discussion with me and the Chief Coroner, coroners' recommendations were included. This inclusion is significant because the government review confirmed my preliminary research findings: coroners' recommendations are one of the most important aspects of the coronial process and the government review.[24] The Minister has also adopted several of my other law reform suggestions. For example, his advisers adopted my findings about the "interested parties" provisions in the Act which I published in an article in March 2014.[25] The data also supports the introduction of Coroner's Court Rules or Guidelines to encourage consistency in coronial practice.

---

20 Moore, above n 11; Jennifer Moore "Coroners' Recommendations about Healthcare-related Deaths as a Potential Tool for Improving Patient Safety and Quality of Care" (2014) 127(1398) NZ Medical Journal 35.

21 For example, see Loughrey, above n 14; Vaimoana Tapaleao "Findings by Coroners Fall on Deaf Ears" *The New Zealand Herald* (Auckland, 18 July 2014); Collette Devlin and Tessa Johnstone "Report Highlights Failings of Coronial System" *Dominion Post* (Wellington, 18 July 2014).

22 Email from Oliver Searle Private Secretary (Advisory) to Hon Borrows and Jennifer Moore "regarding our Law Foundation-funded coroners' recommendations research and the New Zealand Government review" (16 May 2012).

23 Email from Oliver Searle Private Secretary (Advisory) to Hon Borrows and Jennifer Moore "regarding the scope of our Law Foundation-funded research compared to the scope of the New Zealand Government review" (31 July 2012).

24 Cabinet Paper *Coroners Act Review: Proposals for Reform – Paper 1* (2013) at 5.

25 Moore, above n 11.

7.4 LIMITATIONS OF RESEARCH

A limitation of the study is that the interested party participants are not representative. Future research should be undertaken to further explore their views. Although selection criteria were applied, there may be selection bias in the interested party sample because of the high proportion of participants who contacted the researcher.

There may be case selection bias in the analysis of recommendations because the sample of repeated recommendations was limited to those that were identical in wording. Repeated themes were not eliminated, which may have led to an overestimate of the total number of recommendations.

Another limitation of the study is the possible impact of the Ministry of Justice's review of the Coroners Act 2006 (NZ), which began in 2012 during the study period. The review may have impacted the coroners' formulation of recommendations. As this was the first analysis of NZ coroners' recommendations, it is exploratory only and further research should be undertaken.

7.5 DIRECTIONS FOR FURTHER RESEARCH

Given that this was the first NZ study of coroners' recommendations since the introduction of the Coroners Act 2006 (NZ), more research is needed to corroborate these findings. As I discussed in the preceding section, future research could explore the views of interested parties. In addition, the same dataset of recommendations could be analysed for repeated themes (rather than repeated identical wording) for comparison with the results of this study.

This research found that coroners made 670 comments during my study period. Although coroners made more recommendations, 670 is a significant number of comments. It is beyond the scope of this study to provide in-depth analysis of the nature of coronial comments. However, the frequency of coronial comments and the coroners' descriptions of their decision-making suggest that further investigation would be useful.

Coronial recommendations could be a key patient safety resource and reduce the incidence of adverse events, subject to the necessary quality improvements identified in this study.[26] The potential value of the quality of care learning that can be derived from coronial recommendations

---

[26] Moore, above n 20, at 51.

is currently under-researched, but is worth exploring further in future projects.[27]

7.6 CONCLUSION

This chapter's drawing together of the important threads from the preceding chapters has highlighted the strategies for maximising the preventive potential of coroners' recommendations for the benefit of the public. It has also presented a summary of my findings, an analysis of the limitations of my research and a call for further work. The chapter discusses the implications of my findings and how they might inform coronial practice and law reform.

Coroners' recommendations have the potential to contribute to public health and safety. This study described prevention success stories where coroners' recommendations have had a positive preventive impact. However, this study has also demonstrated that while coronial recommendations can be useful tools for intervention and policy development, coroners' contribution to morbidity and mortality prevention at the population level requires further development. Although there is a paucity of research about the relationship between coronial recommendations and prevention, this study's findings are broadly consistent with Australian research on coroners' recommendations. This research seeks to address these gaps in knowledge for the benefit of coroners, organisations and the community.

Coroners' recommendations rarely specified all the elements necessary to adhere to the principles of effective injury prevention. Given that the qualifications and training requirements for coroners are primarily legal, it cannot be assumed that coroners have knowledge of public health principles or the expertise to apply them. Furthermore, the CSNZ is under-resourced, hindering coroners from effectively fulfilling their preventive function. The empirical evidence supports the introduction of a service similar to the Victorian CPU in NZ.

A mechanism to monitor the implementation and impact of recommendations is also crucial for providing coroners with feedback for future death investigations and recommendations. Feedback about proposed recommendations should also occur during the coronial inquiry to enhance the quality and feasibility of recommendations and, thus, increase the likelihood of their implementation.

---

27 At 51.

The CSNZ plays a role in highlighting where avoidable deaths occur and introducing measures to prevent recurrence. Although there have been advances since the introduction of the Coroners Act 2006 (NZ), those who were interviewed consistently expressed the view that further improvements are needed. For example, Coroner Dymond "hoped that the 2006 Act would have been significantly better than it has turned out to be".[28] Research about, and government reviews of, coronial law should be welcomed because by learning from tragedies, coronial systems contribute to public health and safety.

The NZ Minister for Courts has stated that the Government wishes to have a coronial service that can "deliver as high a standard as possible to families and the general public".[29] To enable this, operational improvements to the CSNZ should be considered, such as strengthening resources, support and training for coroners. The Victorian CPU and CLS should be models to consider.

Any reforms for prevention must be balanced against the broader implications of improving a court system already burdened by time pressures. Australian research shows that the efficiency of coronial processes are improved when coroners have easy access to expertise such as clinical information. Moreover, given that a principal purpose of the NZ Act is prevention (and the NZ Government has not indicated any changes to the legislation's purposes), it would be in the public interest to introduce proposals which may enhance coroners' preventive functions. The government review presents an opportunity to initiate much-needed reforms. The reforms could be usefully informed by the empirical evidence in this project.

This book presented a number of factors that posed difficulties for capitalising on the lifesaving opportunities that coroners' recommendations provide. The shortcomings identified in this book are also important for overseas coroner and medical examiner death investigation systems that are considering strengthening their preventive role. Although legislation has been reformed to include prevention as a purpose, and several jurisdictions (for example Australia and the UK) require organisations to respond to recommendations, prevention principles are not adequately integrated into death investigation systems. Death investigation systems continue to evolve, with their level of contribution to public health a matter of much debate. This study is an important step towards improving coronial practice and the contribution of recommendations to injury and death

[28] Interview with Coroner Dymond (Jennifer Moore, 16 October 2012).

[29] Cabinet Paper, above n 24, at 4.

prevention. Future reforms should enhance the preventive functions of coronial jurisdictions to ensure that coroners' recommendations are not a "lost opportunity" to save lives.[30]

[30] Lyndal Bugeja and David Ranson "Coroners' Recommendations: A Lost Opportunity?" (2005) 13 JLM 173.

Appendix: Coroners Act 2006 (NZ) extracts

13 Deaths that must be reported under section 14(2)

(1) This section applies to the following deaths if, and only if, they are deaths to which subsection (2) applies:

Without known cause, suicide, or unnatural or violent

(a) every death that appears to have been without known cause, or suicide, or unnatural or violent:

For which no doctor's certificate given

(b) every death in respect of which no doctor has given a doctor's certificate (as defined in section 2(1) of the Burial and Cremation Act 1964):

During medical, surgical, or dental operation, treatment, etc

(c) every death—

(i) that occurred while the person concerned was undergoing a medical, surgical, dental, or similar operation or procedure; or

(ii) that appears to have been the result of an operation or procedure of that kind; or

(iii) that appears to have been the result of medical, surgical, dental, or similar treatment received by that person; or

(iv) that occurred while that person was affected by an anaesthetic; or

(v) that appears to have been the result of the administration to that person of an anaesthetic or a medicine (as defined in section 3 of the Medicines Act 1981):

(d) any death that occurred while the woman concerned was giving birth, or that appears to have been a result of that woman being pregnant or giving birth:

In official custody or care

(e) the death of a patient required to be detained in an institution pursuant to an order under section 9 of the Alcoholism and Drug Addiction Act 1966:

(f) the death of a child or young person the chief executive has, under section 365 of the Children, Young Persons, and Their Families Act 1989, placed in a residence established under section 364 of that Act:

(g) the death of a child or young person while that child or young person—

(i) is in the custody or care of an Iwi Social Service or a Cultural Social Service, or the Director of a Child and Family Support Service, pursuant to section 43 or 78 or 110 or 139 or 140 or 141 or 234 or 238 or 345 of the Children, Young Persons, and Their Families Act 1989; or

(ii) is in the charge of any person or organisation pursuant to section 362 of that Act:

(h) the death of any patient as defined in section 2(1) of the Mental Health (Compulsory Assessment and Treatment) Act 1992:

(i) the death of any proposed care recipient or care recipient as defined in section 5(1) of the Intellectual Disability (Compulsory Care and Rehabilitation) Act 2003:

(j) the death of a prisoner as defined in section 3(1) of the Corrections Act 2004:

(k) the death of a person in the custody of the New Zealand Police:

(l) the death of a person under the control of a security officer as defined in section 3(1) of the Corrections Act 2004.

(2) This subsection applies only to deaths that occurred in New Zealand or that are deaths on or from—

(a) an aircraft registered in New Zealand under the Civil Aviation Act 1990; or

(b) a New Zealand ship (as defined in section 2(1) of the Maritime Transport Act 1994); or

(c) an aircraft or ship of the Armed Forces (as defined in section 2(1) of the Armed Forces Discipline Act 1971).

(3) Subsection (1)(e) and (f) and (h) to (j) apply to a death whether or not it occurred in the institution, residence, hospital, facility, or prison concerned.

Compare: 1988 No 111 ss 4, 5(2)

Index